The Plantagenet Empire

The Plantagenet Empire

1154–1224

Martin Aurell

Translated from the French by David Crouch

PEARSON
Longman

Harlow, England • London • New York • Boston • San Francisco • Toronto
Sydney • Tokyo • Singapore • Hong Kong • Seoul • Taipei • New Delhi
Cape Town • Madrid • Mexico City • Amsterdam • Munich • Paris • Milan

PEARSON EDUCATION LIMITED

Edinburgh Gate
Harlow CM20 2JE
United Kingdom
Tel: +44 (0)1279 623623
Fax: +44 (0)1279 431059
Website: www.pearsoned.co.uk

First edition published in Great Britain in 2007

© Pearson Education Limited 2007

The right of David Crouch to be identified as translator
of this work has been asserted by him in accordance
with the Copyright, Designs and Patents Act 1988.

ISBN: 978-0-582-78439-0

British Library Cataloguing-in-Publication Data
A CIP catalogue record for this book can be obtained from the British Library

Library of Congress Cataloging-in-Publication Data
A catalog record for this book is available from the Library of Congress

10 9 8 7 6 5 4 3 2 1
10 09 08 07

Set by 35 in 10/13.5pt Sabon
Printed in China

EPC/01

The Publisher's policy is to use paper manufactured from sustainable forests.

Contents

List of plates

Acknowledgements

We are grateful to the following for permission to use copyright material:

Plates 1–7 courtesy of AKG; plates 8–13 courtesy of the Bridgeman Art Library; plate 14 courtesy of the Art Archive/ Dagli Orti; plate 15 courtesy of CESM-Poitiers.

In some instances we have been unable to trace the owners of copyright material, and would appreciate any information that would enable us to do so.

Map of the Plantagenet Empire

Introduction

Henry II (1151–1189) built an empire. More than any other ruler in the twelfth century, the first Angevin king of England knew how to subdue kingdoms, duchies and counties. He was a stockpiler of provinces, a past master of the complex interplay of marriage alliance, manipulation of inheritance and military conquest which were all part of the way new realms were built. It was by these means that Henry II came to control a huge complex of lands along the Atlantic seaboard, from Northumberland to Gascony, and from the heart of Ireland to the Auvergne. The intellectuals of his court found themselves lost for words to describe his empire's growth, it was so rapid and so spectacular. In his *Topography of Ireland* (1188) Gerald of Barry (1146–1223), a priest born into the Norman nobility of south Wales, addressed this eulogy to Henry: 'Your victories swamp frontiers: you, our western Alexander, have stretched out your arm from the Pyrenees to the western shores of the northern Ocean'.[1] According to the clerk Wace (*c*.1110–*p*.1174) – who wrote a history of Normandy commissioned by the man himself – Henry II was 'the one who holds England and all the seaboard between Spain and Scotland, from shore to shore'.[2] More enthusiastic still, an anonymous monk of Saint-Serge at Angers wrote that by 1152 Henry, when he had concluded the wars he had been fighting on all fronts, 'ruled from sea to sea', in a daring and explicit reference to a psalm in praise of the Messiah.[3] The image of the conquering king is a universal one in the writings of authors under Henry II's patronage, men who were ever ready to lavish praise on his political achievements.

Chroniclers used the word 'empire', to characterize Henry's realm. It was a term which in the twelfth century referred only rarely to a type of realm, and was used more in the context of the philosophy of government. Nevertheless, in at least one example drawn from the sources of the time, *imperium* is used to mean a realm greater than the usual run of principalities, a realm based on hegemony. The *Dialogue of the Exchequer* (*c*.1179), a technical manual on the central financial bureau of England written by Richard fitz Nigel (*c*.1130–1198), bishop of London and treasurer of Henry II, says: 'By his conquests the king expanded (*dilataverit*) his empire far and wide'.[4] At a time when knowledge of the classics was growing amongst the educated classes, the word was used on purpose. It did not refer to the sphere of control exercised by any prince, but harked back to the hegemony of the Roman Empire. Besides, the phrase 'expansion of Empire' had been used by chroniclers of the time of Charlemagne, who compared their master to the victorious generals of Rome. Furthermore, was not Henry II himself 'fitz Empress', the son of the second marriage of the empress, Mathilda of England, widow of the German emperor Henry V (1106–1125)? Carrying such a surname, the idea of an empire as a geographical construct, pulling together scattered territorial principalities, should not have seemed all that strange to Henry. Although no king of England since the tenth century had presumed to take the style of *imperator* as his actual title,[5] the instances given of its contemporary use are a good enough warrant for a historian of the Middle Ages to use the phrase 'Plantagenet Empire' or 'Angevin Empire'.

All the same, reservations about the phrase have been raised by historians up until quite recently.[6] The logic of these reservations has to be acknowledged, and they have served the purpose of highlighting a complicated problem. To begin with, they were raised by people who believed that the term 'empire' should be confined to the Romano-Germanic empire, the only institution in the medieval West consistently described as an empire by contemporaries. Yet this objection overlooks the fact that medievalists often use anachronistic but nonetheless evocative expressions like 'feudo-vassalic links', 'banal lordship', 'holy war' or 'urban patriciate'. Then there are more weighty objections from other critics, specialists in law and political science, for whom the power of Henry II, mighty as it may have looked in the twelfth century, seems rather puny in comparison with the Hellenic, Roman, Byzantine, Abbasid, Ottoman or Habsburg empires, not to mention the colonial empires of the nineteenth century. The difference between these great realms and the Plantagenet Empire is a matter of perspective. Such a critic would certainly not approve of the telling comparison which Sir Maurice Powicke suggested in 1913 – in a remarkably innovative book for the time – between King John's lost French province of the Angoumois and the State of Mysore in the Indian Empire (a complex dilemma for the British Empire of Powicke's own lifetime).[7]

Writers who argue against the phrase 'Plantagenet Empire' stress that the characteristics appropriate to great empires cannot be found in the complex of lands of Henry II and his sons. These were characteristics such as absolutism; the use by the supreme ruler of a title greater than that of the rulers of the other states; the varied character of the subject populations; the acknowledgement that one single people were aggressive and dominant over the others; interests spanning one or more continents; and finally, political longevity.[8] Critics would conclude that no Western empire of the Middle Ages answered to any of these descriptions. Analysing what it is that makes an 'empire' an empire has its fascination, as it tells us something about the uniqueness – or even the peculiarity – of medieval Europe, a place whose later political evolution is recognized as being just as eccentric as were its origins. But this process of definition should not be used to discredit terminology which medieval sources openly and freely use, even if the sources use it more in the sense of a ruler's authority than of a diverse conglomeration of territories.

Global questions about the political nature of territorial complexes in the past need to be adjusted downwards when dealing with the more modest scale of the Plantagenet Empire, which is our subject here. Those who are against calling it an empire comment on the fragility of its political foundations and its vulnerability to the circumstances of its own day. If Henry II and his son Richard the Lionheart (1189–1199) succeeded by their unparalleled military exertions in preserving the unity of their domains, John (1199–1216) and Henry III (1216–1272) were powerless to prevent the loss of Normandy, greater Anjou and Poitou, to the king of France's profit.[9] The Plantagenet Empire was incapable of preserving its unity for more than fifty years, from the coronation of Henry II as king of England in 1154 to the fall of Normandy in 1204. It was anything but stable. The facts speak for themselves; its ephemeral nature proves that the Plantagenet 'Empire' was not an empire of the nineteenth-century sort.

These hostile commentators add that such a quick and complete collapse was a consequence of the empire's lack of political, institutional and administrative unity. British historiography in the second half of the twentieth century is full of this idea, almost as if the post-war generation had become aware of the fragility of colonial empires, having learnt first-hand how they can collapse into a myriad of new nations. In a work published in 1963, H.G. Richardson and G.O. Sayles noted: 'what unity this misnamed "empire" had was given to it by the king; but he did not introduce common institutions or a common code of law'.[10] In 1973 W.L. Warren frankly rejected the word 'empire' as a name for the loose federation linking the different territorial principalities ruled by Henry II. At most he would concede that it was a 'commonwealth', a loose federation of seven autonomous 'dominions' whose only common feature was their dependence on the king, shakily based on vassalage and the oath of fealty.[11] Two years later, J.C. Holt took an even more radical view: 'The Plantagenet *dominions* were not designed as an "empire", as a great centralized administrative structure, which was ultimately broken down by rebellion and French attack. On the contrary these lands were simply cobbled together. They were founded, and continued to survive, on an unholy combination of princely greed and genealogical accident.'[12] Summing up (on the French side) the papers presented at an Anglo-French conference in 1984 at Fontevrault – a Plantagenet shrine if ever there was one – Robert-Henri Bautier did not leave it there. He proposed the substitution of the vague word 'zone' (*espace*) for the 'conglomeration of entities' without 'any common structure' called with too much precision 'the Plantagenet Empire' or 'Anglo-Angevin state'.[13] In the eyes of modern-day historians, the 'zone' governed by Henry II and his family was diverse and fragmented.

These subtle distinctions do improve our understanding of the significance of Henry II and his sons within such a variety of territories. The 'Plantagenet zone', a mosaic of kingdoms, principalities and lordships, no more supports a consensus amongst historians in 2000 than it did a single government for its king in 1200. It was a great expanse of lands, vast for the West of those days, each governed in its own way. Its area was subdivided among a number of centres, offering administrative direction, military power and judicial subjection. The title of the most celebrated of the political tracts compiled by a subject of Henry II was the *Policraticus* of John of Salisbury, and in a way, admittedly stretching its sense and orthography a bit, the 'Plantagenet zone' could be called a 'polycratic' world. It comprehended an artificial and temporary union of independent principalities whose forced conjunction temporarily disrupted their tradition of endemic squabbling. The cement which held this union together was naturally to be found in the royal family, for in the twelfth century kinship remained the most stable and secure form of political association. Yet the union was clearly fragile above all because, to borrow John Gillingham's pun, Henry II did not treat his lands as a 'single unified State' so much as a 'partible family estate'.[14] The Plantagenet Empire had been created out of marriage and inheritance, and at the end succession disputes were responsible for its break-up.

The collapse is partly to be explained by the ingrained particularism of the Empire's component principalities. Localization varied the authority of the king of England from one province to the other. The links that he made within each region could indeed vary widely: the links were tight in the Anglo-Norman nucleus, whose administrative efficiency was a marvel to the other rulers of the West, and to a degree also in Anjou, the cradle of the dynasty. The links were loose in Aquitaine; a jigsaw of a land, with many comital, vice-comital or seigneurial enclaves, whose lords regularly rose in rebellion against the king. The links between king and community were indeed tenuous in Ireland, where Anglo-Norman colonists were hard at the work of conquest, and also in Brittany, whose count after 1199 made an armed bid for the English Crown, in alliance with the Capetians. At peace or in rebellion, the different provinces of the Plantagenet Empire varied in their degree of centralization and administrative development. The concentration of authority exclusively on the prince and his household officers[15] in one region contrasted with its fragmentation elsewhere, with authority dispersed among many independent castle-lordships.[16] Plantagenet government was a different quantity depending in which province you were.

A principal concern in respect of government was the problem of castles and their control, for it was a revealing symptom of the nature of Plantagenet power in each province. From Taillebourg (1179) to Châlus (1199), Richard the Lionheart, duke of Aquitaine from his teenage years, committed himself fully to the business of sieges; taking and destroying fortresses in Poitou, the Limousin and Gascony. Meanwhile in England, the 'adulterine' castles, built in the dark times of civil war, had been quickly dismantled following the instructions given by Henry II at a council held at Bermondsey Priory at Christmas 1154.[17] Whether in Britain or in Normandy, the principle of 'rendability' was efficiently enforced, by which a castle's owner surrendered it to a keeper sent by the king.[18] In England and Normandy the Plantagenets were able to undertake expensive projects and build their own castles, the most powerful of all the fortresses in their realms. The fortifications of Château-Gaillard or Dover are the finest examples of this. It was otherwise in Anjou, and even less so in Aquitaine, where the Plantagenets could not often embark on any major programme of construction because of the small extent of their own domain and the poverty of their local revenues. They had to be satisfied with obtaining the temporary allegiance of the castellans amongst the aristocracy, or with strengthening the urban fortifications, which enclosed a populace rather more cooperative with their rule than that of the countryside.[19] The freedom to build fortifications which the lords south of the Loire enjoyed contrasts with the royal control of the infrastructure of castles in England and Normandy, places particularly subservient to the royal prerogative.[20] This regional diversity gave the Angevin political system its characteristic features of flexibility and adaptability.

There is, however, a weighty objection to the current historiographical schema which stresses the flexibility of the power politics of the Plantagenets. It was first put forward by Jacques Boussard, author of a book focusing on the government of Henry II, which appeared in 1956, some years before British and American historians ruled out the idea of the political unity of the domains of the king of England. In sharp contrast to more recent studies, his conclusion was categoric: 'The Angevin Empire was understood to be a powerful state, in the context of its feudal world'.[21] Boussard had a positive idea of the effectiveness of the 'authoritarian regime' of Henry II, which drew on him the resentment of the established local aristocracy.[22] It revealed the sympathy of this practised medievalist for the house of Anjou, his native region, and also the distaste which every French historian born at the beginning of the twentieth century had for the 'feudal anarchy' against which Henry II had conducted so decisive a campaign. Remember that only some fifteen years later W.L. Warren, another historian impressed with Henry, used the term 'federation', rather than the word 'state' which Boussard preferred, to describe the Plantagenet Empire. There is a significance in the different choice of word on either side of the Channel. In his *Atala*, Chateaubriand wrote that 'federalism was the commonest political form in use amongst primitive peoples', so for a Frenchman living in the Third Republic, federalism, which was literally to cost the Girondins and the Communards their heads, was a political step backwards. The word has none of the prestige of the German *Bund*, which embraces any form of human association, from marriage to the global organization of United Nations, or a nation in union with God.[23] The divergence between the way the terms 'federation' and 'state' are perceived by different nations, is an example of how the differing history of each European country forms our perception of medieval political realities.

National concerns show themselves just as strongly with the use of the terms: 'Plantagenet Empire' and 'Angevin Empire'. It first appears as a concept in France. Some British medievalists have criticized it, however, contending that the term 'Plantagenet' only appears in twelfth-century sources as the surname of Geoffrey le Bel (1128–1151), the father of Henry II.[24] This makes all the more significant the identification of branches of broom (Lat. *planta genesta*) on either side of the throne on the 'majesty' side of the great seal of his grandson, Richard the Lionheart.[25] Admittedly it was only in the fifteenth century that 'Plantagenet' became the royal family's surname. At that point in time, the political purpose behind the manipulation of names was to reinforce the political ambitions of the kings of England concerning the throne of France during the Hundred

Years War.[26] Nonetheless the fact that a similar anachronism can be found with the word 'Capetian', is enough to bring the criticism into proportion. It was used exclusively of Hugh Capet in the primary sources, but the use of 'Capetian' is widespread among medievalists. In passing, we may note that Geoffrey le Bel's surname was an allusion to his taste for woods, forests and moors, where he indulged his passion for hunting, an activity which, as we will see, had considerable political implications for his dynasty.[27]

I have kept 'Plantagenet' so as to conform to the entirely reasonable usage of French historians. For their part, with the exception of John Le Patourel,[28] English colleagues prefer 'Angevin Empire', a phrase coined in 1887 by Kate Norgate and reused for the title of books by James H. Ramsay (1903) and John Gillingham (1984 and 2001). This old variant offers the advantage of connecting the domains of the king of England to the house of Anjou, and in this way of putting a greater emphasis of the continental dynasty and the family nature of its rule. The adjective 'Angevin' chosen by Kate Norgate was, furthermore, completely free of any British ethnocentricity, for it stressed the foreign origins of the dynasty ruling England. Norgate's choice, which was destined to have a long-term future amongst British thinkers, was the more far-seeing and creditable as the end of the nineteenth century was so nationalistic.

It is true enough that British medievalists have not always been enthusiastic about the political aims of the Plantagenets, and that they have often looked askance at their continental enterprises. Some of them would rather have preferred the kings to dedicate themselves exclusively to their business in Britain. As an example, a recent biography has put together a collection of texts which, since the middle of the seventeenth century, protested against the heavy taxation imposed on England by Richard the Lionheart in order to support far-flung and pointless campaigns. Two humorous writers of the 1930s considered that it would be a good idea to change his surname from 'Coeur de Lion' to 'Gare de Lyon' because of Richard's attraction to the sunny shores of the Mediterranean and his eager desire to leave for the Near East.[29] For some nineteenth-century English scholars and their successors, detached and ironic as they were, King Richard was not the chivalrous and romantic hero that Walter Scott portrayed with such style.

A degree of isolationism dictated the English point of view. In 1849, Thomas Macaulay went so far as to take satisfaction in the final loss of England's problematical continental possessions, where the Plantagenets squandered their resources in idle entertainments beside the Seine and where the glorious English language was demoted to the status of a rustic dialect in comparison with the French spoken by the higher orders. He concluded: 'England should have fled from such calamities at an event that its historians have so often portrayed as disastrous'.[30] Forty or so years later, William Stubbs, bishop of Oxford, whose works were directed at proving to the world the institutional superiority and benign influence of the English constitutional monarchy, said much the same. He saw in 'the happy incompetence of John Lackland' the chance which let England 'shake free of Normandy', a good riddance.[31] Stubbs's outlook can be explained by his contempt for the latin influence of France, since he maintained that England's origins were purely germanic.[32] Paradoxical though it might seem, there existed in nineteenth-century English historiography a strand of insularity which deprecated the cross-Channel enterprises of Henry II and his successors, and which saw their continental principalities as so much dead weight. For the English establishment, nothing was better in those days than 'splendid isolation'.

The nineteenth century found a prejudice of a similar cast (*acabit*) amongst French medievalists, although for very different reasons. A recent study of these historians by J-P. Genet has highlighted how much they were disturbed by Angevin rule over such a large part of their 'national territory'. It delayed the birth of the Capetian state. In their works Richard the Lionheart is described as a brainless thug, standing in the way of the national hero, Philip Augustus (1180–1223) the architect of France, which had been Balkanized by the feudal fragmentation represented by Richard's domain.[33] These ideas were a result of a deterministic understanding of French history as being directed to one end: the building of the nation within its predestined frontiers. In the passion of his romantic patriotism Jules Michelet (1798–1874) talked of the 'English empire' so as to emphasize the intrusive character of the government of Henry II and his family within the borders of France.[34] His contemporary Augustin Thierry (1795–1856) saw the rebellions of the barons of Aquitaine against Henry II as a patriotic rising against the English invaders, a resistance to the foreigner whose heroic leader was the troubadour, Bertran de Born.[35] The Angevin king and his sons, crowned at Westminster, were very manifestations of 'perfidious Albion'.

In this tradition there could be no appeal against the judgement of Achille Luchaire, leader of a measured but deeply nationalist school of history. To him Henry II was 'as much a tyrant to his family as to his realm'.[36] This is the stance later adopted by Jacques Boussard, of the authoritarian nature of Plantagenet rule over its lands, however widely dispersed. For this school of history, Plantagenet political efficiency was its one and only contribution worth mentioning to the creation of France. It led to the suppression of the as-yet-untamed aristocracy through centralized regional government. In 1941, Louis Halphen talked of his admiration for Henry II's policy in Britain, for 'without him, the English monarchy would have run the risk of lurching back into the feudal rut'.[37] Four years later, Yves Renouard, professor at Bordeaux, used the same argument of a Plantagenet hardline over the aristocracy in their French lands, when he approved of their role in bringing together the north and the south. They gave to their empire an 'overwhelmingly northern feel' and opened up the lands south of the Loire to the Capetians.[38] In this nationalistic tradition of French historiography (the legacy of Jacobinism) the Plantagenets were, on the one hand, an obstacle because of their English Crown and their constant opposition to the Capetians. But on the other hand, it gave them grudging approval for clearing the way for the French state by making war on the instigators of aristocratic risings and overthrowing their troublesome lordships.

The roots of these models of history lie in the old problem of the strong reemergence of 'feudal kingship' in France after a long period of weak central power. Despite their ideological baggage they do have some mileage left in them.[39] But apart from their application to legal and administrative areas, they need to be set aside when considering issues which touch on the wider history of society, such as economy and mentalities. The twelfth century was indeed a time of growing maturity in royal government. It was based on an ideological and technical scheme arising out of the renaissance in Roman law which was taught in a number of Mediterranean schools, and these provided many legal experts to the Plantagenet royal households. But the personal and human face of politics was no less essential. It was as much by his charisma and his own capacities as by bureaucratic and administrative devices that the king influenced and won the loyalty of the nobles, the chief powers in his provinces. He had to influence the hearts of his vassals, projecting by personality and by his deeds an image of himself which attracted their loyalty. The intellectual and literary vitality of the twelfth century helped this programme along. The king attracted writers who, in return for his patronage, wrote favourably about him. On the material level, a fortunate coincidence of events helped the Plantagenets along. At the end of the twelfth century, agricultural expansion and clearances reached their peak. Population rose, towns were developed and the Atlantic trade picked up. The consequent rise in fiscal revenue gave the king the means to pursue new policies. In the continental Atlantic ports, the rising merchant class, intent on securing communal privileges and ready to make mutual trade links with England, also ranged its support behind the Plantagenets. There was no more favourable time for Plantagenet hegemony.

However, the house of Anjou met one major obstacle on its high road to political success. Retaining the loyalty of its subjects was all the more difficult as its kings, though crowned in England, owed homage to the French king for their continental possessions. Too much can never be made of their subordinate status,[40] which deeply compromised the future of the so-called (and that word show its limits) Plantagenet Empire.[41] One example amongst many others: the abbot of Charroux (Poitou) publicly asserted in 1168 that his monastery was a dependency of the French king from its foundation by Charlemagne, and that it had nothing to do with Henry II. This opinion was shared by many Aquitainian monks, who were given to minimizing the comital jurisdiction over their lands by asserting that they were the direct vassals of Louis VII.[42] The homage owed by the Plantagenets to the Capetians reduces to its proper place as a deceptive fiction the big blob of red on the maps of textbooks which marks the huge 'Plantagenet Empire', as opposed to the hemmed-in domain of the French king, represented by some dotted lines and grey shadings, between Soissons and Chartres. Louis VII, and even more so Philip Augustus and Louis VIII, actually had a head start on their Angevin rivals in the race for the final takeover of the decisive areas of the western French principalities.

All this data is necessary for us to understand the twelfth century. It is the seedbed for a reinvented political history, where events are less important than analyses of power, and institutions give way to prosopography and the study of government, pressure groups and their networks of dependants, and the history of ideas is extended into the study of symbols and political theory. The history of the constitution takes second place to the history of the political system. There are any number of examples of such pioneering studies. Only two of them are cited here, ones particularly illuminating for the argument. In 1924, *Les Rois Thaumaturges* of Marc Bloch, a book bearing on the respective sacralities of the English and French monarchies, showed, with remarkable precocity, that the rejection of positivist and empirical history – which is wrapped up in descriptions of princely acts and the battles that they involved – ought not nonetheless to lead to the sidelining of the in-depth history of the medieval political world. In 1955, J.E.A. Jolliffe's *Angevin Kingship* also introduced many new and fascinating avenues of research on the nature of Plantagenet power which, without being absolutist because of its regard for law, was still authoritarian, even arbitrary. Jolliffe's book, dense and difficult, is less like the legalistic constitutional history of the nineteenth century in its originality and more like a leap forward such as the work of Hobbes (1588–1679), for whom power abhorred a vacuum. Jolliffe's method is an example to all those who study political life in the twelfth century. These two books are, in many respects, a point of reference for every research on the Plantagenet Empire. They are in the same vein as the new political history that has been the flavour of the month in France since the 1980s.[43]

The theme of power has to be at the heart of all research into the Plantagenet Empire. It was already pretty much central for contemporary clerical thinkers of the time, who defined it dualistically as on one hand ecclesiastical *auctoritas*, imbued with the prestige bestowed by the sacred and by learning, and on the other hand as lay *potestas*, stemming from armed force. This idea of the force of coercion appeared to them unavoidable if justice and peace were to be made to reign in the breast of sinful man, apt to violence. In contemporary clerical eyes, the order that gave society respect for law and custom – too often imposed by force – made possible eternal salvation for the greatest number. But the clerks also knew that arrogant *potestas* concealed a source of violence, 'for all power has always been, is now and ever will be, hostile to whoever might dare to oppose it to gain his own share', wrote around 1198 the chronicler Richard of Devizes, Benedictine monk of St Swithun, Winchester, when he was explaining the ousting from the Exchequer of Hugh de Puiset, bishop of Durham, by the chancellor, William de Longchamps, bishop of Ely, his sworn enemy.[44] All too often in the twelfth century, power did not just stay where it was put, it moved on. It derived more from the competition for influence and from violence than from the operation of established agencies. At whatever level it was exercised, violence (including the most extreme forms), was integral to the Plantagenet Empire both for its preservation and its expansion. In such a situation, are we dealing with 'politics' as it is understood in modern Western democracies? Using this word for the Middle Ages seems often to be close to anachronism.

The medieval historian who wants to understand the ins and outs of this sort of history is very well-off for sources. For the end of the twelfth century, he benefits from a radical shift in civilization, the object of a brilliant study by Michael T. Clanchy: *From Memory to Written Record*[45] – the movement of book-learning confined to clerics only, to the democratization of reading amongst the laity and of writing devoted to royal bureaucratization. As a result of this change, documentation becomes more plentiful in England, where governmental methods experienced a considerable advance which can be seen in the constant resort of the king and his court to writing.[46] The Plantagenet chancery was never idle. Its messengers carried to its correspondents in all parts of the Empire hundreds of letters, closed by the seal symbolizing the majesty of the king. It was just as frantic at the Exchequer, the central office of finance in England and Normandy, which kept written records of every payment in or out. Already in the reign of Henry I (1100–1135) this financial agency issued some 4,500 letters a year.[47] Under Richard the Lionheart, of whom it has been written that he 'was the creator of English royal record-keeping'[48] Archbishop Hubert Walter of Canterbury, chief justiciar and then chancellor, further perfected the bureaucracy. Right from the beginning of John's reign, and under Hubert's direction, the copying of royal letters on to parchment rolls became routine.[49] To this bureaucratic activity, whose purpose was to issue and record orders, can be added the collection of information by royal agents, who carried out enquiries and even espionage in the modern sense. For example, they obtained not only a copy of Thomas Becket's files kept at Rome but every letter relevant to his case sent by papal legates to England.[50] At the time of the first Angevin kings, Anglo-Norman bureaucracy was increasing its written production as never before.

The extent of the survival of English archives is itself remarkable. Two examples are sufficient to prove it. An average of 120 of Henry II's acts against a score of them for Louis VII (1137–1180) and around sixty for Philip Augustus. Secondly, of the 971 surviving papal decretal letters from the twelfth century whose recipient is known, 434 concern England, where they have been carefully preserved, and besides this fifteen of the twenty-seven decretal collections compiled by European canon lawyers come from Britain. The effectiveness of Plantagenet government, particularly in England and Normandy, involved the diffusion of writing and the keeping of records at all levels of royal bureaucracy. To the great satisfaction of medieval historians, these administrative sources did not undergo the massive destruction which characterize a number of continental kingdoms.

Such a mass of records is exceptional in the West. It is far superior in every way to the archives surviving in France for the twelfth century. Following a recent observation of Nicholas Vincent,[51] this data, allied to the medievalist preferences both of British researchers and the editors of local history societies, is the key to understanding the historiographical divergence on either side of the Channel. In Britain, an unvarying erudition and great chronological and prosopographical precision are more evident than overviews of models and states of the question. On the continent, synthesis triumphs over analysis, as if the meagre historical record was itself creating ideas. It is the source that makes the historian!

The balance of written history also tilts towards Britain. Chronicles and Latin annals are common in England, especially in and after the 1180s. We can add to the names of Gerald of Barry and Richard of Devizes, mentioned earlier, the Augustinian canon William of Newburgh (1136–1198), born in Yorkshire, a very well-informed man; Roger (died 1201) another northerner, retired to be the head of the large collegiate church of Howden, which pertained to the diocese of Durham, where he wrote a chronicle, having served Henry II and Richard the Lionheart, with whom he went on crusade;[52] Ralph, abbot of the Cistercian house of Coggeshall (Essex) between 1207 and 1218, another fervent admirer of King Richard; Ralph de Diceto, or of Diss (1120/1130–1202),[53] dean of St Paul's London; Gervase, monk of Christ Church Canterbury (died p.1210); John of Salisbury (1115–1180), bishop of Chartres after 1176 and the clerk William fitz Stephen, both close collaborators with Thomas Becket. Antonia Gransden, specialist in English medieval historiography, does not exaggerate in describing the last two decades of the twelfth century as 'the golden age of English historical writing'.[54] One of the more significant interests of these English chroniclers is in presenting in their works events concerning the whole Plantagenet Empire, indeed the entire west of Europe.[55]

The geographical range of the historians of the preceding period, from 1150 to 1180, was more local. This shrinking of horizons can be accounted for by the fact that they are for the most part Benedictine monks, originating from Normandy, Anjou, Poitou and the Limousin, where they perpetuated the traditional historiography of their communities. In Normandy, Robert de Torigny (died 1186), prior of Bec and then abbot of Mont St-Michel, left a meticulous account of the events of his friend Henry II's reign; he was one of the godfathers of the king's daughter, Eleanor.[56] It was in Normandy that the king commissioned two secular clerks, Wace, and then around 1170 Benoît de Sainte-Maure, to compose the deeds of the dukes of Normandy in Anglo-Norman verse. Several anonymous Latin annals were kept in Anjou, based at local cathedrals and monasteries. In the Limousin, two accomplished chroniclers, the monks Geoffrey de Breuil, prior of Vigeois (died after 1184) and Bernard Itier (1163–1225), librarian of Saint-Martial de Limoges, reported events in Aquitaine. The same applies to the Cluniac, Richard the Poitevin (c.1110–p.1173). This list of authors shows the exceptional interest of a study of the Plantagenet Empire, which can be based on a plentiful historiography, more extensive than any other part of the twelfth-century West.

The historiography can be complemented with the names of certain professional oral poets, who described in their metrical Anglo-Norman songs things they had often witnessed. Born in the Evreçin, the poet Ambroise, wrote down in the Holy Land, to which he had gone on pilgrimage just after the truce with Saladin, his direct witness of the military exploits of Richard the Lionheart, in whose honour he composed a long poem.[57] The clerk Jordan Fantosme chose the same tongue and a more complicated verse form in which to describe – a little after their occurrence – the conflicts between English and Scots troops in Northumbria, place of his birth, between 1173 and 1174.[58] These two works were entirely and exclusively composed for the glory of Richard the Lionheart and Henry II. It was in the same literary genre that there appeared around 1189 the work sometimes called *The Song of Dermot and the Earl*, telling in 3,459 octosyllabic verses the story of the invasion of Ireland by Norman knights from South Wales between 1169 and 1175.[59] We might mention the famous song of William Marshal (died 1219), regent of England, composed by the trouvère, John, around 1227.[60] Midway between chronicle and epic, these long vernacular songs were composed by contemporary witnesses, who involved themselves without hesitation in the events they were describing. They are similar to the short *sirventes* or vernacular political songs of the Languedoc, by which the southern troubadours praised or criticized the Plantagenets and their political moves. Written hastily to serve as propaganda around a specific event, this sort of poem drew on fictional literature.

Long passed down only by the voice of their creators and interpreters, there were any number of Arthurian romances or Carolingian epics committed to writing around the year 1200 in the Plantagenet lands. They are imaginitive and poetic literature, in which the marvellous, superhuman adventures and supernatural interventions make up the basic plot. But despite appearances, these sources need to be trawled by the medieval historian, for they were all part of socio-political context with which they had some complex relationships. Besides they throw a new light on the collective mentalities and political ideologies of the day.

Nowadays a certain post-structural tendency, tinged with pessimism, doubts the possibility of writing history, for the past cannot be understood. At close reading documents reveal just a discourse, that can be deepened only by an intra-textual approach, exclusively focused on content and ignoring any idea of reality. This method has a few devotees among medievalists, and they apply it to the reading of documents. At its extreme, this approach would prevent any attempt to extract data from fiction to understand humanity and the society in which the authors lived. It has to be acknowledged that structuralism has the merit of having shown the role that invention, manipulation, genre, imitation or myth play in the composition of a text, urging caution on readers. But it would be wrong to sideline the literature of the twelfth and thirteenth century, especially the Arthurian legend, when studying Angevin power, since poetic composition and romanesque fiction had an important place in the Plantagenet Empire.[61] The important thing is to take heed of the application of the method which allows historians to address texts.

Other, strikingly diverse, sources complete the picture. The correspondence of the bishops Thomas Becket (1162–1170), John of Salisbury, Gilbert Foliot (1148–1187), Arnulf of Lisieux (1141–1181), and of Peter of Blois (c.1130–1212),[62] chancellor of the archbishop of Canterbury and archdeacon of London, is all the more easy to consult as each has been lately studied and edited or translated.[63] These letters had been arranged in collections by their authors themselves or by their assistants, for wide publication.[64] They justify the line of action taken by Thomas Becket, archbishop of Canterbury and eager defender of the liberties of the Church against the king, or by Gilbert Foliot, bishop of London and Becket's declared enemy on that score, and also by Arnulf of Lisieux, who after having been chief justiciar of Normandy, fell into disgrace at the royal court for trying to reconcile the king with his sons at the time of the 1173 revolt.[65]

Besides the epistolary genre, technical manuals must be mentioned, such as those to instruct royal administrators, like the *Dialogue of the Exchequer*, mentioned earlier, or the *Constitution of the King's Household*, which described in 1136 the running of the household.[66] Besides these practical works, theoretical works on government attracted the attention of English intellectuals, among which inevitably one thinks of John of Salisbury, whose extensive works include the *Policraticus*, or *Ruler of the City*, the first systematic analysis of politics in the Middle Ages.

On the sociological level, it is interesting to note the increasing presence of secular clerks amongst these authors, which contrasts with the period before 1150, where most of the surviving works stem from monks. From 1150 young intellectuals looked for learning amongst the masters of the teeming urban schools rather than in the silence of monastic cloisters. Their writings form part of the movement which is today called the Twelfth-century Renaissance, following on from the work published in 1927 by Charles Homer Haskins, professor at Harvard, but which Walter Map (c.1140–1209) – another of Henry II's clerks – called 'modernity'.[67] Less man-centred as it was, this new humanism had nothing to envy in the humanism that reappeared in the sixteenth century. In the twelfth century is found an optimism about human nature which God himself took upon him; a fascination for the authors of classical Antiquity; Christianization of Stoic ethics; an increased role for reason in philosophy and observation in the natural sciences; a belief in the unbounded capacity of intellectual knowledge; the partial rebellion against tradition and authority; an austere and considered expression of sentiments, as much as a new place awarded to the vernacular in literature.[68] This laicization of knowledge, for all that it was relative, led any number of clerks to the court of the Plantagenets, who employed their learning in the service of royal power. Study of the humanities had structured their thinking and given them a mastery of written expression, an ideal education for princely service. It was often completed by instruction in legal ideas, indispensable for a lawyer and judge. The intellectual renaissance of the twelfth century undeniably served the political objectives of the king and promoted the influx of lettered clerks into the court.

For the Plantagenet Empire, this process of state formation, which is illustrated for us by sources far more plentiful than at any previous time, worked itself out in a political context which must be sketched in before engaging with the subject head-on.[69] Oddly enough, the empire had its roots in a civil war which, from the death of Henry I in 1135, laid waste the Anglo-Norman kingdom founded by the Conqueror (1035–1087) some decades earlier. Two claimants disputed the succession to Henry I: his daughter, the Empress Mathilda, wife of Geoffrey of Anjou, and his nephew Stephen of Blois (1135–1154). In 1144, the struggle came to a stalemate. Stephen, crowned king at Westminster in 1135, controlled most of England, and Angevin troops occupied Normandy. In the summer of 1151, Geoffrey and his eldest son Henry II went to Paris, where they did homage to Louis VII for the duchy of Normandy, which the king of France then recognized as theirs.

It was on this occasion that Henry II met Queen Eleanor of Aquitaine, whom he married in May 1152, after the decree of annulment at the council of Beaugency of her marriage to Louis VII. By this marriage with the hereditary duchess, a dozen years his elder, Henry II took over Aquitaine, which at the time included Poitou, Gascony and the Limousin.[70] Since September 1151, the premature death of Henry's father had placed him in control of Anjou, Maine and Normandy, though not before he had to fight his younger brother Geoffrey, the legitimate heir to Anjou according to the terms of their father's will.[71] So a third acquisition was swiftly added to this formidable patrimony which Henry acquired by the succession to his father, by marriage and by conquest.[72] Since the 1140s, Henry II had been well known in England, where he had participated as still a young man in the wars of his uncle, the influential Robert of Gloucester (*c.*1090–1147) bastard son of Henry I and an Oxfordshire noblewoman.[73] In November 1153, in the aftermath of the premature death of his eldest son Eustace, King Stephen adopted Henry II according to the terms of the Treaty of Wallingford. The king's younger son William (died 1160) would have to be content with the county of Boulogne and the earldom of Surrey. On Stephen's death, the succession to the English throne was therefore guaranteed to Henry. On 19 November 1154, Henry II and Eleanor were crowned at Westminster. At the age of twenty-one, the new king of England found himself ruling the conglomeration of kingdoms, duchies and counties we call the Plantagenet Empire.

Henry II proceeded to consolidate his position. He reached a settlement with Louis VII who accepted Henry's homage for his continental realms at Rouen in 1154. To ratify this alliance, a betrothal was arranged between the Young Henry, his eldest son, and Margaret of France, Louis VII's daughter, which brought with it the dowry of the Norman Vexin. In the Loire valley, Henry II continued to wage war on his brother Geoffrey who persisted in claiming Anjou. After crushing him militarily, Henry gave Geoffrey the county of Nantes, a city from which Count Hoel (1148–1156) had been evicted by an urban revolt in 1155. Geoffrey died at the age of twenty-four scarcely three years later. His nephew, another Geoffrey, Henry's son, succeeded at Nantes. In 1166 he would obtain the whole of the duchy of Brittany from his father-in-law, Conan IV (1156–1171). In the south, Henry II pursued the traditional expansionist policy of the dukes of Aquitaine, in the direction of Toulouse.[74] In 1159, with his chancellor, Thomas Becket, Henry raised an impressive army to besiege the city, with the help of Ramon Berengar IV (1131–1162), count of Barcelona and prince of Aragon.[75] But Louis VII came to the help of his brother-in-law, Raymond V of Toulouse (1148–1194). The king of England withdrew, not without having annexed Cahors and part of Quercy. He would only receive the homage of the count of Toulouse in 1173.

During the 1160s, Henry II was absorbed by two matters whose consequences would be serious for him in the long run. Firstly, he planned in the usual Angevin way[76] to divide his lordships and realms between his sons: the Anglo-Norman kingdom and Greater Anjou to the Young Henry; Aquitaine to Richard the Lionheart and Brittany to Geoffrey. To accommodate the youngest, John 'Lackland', born in 1166, he had to be content successively with the county of Maurienne through marriage, the county of Mortain, and the eastern region of Ireland, conquered around this time by Cambro-Norman knights.[77] Secondly, Henry II began an open dispute with Thomas Becket, his former chancellor, consecrated archbishop of Canterbury in 1162. Thomas's total refusal to accept the Constitutions of Clarendon (by which the king planned to abolish a number of ecclesiastical privileges, better to control the Church in England) ended in Thomas's exile and then murder in 1170. The assassination in the cathedral considerably undermined Henry II's authority.

It was at this time, in 1173, that Eleanor of Aquitaine and her sons, eager to have untramelled use of their inheritance, chose to rebel against Henry. They counted on the support of the aristocracies of their respective principalities, on the help of the king of France, and the counts of Blois, Boulogne and Flanders, not to mention that of William the Lion (1165–1214), king of Scotland. William's capture at Alnwick in July 1174, at the very moment of Henry II's penitential pilgrimage to the tomb of Thomas Becket, much assisted the crushing of the rebels. The king was reconciled with his sons and imposed a long period of imprisonment on Eleanor of Aquitaine. He had immense prestige in the West, as was proved by requests for his arbitration in the problems between Alfonso VIII of Castille (1158–1214), his son-in-law, and Sancho VI of Navarre (1154–1194) in 1177, and between Henry the Lion (1129–1194) duke of Saxony and Bavaria, another of his sons-in-law, and the Emperor Frederick Barbarossa (1152–1190) in 1182.

But this did not prevent his own children rebelling against him again or fighting amongst each other. In 1183 the Young Henry died in the Limousin, while he was devastating the countryside to signal his displeasure with his father. Three years later, Geoffrey of Brittany met his end in his turn at Paris, where he often stayed to advertise his alliance with Philip Augustus against Henry II. The new king of France showed a firm resolve to face up to his Plantagenet rival, as he assessed Angevin rule over so great a range of continental lands to be a serious danger to the Capetians.[78] In July 1188, he opened hostilities against Henry II. This time he was counting on the military assistance of Richard the Lionheart, who very successfully campaigned against his own father in the Loire valley. John was also in the conspiracy. On 4 July 1189, heading for defeat, Henry II had to recognize Richard as his sole heir in the Treaty of Aizy-le-Rideau. Two days later, abandoned by everyone, Henry died in his castle of Chinon.

In September 1189, Richard the Lionheart was crowned king of England.[79] But his only desire was towards one end: the accomplishment of the crusading vow that he had sworn with Philip Augustus, on learning of the news of the fall of Jerusalem (1187).[80] He proclaimed the Saladin Tithe, raised a great army, and launched an impressive fleet. Mistrusting his Gascon barons and Raymond V of Toulouse, he reached a treaty with

King Sancho V of Navarre, by which Sancho would oversee the Gascons and Raymond in his absence. This treaty led to Richard's marriage with Berengaria, Sancho's daughter, at Limassol (Cyprus) in May 1191. During the winter of 1190–1191, the crusaders stayed in Sicily, where the relations between the kings of England and France began to deteriorate, since they differed as to the direction of the crusade, In the spring, Richard conquered Cyprus. In the Holy Land the victory of Arsur (September 1191) and the conquest of Jaffa (August 1192) secured control of almost the whole Palestinian coast to the Latins.

But Philip Augustus, on his return to France, reached a treaty with John, who ceded the Vexin, lower Berry and part of the Touraine to Philip in exchange for the control of his brother's lands. The situation became all the more complicated in England as the justiciar, William de Longchamps, had failed to maintain his authority in the face of the intrigues of a party amongst the aristocracy, Geoffrey, the future archbishop of York, a bastard son of Henry II, and Walter de Coutances, who in the end seized control of the justiciarship from William. In September 1192, after his truce with Saladin (1171–1193), Richard returned to the West. But he was captured by Leopold of Austria (1177–1194), who handed him over to the Emperor Henry VI (1190–1197). Despite the excommunication by Celestine III of Leopold – who had flouted the basic rights of crusaders – the king's imprisonment lasted a year and a half. Henry VI forced Richard in the meantime to hand over to him his lands as an imperial fief.

In the Plantagenet Empire, Eleanor of Aquitaine encouraged resistance to John and succeeded in raising the enormous ransom necessary to free her son Richard, a ransom equivalent to the revenues of England for two years.[81] On Richard's return in April 1194, the king pardoned his brother. He then began a merciless war against Philip Augustus, his former ally, to recover the lost territories. In the months that followed, his victories at Fréteval and Issoudun, and his conquest of Angoulême with the help of his father-in-law Sancho VI, secured the Vexin, Touraine and lower Berry for him.[82] The treaty of Louviers in 1196 ratified the situation.[83] On a diplomatic level his successes were just as important: an alliance with Baldwin IX, count of Flanders (1194–1206); the marriage of his sister Joan, widow of William II of Sicily, to Raymond VI, count of Toulouse (1194–1222); and the imperial coronation of his nephew, Otto IV of Brunswick (1198–1218). Strengthened by this record of success, Richard could concentrate on pacifying the regional aristocracy of Aquitaine. In March 1199, a new revolt by the count of Angoulême drew the king to the Limousin. It was while besieging the castle of Châlus, held by a vassal of the vicomte of Limoges, that Richard was hit by a crossbow bolt. Gangrene carried him off on 6 April 1199 at the age of forty-one.

Richard's brother John succeeded him. In his early days he assured himself of the neutrality of Philip Augustus by the costly peace of Le Goulet (22 May 1200), by the terms of which he abandoned the Evreçin, part of the Vexin and lower Berry to Philip.[84] But this truce did not last long. On 24 August 1200 John married Isabel, the heiress of Angoulême, with the intention of securing his rule over Poitou. But Isabel had already married Hugh IX de Lusignan, count of La Marche, by means of some *verba de presenti*, or informal spoken contract. She was at the time nine years old and the earlier marriage had not been consummated. Isabel's maternal grandfather was Peter de Courtenay, brother of Louis VII, so she was also a cousin of Philip Augustus. On the one hand her marriage to king John put an end to the pretensions of the Lusignan counts of La Marche as regards the Angoumois, and on the other, it checked Capetian expansion into the region.[85] At the demand of Hugh IX de Lusignan, Philip Augustus retaliated by declaring on 28 April 1202 the confiscation of John's continental domains as being a felonious vassal. He supported Arthur of Brittany, John's nephew, who had been brought up at the French court and who invaded Anjou. King John turned up in time to defeat him in Poitou, capturing him at Mirebeau in July 1202. But it was only a stay of execution. John was unable to exploit his victory and alienated the aristocracy of his own territories. Philip's successes snowballed until the conquest of Normandy, Anjou and the Touraine in 1204. These lands had slipped out of the king of England's hands for good and all.

John experienced similar problems in Aquitaine, where the death of his mother, Eleanor of Aquitaine on 1 April 1204, undermined his interests. The Poitevin towns and aristocracy promptly pledged their allegiance to Philip Augustus. Gascony was invaded by Alfonso VIII of Castille, who claimed it as the dowry of his wife, King John's sister. The marriage contract had provided that he might take control of it on the death of his mother-in-law.[86] But the resolve of Savary de Mauléon, seneschal of Poitou,[87] and of Elias de Malmort, archbishop of Bordeaux, helped to rally a group of local elites into the Plantagenet camp and stabilize the situation. In the summer of 1206, John returned to the continent with substantial forces. He concluded a truce with Philip Augustus which allowed John to keep Aquitaine.

But John had to face just as serious problems in Britain. He opposed the arrival in England of Stephen Langton, elected archbishop of Canterbury, to take possession of his see. In retaliation, Innocent III imposed an interdict on England in 1208 and excommunicated the king in 1209. Philip Augustus was on the point of invading England. In February 1214, however, King John disembarked on the continent with his men. The Norman and Angevin members of his court, who had lost so much,[88] were undoubtedly urging him to pursue this hazardous reconquest, which did at least silence for a while the turmoil in England. But on 2 July this campaign was ended by the defeat of La Roche-aux-Moines. On 27 July, John's imperial allies were also defeated at Bouvines. The five-year truce which Philip Augustus conceded John at Chinon allowed him to retire in good order. On his return to England, John faced a general rebellion which forced him to accept the Magna Carta on 19 June 1215. His enemies appealed to the future Louis VIII (1223–1226), who landed in Kent, took control of Eastern England and entered London on 2 June 1216. But John's death on 19 October provoked a reaction in favour of his son Henry III, which drove Louis out. John's unexpected death probably saved his dynasty, which hung on to the Crown of England.

Henry III, still a minor, and his justiciar Hubert de Burgh, did not escape difficulties. Geoffrey de Marisco, himself justiciar of Ireland, rebelled; Llywelyn ap Iorwerth, prince of North Wales, seized several English castles to the south of his principality. But it was in Aquitaine that the situation became untenable. The widowed Isabel d'Angoulême, now returned to her native land, married Hugh X de Lusignan, count of La Marche, the son of her previous fiancé, creating the big territorial principality south of Poitou, which King John had so much feared earlier. On 2 June 1224, the couple met with Louis VIII at Bourges. In return for Saintes, the Ile d'Oléron, and an annual pension of 2,000*li.*, the king of France would help Hugh to seize Aquitaine. At the same time Louis VIII made alliances with the vicomtes of Thouars and Limoges, and took La Rochelle (a bridgehead for any possible reconquest from England), Saintes and Saint-Jean-d'Angely. Poitou eluded Henry III for good. Only Gascony put up a resistance to Hugh X's troops, preferring the distant rule of England to him. Henry III's resources and opportunities were inconsiderable compared to those of his ancestors. At best his fleet succeeded in retaking Oléron in 1230. The revolt against the French king in 1242 staged by Hugh X and Isabel d'Angoulême – used to reversals of alliance – and by Raymond VII of Toulouse (1222–1249) with the support of Henry III, was heavily defeated. In 1259, the Treaty of Paris recognized Gascony as belonging to the English Crown, but after 1224, without Poitou, the Plantagenet Empire was no more.[89]

The Empire had survived for some seventy years. The reasons it survived for so long are the object of this book. To highlight them, it is unavoidable to begin with the king himself, his family and his household. This closed world, sometimes in harmony and sometimes racked with conflict, deserves a concentrated study, for it was the heart of the government of the Plantagenet Empire. It was the channel for royal ideology and propaganda, intended to promote obedience to the king, whose fiscal and military demands were always increasing. It was in the context of the court that origin myths, recent history and romance fiction were consciously manipulated, as for instance the way the Arthurian legend was. It was from this perpetually itinerant court, into which all information flowed, that decisions were broadcast, having been taken in council and suitably framed by learned clerks. These were unevenly passed on by the local officers of the Angevin dynasty to their respective political and social constituencies. The aristocracy and the episcopal hierarchy were the king's favoured partners in dialogue. Along with the evolving city communities, aristocracy and hierarchy were the only social groups with the power to agree or disagree with the king's orders as they wished. Their compliance or their rebellion accounted for the integrity or the disruption of the Plantagenet Empire. Docility or resistance occurred in a world rarely at peace, where war and knightly violence were universal. They were the heart of the question as to whether a burgeoning state would triumph or fail.

To tackle such questions, we will firstly concentrate on the political 'centre', the place of decision, propaganda and coercion, the place which embodied the king and his court. It was from the court, endowed with a rapidly evolving ideological superstructure, that administrative structures were imposed on the social 'periphery', which will be looked at later. Two groups had the choice of accepting or rejecting royal direction: firstly, the warriors of the nobility, masters of lordships and feudal networks and powerful from their exercise of arms; secondly, there was the episcopate and learned clergy, a great part of whose autonomy was protected by ancient privileges and a particular attitude to power.

Government and royal will

In 1177, Peter of Blois, household clerk of Henry II, wrote a letter to the Englishman, Walter, archbishop of Palermo, someone he had known when he had lived as a young man in Norman Sicily. That same year the marriage between Joan, the king of England's daughter, and King William II of Sicily (1154–1189), once Peter's pupil, had brought that great Mediterranean island and Plantagenet England close together once more. Peter was satisfying the wish of his friend to know more about his royal master. Peter began by comparing Henry II and David, the ideal king of the Old Testament, a redhead, like Henry. He carried on with the physical description. Henry was of medium height, had a round head and square jaw, fierce eyes, was thin on top like Caesar and had a large nose. Peter dwelt on the king's 'rider's legs': '. . . although they might be badly injured and bruised by throws from his horse, he never sits down except when he rides or eats.'[1] The king was a martyr to his constant travelling. His most frequent companions were warhorses and palfreys. Whether trotting along a road with his court, or galloping in the charge,[2] Henry was always the horseman.

Peter's respect for Henry II is a little more equivocal in another of his letters.[3] It is fraught with the scruples of a courtier-priest, torn between the desire to use his political influence to work for good, and his attraction to a contemplative life, which is an impossibility in a secular environment whose many temptations he lists.[4] More prosaically, considering his age, he was weary of the constant travel which prevents the courtier from ever settling down. He describes the trials of the nomadic existence of the court: when the king's servants hang around, uncertain as to what their next stop may be, at the mercy of the royal whim. The order to move takes them unawares. Once the royal entourage is under way, they can look forward to more troubles en route: 'for this "vanity of vanities" (Wis. 1: 2) we courtiers suffer daily weariness and trials from frequent sleeplessness and great dangers, danger of crossings by sea and river, of mountain passes, and of false colleagues (cf. 2 Cor.: 11: 26–7). Courtiers are in frequent fear of death, they injure and exhaust their bodies, and risk their lives.' But unlike St Paul and his apostolic journeys, courtiers do not undergo these tribulations for the sake of Christ: 'They are devotees of worldliness, disciples of the court, knights of Hellequin.'[5] This legendary character, a damned soul whom the devil had forbidden ever to dismount his horse, led a ghostly retinue which, on the run from Hell, purged its sins in this world by forever wandering.[6] This image of frenetic activity also reminded Walter Map (Peter of Blois's companion in misfortune at the Angevin court) of the royal entourage on the road: 'Hellequin's company was seen for the last time on the borders of Wales, at Hereford, in the last year of the reign of Henry II at midday. They travelled as we do, with wagons and packhorses, with saddlebags and baskets, hawks and dogs, men and women travelling together . . . Thereafter it has not shown itself, as if it had passed on to us, poor fools, those wanderings in which we wear out our clothes, lay waste kingdoms, exhaust ourselves and our mounts, and never have time to see to our sick souls.'[7] Peter of Blois and Walter Map seem particularly traumatized by the hellish nomadic life of the king and his court. A demonization of the court runs through their clerkly discourse, the several issues involved in which we will analyse later.

At present the concern is to investigate the negative view of the court by clerks. Despite Peter of Blois's views, the king's travels were not by any means a matter of whim. They followed an itinerary previously agreed, rationally worked out and the fruit of long debate. The royal financial accounts of the Pipe Rolls show that the king's movements were planned six weeks in advance, in consultation with the stewards of the royal manors, from which the royal train drew much of its supplies.[8] Besides this, merchants followed the court and peasants approached it with a view to supplying its needs.[9] Moreover, the stages it travelled of thirty-five kilometres a day by horse or in wheeled vehicles were far from taxing. They were all the less arduous as particular care was taken in managing the travel, as the detailed Exchequer costings reveal. Part of the treasure was transported on a big wagon (the *longa carreta*); the kitchen was carried on one or two single-horse carts, with the provisions on another; weapons, metal-working tools and the liturgical furnishings of the chapel royal were packed up on horses.[10] The court on the road was not the trial that Peter of Blois and Walter Map make out.

Further to this, conditions in the lodging of courtiers were far from being haphazard when the court was on the road. They hardly differed from the lodgings courtiers would have enjoyed if they were resident in a castle, where promiscuity and the lack of private space was the common lot of underlings. When they travelled across open country, the king and his intimates could count on at least one form of comfortable shelter. Henry II's favoured gift for other monarchs was, in this connection, an expensive tent. In 1157 he sent a pavilion, with pulleys and other mechanical contrivances to erect it, to Frederick Barbarossa. The German chronicler, Rahewin of Freising (died c.1175), described it as 'a tent worthy of admiration in the splendour of its decoration', woven in exotic materials and covered with embroidery.[11] In 1177, a 'tent of silk' was likewise a part of the dowry which Joan brought with her to William II of Sicily.[12] So the characteristic gift of Henry II to his fellow-princes was a pavilion, absolutely indispensable in his opinion to any king on his travels. It is a comment on Henry's own perception of the place of travel in his life.

Travel was a necessity in the government of the enormous Plantagenet Empire. During his thirty-four years as king, Henry II celebrated Christmas in twenty-four different places, he crossed the Channel twenty-eight times, and the Irish Sea twice.[13] Counting up the numbers of months which he spent in each of his realms provides us with some telling statistics. He stayed longest in Normandy (fourteen-and-a-half years) and England (thirteen years) where his power was most effective and from which he drew his most considerable revenues. By contrast he spent no more than seven years in Anjou and Aquitaine, that is, a fifth of his reign.[14] The king's itinerary was more frequently along the roads of his northern lands, peaceful and well-governed, than those of the rebellious provinces south of the Loire. It is a matter of fact that his itinerary encompassed and defined his empire, for it was by his own presence that a Plantagenet ruler made his realm a reality. Its feudal relationships depended almost entirely on these face-to-face contacts with its vassals. Prolonged absence weakened his authority; it either fostered the rebellion of a son to whom Henry II had entrusted a region, or the independence of the local magnates. At the king's bidding, the itinerary sparked disputes and rivalries.[15] On the other hand, the mobile court seemed to the king to be a source of justice, good government and patronage. The basic purpose of the royal tours was, essentially, to keep a close watch on the local nobilities and royal representatives, whose work needed to be supervised. Peter of Blois's letter puts it all in plain terms: 'Henry II did not confine himself to his palace like other kings, but travelling through the provinces, he looked into the doings of each man, being the judge of those that he had set to judge everybody else.'[16] The mobility of the Angevin king and his court was directly related to the reliability of his local officers.[17] The king's parade of his own power in all corners of his realm was related likewise to the evolution of faceless bureaucracy.

The evidence about the rise of bureaucracy tallies well with that of Henry II's stays in each of his domains. Most of his officials were recruited from the old Anglo-Norman realm. It was here that there was also the greatest concentration of royal manors, where he could stay with his court to eat up on site what his peasants had produced. Sound administrative practices had existed the longest in the Anglo-Norman realm, as is evident from its organized network of administrative posts.[18] The English sheriffs and Norman vicomtes were given the king's manors, the forests and vacant fiefs within their area of authority at farm. They saw to justice and public order within their areas with the help of sergeants and informers.[19] They levied routine payments, mostly those to do with trade and legal business, and also the extraordinary taxes: the old Danegeld (the tribute anciently given to the Vikings) up to the year 1161;[20] the Saladin tithe of 1188; the carrucage, the tax levied on property under Richard the Lionheart; the scutage, the payment made by knights who could not do service, and other aids levied in time of war. Sheriffs and vicomtes had to answer for their doings before the Exchequers which were held on either side of the Channel from the beginning of the twelfth century. If corruption was proved, the Exchequer fined the malefactor for twice the proceeds of his crime. The officers were in addition regularly inspected by envoys from the royal court, itinerant justices following an 'eyre' (a circuit fixed by custom). Alongside these sheriffs, vicomtes and estate stewards, other officers were employed at the local level of Plantagenet authority. Principally these were keepers of royal castles, men he appointed, transferred or dismissed, just like those officers who were responsible for coining his silver pennies, buying their dies from him. This bureaucratic system involved farming out of assets, bribery and heredity in office-holding. At the end of his reign, Henry II began to shift towards direct appointments and salaries paid to officers by the central administration. This modern approach is only found in England or Normandy, however. It contrasts with the embryonic sort of administration in Anjou and Aquitaine, where some local officers collected revenues from the prince's estates and did their best, for good or ill, to do justice as if they themselves were the lord.

In control of each principality of the empire was a representative of the king. Such a person might be a regent for the king's under-age sons, but was more likely to be someone like a chief justiciar for England or Normandy or a seneschal for Anjou and Aquitaine.[21] In the Anglo-Norman kingdom, the seneschalcy (the office of the steward, nominally responsible for the household and royal accommodation) in practice involved not administration but the command of the army. The king's seal was entrusted to the chancellor, who supervised the issue of royal acts. Part of the financial exactions from England and Normandy were not employed there, but were devoted to paying for the officials of the royal court, funding annual subsidies agreed with the nobility, or supporting military campaigns in the Loire valley and on the borders of Aquitaine. The money was temporarily housed at Caen or at Winchester then, from 1207, at Westminster and in other English towns, under the charge of a treasurer and two chamberlains, before being taken off in the 'great wagon' or shipped on a boat called the 'Serpent'.[22]

The *Dialogue of the Exchequer* provides indications of what would become the standard fiscal policy of English government: 'A supply of money seems as necessary as much in times of peace as in war. During wars, it is spent on fortifying towns, paying wages and other retainers depending on the standing of the recipient; in sum, it is used to maintain the good order of the kingdom. On the other hand, when the rattle of arms falls silent, pious princes build churches; Christ is fed and dressed in the person of the poor man (Matt. 25: 40) and Mammon is dispensed through the doing of other works of mercy (Luke 16: 9).'[23] This policy gave priority to military defence through castle-building and the hire of soldiers; yet it enabled the patronage of churches, social support and charity. Derived from the ancient theology of Augustine of Hippo, the policy presented the king conducting just wars in defence of his realm, supporting the Christian faith and easing his people's sufferings.

We may never know for sure to what degree the Plantagenets had thought through the policy that Henry II's treasurer explained with such care. Nor may we ever know its real political intentions. The Plantagenets did not conduct any fewer wars to preserve their lands, or indeed to extend them, as a result of it. They did build castles, monasteries and churches. They had been influenced by a new sort of evangelical spirituality which emphasized serving the poor. Besides this, they had tried hard to impose their justice, considering that they were more able to pacify disputes and promote peace than could any of their vassals or the Church. To govern effectively and to impose their power, they had to count on the aid and counsel of an existing group of vassals; they had also to legitimize their growing ascendancy by an ideology and propaganda which justified that ascendancy against the aristocracy and clergy. They devoted particular attention therefore to the make-up of their court and the political culture developed by the intellectuals in their pay.

The court, its officers and their skills

For the clerks of King Henry II's household, understanding the court was a tricky business. They actually said that the effort of analysing took more time than they had available. Walter Map wrote to the point: 'Studying the court is so huge an undertaking that any effort to do it would be endless, and there is no mastering it.' He confessed that the size of the task defeated him before he started: 'I speak of the court. But as for understanding the court . . . God alone knows what it is!'[1] It is not very encouraging for the historian of the Middle Ages who might wish to make his own attempt at the task to be confronted by such reflections from medieval courtiers on the methods of their art. However, the court appeared to Map as the principal centre of royal power. It was the very heart from where the monarch and his household governed the realm out as far as its edges. Decisions fanned outwards from the court, which were applied with a degree of success in the different Plantagenet domains. The penetration of its influence down to the local level depended on the court's mobility, on its inquisitions, on the efforts of its envoys, on the reports of its informants, and on the acts drawn up in its chancery and carried by its messengers. In order to grasp the essence of the court, the focus of royal power, it is vital to return to the meaning of the Latin word for it in twelfth-century sources, *curia*. It meant at the same time three things: a court of law, a palace and a retinue.

First, we will consider its judicial function. The centralization of justice was the chief issue between the king and the lords of castles at the end of the twelfth century. On the social level it implied that the king had the monopoly of the 'ban', the power of coercion and constraint, to the disadvantage of the justice offered by magnates. On the ideological level, this centralization was to be found in the Ancient Roman tradition – given a

Christian gloss by St Augustine – according to which there was no peace on earth except the justice wielded with an even hand by the prince. Centralization in the interests of the *curia regis* was very advanced in England.[2] Here, the Clarendon Assizes of 1166 imposed regular annual visitations by royal justices in the shires so as to counteract the abuses of sheriffs in their jurisdictions, and to undermine the former private judicial franchises. After 1166 England would be toured regularly by these justices in eyre, originating from the royal court, sent to monitor the efficiency of the shire courts.[3] The ambitious Inquest of the Sheriffs (*Inquisitio vicecomitum*) of 1170 – which looked into the conduct of the shire officers and which ended in the disgrace of some of them for corruption – was further evidence of the efficiency of the English system.[4] The Inquest represented a turning point for the idea of centralization: the appearance of local justices tightly linked to the court from which they came, men whom English historians unhesitatingly call 'curial sheriffs'.[5] The influence of this sort of sheriff increased further under Richard the Lionheart and John. Did the new sheriffs lessen financial demands and draw back from the old exactions? Not in the opinion of the rebels of 1215, who condemned their abuses in Magna Carta.[6] But they were nonetheless bound to present regular accounts at the Exchequer of Westminster. As well as the general extension of the annual tours of justices in eyre, another measure taken by the Clarendon assizes was its punishment of criminal clerks at the request of the civil authorities. This would be the bone of contention between Henry II and Thomas Becket, the supporter of ecclesiastical law. In short, the centralization of justice was carried out in England for the benefit of the royal court. The situation was essentially the same in Normandy. But the Anglo-Norman examples are a little deceptive. In Anjou and Aquitaine local power retained a wide freedom of manoeuvre in relation to central authority.

The second of the meanings inherent in the word *curia* is as a place of residence. The number of monographs relating to the various homes of the Plantagenet dynasty much increased during the 1990s.[7] They highlight the importance of the dimension of castellology – a study owing as much to architecture as to written sources – to our knowledge of past politics and war. Studies have analysed Gisors, Loches and Chinon on the continent, as much as Orford in Suffolk, where Henry II had a polygonal donjon built between 1165 and 1173, whose design was a break with the old square Norman keeps. But the two most important fortresses of the Angevin dynasty were Dover in England – heavily reconstructed between 1180 and 1189 – and Château Gaillard in Normandy, built by Richard the Lionheart in 1196 on his return from the Third Crusade. These two fortresses are estimated to have cost 7,000*li.* and 11,250*li.* respectively. As a comparison, the annual revenue for the duchy of Normandy amounted to some 14,000*li.* in 1195.[8] Advances in siege technology and the influence of the military architecture of the Holy Land account for numerous innovations in these castles, influenced by the concentric design of fortification, with its inner and outer curtain walls. Relying on three decades of technological progress in comparison with the Capetians, Plantagenet engineers put into practice the cutting edge of military technology: exclusive use of cut stone; banks cut in the Angevin style; jutting, circular mural towers; machicolated battlements on arches; arrow-slits set in niches to command dead zones.[9] As well as these innovations, the older royal castles were reinforced by flanking towers to improve their defensibility. Their donjons were not always spacious, and so the Plantagenets provided themselves with new apartments where they could live in comfort, as at Chinon.[10] It was in these places that the Plantagenets were most often to be found, where they held their courts and attended the liturgical offices. For example, Adam of Eynsham the hagiographer of Hugh of Avalon, bishop of Lincoln (1186–1200), described Richard the Lionheart in August 1198, attending a mass in the castle chapel of Château Gaillard, at the moment when the holy man forced a kiss of peace out of the king, who was at the time annoyed with him and reluctant to give it.[11] This amalgamation of palace and fortress seems unique to the West, when everywhere else royal and noble residences were unfortified, and when younger sons left the domestic hearth of their eldest brother to build their own houses in the countryside.[12] The double purpose of Plantagenet castles, residential and military, are witnesses on a symbolic level to the warrior aspect of kingship and, on a political level, to the difficulty in ruling a realm all too often in rebellion.

Ambition

The third meaning of the word *curia* needs its own more extensive treatment. It describes the royal household, that is, the staff of the court and, more generally, the political community which supported the prince in his decisions and which helped govern his lands. The king was always eager to hear its advice. The *Chronicle of Battle Abbey* portrays its abbot showing Henry II the charter of the abbey's foundation, on the site of the battle of Hastings (1066), which it had from William the Conqueror. The abbot required a charter of confirmation from Henry. The king replied promptly: 'I won't do anything without a judgement of my court'.[13] Perhaps he knew that numerous forgeries had been fabricated at Battle in the name of the Conqueror in the 1150s so as to secure its immunities.[14] The abbot also approached Richard de Lucy (died 1179), the justiciar of England, who argued the abbey's case before the king and his men. It was only after consulting among them that the king issued the confirmation of the foundation charter.[15] There is another example of the influence of the court on the prince. At the beginning of the dispute between Henry II and Thomas Becket, the clergy of the province of Canterbury sent a letter to the pope blaming the royal household for measures contrary to ecclesiastical liberties; there it featured as 'the vassals and intimates of the king who privately assist him in particular affairs, those men who direct the counsels of the king and the business of the kingdom'.[16] The *Dialogue of the Exchequer* talks in similar terms of 'the great men of the kingdom who privately offer advice to the king within his household, so that whatever may have been decided or determined by such great men is established by unbreakable law'.[17] In a monarchy very different from the modern absolutist sort, collective action lent more weight to royal orders; distanced responsibility from the prince, and, if necessary, allowed him to blame political mistakes on one of his advisers. The semantic significance of these texts, which favour words like *fidelis*, *familiaris*, *secreta*, *consilium* and *assistere*, projects the domestic, enclosed and private nature of the household, without which it was difficult to see how the king might govern.[18]

For the reign of Henry II, the study of his household of vassals can basically rely on the sound biographies compiled by the Norman scholar, Leopold Delisle, at the beginning of the twentieth century.[19] Methodologically, however, this sort of study must nowadays follow on from the classic study of Jean-François Lemarignier, published in 1965, *Royal Government in Early Capetian Times, 978–1108*. Lemarignier's great step forward relied on the analysis, counting and identification of witnesses and signatories to royal acts. It has allowed the exposure of the functions of a group of counsellors, so as to put it in the overall context of the changes in power and society. Lemarignier's study has been much imitated, particularly among French specialists in the twelfth century.[20] Lastly, the study of the household has come into contact with a further methodology, thanks to the taste for prosopography, that is, the compilation of multiple biographies so as to uncover accurately the make-up and contours of each social group. This last method of analysis has been most exploited in Britain and the United States in relation to the Plantagenet court, as the works of J.E. Lally,[21] Thomas K. Keefe,[22] Ralph V. Turner[23] and Nicholas Vincent attest.[24] The use of information technology to construct databases and analyse them statistically has helped extend modern research.

Family divisions

When the milieu of the court comes under analysis, it is the king's family – that is, the members of his nuclear kin group linked by relationship and marriage – which comes first to mind. In their day, the members of the Plantagenet dynasty were demonstrably and undeniably aggressive towards each other. Henry II, his wife Eleanor of Aquitaine and their numerous descendants were in constant mutual conflict. This is attested by the huge rebellion of 1173, incited by Eleanor and her sons, the Young Henry, Richard the Lionheart and Geoffrey of Brittany; the subsequent rebellion of the Young Henry in the Limousin in 1183; the harrying to death of the sick Henry II in 1189 by the troops of the same Richard; not to mention the probable murder of the young Arthur of Brittany by his uncle, King John, soon after the battle of Mirebeau (1202).[25] These conflicts startle by their frequency, and they link together into a continual cycle of violence.

Family violence could be found in fiction. Family conflict constantly appears in twelfth-century literature. In his *Estoire des Engleis*, (*c.*1135 × 1138) Geoffrey Gaimar, for example, depicts the dispute between Havelock the Dane and his wife's uncle, who was trying to deprive him of the kingship. Then there was the justified rebellion of Hereward against his own relatives to get back the inheritance of which they had unlawfully deprived him. The *History of the Kings of Britain*, composed in Latin by Geoffrey of Monmouth (*c.*1100–1155), likewise presents Brennius in revolt against his brother King Belin. In the *Roman de Brut* (1155), a French translation and paraphrase of Geoffrey's work, Wace depicts Mordred, Arthur's nephew, as the worst of his enemies. But Wace at least rejects the positive write-up that Geoffrey gave Mordred 'a remarkable and accomplished knight'.[26] You could say that the Plantagenets had climbed straight out of the imagination of a contemporary writer. They were the Atreides of the twelfth century. Although this Classical comparison might seem anachronistic, the chronicler Richard of Devizes, contemporary and admirer of Richard the Lionheart, said much the same when he stated that the Angevin dynasty was 'the dysfunctional house of Oedipus'.[27]

These Plantagenet family disputes were a contrast with the unity of the Capetian dynasty, which was all too conscious that its survival depended on the solidarity of its family members, and their strict obedience to the eldest of the house. Besides this the Plantagenet disputes very often involved a quite exceptional hostility and malice, sprung from those passions which the clerks of the court tried so hard to moderate by their counsels. Despite the fact that he had often pardoned them and endowed them with possessions, Henry II's animosity towards his sons did not in any way lessen. At some time in 1188 or 1189, when the rebellion of Richard the Lionheart was in full swing, Peter of Blois composed a 'Dialogue between King Henry and the abbot of Bonneval' in which the king cursed his children and damned them to hell, when confronted by a clergyman who tried to recall him to a more reasonable outlook.[28] According to Sir Richard Southern, this conversation between Henry II and Christian, Benedictine abbot of St Florentin of Bonneval, in the diocese of Chartres, might very well have taken place at that time, Peter merely sketching in the details.[29] But it seems more likely that the abbot in question was simply a representative figure, a compilation of views attached to the name of a monastery with family connections to the Plantagenet court.[30] Peter of Blois was using this particular scenario to encourage his readers in their charity towards their neighbours and in attending mass. Still, the aristocracy gave all the more weight to these calls to repent when the scenario of disputes in which the imagined conversation took place did not diverge too much from reality. The hatreds which smouldered at the heart of the Angevin royal family were genuinely bitter.

A chronicler as well-read as Ralph de Diceto endeavoured to show that the Plantagenet family fights had many historical precedents. He cited in his support the Biblical characters Jephthah son of Gilead, Absalon son of David, Addramelek and Sharazer, assassins of their father Sennacherib, king of Assyria. The *Epitome* of Trogeius Pompeius by Justin (3rd–4th century), the *Jewish Antiquities* of Josephus (37–95AD), or the *Scholastic History* of Peter Comestor (1100–1179) were his material for evoking the parricides amongst the ancient Persians and Herodians. Thanks to Sigebert of Gembloux, Ralph could marshal in his case the dynastic disputes of the Merovingians, Visigoths and Carolingians. Geoffrey of Monmouth and John of Worcester (died *c*.1141) were his basic sources for the Norman and Anglo-Saxon kings. By contrast, oral tradition, probably picked up at the court of Henry II and Eleanor on the continent, seems to underlie Ralph's description of the family troubles between William IX (1086–1126) and William X (1126–1137) of Aquitaine, and between Fulk Nerra (987–1040) and Geoffrey Martel (1040–1060) of Anjou. History came to the aid of intellectuals close to the Plantagenets, like Ralph, who were trying to demonstrate the fact that the quarrelsome nature of their masters, if not exactly commonplace, was nothing out of the ordinary in great royal or princely dynasties.

All the same, these apologists were not fools, and they did not fail to describe what happened as a result of these quarrels as being a disaster.

The annals of St Aubin of Angers write of the year 1173: 'The three sons of King Henry rebelled together against their father: the kingdoms of the earth were overthrown, churches laid waste, religion dragged through the mire and peace lost throughout the land.'[31] The impact of the Plantagenet family disputes on the integrity of the kingdom was in this way precisely analysed. What was in essence a domestic conflict took on a disproportionate scale. Walter Map wrote that a king as capable as Henry I ruled his lands 'like a good father of a family presiding over hearth and home'.[32] Map believed that domestic harmony in the house of Anjou was a necessary preliminary to the pacification and security of the Plantagenet empire. His admirer and plagiarist, Gerald of Wales, hardly differed in his own analysis[33] when he considered the poor record of the reign of Henry II and his sons, when he emphasized the number of their disputes – a punishment imposed by God – and when he delivered his judgement upon the tyrannical history of the rulers of Britain, and of England in particular.[34] For Walter and Gerald, who were taught by the Gospel lectionary that a kingdom divided against itself could not stand, the final defeat of King John by the Capetians was ultimately due to the sad family divisions of the Angevins.

When they pondered the deeper causes of the endless and recurring family arguments, the clergy attached to the court adopted a style of language where Christian providence was mixed up with pagan superstition. Roger of Howden's account of the last war between Henry II and Richard the Lionheart, for example, is saturated in a supernatural aura. So as the two men talked in a harvested field, lightning struck between father and son, although the sky was cloudless. Just as Richard entered the room in the castle of Chinon where his father's body was laid out, it began to bleed suddenly through the nostrils, a phenomenon which identified a murderer according to the judgement of the medieval God.[35] Even according to as sober a commentator as Roger of Howden generally was, the supernatural intruded into the family dispute. The unusual nature of the bitter dispute between father and son grew so alarming that nothing could account for it except magic.

Several commentators could only account for these family conflicts by placing them on the level of mythical origins.[36] Gerald of Barry mused on the fact that the counts of Anjou descended from a malevolent fairy – identifiable perhaps as Melusine[37] – who disappeared into thin air when she was forced by her husband to be present at the consecration of a mass, which she had always refused to do.[38] Caesarius (c.1180–1240), prior of the Cistercian abbey of Heisterbach and native of Cologne, took this legend (widely spread throughout the West) as his reason for comparing the kings of England to Merlin, like them a Briton and the son of a demon incubus, because 'it is said that they are descendants of a supernatural mother'.[39] Gerald of Barry says that Richard the Lionheart quoted this legend to explain the rows within his family, and the king made this conclusion: 'We Plantagenets, who descend from a devil, will return to the devil'. Gerald also said that Heraclius, patriarch of Jerusalem, annoyed by Henry II's refusal to go on crusade in 1185 because his sons might rebel in his absence, described the origins of the dynasty in identical terms. For these two churchmen the conduct of the Plantagenets would lead them straight to hell, although not before they had first acted the tyrant to their people.[40] The uncanny marriage to a demon wife in the distant mythical past of the foundation of the house of Anjou was by then held to account for the bloody quarrels of her descendants.

We also find some influences nearer to popular and profane culture than intellectual and clerical in the use of the 'Prophecies of Merlin' to account for the origins of these family hatreds. Merlin, despite being born of a demon, worked for the cause of good and favoured the victory of his protégé Arthur, the king of the Britons. His magical powers, gained from his descent from a fallen angel, allowed Merlin to predict the future. Derived by Geoffrey of Monmouth, bishop of St Asaph or Llanelwy, from a variety of sources and fragments, and compiled supposedly from a Welsh original, Merlin's predictions were first written down in Geoffrey's 'Prophecies of Merlin' (1134) and recopied soon after into the third section of his *History of the Kings of Britain* (c.1136), one of the most widely known works of the Middle Ages.[41] Merlin's predictions are distinguished, as the genre of prophecy tends to be, by their obscurantism, which left to their later commentators a wide liberty in interpretation. The prophecies delight in employing a large cast of beasts, whose mysterious nature stretched the interpretations further. So the chroniclers, Ralph de Diceto and Richard the Poitevin, on the one side, and Roger of Howden, on the other, respectively identify the eagle and its joy for its third brood as a prophecy about the breaking of the alliance, and the revolt of the offspring of the raging beast as a prophecy about the dreadful relations between Henry II and his sons.[42] According to the evidence of Gerald of Barry, Henry II ordered a fresco to be painted in his palace of Winchester which represented a great eagle attacked by its four eaglets, which was to be identified with his own treacherous offspring.[43] The painting was not without its resonances with the two preceding prophecies.[44] Walter Map drew from Merlin's many oracles one which said that 'the clever lynx will everywhere threaten his own race with destruction' to recall the opposition to his own father by the Young Henry, who he compared to Absalon. His death at the age of twenty-seven was the proper penalty for his rebellion.[45] In short, the Plantagenets and their court resorted all too readily to Merlin's prophecies as an excuse for their internecine wars.

The prophecies compromised their individual free will, but at the same time they limited the Plantagenets' moral responsibility over their feuds, their fits of anger and other violent acts. Their destiny was inescapable, foretold in the dark past where it had been perceived by the British prophet. It would be fulfilled whether or not they liked it, even the prophesied parricide. Finally, the oracles of Merlin, just like the supernatural ancestry of the counts of Anjou, belonged to the folk-tale canon of demonic and spirit possession, whose influence lessened the place of free will in human actions. No one expressed this better than Gerald of Barry, one of the promoters of the idea of a curse weighing heavy on the Plantagenets. Gerald attributed to Geoffrey of Brittany (whose son Arthur would be murdered one day by King John, his brother) the reply given to Geoffrey de Lucy, future bishop of Winchester (1189–1204), the envoy of his father who was asking for a reconciliation with him: 'You mustn't ignore what has been given us by nature, that is to say by inheritance from our ancestors, who have bequeathed to us and made it innate in us that we cannot love each other, that brother will always fight brother, and the son the father with all the energy that he can. So do not attempt to talk us out of our inheritance, you would be trying in vain to change our native disposition.'[46] If we are to believe Peter of Blois, Henry II said no less: 'Nature has made me the child of wrath, so how could I ever not be angry?'[47] A superhuman determinism lay behind the Promethean defiance directed by the Plantagenets at Christian morality, accepted inheritance customs and at political stability. This inescapable destiny identified by Gerald of Barry and the other court intellectuals derived largely from a pagan subculture that sucked into itself the demon succubi and incubi of Celtic legend (which they had heard tales of as children) and Fate as described by the ancient Roman Stoic writers (whom they read assiduously).

Do we need to draw any significance from the blasphemous nature of assertions made in throwaway remarks attributed to the Angevins, as the historian Karl Leyser suggests,[48] and put them down to the increased laicization of a royal family whose secular administration was becoming daily ever more effective? The problem of the mocking of sacred things by the Plantagenet royal family is a complex one, and we will try to get to the bottom of it later. Let us stay for the moment with the fact that, for all the irreverence that they might have felt towards the traditional teaching of the Church on human free will, the Plantagenets' deterministic assertions were drawn from a world of demons, spirits and magicians, that it is not convincing to call either secular or hostile to the sacred. It seems pointless, whatever the case, to put on the same level the modern ethos of twelfth-century state formation and the misty paganism of the same period, as it was partly preserved by the writings of contemporary theologians.[49]

If the Plantagenets looked towards folk tales to understand why it was they could not stand each other, they did not for all that neglect more orthodox explanations. So they questioned the wisdom of marriages made more recently than the one with a demon with a phobia for the eucharist, who vanished at the moment of consecration. Despite their Christian nature, these questionable unions were quite as damaging as the one with the demon. They brought into the house of Anjou women as wicked as their alleged founding ancestor. They were notorious for the children they produced. Whether they were Norman or Poitevin, they were the source of bad luck. By one view, the prestigious marriage with a woman of the ducal house of Normandy, who would bring to them eventually the Crown of England, was ill-fated from the beginning. According to Geoffrey of Vigeois, Roger of Howden and Walter Map, the first husband of the Empress Mathilda, Henry V, had not in fact died but had slipped away by night from his wife.[50] Gerald of Barry said the emperor had become a hermit near Chester, where he did penance for his sins. Gerald therefore accused Mathilda of bigamy when she married Geoffrey of Anjou, and their son Henry II was the issue of an adulterous liaison.[51] By another view, common to those writers closest to the Plantagenets, the Aquitainian alliance of their masters was as tainted as that with the Normans, if not more so. The debauchery of earlier generations of the house of Poitou was equated to the similar lapses of Henry II. According to Ralph de Diceto,[52] William IX of Aquitaine, the troubadour prince whose marital infidelity was unanimously condemned by the Anglo-Norman chroniclers of the beginning of the twelfth century,[53] abandoned his wife for a woman called Maubergeonne. His son William X began a seven-year war against his father in retaliation, before dying on a pilgrimage to Santiago de Compostella. Interred far from the traditional burial places of his family, his body never found proper rest as a punishment for his rebellion. In his research into the causes of the Plantagenet disputes, Gerald of Barry turned to the theme of the sinful affair of the duke of Aquitaine with the viscountess of Châtellerault, which he attributed not to William IX, as the other writers preferred, but to William X, father of Eleanor of Aquitaine, as if he felt it necessary to discredit particularly the wife of Henry II through her nearest relations.[54]

Scandal focused particularly on this last woman, Eleanor. According to a deathbed prophecy attributed to St Hugh of Avalon, Carthusian monk and bishop of Lincoln (died 1213) her marriage with Henry II would become the cause of the fall of the Angevins.[55] Arranged in dubious circumstances, the marriage with Eleanor could do no other than give the king of England the unsupportive offspring which was to be expected. Most writers blamed the revolt of 1173 against Henry II on Eleanor's intriguing.[56] To repeat the rather lame pun of Robert de Torigny on her name, she was the 'alienator' of the king's sons.[57] Her image at her husband's court, just as with every other wife of princely rank, suffered from her distant and foreign birth, which made her a stranger in relation to her past and created suspicions about her family connections, as she was born to a rival dynasty with which the marriage accomplished a temporary truce.[58] But in the eyes of the clergy, Eleanor's situation was even worse. Her second marriage should never have taken place, for it was at one and the same time bigamous, incestuous and criminal. The chroniclers William of Newburgh and Gervase of Canterbury, and a Parisian moral theologian, Robert de Courson, asserted that the annulment of her marriage with Louis VII was indisputably unlawful. According to them the grounds of consanguinity brought for this annulment was just as applicable to her marriage to Henry,[59] for he and she were cousins in the fifth degree.[60] Court gossip, echoed by Walter Map and his imitator, Gerald of Barry, alleged that Eleanor had slept with Geoffrey Plantagenet before her marriage with Henry, so committing the deeply serious offence of incest.[61] Finally, Henry II had married the wife of his overlord so as to gain advantage over him, an act of felony of the worst sort for a vassal.[62] Adulterous, incestuous and disloyal, the marriage of the count of Anjou and the duchess of Aquitaine could not turn out well.

In any case Henry II proved deceitful with his many mistresses. As an adulterer, he was scarcely unique as a king. The Norman ducal dynasty had long practised marriage *more Danico* 'in the manner of the Vikings': an institutionalized bigamy which allowed full rights of succession to sons born of concubines.[63] William of Newburgh remarked that Henry II followed his maternal grandfather in his marital unfaithfulness; indeed he speculated that Henry I was a victim of his own lust,[64] a suggestion corroborated by the existence of at least nineteen of his bastards discovered by modern scholarship.[65] Gerald of Barry reckoned that Henry II's adultery was among the reasons why his sons hated him.[66] Gerald alleged that Henry II's mother, and Eleanor's father, had both been guilty of bigamy, a double adultery which resulted in the misfortunes of their descendants, according to the prophecy made by a Poitevin hermit whom Hugh of Avalon is often said to have quoted.[67] Adam of Eynsham, Hugh's hagiographer, puts in the dying bishop's mouth a prophecy of the overthrow of English kingship at the hands of the Capetians because of the unlawful marriage of Henry II and Eleanor: 'the shoots arisen from bastardy do not enjoy deep roots . . . the seeds of an adulterous union will be uprooted'.[68] Hugh wished the same on the Anglo-Norman dynasty all the more as its founder, William the Bastard, was born of a liaison which did not conform to a Christian ethic.[69] The view that related the dynasty's promiscuity to its internal conflicts, indeed to the general anarchy within society, was as old as it was widespread.

If it related to extramarital adventures, this view associating family feuds with civil conflicts related even more generally to 'incestuous' unions, that is, marriages with a close cousin. In the house of Anjou, for example, a consanguineous marriage celebrated in 1032 between Geoffrey Martel and his cousin Agnes of Poitou provoked a war between Geoffrey and his father, Fulk Nerra, according to the chronicler of Saint-Aubin.[70] In identifying incest as the root of the family dispute, the monk-annalist was repeating a contrario an old argument developed by St Augustine. The purpose of marriage was to radiate charity, to send out love from the closed and limited circle of the close kin. The more widespread was that love the wider was the sway of the kingdom of peace and concord. At the time of the Gregorian reform, theologians and moral philosophers developed a more specific version of this argument, suggesting from case studies that a consanguineous marriage could give rise only to feuds, argument and war.[71]

We have already seen how several chroniclers – following in the wake of an already ancient debate – pointed to the closeness of kinship which forbade the marriage of Henry II and Eleanor of Aquitaine, rulers of the neighbouring counties of Anjou and Poitou. Their reasoning was so much the more effective as the duchess had ended her previous marriage through precisely that same pretext of consanguinity. Their justification was the rebellion of her children, encouraged by herself, which erupted scarcely twenty years after her marriage. It was one of the more spectacular and convincing examples to support the sort of exogamy pursued in Biblical pastoral societies. The texts of Gerald of Barry and Walter Map accusing Eleanor of having married the son of her lover are part of this context. Written in the reign of King John, after the deaths of the chief characters of the internal family wars, they offer an explanation of the unparalleled intensity of the feuding within the Plantagenet family. Like any clergyman imbued in the preaching of their day and imprisoned in his mental outlook, Gerald and Walter found this explanation for the worst of the outbreaks. So they repeated *a posteriori* the idea of Henry and Eleanor's incest to account for the hatreds between the Plantagenets in the manner of an exemplum, as another moralizing anecdote for the condemnation of endogamy. However valuable is their evidence on the level of the history of mentalities and religious feeling, it is worthless in relation to the love life of Eleanor, a rather futile subject to try to pin down.[72] But at best their histories, analyses and ethical arguments show that in the twelfth century, every English cleric held that the sins of the flesh, and most particularly consanguineous marriage, were responsible for family breakdown.

It cannot be any surprise that contemporary medievalists' explanations for Plantagenet family problems are on an entirely different level. They account for the feuding by means of psychological, relational or educative frameworks.[73] As a result, they trace back the unresolved animosity within the family to the disturbed childhoods of Henry II's sons, noting under this heading the small role of the king in their upbringing, always on the road. The role in their education of Eleanor, often called away to Aquitaine, was also limited. Nurses, indispensable servants at court, replaced their parents. One of them, Hodierna, remained the object of Richard the Lionheart's affections. He showered her with goods and marks of distinction. Another, called Agatha, who took care of the infant John, did equally well out of the generosity of Eleanor.[74] It follows from these theories – whose authors sometimes project them as psychoanalytical – that of them all Eleanor would only have experienced a conventional mother's love for Richard, and for him only from his adolescence onwards, when he was named duke of Aquitaine. This is why Elizabeth A.R. Brown wrote that the queen was more queen than mother in her relations with her sons.[75]

Besides these influences, after John's birth and Eleanor's menopause, Henry II openly took the young Rosamund Clifford as his concubine. According to the same theories, Henry II's peccadiloes, his wife's jealousy, and their invisibility when it came to their children's emotional life and upbringing, would be at the root of the conflict between the generations, of the disputes between the children and their various mental complexes, which were most obvious in the case of John, whom this sort of scholar suspects of paranoia, persecution mania, emotional instability and control freakery. There is some truth in these speculations. Nowadays, in explaining the defeat of 1204 – even though English revenues were still at that time greater than French[76] – almost all English medievalists cite King John's troubled persona, which added to his unpopularity and alienated the nobility of his provinces. The problem with these theories is that they sometimes lean too heavily on the psychology of individuals, all the more unreachable for being eight centuries away as for the fact that their mental and social milieu was so very different from our own.

It seems more fitting to leave the area of personality alone – always obscure because of people's erratic wilfulness – and stick rather to the fields of society and social conduct, where general rules and a certain degree of rational behaviour can be reconstructed. So it is appropriate to look for the political causes of these internecine wars and to lay the stress instead on the composite character of the huge area controlled by Henry II, where territorial principalities had neither common history nor tradition of cooperation and were heavily burdened with ancient enmities. The Angevin Empire was divisible by its very nature; its integrity was fragile. Powerful centrifugal forces threatened to break it apart. According to his biographer, Geoffrey Plantagenet on his deathbed urged on his son and successor this warning, which might be said to have been prophetic. He was never to press the customs of one of his principalities on another but should preserve its legal character, drawing back from any pointless scheme of unity.[77] In the light of this advice, Henry II's policies – which aimed at focusing his assorted territories on a single government and on a single ideology in opposition to the king of France[78] – seem overambitious, maybe even unrealistic. A similar policy was adopted by Richard the Lionheart soon after his coronation.[79] This desire to centralize was manifested in several edicts, assizes and inquisitions concerning the entire Anglo-Norman kingdom, indeed, the whole of the Plantagenet Empire.[80] Centralization appeared in each of the principalities where one of Henry's sons ruled in the guise of a stream of edicts and frequent royal progresses, and it was both humiliating and peremptory.

The king had to face the opposition of local nobilities, above all in Anjou, Aquitaine and Brittany. To maintain their independence the nobles allied against Henry II with the son who was put in power over their principality. The records of the time say much the same. The regional nobles feature in them as the 'bad counsellors' who led the king's sons into treason. In the *Roman de Rou*, Wace launches into a diatribe against certain Norman 'provincial barons' (whom he did not care [sied] to name) for having undermined relations between Henry II and his children at the beginning of the 1170s by fanning their mutual hatreds.[81] In doing this they had copied the French who 'led the sons astray so as to bring down the father' (v. 69). This view, which adopts the official Angevin line, is repeated in a letter collection. In a letter which Henry II addressed in 1173 to Pope Alexander III (1159–1181) asking him to excommunicate the rebels, the king indulged in an exegesis, as lengthy as it was rhetorical, on the verse of the Book of Proverbs (17: 2) 'Where the son is a wastrel, a prudent slave is master'.[82] This sort of analysis of the leading role of advisers drawn from the regional nobilities in unleashing rebellion is very distinct, in its reasonableness, from the supernatural or marvellous explanations of the courtiers' tales. Its superiority in political terms is in transferring moral responsibility for revolt on to the aristocracy, which the king was seeking to reform.

Pointing to the bad influence of ministers over the young princes allowed their acquittal from any blame for the revolts. According to the archdeacon of Lisieux, on Richard the Lionheart's return from captivity, he met John, who threw himself at the king's feet. He raised him from the floor and said: 'John, relax. You are only a child. You have been keeping bad company, and your advisers will pay for it.' The two brothers promptly sealed their reconciliation with a meal of salmon.[83] John was at the time twenty-seven years of age. But by this white lie about his age, Richard may have been recalling that he had himself been fifteen years old when he first rebelled against Henry II. If accounts of rebellion and subsequent pardon make a point of the youth of the rebels it is, on one level, to highlight that they were so much more susceptible to bad influences when they were emerging from their adolescence. On another level their time of life 'Youth' – in the sociological sense of the word[84] – made them particularly open to the appeal of fighting against their father or their oldest brother. As a *juvenis*, fuming with impatience for an inheritance slow to arrive, each of the Plantagenet princes chose the way of action and took up arms against the head of the family. This temptation, a mixture of greed for a share of the family wealth and jealousy of the father's authority, seems to have been very marked in the heart of the Plantagenet dynasty, where the concept of patricide had a significance quite different from the Freudian.

In conclusion, there was a radical incompatibility between the modern concept of kingship and the patrimonial understanding of power; between the emerging public dimension of the state and the private aspect of the princely dynasty, paradoxically too concerned and anxious about maintaining at all costs the rights of younger sons. The archaic nature of the system did not in that respect become any less burdensome. So when the peripheral aristocratic revolts of the 'Plantagenet zone' provoked domestic disputes within the royal family, the court would not be like an epicentre from which palace intrigues might wash outwards, just like concentric waves, to the provincial margins where they might in due course subside.

Quite the opposite, it was the pressure from the edges of the empire that destroyed the unity at the centre.[85] The king's sons took up the causes of the provincial nobilities that they governed. The influence of their entourages counted for a lot. The *mesnies* (military households) of the princes caused trouble at the expense of their father's court.

Was the history of the Plantagenets exceptional in Western history in the eleventh and twelfth centuries? The frequency of internal rebellions within the family was not typical of the time. Louis VII (with only one son, it is true) and Frederick Barbarossa encountered no such problems from their children. But Henry II's families on his mother's and father's side did experience upsets similar to his. Violent conflicts, imprisonments for life and perhaps fratricides were to be found in the Anjou of the time of Fulk Nerra and his son Geoffrey Martel, or in the Normandy of the time of the brothers Richard III (1026–1028) and Robert the Magnificent (1028–1035), and again amongst the children of William the Conqueror. The American historian, Bernard S. Bacharach indeed reconstructs a sort of 'Angevin inheritance of behavioural strictures' in the 'violent and hostile interaction' at the heart of the family of Henry II.[86] But it is always necessary to emphasize that this sort of appeal to a genetic inheritance of conflict is probably illusory, for the Norman and Angevin ancestors of the Plantagenets were not unique in their behaviour.

At that time disputes amongst close kin were not as rare as one might think. In the comital dynasty of Barcelona, countess Ermessenda of Carcassone (died 1058) suffered during her widowhood the revolt of her son. Then her grandson, Ramon Berengar (1076–1082), was assassinated, probably at the instigation of his younger twin brother Berengar Ramon I (1076–1096). Fratricide indeed was a frequent occurrence in the house of Léon-Castille, where King Alfonso VI (1065–1109) was forced by the Cid to take an oath to clear himself of the murder of his elder brother Sancho II (1065–1072). Less shockingly, in the twelfth century Alfonso VIII of Castille (1158–1214), Henry II's son-in-law, fought against his first cousin, Alfonso IX of Léon (1188–1230) to the detriment of the *Reconquista*. Sancho, count of Provence, rebelled in 1185 against his brother Alfonso II (1162–1196), king of Aragon and count of Barcelona.[87] Finally, during the course of the Albigensian Crusade, Count Raymond VI of Toulouse, another son-in-law of Henry II, was obliged to fight his own brother Baldwin, a soldier in the army of Simon de Montfort; in 1214 Raymond captured him and sentenced him to hang.[88] Examples of family conflicts are numerous. They prove that harmony was all too often the exception rather than the rule in princely dynasties. In fact, the case of the French royal dynasty is unique, as if a 'Capetian miracle' was at the root of the respect that the eldest son understood that he could impose, generation after generation, on his younger brothers and sons. It was precisely these Capetians who are usually picked by medieval historians as the sole comparison with the Plantagenets, their ancient enemies.

Capetians and Plantagenets alike maintained the transmission of their paternal and maternal inheritance to the eldest son, and other acquisitions to younger sons, as apanages. In 1225, the testament of Louis VIII alienated a third of the royal domain to the benefit of his three younger sons.[89] This system of partition gave priority to the eldest son, for the eldest received the entire ancestral patrimony of his parents and the crown, which involved the homage of his younger brothers. The same rule of succession prevailed among the Plantagenets, with some slight differences.[90] Furthermore, the same rule was common in aristocratic families at the end of the twelfth century, and the kings of France and England were doing no more than following a general custom. It was the sort of succession frequently found in the Latin works written by clerks of the Plantagenet court, who harked back to an older Britain, before even Arthur, and the partitions which took place in the legendary royal houses of those days.[91] The reasons for the Plantagenet family quarrels need not be looked for in the divisions of lands made in the lifetime of the king or in Plantagenet succession customs, which were more or less standard for royal and noble lineages. The reasons are more to do with the power of the aristocracies in the outer provinces of the empire, and their fondness for rebellion.

Faithful servants

The expression *familia regis* in the writings of those close to Henry II is not only used for the king's immediate nuclear family,[92] and here there is scope for misunderstanding. Roger of Howden talks, for instance, of a hundred knights of the 'family' of the Young Henry.[93] The word encompasses a large group: soldiers, advisers, domestic servants and chaplains in the household of the prince. The word also includes a group of royal kinsfolk, close or distant from the king, among which his illegitimate children were held in particular favour. They were by no means marginalized at court, as bastardy did not yet constitute a social handicap.[94] Such was true of Geoffrey, the future archbishop of York, who resigned the see of Lincoln to be the chancellor of his father, Henry II. The king said of Geoffrey at the time of the last, fatal rebellion of his legitimate children: 'He is my true son. It's the others who are the bastards!'[95] On the same subject, William Longespée, who married the heir to the earldom of Salisbury, was very active in the following of his half-brother, King John. He had an outstanding political career: sheriff of eight counties, royal lieutenant in Gascony, keeper of Dover Castle, warden of the Welsh Marches, a man charged with any number of diplomatic missions.[96]

Domestic attendants and servants were another part of this inner circle of royal intimates. An entire microcosm of guards, cooks, bakers, falconers, and even jesters and musicians, lived side by side with the great men of the kingdom. Although they were in theory lowly functionaries with modest responsibilities around the household, they often did quite well out of royal favour. The theologian Alexander Neckam (1157–1217), son of the royal nurse Hodierna and foster-brother of Richard the Lionheart, turned this background to account in funding his studies at Oxford, receiving the abbacy of Cirencester near Bristol.[97] As in many medieval courts, where power was concentrated at the very heart of the household, around the head of the dynasty, the scope of certain officers trespassed into politics. It is well understood how, in the twelfth century, the high-ranking officers, the butler, marshal, chamberlain and constable – men simultaneously humble and powerful – had begun as domestic menials of the king.[98] The offices had become hereditary and some great families had acquired them. There were for instance the butlers of the house of d'Aubigny, one of whom was William, who became earl of Arundel on his marriage with the widow of Henry I.[99] The weighty responsibilities of the great household officers arose from their being servants. The rise in status was not just a matter of household reorganization, it was a social movement. This is attested by the rise of many families involved in service in a time when the power of the king, patron as much as monarch, was still focused on his person.

Besides these servants, the *familia* included the intimate advisers of the king, who accompanied him on his tireless travels. The Plantagenet itinerary has been a godsend for medieval historians, who can analyse his 'permanent entourage' from the list of witnesses to the acts of his chancery. This restricted group of followers, who accompanied him everywhere he went, should not be confused with the 'occasional entourage' made up of distinguished people who attended on the king when he passed through their land, and are simply there in that capacity at the tail end of his charters. Many of the members of the king's inner circle, those who travelled with him, might be entrusted with local offices or distant missions. There was not much in the way of administrative specialization, and they might become sheriffs as well as judges in eyre, ambassadors or soldiers. But it was on the shoulders of these men that the apparatus of the state rested.

What were the geographical origins of this inner circle? The common-est suggestion, articulated particularly by Lucien Musset,[100] contradicts the old theory which maintained that Normandy was the traditional nursery of followers, soldiers and faithful administrators of the king, who imported them into Britain. But by Henry II's time it was England which provided the principal servants and officers of the king. Under Richard the Lionheart the English contingent grew further, at the expense of the Norman court nobility.[101] Since the English aristocracy answered the call of the Plantagenets, it is permissible to conclude that the dynasty had managed to integrate successfully into the English political world. Wanting above all to be royal, and thus English, they had grafted themselves neatly into the English system. Normandy's feeble resistance to Philip Augustus perhaps betrayed a feeling of alienation within its aristocracy towards a king who had become an Englishman amongst the English. The nobility of Anjou, although it was the cradle of the dynasty, and that of Aquitaine, were barely evident amongst the close counsellors of Henry II, Richard the Lionheart or John.[102] It was the Angevins and Aquitanians who plotted rebellion against the Plantagenets and sought alliance with the Capetians. Their unreliability provided yet another reason for Henry II and his sons to concentrate on the English, or failing them on the Normans. It was only after 1204, with the loss of the lands in the Loire valley, that a few Angevin nobles who had taken refuge in England began to enjoy some influence in the entourage of John and Henry III, influence they used to press for military campaigns on the continent to recover their lost lord-ships.[103] In conclusion, whereas Plantagenet power was fully accepted in Britain, it was often resisted on the continent. This fact had its conse-quences for the geographical origin of their entourage.

A social (rather than spatial) study of the royal court leads to the conclusion that the careers of its members were often chancy, because they depended entirely on the king's whim. Walter Map, one of those very courtiers, justice in eyre 1172–73 and 1184–85 and ambassador to the pope in 1178, expanded on the precariousness of a career where disgrace could follow on from royal favour for no very obvious reason. 'Should I come to describe the court as Porphyrus defined genre, it would be no lie to say that it is a multitude linked in a certain way to a single principle. We are indeed an infinite multitude, but which strives to bring pleasure to one man. Today we are one multitude; tomorrow we may be an entirely different one. But the court never changes, it is always the same. It would be as just if we were to say of the court what Boethius said truly about fortune, which is only dependable in its undependability'.[104]

Boethius was the object of the unconfined admiration of John of Salisbury, who resorted to the image of the wheel of fortune he used to criticize the epicureans: power-obsessed hedonists, tainted by their frantic search for transitory material goods who would never find fixed and eternal happiness.[105] For Walter and John, their approval of Boethius, the fallen courtier condemned to death by his master Theoderic the Great (474–526), had a contemporary point.[106]

The wheel of fortune turned very quickly at the Plantagenet court. Medieval historians maintain that almost every social level was represented in the royal household: great barons, lesser knights and commoners. There was present within the entourage the high Anglo-Norman nobility, the king's tenants-in-chief who owed him military assistance and counsel, according to feudal custom. So Robert II earl of Leicester (died 1168) was appointed chief justiciar of England in 1154, the man who was probably the most powerful baron in the kingdom.[107] William de Mandeville (died 1189), hereditary earl of Essex and count of Aumale by marriage, belonged to the same official circle. Henry II made him ambassador to the king of France and the emperor of Germany and repeatedly put him in command of his armies. At the coronation of Richard the Lionheart William carried the royal crown, and he too took his turn as chief justiciar.[108] Richard de Hommet (died 1179), constable and perhaps justiciar of Nomandy, was a descendant of Odo, bishop of Bayeux, brother of William the Conqueror. His son William succeeded him as constable of Normandy. The considerable possessions of the Hommet family spread across several Norman and English counties.[109] The examples of rich and powerful court magnates whose ancestors had served the king of England since at least the conquest of 1066 could be multiplied. They were drawn from the group of tenants-in-chief, the greatest subjects in the kingdom. The small nucleus of courtiers included in it held 74% of the knights' fees of Normandy and 68% of those of England. Nine out of twenty-five most frequent witnesses to the charters of Richard the Lionheart in 1189 were holders of earldoms. The compiler of these statistics, Thomas K. Keefe, deduced from this that the high aristocracy formed the majority group in the royal entourage, and that it was indeed the foundation of the government of Henry II and his sons.[110]

The prosopographical studies of Ralph V. Turner show, however, that the high aristocracy did not monopolize royal favour. It could also fall on 'men raised from the dust' – the scornful phrase coined by the chronicler Orderic Vitalis (1075–1142) – that it is tempting to translate as 'men risen from the gutter'.[111] Some simple calculations support this view.

Only one out of the fourteen royal justices of Richard the Lionheart was of baronial rank, compared with seventeen out of forty-six sheriffs appointed by King John.[112] The king preferred to choose most of his officers from the ranks of the lesser knights, holders of minor fees, which were their modest point of entry into the brotherhood of arms.[113] In England, this level of men, used to feudal service and obedience to the king and his court magnates, exhibited an immovable loyalty to the Crown. The irresistible rise of Richard de Lucy began from out of this group during the reign of King Stephen (1135–1154), who granted him a number of fees. Richard occupied numerous offices: constable of the Tower of London, sheriff of Essex, royal justice in Cumberland, president of the Exchequer and chief justiciar.[114] Ranulf de Glanville, who was Richard's successor as chief justiciar, belonged to the same group of lesser nobility, clients of the court magnates.[115] The tract called *The Laws and Customs of the Kingdom of England* (*c.*1187 × 1189) has been attributed to him, probably erroneously.[116] The quality of Ranulf's political judgement, which was praised by Walter Map and Gerald of Barry,[117] reveals that a high level of education was not incompatible at that time with lay status. Study increased the efficiency of those officers who had embraced literacy.[118] Knighthood and learning were not mutually exclusive at the Plantagenet court, where knowledge, secular and religious alike, was deployed in the king's service.

Careful reconstruction of the careers of courtiers from royal charters and Exchequer accounts allows us to go further, and to affirm the presence of non-nobles in key posts in the English government. The chancellor, Thomas Becket (died 1170) was the son of Gilbert, a merchant of Rouen, who did well in business in London where he became one of the two provosts of the city. Thomas's education at Merton Priory and Paris led to his becoming a clerk of Osbert Huitdeniers, a London financier and sheriff, before entering the household of Archbishop Theobald of Canterbury (1139–1161), who recommended him to Henry II in 1154 as a confidential clerk.[119] An even more spectacular rise was that of John of Salisbury, right-hand man and strategist of Becket, ambassador of Henry II to the pope, but born probably to a peasant family. Although he came to be known in the best cathedral schools on the continent, he began his training at the feet of a village priest, who taught him to read out of a psalter.[120] A similar example is Richard of Ilchester (died 1188), who would be the nemesis of Becket through his stout defence on the king's part of the Assizes of Clarendon. Although Richard had contacts and kinsmen in the episcopal household of Bath and even the royal court,[121] he came from a lowly background. Born within the diocese of Bath, he began his career in a humble way around 1156 as scribe in the royal chancery under the orders of Becket, who would soon learn to hate him. He was prompt to exchange his modest family names (Toclyve, Tokelin or Poore) for the title of 'archdeacon' following his appointment to the chapter of Poitiers, and for the surname of Ilchester, the name of the royal estate which Henry II gave him as a reward for his countless services. Justice in eyre, central character at the Exchequer, tireless ambassador and justiciar of Normandy, Richard was appointed bishop of Winchester by the king in 1173, after Becket's death. His sons Herbert and Richard Poore occupied bishoprics in their turn: Herbert had Salisbury and Richard successively Chichester, Salisbury and Durham.[122] There is no denying that non-noble people rose through royal service, and it was deplored on many occasions by the satirists of the court. We will later have occasion to analyse their arguments in favour of a society of fixed social levels.

William de Mandeville, whose correspondence in French survives and who was possibly one of the patrons of Marie de France[123] was one of the group of *milites litterati* ('literate knights'),[124] just like Ranulf de Glanville. Their knowledge of Latin was a step beyond what could be picked up from the parish church or the liturgy.[125] Some courtiers had acquired a legal culture highly compatible with their administrative duties. It was superior to the empirical knowledge and experience of the law and custom which every free Englishman acquired when he sat in the local law courts.[126] Archbishop Theobald of Canterbury invited Master Vacarius of Bologna to England, where he entered the royal government.[127] Peter of Blois was educated at Tours, Paris and Orleans, noted centres for acquiring the *ars dictaminis*, a method of drafting very fashionable amongst chanceries. He went on to study law at Bologna and served in the court of Sicily before moving to England. Gerald of Barry, for his part, says without much modesty that in 1176 his teaching of canon law at Paris excited such enthusiasm that it was believed that he and his teaching both came from Bologna. He had in fact learned the decretals from Matthew d'Angers.[128] Before becoming chancellor, William de Longchamps had compiled a *Practice of Laws and Decretals* (*c*.1183 × 1189).[129] Many courtiers possessed a solid knowledge of jurisprudence and legal theory.

Other royal officers were noted for the technical accomplishment of their knowledge of accountancy and finance. The treasurer, Richard fitz Nigel was sent as an adolescent boy to study at Laon, one of the most renowned centres for the teaching of mathematics. His continental studies had possibly been decided on by his uncle, Roger, bishop of Salisbury, a very close servant of Henry I.[130] On the death of King Roger II of Sicily,

Henry II invited a certain Thomas Brown from Palermo to work in the English Exchequer.[131] The hunt for talent could draw the Plantagenets as far as southern Italy. They knew of its bureaucratic precocity because of its long rule by the Byzantines.[132]

The majority of royal officers were alumni of the cathedral schools of northern France. It can be calculated that the Capetian king of France's household included only half the number of the 'masters' (men holding the *licencia docendi* awarded by the head of a chapter cathedral school) the king of England had, even though the schools were in Capetian territory.[133] The end result was a court and a royal administration whose personnel, largely clerical, was better trained that any other in the West. The high ratio of intellectuals in the government of the king of England was no accident. It was the result of a political environment where knowledge and technical skill were deliberately sought out and applied to the effective execution of royal orders and to the collection and processing of the information needed for government. Rhetoric, law and mathematics were all indispensable for the centre to be able to impose itself on the margins. The Plantagenets were pioneers of this application of theory to practice. They were decades in advance of the other European monarchies.

This quick prosopographical tour has introduced us to a political society both varied and homogenous. Royal officers were varied in their social origins. Some Anglo-Norman barons related to the king made links to the court, others were lesser knights with modest estates in England and others were sons of London merchants. Were the first more numerous than the last? Using genealogical indexes and analytical lists of charter witnesses, historians are working to discover whether the hereditary nobles, parvenu knights or non-nobles played a greater part in the Plantagenet government. Whatever the case, the presence of the higher nobility in the English royal household is markedly higher than in that of Philip Augustus. In France, by contrast, the lesser nobility and the urban elites took the lion's share of the conduct of government.[134] The reasons for so marked a difference in the composition of the royal household have been analysed by John Baldwin and C. Warren Hollister.[135] In England and Normandy the king had effective control over the honours of the great barons, a fact which guaranteed their feudal loyalty, military aid and counsel. The king continued to maintain his right of wardship over the lands the barons were enjoying by royal grant. The Anglo-Norman linkage of royal patrimony and aristocratic honours contrasts with France. Here the royal domain and the ancient noble lordships were quite separate, and the French king had no control over them. The great noblemen, whose estates had escaped from royal supervision, had long deserted the royal court. This fact obliged Louis VII and Philip Augustus to concentrate instead on the lower nobility, which was the more cooperative as it owed everything to the king. The Plantagenets controlled their great tenants-in-chief, but they also owed more to them. The foundations of French absolutism and English parliamentarianism can possibly be found in this distinction. The cooperativeness of the political classes of Philip Augustus and Louis VII is a contrast to the rebelliousness of the magnates of King John, from whom they extorted Magna Carta.

However socially varied, the Plantagenet household was homogenous so far as geographical origin was concerned. Native English and English of Norman descent predominated. There was a similar homogeneity in the education and common culture of Plantagenet bureaucrats. The family background of Gerald of Barry, a Cambro-Norman nobleman, was worlds away from that of Thomas Becket, a merchant's son. But the two courtiers both attended the schools of Paris in their youth. A Latin and legalistic culture, tailored to the administrative class of the royal household, helped maintain control of the enormous complex of lands the Plantagenets had inherited. Whether lawyers, dialecticians or mathematicians, the intellectuals used their pens, their eloquence and their accounting skills to further the success of the kingdom and the establishment of its bureaucracy. This was why – despite their frequent low birth – Henry II and his son entrusted so many responsibilities to these scholars. The Plantagenet system of government betrays a remarkable effectiveness and modernity.

At the king's mercy

The king had to find means of attracting competent advisers and officers to his court. So he offered them some material inducements. Back in the past, the grant of a landed estate had been a frequent form of reward, but feudal institutions were changing rapidly at the end of the twelfth century. During the civil war (1135–1153) rigorous control of English honours, which had formerly been admired by Western rulers, eluded the prince both in England and Normandy. Anglo-Norman feudal landowning stopped being a matter of life interest and abrupt recall. The military service it involved was barely observed any more. At the time of his succession Henry II was obliged to acknowledge the Treaty of Westminster (1153), which allowed that honours should be hereditary, much to the benefit of the aristocracy. King Stephen was by then in a weak position and, after a long war of succession, he had to accept the hereditary nature of kingship. In order to consolidate his succession to the throne of England, Stephen had been obliged to parcel out his demesne, in the form of fees, to reward his supporters: concessions of which the *terra data* section of the Pipe Rolls kept a systematic account.[136] These alienations were perpetuated by his successor. They chiefly concerned properties in the Thames valley and the west of Wessex, regions of strong loyalty to Henry II where ancestral royal demesne lands were heavily concentrated.[137] Richard de Lucy, Ranulf de Glanville and the chamberlains Warin and Henry fitz Gerald constructed imposing lordships in that way.[138] But the number of such alienations of royal land never again reached the level of 1154. The new king progressively reduced these grants, which had compromised the integrity of his own estates. His preference was to maintain and expand the royal demesne rather than dismember it for the benefit of his courtiers and soldiers. The revolt of 1173 gave rise to several commissions on alienations, at the same time as inquisitions were regularly conducted on his own lands or on the fees held by his vassals.[139] Henry II contrived to continue the collection of part of the dues of these alienated lands and to recover those whose holders died without heir.[140] Feudal landholding still delivered the balance of local power to the aristocracy. Henry's government would consciously work to encourage the slow replacement of feudal military service by scutage – a tax levied on the vassal who could not fulfil the service for his fee – and the unprecedented recruitment of a paid army which made feudal service redundant.

It was completely different with the control of the marriage of female feudal landowners by the king, which offered the possibility of rich inheritances to his most faithful advisers.[141] It prevented, at one stroke, marriage alliances and estate-building to the benefit of untrustworthy families.[142] Richard the Lionheart rewarded in this way the loyalty of William Marshal, then in his forties, by marriage to Isabel de Clare, the wealthy countess of Pembroke, with great estates in England, Wales and Ireland.[143] The same applied to the family of Lusignan, his unfailing supporters in the Holy Land. On his return from captivity in 1194 Richard gave the heiress of the Norman county of Eu to one of the Lusignans, Ralph d'Exoudun, brother of Hugh IX le Brun.[144] A list of the most prominent widows and orphans of twelve English counties is a feature of a significant document, the *Rotuli de Dominabus*. It was compiled around 1185 on the orders of Henry II, who was intending to use it to exploit their marriages.[145] The wardship of orphans was just as much sought after by the aristocracy, as it seems from those who succeeded in exercising it, who were sometimes punished for *wastum*, the penalty for failing to maintain possessions entrusted to them.[146]

Every lay courtier wanted to get hold of estates from the king. The most usual way was to become the husband of a great heiress or the keeper or guardian of a child heir or someone unfit to manage his lands. At the last need, a courtier might even succeed in winkling out of the king a direct enfeoffment, despite his reluctance to deplete his royal demesne.

The king's advisers received roof and board at court. The English Exchequer registers preserve the *Constitution of the King's Household* (*c*.1136) which lays down the total in cash or kind of the daily payments owed to the officers of the household.[147] Courtiers benefitted from other gifts that the king gave away from time to time, in money, fabrics, robes, arms and horses. These were rewards in movable goods whose value should not be underestimated.[148] Two moral allegories written in Latin verse by clerks who had visited the court of Henry II satirize this sort of gift. The *Mirror of Fools* (1180) of Nigel de Longchamps, called Wireker (*c*.1130–1200), monk of Canterbury and probably a nephew of Bishop William of Ely, features a long tirade on the immorality involved in the king's gifts.[149] The *Archipleurer* (1184) of John de Hauville, master of the schools at Rouen cathedral, talks of the yoke that 'Queen Money, the fertile mother of Vice' and 'Avarice, her inseparable companion' imposes on courtiers.[150] The examples of Stephen de Marzai, seneschal of Anjou, and the treasurer Ranulf de Glanville, demonstrate that closeness to the king could be all too profitable. At Henry II's death in July 1189, Richard the Lionheart forced the pair to pay respectively 4,500 and 15,000 pounds 'because they were suspected of having taken advantage of their intimacy with the king', as Richard of Devizes puts it.[151] Richard's evidence, which may possibly be a little untrustworthy because of his admiration for the new king, is, however, confirmed by an earlier scandal of Ranulf de Glanville when he was sheriff of Yorkshire around 1170.[152] There is more reliable confirmation from John the Trouvère, when he puts in the mouth of William Marshal this reply to Stephen de Marzai, who was refusing to pay for the transport of King Henry II's corpse to Fontevraud: 'My lord, you might have none of the king's money, but you have plenty of your own which you have amassed while in his service'.[153] This exchange cannot be explained away as a spiteful remark made to pay off a political score; it was a result of the bureaucratic culture of the twelfth century.

Royal generosity was more likely during military expeditions – very productive of plunder – than in peacetime. Richard the Lionheart passed for the most liberal of kings amongst his circle, to whom he wanted to appear as the model of a generous knight.[154] This is what Roger of Howden had to say about the king's stay in Sicily during the winter of 1190–1191:

'He gave away his treasures profusely to all the knights and squires of his army. Well might they say that not one of his predecessors had given as much in a year as he gave in a month'.[155] Ambroise, a poet of the district of Evreux who followed the king on crusade, described Richard's Sicilian munificence with great enthusiasm: 'Richard, a man neither stingy nor greedy, bestowed on them such rich gifts – plate, silver bowls, gilded cups – that they were carried in bulging bags to his knights according to their rank, so that great men, men of middling rank and lesser men alike praised him for his fine gifts'.[156] These presents left his soldiers all the more indebted to their master. But they were haphazard and depended on the goodwill and the plunder which the king disposed of in response to the successes of his victorious campaigns. Courtiers and royal officers would have little experience of regular pay, and would as a result consider looting, protection money and extortion a fair return for their service to the State.

In legal matters, a system like this made much of royal favour. To take one of several examples – Geoffrey fitz Peter, son of a plain forester, rose steadily through the ranks of the English administration: justice of the forest and sheriff of Northampton, he was associated with William de Longchamps, the chief justiciar, during Richard the Lionheart's absence, before being himself named as chief justiciar in 1198. He achieved a profitable marriage with his betrothal to Beatrice de Say, whose first cousin was none other than William de Mandeville, chief justiciar and count of Aumale and Essex. At William's death without children in 1189, Geoffrey's influence at Richard's court was such that he ended up acquiring the county of Essex over the head of his brother-in-law, Geoffrey de Say. Geoffrey de Say did not secure either the loans to buy the transfer of the earldom or the king's favour. The favouritism by which Geoffrey benefitted over the succession to Essex was quite open. His close relationship with the king, his influence at court and his access to the Exchequer allowed him to carry it off.[157] Partisan decision-making like this reveals that royal justice was far from impartial. Royal favour was the source of many legal victories, offences pardoned and fines waived to the benefit of courtiers and the king's local officers,[158] who might well regard these favours as a lawful form of reward. This favouritism is also encountered in the ease with which sons of royal servants made their careers in administration. Such was the case, for example, with the Mauduits, a dynasty of chamberlains of the Exchequer.[159] De facto inheritance of offices was informal and never institutionalized. But it was so far admitted to be customary at this time, that John of Salisbury, for example, acknowledged its existence in his *Policraticus*,[160] a treatise otherwise highly critical of the behaviour of courtiers. The

Policraticus argued in favour of the transmission of technical know-how by father-to-son succession. So Hubert Walter, one of the most efficient royal officers of his day, for all he was devoid of any knowedge of theology or canon law, had at least been thoroughly educated in fiscal matters by his cousin, the treasurer Ranulf de Glanville.[161] Favouritism, clientage and inheritance were underhand means of rewarding the efforts of many of the lay officers, but they were very effective.

Rewarding courtier-clerics was much easier. At all events, it was not very expensive for the king, who had a monopoly on the patronage of bishoprics, chapter offices and royal churches in Normandy and England, two realms where he directed ecclesiastical elections as he pleased. On the other hand, in Anjou and Aquitaine the choice of church leaders remained less supervised, another indication of weaker royal control there.[162] The list of *clerici regis* who became bishops or canons after the intervention of Henry II is very long.[163] On the other side of the process we should remember the fall of Arnulf (before 1109–1184) bishop of Lisieux, who was forced to resign by the king after the rebellion of 1173, all to the benefit of Walter de Coutances, the vice-chancellor, a more reliable sort of cleric.[164] Richard the Lionheart was quite as decisive as his father in his interventions in episcopal elections. During the synod of Pipewell in September 1189 Richard placed his most loyal officers, or their kinsfolk, in the vacant episcopal sees of England. He managed to get Geoffrey, his bastard half-brother, elected to the archbishopric of York. While still a captive in Germany in 1192 he managed the election of the archbishop of Canterbury.[165] In 1197 and 1198 he succeeded in placing his chamber clerk and crusading companion, Philip de Poitou, in charge of the see of Durham and Eustace, vice-chancellor and keeper of the seal, in Ely.[166] The king's control of these ecclesiastical offices was inextricably linked to the workings of a State where ties of client-age remained important. This complex interplay of power struggles and favouritism around the king so as to gain his goodwill surfaces frequently in the letters of the courtier-clerics.[167]

There is little precise information as to how local officers of the Plantagenet Empire were paid. The English sheriffs took their offices at farm, and received an annual fee from the subordinate officers of their counties. They presented their accounts annually at the Exchequer and they were also inspected by the justices in eyre, or travelling courts, as they passed on their circuit. In Anjou and Aquitaine, the provosts, *vicarii* or bailiffs responsible for a lordship in the king's hand, bases from which they exercised police and judicial functions in the surrounding country, kept for themselves most of the lands under their supervision.[168] Their behaviour was less well monitored by the king and his counsellors than those of England and Normandy, realms which were exceptionally well administered for the time.

This analysis of the system of rewards for courtiers and of a number of clerical careers matches the bitter remarks of the Latin satirists on ambitious prelates at the Plantagenet court and their frantic pursuit of bishoprics and prebends. The same applies to their denunciations of the corruption of royal officers, men who were often paid in an erratic way. Some of their rhetoric will be looked at a little later, but for the meantime it needs to be stressed that there was a reality that underlay their discourse. Royal officers, unhappy with their rewards, did make use of their position to profiteer ruthlessly. Apart from this, administrative office brought them more than just material possessions. It gave them the prestige, influence and connections by which they made their fortune.

To conclude, the men who furthered the Plantagenets' interests belonged to a range of social backgrounds. Often they came from the upper levels of the old aristocracy, sometimes from the lesser, educated knightly families, but also from the urban bourgeoisie and even the free peasantry, who were exploiting their links of clientage with greater men to get an entry at court. The intermixing of these diverse social groups of men, nearly all English or Norman, in the circle around the king, was not without its problems. The coming together of different and competing levels of vassality and fealty in one place was a frequent cause for conflict. The ambition of courtiers gave rise to scheming for personal and family advancement. All this was in addition to the plotting going on within the Angevin family itself, where the sons, *juvenes* insecure about their inheritance, sought to take their principality in the Plantagenet empire from out of their father's control. The court was a stormy place. Its hothouse atmosphere was often deplored by its own officers themselves. But it would not do to leave the image of courtiers as only one of a group at war with itself. Because they often pursued long courses of study, and because they shared general skills or techniques, these men were capable of cooperating in the building up of an effective administrative system, capable of imposing justice and order, and of securing the money needed to finance distant wars.

Improving manners

The Plantagenet court was remarkable for the number and quality of the Latin writers who were its members: John of Salisbury, Peter of Blois, Gerald of Barry, Walter Map, Arnulf of Lisieux, Nigel de Longchamps,

Walter de Châtillon (*c*.1139–*c*.1179) and Ralph Niger (1140/6–*c*.1199). All of them were attached to the household of the king of England, in one capacity or other, and benefitted from his patronage. This remarkable concentration of talent was an exceptional feature in the cultural panorama of the twelfth century. It was a response to a political impulse of raw power, which alone could have succeeded in mobilizing these intellectuals, who were otherwise natural critics of the court. These clerks described an environment notable for the rigidity of its social codes. They reflect a specifically courtly culture, combining elements as much Christian as knightly, as much sacred as profane. To understand them fully it is first necessary to examine the moral reflections that these courtier-clerks themselves composed on the social world of the royal palace. After this we need to move on to survey those attitudes typical of knights which are encompassed by the broad, if vague, word 'courtliness'. On the way, we will discover that the dichotomy between 'clergy' and 'knighthood' was not quite as deep set as might be believed, and that the courtly behaviour of the laity came under a heavy clerical influence.

Clerical morality put to the test

The intellectuals who served Henry II, Richard the Lionheart and John often liked to pose as satirists. In this way they affected the literary genre and the rhetoric of those Classical writers who had long ago declaimed against the morals of the decadent Roman Empire. They talked paradoxically in a disengaged, jaded and pitiless way about the court where they made their career and also about the sort of people they met there. They often talked of the hellish court of Hellequin in their works. Egbert Türk has published the best and broadest study of their genre.[169] But sticking to social history, we will limit ourselves just to the re-examination of some of the criticisms these intellectuals made of courtiers and their world – the world they knew so well – so as to give them their true political and social context.

The first thing is to highlight one particular theme to which they return again and again: the wickedness of parvenus in the Plantagenet bureaucracy. Being as contrary as he usually was, Walter Map insisted on the link between the low birth of certain judges, sheriffs, serjeants and foresters and their excessive force and harshness. They were scourges on the backs of those innocent parties who came within their power.[170] An identical prejudice against the lower orders can be found in the writings of Gerald of Barry, descendant of a constable of Henry I and member of a noble Norman family settled in Wales. Henry II, 'the oppressor of the nobility' encouraged the promotion of foreigners, of low born and unknown men, for 'he raised the lowly and humbled the proud'.[171] The same criticism is found in the work of Ralph Niger, a fierce partisan of Thomas Becket against Henry II, whom he accused of having entrusted important offices to 'peasants, bastards and mercenaries' and chosen bishops and abbots from amongst his 'flunkies'.[172] Some of these shots were aimed at particular historical characters. Fawkes de Breauté, one of the most prominent soldiers of the minority of Henry III, was criticized by the contemporary Barnwell chronicler on the grounds that he had abused the favour of King John 'who had made him a knight, and indeed the equal of an earl, from the domestic servant he had been, all because of his assiduous obsequiousness'.[173] Ancient commonplaces and long-ago discontents, which reached the twelfth century from Classical rhetorical techniques, certainly affected the modes of expression of those stern critics of contemporary morals. But even so, prosopography proves that the presence of 'new men' at the Plantagenet court was not just their imagination.

Once they had pointed to the dominance in the administration of 'lesser folk', every Plantagenet satirist analysed how they had achieved their 'unlawful' rise. One of their favourite targets as the cause of their irresistible rise was the democratization of knowledge. Nigel de Longchamps, author of the significantly-named *Tract against Courtiers and Clerical Officers* (1193 × 1194) highlighted the open ambition of a large number of highly-educated clergy to enter the court so as to gain a bishopric.[174] In a conversation he claimed to have had with Ranulf de Glanville, Walter Map also argued against the way commoners rose by means of the schools: 'The nobles of our lands do not care for study or they are too idle to put their children to learn. Now, of right, only those who are freemen (*liberi*) can devote themselves to those arts called "liberal". Serfs, or peasants as they are called, push themselves to educate their ignoble and obscure offspring in the arts which are forbidden to them, not so as to distance them from their vices, but that they might gather riches; and the more skill they gain, the more damage they do.'[175] If we believe Walter on the subject, education had a cash value. Here again his outlook betrays aristocratic prejudices allied to the need to defend a society of ordered levels. He overreacts to a phenomenon whose significance we know to have been actually quite limited. What makes it all the more interesting on the psychological level is that Walter was not himself from an aristocratic background. Whatever their family background, intellectuals had become a necessity.

For their part, these intellectuals-turned-administrators betray a deep malaise. In their writings they assert the independence of culture and literary endeavour, and they distance themselves from their employment by the powers-that-be for political purposes. Yet the facts reveal they did engage in politics. They all go on as if theoretical knowledge was incompatible with practical activity. An aphorism of Alexander Neckam says it all: 'The philosopher who laboured often late into the night over the vagaries of mathematics, is now employed as an accountant at the Exchequer'.[176] The *trivium* and the *quadrivium*, whose independence and freedom intellectuals asserted, were to be deployed directly in the king's service. They said that such sublime forms of learning should not be contaminated by their subordination to the State, and should not be reduced to governmental hack work. Yet for all that, John of Salisbury betrays a certain anxiety of the increasing number of clerks – stigmatized as 'Cornificiens' – who were looking for a professional and profitable return from their studies, which they hoped to be brief and cheap.[177] Gerald of Barry deplores the corruption of literary studies in much the same way as John. Young students were flocking in their superficiality to the law and other 'profitable studies' to the detriment of the liberal arts, which would supply them with the deeper knowledge that underpinned all else.[178] Careerism alone dictated their choices. This is why Gerald tartly criticized the rift between the court and the schools. He contrasted the body, the death and the hell of the court with the spirit, eternity and the happiness of the schools: 'the court, the source of all cares; the schools, the source of all delights'. It was not lightly that he asserted that life had no more heady pleasure than the reading and writing of books.[179]

Peter of Blois talked in the same terms when he criticized Master Ralph of Beauvais in one of his letters for having given up education for the court (*curia*), a word he made out had derived from *cruor*, 'bloodshed, murder'.[180] He composed a long oratorical exercise in Latin verse which contrasted the courtier with his critic. It took on a moralizing tone. The faulty arguments of the courtier, who put forward in his worldly way the delights and refinements of the court, had been knowingly exposed to the benefit of the critic.[181] In later days Peter, who had decided to retire from the world of affairs, reassessed his previous life. Self-obsession, blind ambition and the wish to make his fortune had pushed him into Henry II's service, the root of all his unhappiness.[182] A contemplative life is entirely incompatible with the active life, which drives every royal officer into a frenzy, according to the writings of every one of these clergymen, highly placed in the royal bureaucracy. It was not a good thing for a priest to risk himself in the court. Beset by countless daily worries, he would not only lose the intellectual calm which leads to contemplation in this world, but he would risk losing the beatific vision of Christ for all eternity in the next.

Such was the corruption at court that it put at risk the eternal salvation of its members. The satirists were quite of this opinion when they criticized the misdoings of royal officers. So far as they were concerned, justice – expensive for the poor and free for the rich – was just a sham.[183] Embezzlement was everywhere: no public official would do his job without first taking a cut for himself from his clients. Peter of Blois cited the fees of justices in eyre, chief foresters and sheriffs; always ready to make money and to rule in favour of the one who offered most. Their victims dared not complain to the king in fear of reprisals, for the court may have been deeply divided against itself but soon rallied against any exterior threat, as he said. The culture of bribery reached down to the doorkeepers and servants of the royal palace, who let no one near the king unless they paid handsomely first.[184]

As well as corruption, a climate of fear dominated the court. There was a merciless rivalry which pitted one courtier against another in climbing the steps of power. Sometimes it led to war: in the absence of Richard the Lionheart on crusade William de Longchamps, bishop of Ely and his chancellor, confronted Hugh de Puiset, bishop of Durham and chief justiciar of England; the two chief government officers in England went so far as to exchange hostages and royal castles as a result.[185] More routinely, these power struggles could be seen in the relentless pressure kept up round the king to overthrow rivals. In 1155, in a letter addressed to Thomas Becket, Bishop Arnulf of Lisieux, justiciar of Normandy, complained that he was the victim of the plotting of sycophants he had himself brought into the court.[186] In the same way, John of Salisbury condemned jealousy as the characteristic sin of courtiers, who were drawn irresistibly towards deceit and hypocrisy.[187] Walter Map told the story of a young warrior whose courage won a great battle for the king of Portugal. But he did not keep his favour for long, since courtiers invented charges of his adultery with the queen before being allowed to arrange his death during a hunt.[188] Malicious gossip went along with outrageous flattery at the court. John of Salisbury devoted long chapters to the subject in his *Policraticus*: 'The flatterer is opposed to all virtue and produces a sort of cataract in the eyes of the man to whom he talks.'[189] Powerful moral distortions were inherent in the world of the court, where any and every strategy was permissible provided that it might deliver the public office which was the object of every courtier's desire.

Once power was obtained, jobs were sought for relatives. Nepotism and clientism were at the time the surest means of political advancement. According to Peter of Blois, the leeches who specialized in local administration shared their power only with kinsfolk and a few lucky friends.[190] These sorts of link, which were not to the general benefit of society, were particularly criticized in the *Architrenius* of Jean de Hauville.[191] Examples of networks of kinship and clientage based on political offices were not uncommon among the intimates of the Plantagenets.[192] The protection, favour and support of a magnate allowed a man to climb very high indeed. If kinship connections were lacking, money could do the same. John of Salisbury in this way laid into 'those who resort to great men carrying gifts, furthering their kinsfolk and connections and looking for the favour of the higher clergy.' Later on, he derides their unbridled ambition: 'They become the nurses of aged and powerful men and make the most of their grey hairs. They consult physicians and astrologers about the fate of princes.'[193] In passing, John castigated astrology, in his view, alongside magic, a widespread vice in the world of the court, and devoted long passages of the second chapter of his *Policraticus* to it.[194] Kinship, relationships and friendship stood in the way of equal opportunities in the pursuit of a career. These connections penetrated the framework of the State. They swamped it in such a slough of vested interests and family politics that they put all idea of fairness out of the question.

Apart from corruption, the venality and the ambition that they said they met everywhere, the clerks compared the court to hell or at least to its portals. The spectres of Hellequin's Hunt were their chosen examples. John of Salisbury's judgement on the sinners of the court admitted of no appeal: 'The law invites specialists in folly and crime to court, and it expels from court the true scholars.'[195] He addresses himself then to the vices of courtiers, every coward, traitor, criminal, liar, homosexual, glutton, addict of the hunt, gambler, mime and every other abomination, to everything which was contrary to the ideal of the austerity, seriousness and abstinence of a true philosopher: 'Love of knowledge has made no man rich.'[196] Walter Map pushed the logic further. The court was for him not only a place of damnation but also of suffering, an echo in the world of the final damnation, a true hell where was to be found all the known demons: Pyriphlegethon (or Envy), Lethe (or Forgetfulness of God), Acheron (or Regret for Unassuaged Desire) . . . 'What torture is there in hell which is not worse in the court?'[197] The worst of them all is the impossibility of literary creativity or any deep and sustained reflection in an environment completely abandoned by the Muses.

Looking back over several centuries and taking a chance on anachronism, a researcher has to grasp at the meaning of these complaints. They betray the dissatisfaction of the intellectual who wanted to devote the chief part of his time to his mental endeavours rather than to time-consuming administration.[198] Other psychological factors could have entered into the equation, such as the ill-feeling against the king and his court of a clerk who had not obtained his proper due and who brooded on his unfulfilled career in the evening of his days.[199] The writings of Gerald of Barry (frustrated by Henry II and the chancellor Hubert Walter in his succession to the diocese of St David's, to which he had been elected in succession to his uncle by the cathedral chapter) or those of Arnulf of Lisieux (deposed from his see because of his stance during the revolt of 1173) perhaps betrayed this sort of resentment, but no medieval historian could ever penetrate their true motives.[200] As in many cultures, critics of the prince's counsellors have a particular ideological function: to save the king's face by blaming his ministers for abuses and unpopular actions.[201]

Should we take the criticisms of these authors literally? Walter Map, who generally had little time for his colleagues at the court, had more respect for the justices of the Exchequer.[202] The modern study of the Exchequer accounts confirms their severity towards some of the less competent sheriffs. All the same, as Walter Map or Peter of Blois emphasized, abuses and impositions had spread throughout every level of the administration. Embezzlement, greed and favouritism, so deplored by the Plantagenet court clerics, seem endemic in an administration which paid its officers in a haphazard way and which had little control over their activity or information about it. Educated in legal studies, the satirists of the court thought in terms of institutions, law or offices. The same was not true for many of the bailiffs and sheriffs who behaved, not so much as officers who had to give a strict account of their charges, but like lords. Their morality was hardly that of austere public servants when they served societies where there was not yet any sensibility of the common good, of the separation of public and private spheres and of political culture.[203] At the heart of the structure of the Plantagenet State, venality triumphed over fairness, private over the public, and family and hereditary concerns over the common good.

When they composed their attacks on the court, the satirists cited classical references and used ancient rhetorical devices. From the perspective of comparative literature, philologists have shown how, well before the twelfth century, the satirists found many of their themes in the Latin classics and that these themes can be, if necessary, analysed apart from their chronological context.[204] The ideal of the leisure and calm (*otium*) necessary to a philosopher so as to reach and to contemplate truth divorced from all wordly distractions and business (*necotium*) goes back, at least, to Socrates. The seat of power and authority would hardly be understood to favour such conditions. Under the Roman Empire, Seneca and the Stoics had composed criticisms of the court that Christian thinkers, persecuted by the state, had promptly revived.[205] The personal journey of Boethius, the intimate of Theoderic the Great, his disgrace and the composition of the *Consolation of Philosophy*, showed, if it was necessary, what John of Salisbury, Walter Map, Gerald of Barry or Peter of Blois could not have failed to take note of: how such topoi were common to intellectuals torn between their duties at court and their craving for knowledge, beauty and spirituality. Plantagenet clerics knew the classics all the better as the renaissance of their time revealed them in their original form, rather than in the ancient florilegia of former days. Their interest in the *Consolation* of Boethius is made obvious by the *Romance of Philosophy*, its Anglo-Norman adaptation by Simon de Freine (died 1224/1228), the friend of Gerald of Barry.[206] There is no doubt of the influence of ancient authors on Plantagenet thinking.

After the regrets of the philosopher, the priest did not spare his strictures on the ineffectual ethics of courtiers. This was his basic pastoral function: to improve the conduct of layfolk and point out their vices so as better to correct them.[207] According to Matthew, dean of Chichester between 1180 and 1197, this was the only thing that excused clergy of being at court: 'There is nothing to criticise in clerks serving princes with integrity; we only chastise them for doing it obsequiously and for material reasons, and enjoying their time at court too obviously . . . Ecclesiastics can join a princely court and follow its progress, provided that they are moved to do it by love and the desire to correct princes and further the cause of the churches.'[208] On the other hand, for John of Salisbury the most despicable of the clergy who were royal councillors was the flatterer, a 'dog of the court' yapping his praises to please his royal master, whose adulation – his principal vice – is dissected in several chapters of the *Policraticus*. The opposite of the flattering clerk was the type who, like the priests of Deuteronomy, were vigilant that divine law be always respected, and did not hesitate to rebuke rulers.[209] There could be no reproach to him over his instruction of other courtiers by moral rebuke or preaching.

This sort of clerk was in no danger of being punished by the king in pursuing one of the missions of his priestly office. This freedom of speech at court was illustrated in the first preface of Gerald of Barry's *Instruction of the Prince* (1192–1218): 'I find much to criticise in the actions of princes and prelates set to govern and instruct others as much by their example as their power.' To show up those who grieved him by flattering the great of this world and by lacking the nerve to criticize them to their face, Peter of Blois recalled his freedom in addressing Henry II in his *Breviate of the Book of Job* (1173) and his *Dialogue of the Abbot of Bonneval* (1188–1189).[210] He undoubtedly exaggerated his advocacy: these two collections of biblical quotations may be addressed directly to the king, but they maintain a respectful and indulgent tone towards him. At the most, these two collections suggest to the king a conventional enough ideal of the Christian life, stressing patience in the face of adversity, charity when faced with filial ingratitude, attendance at the sacraments, penitence for one's own sins, the practice of virtue and generosity to the poor. There was nothing more natural, in conclusion, for a courtier-clerk than to criticize what was wrong with his world, in pursuit of moral reform.

This attitude was so much more marked in the reign of Henry II that his dispute with Thomas Becket reignited the century-old rivalry between spiritual and temporal authority. Had not one of the most influential minds behind the Gregorian reform, Peter Damian (*c*.1007–1072) written a treatise called *Against Courtier-clerks and the Pursuit of Office*, all in furtherance of the strict separation between God and Caesar? In 1179, did not the Third Lateran Council move to condemn clerks in higher and minor orders who lived off ecclesiastical revenues but continued to act as justices in secular courts, a thing very widespread in England?[211] For John of Salisbury and Ralph Niger, committed body and soul to the support of Thomas Becket, criticism of the court was aimed at those who were helping the king to suppress ecclesiastical liberties. It was the same with Gerald of Barry, less radical a partisan than they were, who still did not hesitate to brand Henry II as 'a son of perdition' and 'a hammer of the Church' and to see in his undignified death divine punishment following on the murder of the archbishop of Canterbury, 'perpetrated by four dogs of the court'.[212] Almost all Becket's hagiographers embrace this view, accusing the king's 'thieving councillors' of planning the crime: the 'lies of informers', 'gnawing of envy' and 'enormities of ambitious men' of driving the quarrel to the brink.[213] For these intellectuals, the king and his wicked councillors were as much worthy of damnation for the murder in the cathedral as for the suppressing of the Church's liberties. As Natalie Fryde has demonstrated, hostile clerical posturing against the Angevin monarchy was in the direct line of the long struggle to preserve Church liberty;[214] it was restated in the text of Magna Carta, extorted by force of arms from the king, who was forced thereafter to respect it. In a context not unlike the Investiture Contest, the anti-curial criticisms, however much derived from Classical models, adopt a new stance and a new sort of bitterness.

Moral condemnations of the Plantagenet court are at the heart of the work of the intellectuals who worked there. Their essential aim was to rein in the human faults of the State.[215] The strong ethical standpoint of their criticisms may seem rather antiquated to a modern medievalist who looks at them in the light of the sorts of analysis inspired by Machiavelli, Hobbes or Hegel in the name of the ineluctable development of the means of government following their own intrinsic logic.[216] One of their philosophies stressed the moral autonomy of the rising modern State, an autonomy which the courtier-clerks of the Plantagenets would have judged to be harmful to the common good and which they would not have hesitated to judge to be tyrannical. We are in no position to stand in judgement on the thinkers of the twelfth century as the worse atrocities of the twentieth century have shown how much the interest of the State and political ethics might not always be incompatible. The Plantagenet court intellectuals, deeply sensible of their reforming mission, worked to change the conduct of aristocrats, impressing on them a self-awareness and manners able to offset the group and individual manifestations of their aggressiveness.

The fashion for courtly knights

In the twelfth century, the increase in royal power was all too often at the expense of the nobility, whose culture was primarily that of the warrior. Thereafter a showdown between the embryonic State, the sole lawful employer of violence, and the aristocracy, whose behaviour was frequently brutal, became inevitable. Noble education was based on the acquiring of physical techniques which fitted the young to fight on horseback. More-over it included the transmission of military values like courage, loyalty, camaraderie, honour and discipline. Violence was integral to the aristo-cratic lifestyle, of which the principal pursuit and justification for its social dominance was war, private so much as public and to do with their lordships as much as the State. There were more or less daily examples of aristocratic savagery, but it might just suffice to note the pattern of noble nicknames: it usually involved taking names and surnames inspired by wild beasts.[217] The murder of Becket was in this sort of spirit. When they had wounded the archbishop, his four assassins hacked at him on the ground with their swords; they wounded the unarmed clerks who tried to defend him; they looted the archiepiscopal palace and commandeered the horses in his stables.[218] It was all done without any scruples, as if a life of arms and pillage had rendered violence commonplace among the knights close to Henry II.[219]

The Becket affair was significant for another reason. As it unravelled, it crudely restated the ancient dialectic between unrestrainedly violent warriors and priests, pledged to the worship of God and keepers of written knowledge, to whom canon law forbade the shedding of blood. Clergy worked towards the pastoral objective of restricting noble violence through a strict framework of the 'just' war, legitimate and defensive, along the lines of St Augustine's definition, and of limiting war by a Christianization of noble conduct. The priests persuaded the aristocracy to assume an ideology, formerly the preserve of royalty, which stressed the restoration of justice and peace in the land by the protection of the powerless. It was in fact no less than chivalry, in the ideological rather than social meaning of the word, that is, an ethic saturated by ecclesiastical virtues, a construct offered by the clergy to professional warriors.[220]

Texts produced by clergy at the court of Henry II are witness to this wish to soften aristocratic conduct. In one of his letters, Peter of Blois holds forth about the decadence of chivalry. As soon as they were knighted, the nobles turned their weapons against the Church.[221] The same applies to the *Book of Conduct* (*c.*1175) – note the title – of Stephen de Fougères (died 1178), chaplain of Henry II and chancery clerk, raised to the see of Rennes in 1168. His work, written in Anglo-Norman French, borrowed from the technique of preaching *ad status* (to different conditions of life) which criticized each social category by pinpointing its particular vices. He was unsparing towards the knights, who wilfully misused their power to mistreat and exploit their inferiors, and towards noblewomen, their adulterous wives.[222] Following Stephen, many authors took the same tone in chastising the warrior aristocracy.[223]

John of Salisbury is the writer who reflected deepest on the problem of the conduct of warriors and on their role in the social structure.[224] He gives a long list of the duties of a knight, which repeated the ecclesiastical model: 'Protect the Church, oppose wickedness, respect the priest, defend the poor from injustice, make peace to reign in the land, spill his own blood and, if need be, lay down his life for his brother.'[225] The role of the knight was to defend the unarmed and cause peace and justice to reign. This gave the knight a particular place within his society, which John does not explain by means of the trifunctional scheme of the Three Orders, long since marginalized by the increasing bureaucratization of the English government.[226] According to John, humanity was an organic entity:[227]

knights were its hands and blindly obeyed the prince who was its head. They were entirely at the king's disposal. There could be no justification if they rebelled against him.

The theory of tyrannicide presented in the *Policraticus* has been wrongly interpreted as a call to resist Henry II,[228] who would be responsible for the murder of Becket, John of Salisbury's patron, a dozen years after its publication.[229] In mitigation of the interpreters of his work, it has to be said that it is not easy to interpret John's thought. His method is not scholastic, but encyclopaedic. It was rooted in the comparison of contradictory anecdotes (or *exempla*) and did not pick arguments according to the principles of non-contradiction or dialectic.[230] Influenced by Gregorian scholarship, it tried vainly to bring together 'the agreement of opposites' (*concordia discordantium*). This sort of thought had been devised around the year 1000 so as to reconcile contradictions, sidestep them and draw them into agreement. Musical harmony was one of its inspirations, for it allowed, by means of keys, a unity of sound to proceed out of variety.[231] In the case of John of Salisbury, he put his argument on tyrannicide within the chapter which condemned the outrageous flattery of courtiers, just so as to highlight the contrast between the two attitudes. As was his custom, he buried his thoughts on political assassination in such a mass of counterexamples (like the patience of David with Saul) and exceptions (like the ban on killing a man to whom had been sworn an oath of allegiance and to whom one owed loyalty, or the forbidden use of poison), that the doing of the act itself is next to impossible.[232] John emphasized, on the other hand, the divine justice implicit in the acts of men, which explained the grim end of all rulers who abused the power which had devolved on them from on high, who had ignored higher laws and had violently oppressed their people. Because John was subtle and enjoyed paradoxes, his arguments presented political problems in all their complications.[233] He was truly close to a modern thinker in his intuitions.

Despite the subtleties which his form of thinking introduced, there is no doubting the innovatory and revolutionary nature of John of Salisbury's theory of tyrannicide in the history of Western political thought. It burst on to the medieval intellectual stage after many centuries of obscurity.[234] It would be repeated by John's contemporary, Gerald of Barry, who put it in a clearer and sharper way than he did, though posterity has been rather less grateful to him than to John: 'He who strikes down a tyrant ought to suffer no punishment, but rather a reward, as it is said: "who kills a tyrant deserves a prize".'[235] Plantagenet thinkers were definitely ahead of their time.

The theory of John of Salisbury had nothing to do with the short-term circumstances of the time it was written. It was in no way directed at Henry II. The *Policraticus* was finished in 1159, when relations were excellent between the king and his chancellor, to whom it was dedicated. In that year Thomas led the royal army against Toulouse. An entire chapter of the book contained a eulogy on the way that the new king Henry had managed to pacify England after the long civil war. The most the book does is close with a short passage alluding to a man who had reached maturity, which one modern translator has interpreted as a veiled criticism of the high level of scutage collected by the king for the Toulouse campaign.[236] John was temporarily in the bad books of the king, who had forbidden his return to England. He was trying to get into his good graces by complimenting him in this sort of way and by working on his chancellor, the dedicatee of the book, to intervene in his favour at court.

John described as 'tyrants' those magnates who had previously rebelled against King Stephen of England. He did the same for the nobles who had profited from the civil war by occupying the lands of the see of Canterbury.[237] He paralleled here a tradition of monastic historiography, which went back at least to Carolingian times, in which the 'tyrant' was none other than the man who defied royal authority. The *Annals of St-Serge* praised Henry II who, in 1154 'imposed peace on a certain tyrant, Hugh de Mortemer, who had rebelled'.[238] John's mode of expression never undervalued Plantagenet state-building at the expense of the independent castle-lordships and the jurisdiction of the aristocracy.

One last aspect, apparently secondary, of the *Policraticus* concerns noble violence. It concerns his harsh strictures against the hunting to which courtiers devoted themselves single-mindedly. 'The hunt is a foolish occupation and blameworthy, and its benefits do not outweigh its inconveniences.'[239] John of Salisbury was surely here putting into words the prejudices of the clerical world against an amusement which involved bloodshed, a thing forbidden by canon law to clerks. He also knew the hunt might be a training ground for murder, and how much the royal forests (covering a quarter of England) impoverished the peasantry, who were forbidden from making use of them. This sort of reproach was a characteristic of a broader current of thought found amongst exegetes, who made the hunt a metaphor for bloody meat the king ate – a hidden allusion to the royal taxes which ate up just as greedily the fruits of the people's labour. Gerald of Barry described King William Rufus in the act of eating raw human flesh the night before going on a hunt.[240] Philippe Buc makes the point that this cannibalism was the repulsive counter-image to the eucharist which built up the unity of the Church, rather than destroyed it. It alluded to a cruder dimension of the monarchy, which was in its way also that of the aristocracy, growing fat through its impositions on the peasantry.[241]

For John of Salisbury the dividing line between clerk and knight is elsewhere. It lay in the knowledge of letters. 'Who ought to expect an *illiteratus* to employ literacy, when his duty is to know his trade as soldier not letters.'[242] *Illiteratus* needs to be understood here in its medieval not modern sense, the unlettered man being one whose incapacity in Latin prevented him reading the available works in scholarly disciplines of the highest sort, that is, philosophy and theology. It was also impossible to work as an administrator without Latin. At that time the literary use of the vernacular excluded scholarship and was confined to fiction and reminiscence, then believed to occupy a different sphere from reality.[243] At the time we are looking at – with just a few exceptions – the *illiteratus* was interpreted as a layman. Clergy and knighthood possessed entirely separate cultures. But is that to say they were incompatible? Were the bridges between them completely down? The prologue to the *Romance of Thebes*, written in Normandy around 1150, puts these two categories on the same level, and considers that they alone would be able to follow the romance: 'As everyone is silent on this subject, except only clerks and knights, for the rest have no value for it, any more than an ass would for a harp.'[244] A certain elitism linked clergy and noblemen in literature, and excluded merchants and peasants.

It was not out of the question for lay noblemen to participate in learned culture, even if it was not always in the shape of the written, Latinate and sacred sort, but instead, oral, romance and profane. The cases of Ranulf de Glanville and William de Mandeville already mentioned show that the *miles litteratus* was not a contradictory concept or irreconcilable with the facts of aristocratic society at the end of the twelfth century.[245] The emergence of educated knights was not necessarily a symptom of a crisis of military values within the nobility.[246] Gerald of Barry tells the story of a learned knight who returns to earth as a ghost so as to swap improvised Latin verses with his old master Maurice as he had done when he was alive.[247] The learned knight was nothing less than an ideal social type widespread at the Plantagenet court within the middle-ranking nobility, where education assisted in getting careers in royal service.[248] The higher nobility was just as educated, maybe more so. Robert, earl of Gloucester (died 1147), bastard son of Henry I and supporter of the young Henry II, was a generous patron of the arts. He was a dedicatee of William of

Malmesbury, Geoffrey of Monmouth and Geoffrey Gaimar.[249] Equally, Robert II, earl of Leicester (died 1168) – praised by John of Salisbury for his views on kingship and by Richard fitz Nigel who called him *litteris eruditus* (a man learned in letters) – and his twin brother Waleran, count of Meulan (died 1166) – who wrote Latin verse and himself read charter texts – both received as children a careful education at the monastery of Abingdon.[250] Waleran, one of the dedicatees in several manuscripts of Geoffrey of Monmouth's *History of the Kings of Britain*, may have been the father of Marie de France, author of the *Lais*, who may have been the wife of Henry Talbot, a Herefordshire landowner.[251] Gilbert fitz Baderon, a kinsman of the Clares, collected a library of French and Latin works in his castle of Monmouth: the Cambro-Norman poet, Hue of Roteland, borrowed one of them.[252] Constance, wife of Ralph fitz Gilbert, a Lincolnshire landowner, entrusted Geoffrey Gaimar with the French translation of the Anglo-Saxon chronicle.[253] All these people were undoubtedly members of the higher Anglo-Norman aristocracy, and were just as likely to recruit the lesser literate nobility into their service. For such courtiers neither careers in war or the law ruled out love of letters.

The rise of civilized behaviour

Most knights may well not have acquired quite so formidable a cultural background, but they still mastered a pragmatic level of literacy. They did not devote their spare time to reading works of fiction and scholarship; they knew the basics of writing and calculation, hardly sufficient for understanding learned tracts, but fine for royal charters or untangling the accounts of their domains. In England, many of the sheriffs and local justices knew how to read and dictate Latin documents, sometimes even to write them, as is proved by the autograph act of one Richard, who presided over Hampshire under Henry II.[254] Walter Map mentioned of one of his young English relatives that his desire to carry arms drove him to Flanders with the intention of finishing his military education at the court of Philip of Alsace, and that he 'with no knowledge of Latin, which was a pity, could still write out the alphabet'.[255] This seems a significant indicator of the general level of education of knights.

Knights developed a culture all of their own, where oral composition and the vernacular replaced the written composition and Latin of the clergy. Walter Map talks of Waleran d'Ivry, who despite being a *miles illiteratus* – that is, ignorant of Latin – could still compose French verse.[256] Using Latin became a matter of considerable prestige amongst the nobility of the whole Plantagenet Empire. Gerald of Barry, son of a Norman aristocratic family, was not being ironic when he wrote: 'For us Latin and French are more important than any other languages.'[257] In Britain, Anglo-Norman (the French dialect spoken on either side of the Channel) became the language of the social elite after the Conquest of 1066, which had extinguished or marginalized the native aristocracy speaking Anglo-Saxon (at that time, Middle English). Throughout the twelfth century the prestige of Anglo-Norman continued to grow amongst the nobles, clergy and jongleurs of England. It is a fact that it was in England that the first French romance, historical work, Biblical translation, monastic rule, scientific text, administrative treatise and octosyllabic couplets can all be found. It was also in England that a woman is first found writing French. Ian Short attributes this precocity to the trilingualism and multiculturalism of the British elites which adopted Anglo-Norman, more useful as it was than Latin and wider in its expression than Anglo-Saxon.[258]

In this world, Anglo-Saxon was demoted to a lower social level, becoming a day-to-day language, the tongue of the hearth and the servants' quarters.[259] Thanks to one of the Lives of Thomas Becket, we know that at the home of one of the assassins, Hugh de Morville, his wife talked to him in English. But the final argument between the archbishop and his murderers was conducted in French.[260] This situation of 'diglossia' where one more prestigious language consequently squeezed out another from anything except daily use, leaves its traces in the anxieties which plagued Anglophones who had to use French, such as the nun of Barking, who excused herself to the readers of her Vie d'Edouard le Confesseur: 'I know the quasi-French of England, for I've never gone overseas to find a better.'[261] Nigel de Longchamps advised his uncle, Bishop William of Ely, to use the speech of his father, a Frenchman, rather than that of his mother, an Englishwoman.[262] The former was the language of king and court, the one which assisted careers and social climbing.

At court it was the grammar, syntax and speaking of Anglo-Norman which powered social codes. It was a source of prestige and reputation to master them well. There was no easier way to poke fun at a political enemy than to mock his accent. Walter Map satirized the bad French of Geoffrey of York, the natural son of Henry II, who spoke the dialect of Marlborough, a barbaric tongue, he said, which belonged to those who had drunk from the well of that town.[263] Other references to language are not so easy to interpret. In the prologue of the Policraticus (once thought wrongly to be a handbook of conduct written by Nigel de Longchamps)[264] John of Salisbury gives this advice to a young man on the make who wanted to succeed at court: 'That your deportment, clothing and appearance assume a foreign air. Your own way of talking should be remarkable for its odd accents. Tell everyone that you're a native of Poitou, where the speech is freer.'[265] Would social distinction be conveyed from now on by a continental and romantic accent, free of the accent and distinctive grammar that bilingualism had given the English, now feeling inadequate because they spoke a dialect Gerald of Barry called 'gutter-French'?[266] In Britain, the triumph of Anglo-Norman as the prestigious language of a warrior aristocracy, and as a sign of their refinement, coincided with the establishment of the Angevin dynasty. To be part of the court, it was necessary to speak adequately in Anglo-Norman French, which more than ever now had superseded Anglo-Saxon, which Henry II himself never mastered. Under him, the use of French, imposed by the Conqueror and his men on the English, remained a means of expressing royal hegemony over the native nobility.

In the other direction, in the Occitan lands of the Plantagenets, it did not seem that the Angevins found the need to resort to the language of the north to assist their government. Their legitimacy was never questioned as dukes of Aquitaine, as traditional protectors of the literature of Languedoc, and they made sure to continue this artistic patronage so as to draw prestige from it. Following the example of William IX, the first-known troubadour and his maternal great grandfather, Richard the Lionheart himself composed Occitan poetry.[267] During his long period as duke before assuming the Crown of England, Richard kept up particular links of patronage and friendship with numerous troubadours, who consequently acknowledged their obligation to him in their songs. They composed *sirventes* – political works as opposed to love songs – that any number of poets sang to praise the Plantagenets in their lands south of the Loire. Amongst the southern aristocracy – which listened to, interpreted and composed these *sirventes* – there was not the fascination with the French of the north that the English had. The troubadours, knights and servants of princely and noble courts, carried on composing in Occitan right up to the time of the Capetian conquest.

These regional modes of speech feature as essential elements of a socially codified system, along with modes of behaviour. At the end of the twelfth century, knightly literature and clerical preaching both carry echoes of a way of behaving at court so as to attract the king's good opinion, increase one's reputation amongst other men and win female admiration. It was all about *courtliness*, a critical factor in the process of building the Plantagenet State. It was no less than part of a social revolution, a programme devised by the king and ecclesiastical intellectuals with the purpose of softening the way that warriors behaved, teaching them self-control, as the innovative work of C. Stephen Jaeger argues.[268] The appearance of handbooks of good conduct in the Occitan lands of the Plantagenets is a good indicator of this process. In Gascony, around 1200, Arnaut Guilhem de Marsan composed his *Ensenhament* (Instructions) which offered to knights who want to charm ladies advice on conduct, dress, running households and spending.[269] It is evidence of increasing sophistication in the business, dress and conversation of the nobility. It also reflected the part played by women in courtly love, where learning to control sexual passion was part of the process of mastering aristocratic violence.

The analyis of social conduct and the instructions on it presented by the handbooks match well the reality of the Plantagenet court. Around 1175, Herbert of Bosham gave a particular description of the manners that Thomas Becket, the tutor of the Young Henry, taught the adolescent aristocrats whose upbringing had been entrusted to him. For Thomas, even dinner was a school. The young folk sat round him for a philosophical banquet; they ate with control and moderation; they followed a hierarchical order when they passed dishes or served the other diners, course by course.[270] There were strict rules of precedence at the royal court. The marshals, for example, might throw a nobleman out of his lodgings in the middle of the night if a greater nobleman arrived unexpectedly.[271] Such incidents gave rise to sometimes quite spectacular disputes. Walter Map talks about the confrontation between William de Tancarville, the high chamberlain, and the king's domestic chamberlain to secure the silver bowls used by Henry II to wash his hands.[272] The archbishops of Canterbury and York fought with fists and clubs to gain the place of honour next to the cardinal-legate at the synod of Westminster (1176).[273] Here for once the sense of precedence outweighed good manners!

Etiquette was all important at the Plantagenet court. It was so important that French medievalists ought to abandon for good their reservations about translating *curialis* in texts of their period as *courtisan* (courtier) under the pretext that this term belongs to Versailles and the pomp of the seventeenth-century monarchy. But it is not necessary to wait for the age of powdered wigs and lace cuffs for Western monarchies to have discovered the 'rise of civilization' so dear to the heart of Norbert Elias. The Plantagenet court proved that education in self-control by manners and obedience to precedence, imposed on a nobility by the king who had attracted it to his court, was not a modern discovery. Long before Louis XIV, princes had made the connection that the control, subordination and the subjection of the aristocracy could be achieved by 'curialization'.

At the end of the twelfth century, this domestication of men by manners evolved into a branch of intellectual thought. It was part of the intellectual renaissance, furthered by the rediscovery of the Latin classics and a level of humanistic thinking. A Stoic ideal of knowledge and education, emanating from the schools of Chartres and Paris, influenced the intellectuals of the court. Seneca, whose political ethics were taught by William de Conches, the tutor of Henry II, was as admired as Cicero, on which subject John of Salisbury (another pupil of William) wrote that the world produced nothing finer.[274] John borrowed from Cicero's work – tolerably well Christianized since Ambrose, Isidore and Bede – the ideas of *civilitas*, *cultus virtutum* and *honestum*. The last of them comprehends a moral idea of service to the State, which should be entrusted only to honest men and virtuous citizens. This governing class had all been educated, not by a distant and remote teacher handing down technical and pragmatic precepts, but by a practical tutor deeply forming his pupil's personality through his own virtue, humanity and good manners. A maxim of Seneca summed up this sort of teaching: 'Theoretical instruction takes time; but example is quick and effective.'

Thomas Becket's instruction of his wards falls within this rediscovery of rhetorical culture. The chancellor put the stress on the use of conversation and bearing by his pupils to achieve a strictly moral end. His idea was that the formation of a person was the product of a double grace, human and divine: the goodwill (*benignitas*) 'which appealed to this world' and the moral goodness (*bonitas*) 'which appealed to heaven'.[275] The humanistic aspect of education was basic for John of Salisbury, just as it was for Thomas Becket. John stressed 'civility', through which was attained true happiness, by the single way of philosophy and virtue, although of course he left out the agency of the supernatural in attaining it.[276] In emphasizing the benefits of a worldly culture Peter of Blois made much of its understanding, 'The work of the scholar is of no use to the god of his soul, but he does at least have the benefit from it of a worldly honesty, a secular innocence.'[277] At the end of the twelfth century, these themes arising from the classical Latin authors were not just to be found among the intellectuals of the Plantagenet court through their literary tastes or unconscious imitation of classical forms. They were taken up in a precise cultural and political environment where the king was attempting to impose his own coercive power on the feudal lords. Physical control, intellectual endeavour and the pursuit of knowledge were all combined into a broad programme for the domestication of the nobility, which at court taught the mastery of one's emotions; while private violence was from now on outlawed, since it had become a royal monopoly. Within this context appeared the themes of *fin'amors*, a phrase translated since the nineteenth century as 'courtly love' that William IX of Aquitaine had established in his songs for the first time in the West. Civility and courtliness were therefore a matching pair.

Throughout our period, the significance of book learning, chivalrous values and courtly affectation grew in the mentalities of the aristocracy of the Plantagenet Empire. But the problem of where this new noble culture began is one that still needs to be tackled. Although it may seem unimportant, and indeed insoluble, the question has some clear implications for the political history of the twelfth century. The theory that it diffused outwards from a French point of origin to the outer edges of Europe still prevails among the better historians of the medieval court. For Joachim Bumke, beginning from 1100, trading routes, the movements of clergy and dynastic links, would have imported the aristocratic culture from the royal court of France into Germany.[278] The superiority of the Capetian world in intellectual culture and the general triumph of its models of behaviour, underpins this sort of idea, which, however, takes no account of the energy of the English, Flemish and Champenois courts.

Remarkably enough, the English nobles of Henry I's court developed just the same outlook as the French. In the aftermath of the fall of Normandy in 1204, Gerald of Barry described an imagined conversation he said he had with Ranulf de Glanville (who had in fact died on crusade a dozen years earlier) on the way that Philip Augustus had so little trouble with the conquest. He put the emphasis on the French love of knowledge, which gave them an edge over other peoples, as it had done in their day to the Ancient Greeks and Romans.[279] If we follow this analysis, written down around 1216 when Gerald was supporting the invasion of England by the future Louis VIII, the schools of Paris and Chartres had the last word in the dispute between the kings of France and England. It is true that among English inellectuals, these schools evoked a blind admiration, close to a Francophilia hard to reconcile with the war between the two kings. They liked the wordplay of 'Paris' and 'Paradise'.[280] Gerald of Barry affirmed that 'the transfer of Empire and of scholarship' (*translatio imperii et studii*) from Greece, then to Rome had ended up in France.[281] John of Salisbury said that he was so struck by Paris, by the goodwill of Parisians, by their respect for clergy, by the splendour of the Church there and by the philosophy of its students, that he could have been Jacob watching the angels climbing and descending the staircase; and he could say with Jacob, 'surely the Lord is in the place, and I did not know it!'[282] The impressive cultural models that the cathedral schools of the north of France were able to offer increased the renown of Philip Augustus, and this intellectual predominance suited the king's political purposes. The intellectual fad for Frenchness stretched the links between the Norman elites and King John. It also undermined their will to resist the Capetians.

It would not fully describe the mentality of the Plantagenet court if no mention was made of its religiosity, influenced in turn by the most innovative spiritual developments of the end of the twelfth century. The monastic and episcopal reform which we call Gregorian had not been sufficient to dislodge the English or Norman Church from its dependency on the king. However, its ideas, insights and attitudes influenced the political elites of England. This seems to be confirmed by a renewal of religious devotion amongst clergy and laity, which emphasized spiritual independence, interiority and devotion to the person of Christ.[283] In paraphrasing the Stoic, Lucian, Seneca's nephew ('If you want to be pious – leave the court!'),[284] John of Salisbury may well have exaggerated the indifference to religion of those circles, where, despite his aphorism, some particular forms of spirituality very much flourished.

A particular attachment to the Cistercians marked out the court of Richard the Lionheart, whose confessor was the Cistercian monk, Adam de Perseigne (c.1145–1221), and to whom Milo, abbot of Le Pin, gave the last rites.[285] Richard founded Bonport, rebuilt Le Pin and re-roofed Pontigny.[286] On his part, William Marshal founded two Cistercian houses in Ireland, Tintern Parva and Duiske.[287] The white monks played an important role in his diplomacy, as papal legates, and ambassadors or observers of truces between the kings of France and England.[288] They enjoyed still an undeniable prestige, even though the criticisms of Walter Map and Gerald of Barry betray a certain hostility to the Cistercian order.[289] But it has to be remembered that from 1152 their general chapter called a halt to any new foundations,[290] and that the needs of the monks made tracts of wasteland desirable for their monasteries, which did not make grants to them any the easier. Besides this, the attitude of Geoffrey of Auxerre, abbot of Clairvaux, in the Becket affair could do nothing other than harm the order's reputation. In 1166, Geoffrey had secured from the general chapter the expulsion of Becket and his companions from Pontigny Abbey, where they had found refuge. The Cistercians who followed the example of the theologian, Isaac, abbot of L'Etoile, near Poitiers, and argued against this decision, were then persecuted by the king of England.[291] Four years later, the murder of the archbishop of Canterbury and the popularity of the cult that he inspired had beyond all question damaged the prestige of Cîteaux and its houses.

Plantagenet preferences fell on other sorts of institution. Henry II supported the growth of the forms of eremitism encouraged at Grandmont, in the Limousin. Walter Map echoed his generosity but, for all that he praised the poverty of this new order, he nonetheless believed that it was sinking into avarice.[292] The Grandimontaines, along with the Carthusians, met with the sympathy of John of Salisbury, who, however, was critical of the Cistercians.[293] The canons regular – who combined in one, pastoral mission, conventual life and advanced study – had more of an advantage over monks, black or white. This was the reason that Richard the Lionheart began many houses of Premonstratensians in Aquitaine. The Augustinians, who accounted for seven out of twenty-nine foundations by royal officers between 1170 and 1239,[294] were highly valued at court. According to Gerald of Barry, who was harsh towards other orders, the Augustinians were far and away the best of all the regular clergy.[295] Some months before he died, Richard de Lucy, for example, abandoned the justiciarship of England in order to retire into the Augustinian abbey of Lessness in Kent, which he had himself founded. It was the same with Robert de Beaumont, buried in the choir of a house of the same order, which he had set up in his honour of Leicester.[296] These conversions *ad succurrendum*, in the closing days of their lives, happened a lot with the military orders, in an age where the crusading ideal obsessed many – as one remembers from the death of William Marshal as a Templar, described magisterially by Georges Duby.[297] The clergy did not seem often to have shared the enthusiasm of noble laity for warrior monks, as the well-known words of John of Salisbury prove: 'The knights of the Temple, who are supposed to administer the blood of Christ to the faithful, have taken an oath to shed human blood.'[298] Criticism of the military orders and the incongruity of their mission was beginning to appear at this time.

Foundations which were principally charitable, with the intention of assisting the poor and the care of the sick, were frequently encouraged by the aristocracy. In England they accounted for eleven out of twenty-nine foundations by royal officers. Walter Map repeated a sermon example which, despite being discredited, is nonetheless significant as evidence of a new attitude towards sickness and poverty: 'For the sake of their good names, many men and women leave their patrimony to hospitals, and several go so far as to enter these institutions so as to assist the sick and aged. A nobleman, accustomed to be served, gave himself up to serve others there (Matt. 20: 28; Mark 10: 45); while he washed the horribly ulcerated feet of a sick man he was overcome with nausea: he swallowed the water with which he was washing them, to force his stomach to get used to what was disgusting it.'[299] It was among the needy that some courtiers came closer to understanding the humanity and suffering of Christ.[300] In the circumstances, this reception of very advanced ideas on poverty reveals that the court was not at all a closed world, but that it was on the contrary sensitive to the changing ideas of society.

The court was a place of knowledge, where traditional learning, drawn from the Bible and its exegesis but also the Latin classics, blended together thoroughly with a vernacular culture regenerating itself fully. This new sensibility was personified by the *miles litteratus* that we meet more and more at the Plantagenet court. Warrior and scholar, courtier and knight, administrator and soldier, the literate knight was an agent in erecting the embryonic State. He knew that war was the reason for his social eminence, so long as it was practised in the royal army, properly constituted and indeed 'regimented'. He must be besides this an agent of government either at the king's side or as his local representative, weakening the foundations of the aristocratic honour by new forms of justice and taxation. In doing this, he undermined the autonomy and privileges of the nobility, with for all that no desire of losing the loyalty of the nobility as a legal class.

The contradictions of this attitude leap out at us. The *miles litteratus* worked, out of the centre which was the court, at the dismantling of aristocratic power, established, so far as the court was concerned, at the periphery represented by private lordship. He certainly earned his keep at court in the fees, board, wardship or marriages that the king offered him. This behaviour, increasingly widespread, touches on a sort of social schizophrenia: the double personality of a knight who was at one and the same time a warrior and a scholar, and, what was most difficult to accept, both the heir of an ancestral estate and at one and the same time its nemesis as a royal officer. What followed was violence, private and not public, exercised outside the new feudal structures controlled by the royal government. There were many knights ready to follow the king's sons to take arms along with them against the king. This treachery was a manifestation of the rage of the younger sons disadvantaged in terms of inheritance, but also that of their more mature elders who saw the power and resources of their lordships contracting little by little under the attacks on it by agents of the Crown, among which were numbered certain of their own relatives. Internecine war, so frequent in the Angevin family itself, became common enough in families disrupted by interests and political choices all too often irreconcilable. The construction of the Plantagenet State shattered family solidarity and traditional feudal society.

Kinship, government, mobility, knowledge and civil conduct: these facets are all to be found in the phenomenon of the court. They formed elements of a coherent system of state formation. They attracted to the court numbers of warriors, caught up in the process of civilization of conduct, and also of clergy, who put their knowledge in the service of a growing bureaucracy, but who meditated also on politics and ethics. Was the Plantagenet court then a 'hell on earth' thanks to these deep changes? The clerical intellectuals of the households of Henry II, Richard the Lionheart and John did perhaps misuse this diabolic metaphor, with the intention of influencing courtiers in the direction of a religious conversion. Like other household officers, they were often conscious of building a long-lasting monarchy and giving effective institutions to the king's provinces. Influenced by a political Augustinianism, they knew that the first vocation of the *curia* – in the judicial sense of the word – was to make Justice reign and, as a consequence, Peace also. Their legacy endures to this day.

Plantagenet ideology

L earned clerks and literate knights laboured day by day to shore up Plantagenet power. They held the judicial, military and fiscal offices of the central and local administration at the heart of the bureaucratic framework of the monarchy. But their calling to the service of the king did not just stop at the role of officer and functionary. Their intellects were mobilized in pursuit of a far more ambitious plan: to exalt the Angevin dynasty and its government in the minds of its aristocratic subjects, to make them sympathetic towards its policies of expansion and territorial unity, and to get them to identify personally with the enterprise. Influencing the minds and will of the elites of the Plantagenet Empire was also the best way to secure royal ascendancy.

The satirists may often have scoffed at the doings of king and court, but that did not stop them composing eulogies on them when circumstances required. Walter Map conveniently forgot his own criticisms when he wrote: 'Our king Henry, whose power is known throughout almost all the universe'. He claimed that Louis VII had once said: 'Your king of England lacks nothing. He has men, horses, gold, silk, gems, hunting and all the rest. In France, we have only bread, wine and good cheer.'[1] If the comparison with the Capetians favoured here the Plantagenets, it is because the battle had already been won in the minds of men.

With these aims in mind, the court intellectuals were more likely to defend than to attack royal policy. They created propaganda in their master's service. Their work was all the more useful as the kings of England, engaged in a costly rivalry with Louis VII and Philip Augustus, asked for total commitment to the war. It was particularly true on the eve of the fall of Normandy in 1204. The Cistercian Ralph of Coggeshall, historian of Richard the Lionheart, asserted that, in the five years that followed his return from captivity up to his death, Richard asked for more money than any king had required in living memory. He portrayed his premature death as a divine punishment for these demands.[2] Such fiscal demands could not be made without a campaign of propaganda, which was just the mission to be assigned to his ideologues at court.

The king as master of propaganda

As modern as it may seem, the term 'propaganda' does not appear misplaced or anachronistic here – far from it.[3] Propaganda simply implies the broadcasting of a political message out from the centre, that is, the royal court, and its reception by the periphery, where the aristocracy still had an ability to make up its own mind, an ability the king wanted to influence. It recognized that there was public opinion in the complaisance of the aristocracy, which it was necessary to convince about the good sense of the actions of the king and his officers. 'Propaganda' assumes a sharp consciousness of the role of communication amongst the governing classes, who were intelligently furthering the spread of favourable ideas when they funded professional thinkers, writers and performers. It implies also an infrastructure, however primitive, even if it only mostly conveyed 'diffuse propaganda',[4] uncontrolled and spontaneous, on themes originated at the court and broadcast by it, limited and modified at the local level far from the royal household.

All these conditions were to be found at the Plantagenet court, which used these very diverse means to spread ideas and images favourable to the dynasty. This publicity appeared, for example, in Latin epigraphic inscriptions put up in public view. It was of course difficult for most passers-by to read and understand these stone plaques.[5] But they did not any the less convey weighty political matters. Proof of this is a story, repeated in a royal charter, of a stone slab placed in the abbey of Varennes to exalt the patronage of Ebles de Déols, the most important lord of lower Berry. When he heard about it, Henry II had promptly ordered it to be taken down, as he believed that he was the sole 'founder, guardian and advocate of the abbey'.[6] This high-handed act is evidence of the king's desire to leave in the collective memory the marks of his patronage and his generosity towards ecclesiastical foundations.

Iconography, on open view to all, also played a propagandist role. Between 1168 and 1170, Henry II and Eleanor of Aquitaine caused themselves to be depicted, with their four sons, as donors in the great window showing the crucifixion of St Peter at the cathedral of Poitiers, whose improvements they had patronized.[7] Just as at Varennes, royal generosity towards the Church found its expression here. Is this same desire to promote the royal dynasty just as apparent in sculpture? Some recent research emphasizes the coherence of sculptural programmes on the Gothic facades of the cathedrals of Angers, Le Mans and the collegiate church of St Martin of Candes. It emphasizes the iconographic purposes of Henry II and Eleanor, who would have wanted the representation of Christ the King, of a royal couple and the kings of the Old Testament on these churches so as to promote the legitimacy of the house of Anjou.[8] Theories such as this cannot be verified, as they are not supported by written evidence. But still, the convergence between royal themes in the first Gothic of the Loire valley and the accession of Henry II to the throne of England remains nonetheless striking. Apart from its christological character, it seems to be a good example of the wish to make political propaganda.

Two further examples, more profane than sacred, are to be placed on a different level. One is that of a lost fresco at the palace of Westminster, painted for Henry II, showing a great eagle attacked by four eaglets, symbolizing the rebellion of the king's children against their father.[9] The other is the wall of the hermitage of Sainte-Radegonde, hollowed out of the rock at Chinon, which preserves a painting of five riders, richly clothed, of which two are crowned. Specialists agree on seeing in them members of the Angevin dynasty at the end of the twelfth century, or the beginning of the thirteenth. They suggest, however, widely varying ideas in interpreting the significance of the scene. These range from King John and his wife Isabel of Angoulême hunting, with a falcon carried on the wrist of one of his knights;[10] Eleanor of Aquitaine, carried into captivity by her husband, taking leave of the Young Henry and Richard the Lionheart;[11] to Henry II and his four sons, reconciled after the rebellion of 1173, on a pilgrimage to Sainte-Radegonde.[12] Whether viewed as promoting the harmony of the house of Anjou or, quite the opposite, as recalling their family quarrels, the paintings commissioned by the Plantagenets witness to their mastery of the visual image to present themselves.

Song seems a more effective means of communication than epigraphy, sculpture or wall-painting. This is why the Angevins attempted to control the *sirventes* or political songs, the pre-eminent political media of the time.[13] The chronicler Roger of Howden has left us exceptional evidence of the means mobilized by William de Longchamps, bishop of Ely and chancellor of the absent Richard the Lionheart, so as to promote himself: 'William, so as to glorify and distinguish his name, caused sympathetic poems and flattering songs to be composed. He caused singers and entertainers to come from France, attracting them by gifts, so as to go around singing his praise in the market places. Soon it was said everywhere that he had no equal in all the world.'[14] An extract from a very critical letter of Hugh de Nonant, bishop of Coventry, tried to discredit Longchamps as patron of the arts. He poked fun at the megalomania of a chancellor who in order to improve his reputation looked for the support of entertainers. There is no call to reject this evidence out of hand, as its authenticity is confirmed by Gerald of Barry who says in 1195 – some months after the fall of Longchamps – that if recently the poets had sung in his praise, now there were as many who attacked him in their writings.[15] Such were the fortunes and misfortunes of the arrogant leader.

The king was not slow to use this sort of strategy. Following the example of his chancellor, Richard associated with minstrels, granting them lands. Such a man was Warin Trossebof who had from Henry II a field at Dol for life to hold from Archbishop Roland.[16] Likewise, royal accounts mention payments to the storyteller Maurice in 1166 and to the harpist Henry in 1176.[17] In their attacks on the court, Peter of Blois or John of Salisbury, talked of the large number of entertainers in the royal household, where they encouraged debauchery and played out a comedy of pointlessness and duplicity.[18] Their presence at court, well attested as it is, is good evidence of the readiness of the Plantagenets to use entertainers for political ends.

Few *sirventes* entirely dedicated to the praise of the Angevin dynasty have come down to us. But what has done represents the tip of an iceberg of songs now lost. Medievalists are well aware how much of this oral literature – composed for contemporary political purposes according to how events developed – was ephemeral. Such brief and passing songs were rarely transcribed into serious manuscripts, and few survived the test of time.[19] But we do have the poem of Richard the Lionheart, reviving the literary tradition begun by the troubadour William IX, his maternal great grandfather, in a bid for his release from an imperial gaol. Passed on by singers, the song must have encouraged the collection of his ransom.[20] Two troubadours are known – Peire Vidal (*fl.*1184–1207) and the monk of Montaudon (*fl.*1193–1210) – who asked for the king's release in their poems, each in their turn. In these songs, in passing, they praised his recent exploits against the Turks.[21] Between 1197 and 1199, well after his release, Richard addressed a *sirventes* to Guy, count of Auvergne and his cousin the Dauphin, criticizing them for doing nothing to avoid the addition of the town of Issoire to the lands of the king of France.[22] Then, ten years later, a short and anonymous composition in northern French urged Savaric de Mauléon and other Poitevin vassals of King John to defend the town of Thouars against the army of Philip Augustus.[23] All these compositions take a clear contemporary perspective. They further the political and military success of the Angevins. They work on the sympathies of the aristocracy, presenting the Plantagenet king as an ideal and courageous warrior, the very antithesis of Capetian villainy.

We need to add to these political songs the *planhs* or funeral elegies, composed respectively by Bertran de Born (*a*.1159–1215) and Gaucelm Faidit (*c*.1150–*c*.1202) in memory of the Young Henry and Richard the Lionheart.[24] Their brother Geoffrey of Brittany took part in a *tenson* (an exchange between two poets) in northern French with Gace Brulé (*fl*.1159–1211). He did the same bilingually in northern and southern French with Gaucelm Faidit.[25] Some brief allusions to the Plantagenets appear, in a roundabout way as digressions and dedications in other poems, whose principal theme is love. For example, Arnaut de Mareuil (*fl*.1170–1190) dared to assert that Julius Caesar was far from being as noble in birth as 'the king of Ireland, count of Anjou and duke of Normandy'. He goes on to say much the same about the gulf which separated Henry's undistinguished looks from the magnificence of Eleanor, whose heart nonetheless he would come to win, just as the Roman emperor and the king of England had conquered their lands.[26] Peire Vidal, always caught up in his own art, wrote these verses addressed to Richard the Lionheart: 'Your renown and mine surpasses that of all others: you for your great deeds and me for my fine words'.[27] Giraut de Borneil (*fl*.1169–1199) and Foulquet de Marseille (*a*.1178–1231) composed some verses to praise the commitment of Richard to the crusade.[28] The language of courtesy was more suited to Bernart de Ventadorn (*fl*.1147–1170), who dedicated one of his songs to Eleanor of Aquitaine, 'the queen of the Normans'.[29] There were many poets who declared their admiration of the Angevins, from whom they could have occasionally benefitted from patronage.[30]

Their songs, most of them eulogies, made Henry II and his sons very popular subjects among the troubadours. After their death, the memory of their courage and their courtliness seemed to become a literary topos. Between 1199 and 1213 in Catalonia, Raimon Vidal de Besalù recalled them in an *ensenhamen*, a sort of handbook of courtesy for the information of a poet, while he was dealing with the three nobilities of heart, mind and knowledge: 'These three virtues added to the merit of the lord King Henry of England and his three sons, as I do not forget, the lords Henry, Richard and Geoffrey. There was in each twice the number of qualities than it would take a year to tell; I saw them coming into court at his side, making love and war. Those were the days for a man who wished to do noble, valorous and well-judged deeds.'[31] It was at this time that Guiraut de Calanson composed a *planh* (lament) in honour of the young Ferdinand (died 1211), heir of Castille and a Plantagenet through his mother, whom he did not fail to compare with King Arthur, his ancestral and mythical ancestor, but also with his uncles: 'the Young King, the accomplished Richard and the count Geoffrey, the three valiant brothers, whom he resembled in body, conduct and generous heart.'[32] Again, in 1241, Peire de Vilar, who by his poem was fostering a great southern rebellion against Alfonso of Poitiers and the king of France supported by Henry III, said that the English leopard was the equal 'of the dynasty of which came the brave brothers, Henry, Richard and Geoffrey.'[33] The image that the Angevins left for decades to their descendants through the southern poets was very flattering indeed.

In northern literature there survives at least two very long works composed by poets with the principal intention of celebrating the military achievements of the Plantagenets. They construct an epic of the Angevin kings of England, who, in the British Isles and the Near East, defeat the 'barbarians', be they Welsh, Irish or Saracen,[34] all the while fighting on the continent with the king of France, their perpetual enemy. This is the open aim of the first of these two poems, the *Histoire de la Guerre Sainte* (1192–1199) that Ambroise composed at the request of Richard the Lionheart with the purpose of glorifying his deeds of arms against Saladin.[35] Ambroise took advantage of the truce of 1192 with the Seljuk Turks to return to the Holy Land a little after the departure of Richard, whose exploits were told him by eyewitnesses. He also drew on an older French source in prose, which the anonymous Latin author of the *Journey of the Pilgrims and the Deeds of King Richard* also copied.[36] Ambroise was a professional poet; he revealed his mastery of the traditional repertoire, 'the old *chansons de geste* of which the poets make great play.' It is very probable that not just the cycles of Alexander the Great, Arthur, Pepin and Charlemagne, but also the Songs of Aspremont and the Saxons were well known to him.[37] He was born either at Pacy or Breteuil, towns in the south-eastern marches of Normandy, which suffered particularly harshly from Capetian attacks.[38] He had no hesitation in giving free rein to his animosity against the French when he tells the story of the rivalry between Richard and Philip Augustus during the crusade.

The second poem, also written in Anglo-Norman but twenty or so years before Ambroise, had rather more northern concerns. This is Jordan Fantosme's *Chronicle* (1174–1175), a tale of the war against William the Lion of Scotland in Northumbria, the native border province of its author. Following a period of study at Paris under the great theologian Gilbert de la Porée (c.1075–1154), Jordan became master of the schools at Winchester.[39] In this post he was associated with Richard of Ilchester, recently elected bishop of the see, one of the most influential counsellors of Henry II. There is a strong likelihood that the king himself was the patron of Jordan's work.[40] Right from the beginning, the poem says its intention is to tell 'the true history . . . of the best king who ever lived . . . the noble king of England with the right bold countenance' (lines 1–5). Henry II became 'the most honourable and the most victorious' (line 111) of kings since the time of Charlemagne and his twelve peers. The propaganda is shameless in its praise of the king's piety, in its discussion of the devotion of the vassals of his army ('He thinks more longingly of his absent lord than does a knight of his mistress', line 548), in his animosity towards foreigners – Flemish mercenary or savage Scotsman – and in his celebration of the heroic Anglo-Norman warriors whose brotherhood made victory possible.[41] The propaganda positively leaps off the page when Jordan juxtaposes the penance of his king at Canterbury in expiation of the murder of Becket, with the simultaneous capture of William the Lion at Alnwick, the victory being a manifestation of God's forgiveness.[42] There are very evident ideological consequences in this sort of reading of history, full of providentialism.

Jordan Fantosme's criticisms of Henry II's attitude to the Young Henry ought not to be interpreted as an argument against his royal patronage,[43] but more as a flattering encouragement of the father to demonstrate even more of his generosity and indulgence. In the Middle Ages, the freedom of speech and content in the poetry of the court and official court history was perfectly compatible with working for a patron. It did not demand a slavish flattery towards the man who had commissioned the work.[44] In dedicating the *Policraticus* in 1159 to the chancellor, Thomas Becket, then everybody's ideal of the worldly courtier, did not John of Salisbury devote his work to criticism of 'the vanities of courtiers', the subtitle of his work?[45]

One reason for the wide popularity of poetry in the vernacular was its performance to the accompaniment of musical instruments. Those who sang in this way were to be found in the presence of the king, who could get enthusiastic about their playing, as Richard the Lionheart was, according to Ralph of Coggeshall: 'He enthused the singers in their songs by his gifts and urging; he would encourage them to sing with more spirit and, often entering the choir and chapel, he urged them on by voice and gesture

to a more profoundly resonant performance.'[46] It was just as natural that
Jordan Fantosme, to conjure up the nocturnal silence of the palace of
Westminster, wrote that 'no harp or viol played'.[47] Whether sacred sounds
or profane, everything was dominated by the music which pervaded all
the royal residences, places to which composers and performers flocked.
The clergy took against the debauchery which provoked the rude songs
of the entertainers and their improper dances. John of Salisbury for this
reason criticized the dangers for the soul in secular music, voluptuous
and hostile to all moderation, as seductive as the song of the sirens, and
particularly dangerous during state banquets.[48] Peter of Blois fulminated
against the women who sang at the court of Henry II.[49] Behind these
acidic comments we cannot fail to discern the real existence of a large
corps of professional musicians at court.

William fitz Stephen's description of the embassy of Thomas Becket
to Paris in the summer of 1158, to negotiate the marriage of the Young
Henry and Margaret of France, is significant evidence of the political
implications of works of art. Throughout the journey, 250 attendants
in his magnificent entourage performed compositions, each in his own
maternal tongue.[50] Their songs, mostly to the glory of Henry II and his
family, added to the dignity of the embassy and made a great show on the
road to Paris, where he needed to negotiate the marriage contract from
a position of strength. The music masked an important Angevin resource
– the spread of *sirventes* – giving them a life and vitality of their own. The
sirventes was all the more easy to remember as it was sung to a current
melody line, borrowed directly from a popular love song. The humorous
effect of this popular borrowing helped those who heard the *sirventes* pick
them up directly from the live performance of minstrels who came from
the court to perform them in public places. Music was the best way to
broadcast these songs.

The political purpose of the Latin literature which apotheosized the
Angevins is less obvious. At the least, the circulation of these works must
have been more difficult than that of vernacular songs, sung by professional
entertainers and understood by everyone. But there still survive a dozen
Latin poems dedicated to Henry II, the Young Henry and Richard the
Lionheart. One is a poem in hexameters celebrating the coming of Henry
II to the English throne.[51] Another is a curious lament on his death, which
concludes with a eulogy on his successor because of the radical change
that it brought to Henry's policies.[52] A third was a lament for the Young
Henry, comparing him to Paris and Hector, which was quoted by Gervase
of Tilbury (*c*.1140–1220).[53] A fourth is a more conventional one to the

memory of a young prince dead before his time, again probably the Young Henry. Two more poems agitate for the release of Richard the Lionheart, and attack the Germans, England and Rome; they, like the previous one, were quite likely composed by Peter of Blois.[54] There are eight couplets honouring Richard[55] and several epigrams lamenting his death.[56] There is another elegy, sixty-three hexameters and three couplets long, dedicated to Richard as defender of Normandy assassinated by a treacherous knight, and composed with a certain style by Geoffrey de Vinsauf (died *c*.1220), teacher of rhetoric at Northampton, who copied it into his *Poetria nova* (1208–1213), a treatise on poetry directed at the promising amateur.[57] With two exceptions, all these Latin poems on Richard belong to the genre of elegy. They are laments composed on the imprisonment or death of the king. Roger of Howden had himself copied down funerary verses in memory of Henry II and Richard the Lionheart, as a sort of epilogue to bring the story of each reign to a close.

A few courtiers, friends and officers of the king are found amongst the numerous chroniclers and Latin writers who not only expressed their respect for the Angevin dynasty but also described its deeds, notably Walter Map, Roger of Howden, Robert de Torigny and Ralph de Diceto. Gerald of Barry is more direct and open than the others about what made him write and how he did it. In his two first works, composed in 1188 to celebrate the invasion of Ireland, he did not hide his support for the cause of Henry II. On the one hand, his *Conquest* tells the foolish and envious people who asserted that the kings of England had no rights to Ireland to keep silent.[58] On the other, the prologue of his *Topography* says without equivocation that he wanted to preserve for ever the deeds done by Henry II during the course of the invasion. It was a good strategy to offer such a high-minded prince, rather than gold or falcons, an imperishable book which praised for ever the great deeds of this new Alexander, builder of an empire and subjugator of a cruel and barbarous race in the name of divine vengeance.[59] In this way Gerald lifted the veil on his self-interested relationship with his king, and the subordination that this entailed for his intellect.

In his autobiography, Gerald said that he had widely publicized his *Topography* by staging public lectures alongside dinners offered at his own cost over three days at Oxford. On the first day he had invited the poor of the town, on the second the teachers and brighter students and, on the third, the knights and the urban elite. Many of them promptly asked for a copy of the book, of which there remain twenty-four manuscripts, a higher than usual figure for texts of the time.[60] Gerald himself said that the public lecture was unusual in his day. Frequent in Antiquity, it seems to have been coming back into fashion in the Parisian schools already for some decades.[61] But it was not sufficient to increase the thin circulation of Latin prose historiography, confined to a small circle of courtiers and intellectuals who, for all their influence within society, were not by any means numerous.

The corpus of books of Gerald of Barry – which also included a *Book of Prophecies*, now lost – was rich in political prophecy.[62] In the Wales of which Gerald was a native, the bards (called in Welsh *cyfarwydd* or *awennithion*, a word derived from *awen* 'poetical gifts or inspiration') still formed an influential group, both professional and hereditary. They were not simply tellers of tales and singers: they were believed to possess powers close to sorcerous and their talents gave them a social eminence that often raised them to the position of judges. Foretelling the future was part of what they did. When they did this they followed the traits common to Eurasian shamans: as soon as they had been consulted they went into a trance to make their predictions; always they were in an ecstasy, and invariably they masked their oracles in obscure allusions.[63] The Welsh prophecies quite often fostered resistance to the Anglo-Normans. Gerald, in the service of Henry II, exploited this old tradition of prophecy so as to further the military supremacy of the king over the Welsh and Irish. Here are two examples from the 1180s: 'The bipartite warrior will march first within the confines of Hibernia', an allusion to the landing in Ireland in 1169 of Robert fitz Stephen, a Norman raised in Wales; 'The white warrior riding on a white horse carrying a bird on his shield, will first attack Ulster,' referring to the campaign of John de Courcy in 1177. Gerald also made use of these predictions to explain the struggles within the Angevin dynasty. He gave a transcendent character to their internecine fighting which had little to do with the motives of the antagonists themselves. In the thirteenth century, King John paid particular attention to prophecies, whose implications he assessed carefully. In 1213, he ordered that Peter of Pontefract, a Yorkshire hermit, should be dragged by horses and hanged, along with his son, for wrongly predicting that John would not keep his throne beyond the feast of the Ascension.[64] There is no doubt that prophecy was widely and consciously used by the Plantagenets for the purposes of propaganda.

In the twelfth century, letter-writing experienced an unheard-of level of development as a literary genre amongst intellectuals for whom the letters of Cicero and Seneca were the definitive rhetorical model. Grammarians developed a framework for analysing each letter, which they composed in a rhythmic Latin, light and easy to memorize, responding to the rules of *cursus* or *dictamen*. They were supposed to have five parts: the salutation (where the author defines his standing relative to the addressee, whom he flatters with distinguished titles), the exordium (designed to secure the addressee's goodwill), the explication (laying out the reasons for the request he was making), the petition and conclusion (bringing the matter to an end).[65] Correspondence was not then a private business, but very often belonged to the public domain. It is known that certain letters, once written, experienced a rapid general circulation. An example is the *Ex inesperato*, which John of Salisbury composed a few hours after the murder of Thomas Becket, an event he witnessed. The same was true of three letters, probably drafted by Peter of Blois on behalf of Eleanor of Aquitaine and addressed to Celestine III (1191–1198), whom she begged to involve himself in the freeing of her son Richard the Lionheart, the prisoner of the emperor.[66]

If they accumulated, letters might be made into collections, then copied into manuscripts so as to safeguard the rights of the author. The friends of Thomas Becket had made a preliminary collection of his letters around 1164, at the high point of his struggle with the king. Around 1175, some years after Becket's death, Alan of Tewkesbury (died 1202) edited and expanded this first collection with the purpose of widening the knowledge of the recently-canonized archbishop's agenda and thinking. The volume of letters of Gilbert Foliot, bishop of London and supporter of Henry II against Becket, had probably been drafted in response to the Becket manuscript of 1164. The letter collection of Peter of Blois, who often proclaimed the merits of the government of Henry II, furthered the interests of the king, just as Gilbert Foliot's had done. Letters, whether individual or collected, were read widely, and the reason why they were written was quite often didactic and propagandist.[67]

All the examples given above, taken principally from political poetry in Occitan, historical epic in northern French and from Latin literature, may not really be sufficient fully to illustrate something as complex as propaganda. The nature of the sources of the period barely allow us to glimpse the importance of the Plantagenet programme, its sophistication and the extent of work behind it. But they tell us at least that the Plantagenets had mobilized professional writers to sing in the vernacular and write of their exploits in Latin, with the purpose of giving extra lustre to their dynasty, as it fought the Capetians, crusaded against Saladin, and conquered new British lands from the Celtic peoples. One of the clear purposes of these intellectuals was to exalt their master through their propaganda. What we need to look at next are the principal themes and ideological concerns which characterized their compositions and their commentaries.

The king as literate knight

There was no single image that the Plantagenets wanted to leave to posterity. It formed around no less than two themes: learning and war. In Touraine, John of Marmoutier described Geoffrey Plantagenet as 'devoting himself to civil arms and also to liberal studies.'[68] In much the same way Gerald of Barry asserted that Geoffrey's son, Henry II, devoted himself 'as much to the business of arms as to the toga; to war as much as to books.'[69] For these authors, the prince seemed as learned and wise as he was ready and courageous in battle. The prince achieved in his person, a perfect synthesis of clerk and knight. He had become a *miles litteratus*: the prestigious model already emulated by so many of the lay courtiers.

A model of wisdom and culture

Knowledge is power. Henry II went looking for men of genius. He promoted a genuine brain drain so as to staff his palace and administration with intellectuals. He could not imagine a servant of his State who was ignorant. He practised what he preached. He projected himself as an enlightened ruler.[70] His childhood tutors must have often hammered home to him this judgement, from which there was no appeal: 'An illiterate king is no more than a crowned ass!'

This maxim first appears in the writings of the historian William of Malmesbury (c.1080–c.1142), who attributed it to William the Conqueror, very keen that his son Henry I should be well educated.[71] In the next generation, influenced by the rivalry with the Capetians, it was used as a barely disguised criticism of the kings of France by English and Angevin clerks. Breton d'Amboise, a chronicler of the counts of Anjou working early in Henry II's reign, puts the same words in the mouth of Fulk the Good (*fl.*940–60), whom he praises for 'his wisdom, eloquence and literacy'. They were used as a reply to the mockery of King Louis IV d'Outremer (936–954) who abused Fulk for singing the psalms in the choir amongst the canons.[72] In his *Policraticus* (1159) John of Salisbury used the phrase as a way of promoting the superiority of an education that was intellectual and biblical rather than simply military. He uses it by way of a moralizing story in an imaginary letter in which a German emperor advises the king of the Franks to get his children well educated.[73] The Cistercian writer, Helinand de Froidmont (1160/70–c.1229) also quotes the same letter. He does not stop at quoting a phrase which pokes fun at the French kings, who had been his employers when he had worked at the court of Philip Augustus as a poet.[74] Gerald of Barry insinuated the same maxim into the first preface of his *Instruction of the Prince*, whose title and content both reflect the sentiment without applying it to any ruler in particular. Gerald illustrates all the lessons in governing and making war that a king can learn from the study of history.[75] For him, as for the rest, the aphorism serves to confirm that every king needs to acquire the experience and knowledge built up as century succeeded century, so as not to repeat the errors made in Antiquity, as viewed through a mirror of the past.

Was the fashion for this maxim stimulated solely by the ambitions of the clergy to insinuate themselves into a place in the sun near the king, as payment for the learning which they had acquired in the schools?[76] It is unlikely. Ambition was not the chief motive of those intellectuals who, once at court, got nostalgic for the spiritual life under the pressure of the harsh acquisitiveness of their new jobs. It would seem that the popularity of the maxim was a symptom of a rather wider double phenomenon, of the rise of the state (which led to technical advances in the royal bureaucracy) and of the intellectual renaissance. The court, which more than ever attracted scholars educated on the continent, had become a place of science, and the king could not seem to be less intelligent than his household. It was on this that a great part of his authority rested if he wanted to make himself obeyed promptly. If he possessed no culture, his prestige would fade among the clerks of his court.

The king had to excel in wisdom if he were to govern effectively. Only study under scholars and steady reading would allow him to acquire the extensive Christian culture, enriched by the moral content of biblical study; the secular learning of the classics and a sufficiently deep knowledge of ancient history. In a letter encouraging the king to give his son the Young Henry (then aged six) an education quite as careful as the one he had received – a letter that Peter of Blois sent to Henry II on behalf of Rotrou of Rouen and the other bishops of his realm – we find a phrase which (although less often quoted than the 'crowned ass' tag) was no less effective: 'an illiterate king is a ship without oars and a bird without feathers'.[77] Peter gave examples like Julius Caesar, a master of literature, civil law and philosophy; Alexander, taught by Aristotle; as well as the learned rulers of the Old Testament (Solomon, David, Hezekiah, Josiah) and the Christian Roman Empire (Constantine, Theodosius, Justinian, Leo), all as good scholars as they were soldiers. The Plantagenets were presented with a biblical and classical model of the wise king so as to heighten their appreciation of justice, equity and peace. The dynasty accepted it all the more happily as it increased their reputation and the respect with which they were treated.

This Plantagenet taste for reading the ancient authors is demonstrated by a story to be found in Angevin historiography. It pictures Geoffrey Plantagenet finding in reading Vegetius (c.400AD), the great Roman military theorist,[78] a way to capture the fortress of Montreuil-Bellay by using Greek fire. The need to excel at court and avoid ridicule is just as apparent in a discussion between Richard the Lionheart and Hubert Walter, archbishop of Canterbury, on the use of the accusative or ablative to agree with the Latin preposition *coram* ('in the presence of'). If we believe Gerald of Barry, it was the king's ablative that won out over the faulty grammar of the highest cleric in England.[79] Richard was just as combative in vernacular poetry, where he proved himself a born versifier. During the crusade, he improvised a rhymed reply to an insulting song that Duke Hugh of Burgundy had addressed to him.[80] Theology and exegesis were other interests of his. In the winter of 1190–1191, at Messina in Sicily while travelling to the crusade, Richard held forth at length to the Cistercian abbot Joachim of Fiore (c.1130–1202), famous for his eschatological commentaries on Scripture, on the success of his imminent campaigns against Saladin, the seventh head of the dragon of the Apocalypse, and also on the end of time, and he did so undoubtedly in Latin.[81] There is no denying the extent of the literary cultivation of Richard the Lionheart.

He was in no way superior to his father Henry II, whose education was the wonder of contemporary clerks. As a child Henry was confided to the Master of Saintes, reputed at the time to be the best Latin poet in the West.[82] At the age of nine, in 1142, he was sent to England to live in the household of his uncle, Robert of Gloucester, a devotee of literature, with his son Roger, the future bishop of Worcester. For four years he was tutored by a master called Matthew, whom some identify as Henry's future chancellor and bishop of Angers.[83] On his return to France at the age of thirteen, Henry's education was entrusted to William de Conches (c.1080–1154), pupil of the grammarian, Bernard of Chartres (died c.1126), whose famous phrase that 'we are like dwarves sitting on the shoulders of giants' summed up the 'Renaissance' of the twelfth century. William was master also of John of Salisbury who gave him full credit as a teacher.[84] William dedicated at length to the new king his *Dogmas of Moral Philosophy*, a work inspired by Cicero which discussed the cardinal virtues and expanded on the conflict between honesty and pragmatism.[85] This sort of teacher proves that the young Henry II received an advanced intellectual education.

Henry's educational achievements emerge in his mature years. In a letter written to the archbishop of Palermo, Peter of Blois emphasized that the king read for relaxation. Beside this he praised the king's resolution: 'With the king of England each day is like being at school, he is constantly debating with the best masters and discussing intellectual problems.'[86] It is hardly suprising that so flattering a letter was carefully preserved in a collection that Henry II had asked Peter to prepare for publication.[87] In the part of the *Instruction of the Prince* written in his old age, which was particularly hostile to Henry II, Gerald of Barry still acknowledged Henry's great eloquence and his erudition as exceptional for his day.[88] These remarks of Gerald's match nicely with Walter Map's pen portrait of Henry: educated and literate enough to govern well, he spoke Latin and French and understood every language from the Atlantic to the river Jordan (although on the last point Walter is exaggerating).[89] Many of these appreciative comments are confirmed by charters and legal records, which show the king as a quick and efficient reader of the documents presented by the abbeys of St Albans, Battle and Bury St Edmunds.[90] Henry II possessed an undoubted mastery of Latin and gave evidence of a genuine intellectual curiosity. His culture and taste for literature was soon identified by the clerks of his court, who found him to be the very model of a learned king, a 'second Solomon' to quote a phrase of Gerald of Barry.[91]

Several treatises are dedicated to Henry II as a consequence of his learned reputation. Their prologues or passing comments in the text praise the culture and education of the king, more or less explicitly. So as to stand well with the king, the authors make little of their own abilities. Their own expertise was a mere gloss on the king's knowledge, which would better help him to fulfil his role. This is so for three handbooks directly linked to Plantagenet government: the *Dialogue of the Exchequer* of the treasurer, Richard fitz Nigel; the *Laws and Customs of the Kingdom of England* (1187–1189) written by a specialist in law in the household,[92] and the *Notarial Art*, probably by John of Tilbury.[93] The first of them describes the workings of the English royal government's financial office; the second is a compilation of laws and legal commentaries, which amount to a buttress to royal authority; the third gives a definition and short history of the notary's art, before going on to present technical advice and abbreviations. The association of these books with the daily business of the king and his friends is quite obvious.

Other treatises dedicated to Henry II are more scientific and less pragmatic or less obviously useful to the king. Such is the *Treatise on the Astrolabe* (1149–1150) of the famous Adelard of Bath (c.1091–c.1160), mathematician, astronomer and falconer, the man who introduced the concept of zero to the West. He studied at Tours, Laon and in Sicily, and travelled in Cilicia and Syria before returning to the household of the bishop of Wells in the 1120s. The book begins with a long prologue praising the qualities of the future Henry II, encouraging him to explore the astronomy of the East:[94] 'Henry, I know that you, the king's grandson, were educated in all aspect of philosophy. It is said that the commonwealth is happy when ruled by philosophers and its people pursue the subject . . . This is why you must learn not only what Latin texts have to tell but also what the Arabs have to teach us about the movement of the earth and the orbits of the stars.'[95] The same applies to the preface of the anthology of Pliny the Younger's *Natural History* which Robert of Cricklade (*fl.*1140–1174), Augustinian prior of St Frideswide, Oxford, wrote for Henry some years before he was king. He said that the lord who governed so large a part of the world, undefeated in war and devoted to the liberal sciences in peace, should not ignore the nature of the land, sea and air, and of objects animal, vegetable and mineral.[96] Eleanor of Aquitaine was the dedicatee of another of these works, as if her association with the throne of her husband might allow her to aspire to the learning which assisted in its government. Philip de Thaon, the first translator of a scientific work into French, dedicated to her a copy of his *Bestiary*, his Anglo-Norman adaptation of the *Physiologus* (1121–1139), which he had already dedicated in its original version thirty or so years before to Adeliza, the second wife of Henry I.[97] Finally, according to the late witness of Daude de Prades (died 1282), canon of Rodez, Henry II was supposedly the author of a treatise on falconry, of which no trace now exists. If we are to believe Daude, the originality of this work lay in the fact that its theories were solidly based on practical observation.[98] We may never know how accurate was this attribution, but it matches curiously the nature of another treatise on falconry that Adelard of Bath issued, around 1130, with a dedication to the late King Harold.[99]

The fact that a later period was ready to believe that Henry II was capable of writing such a book is not only due to his love of hunting and his fondness for animals, widely confirmed by other sources (he had, for instance, his own zoo).[100] The theme of the king's knowledge of the natural world fits within a wider frame of reference. In the first place, in medieval Christianity, the idea of the wisdom of the king refers back to the books of wisdom in the Old Testament and to King Solomon, assumed to have been the author of the Book of Proverbs, but it also referred back to Greek and Latin thought. The letter and poem of Osbert de Clare, prior of

Westminster, dedicated c.1154 to the praise of Henry II on his recent arrival in England, drew on this Old Testament theme to characterize him as personified wisdom: the source of peace, because wisdom was opposed to vice.[101] Even at that time it was known that Classical culture, indispensable to good government, had been valued by the Emperor Charlemagne and the intellectuals of his court, and even more so by Alfred the Great, king of Wessex (871–899), who undertook the restoration of the English schools, attracted foreign scholars to his court, and did not shrink from personally translating the psalms and key texts of the Latin fathers into Anglo-Saxon. Charlemagne and Alfred were the inspiration for Henry II and the clergy whom he took for counsellors. His classically-inspired affinity for wisdom is not then much of a surprise and shows him to have been tugged along in the wake of the Gregorian thinking on the Peace of God.

In the circumstances, what is really surprising for the period are the remarks on the happiness of a commonwealth ruled by philosophers, as expressed particularly in the prologue to Adelard of Bath's treatise on the astrolabe. The idea, drawn from Plato, had already been played with by some Latin theoreticians, as for example Alcuin of York, who correctly traced it back to Athenian philosophy in a book addressed to Charlemagne.[102] In the same way Stoic philosophy stressed the importance of wisdom for a man whose duty it was to rule. So Cicero and Seneca made intelligence a higher virtue, and made a science out of human and divine conduct which directed it towards Universal Good.[103] Even if these ideas were already to be found in earlier writings, the intellectuals of Henry II's household produced something new in their direct borrowing from the Neoplatonic and Stoic classics concerning learning and good government. Here their writings undoubtedly reflect the intellectual renaissance of the twelfth century.

The originality of these men is evident in another way. This was in the link that was suggested between the king and natural science, and in particular between the king and practical knowledge gained by experiment. Henry II's appearance as scientist is remarkably precocious. It prefigured by a half century the reputation the Mediterranean rulers, Emperor Frederick II (1212–1250) and Alfonso X of Castille, or Alfonso the Wise, (1254–1284) had wished to make. This idea of the omniscient monarch was perhaps the ancestor of the enlightened despot of the eighteenth century, whose great learning justified his absolutism. Enlightenment knowledge, based on a scientific method, seemed vastly superior to the learning of the clergy whose scriptural and theological knowledge were quite useless in efficient government. Naturally, neither Henry II nor his followers had gone as far as that in their political theorizing. But nonetheless their characterization of the scientific king was one of the first the medieval West had encountered.

Some Latin and Anglo-Norman histories and works of fiction with flattering prologues dedicated to the Plantagenets need to be added to the technical works mentioned above. More will be said about these later. Their numerous eulogies on Henry II and his family need care in interpreting.[104] Are they the result of the sort of patronage, strictly speaking, by which the author was paid for his commission? Do they reflect the wish of the writer to attract the king's goodwill, to which up to that time he had had no access? Rather than opt for one or other of these interpretations, it seems a more sensible idea to look at the circumstances of each individual as to what attached or distanced him from the king so as to work out the degree of attachment in their relationship. The diversity of these men is demonstrated by the well-known story of Gerald of Barry – toadying courtier of the Plantagenets whose refusal to give him the diocese of St David's in spite of many services he did them stirred his resentment – and also of Wace, for whom Henry II obtained a canon's stall at Bayeux so that he could write the history of the dukes of Normandy without any material distractions. Many of these intellectuals benefitted from the gifts, sometimes valuable, that the king gave out in great quantities to his closer servants, even if they did not enjoy the temporary hospitality of the court. But sometimes these beneficed clerks, monks living on their abbey's income, or literate knights well-provided with lordships, did it of their own free will, good-naturedly, simply through good feeling towards the king. Whatever their deeper motives in doing it and however they were rewarded, it remains nonetheless the case that ideas helpful to the ruling dynasty were put in circulation by means of their propaganda.

These writers added to the prestige of the dynasty, which had a reputation thereafter as the very apex of artistic patronage, sponsorship and magnanimity. Already in 1154 Osbert de Clare pictured Maecenas in company with Horace and Augustus with Virgil, in a poem that he addressed to Henry II, then only recently crowned king of England.[105] Around 1230, forty years after the king's death, the prologues of the *Quest of the Holy Grail* and the *Death of Arthur*, and the epilogue of some manuscripts of *Lancelot of the Lake*, anachronistically attribute the origins of the works to Walter Map (died *c*.1209) and imagine that he had been commissioned and encouraged by Henry II.[106] The homage by the writers of the Arthurian vulgate cycle to Henry is easy to explain. It matches the idea, widely accepted at the beginning of the thirteenth century, of his generous patronage and his commitment to literary creativity. It does not seem that his reputation was exaggerated, despite some recent attempts to minimize its range. It has been affirmed by many philologists and historians during the twentieth century. In 1963, Reto Bezzola, whose knowledge of texts relating to the chief medieval courts was, to say the least, impressive, wrote: 'Since the time of the Carolingians, indeed since Antiquity, there had never been in the west a literary centre of more significance than that of the court of Henry II.'[107] Today the indexes of sources which can be trawled quite agree with Bezzola's assessment. They allow us to adopt it without any reservation.

The sons of his anger

At the end of the twelfth century in the aristocratic world, arms were still as often as not the inevitable conclusion of any conflict. Adjudications by ecclesiastics, border conferences, embassies, temporary truces and marriage alliances sometimes prevented disputes from degenerating into open violence, or rather, they put back the explosion for a few months. The list of wars between kings, territorial princes and castellans during the years between 1154 and 1224 is not short. In this age of warfare, the Angevins wished to appear to their enemies and their subjects as bitter and unbeatable adversaries. But some of them were indeed very talented on the field of battle, where they showed themselves to be daring knights, accomplished generals and true leaders of men. This is at least the image that sympathetic chroniclers projected, with a narrowly propagandist purpose, hoping that it would be all the more widely circulated. Wars are always psychological, won as much in the collective mind as on the battlefield. The problem here is to assess the importance of the theme of warrior in the political culture of the Plantagenets, their particular warrior qualities and the use made of them in their wars.

There was no question that memories of the dynasty of Anjou emphasized its knightly activities. At the end of the twelfth century, the chronicles of the Angevin heartland located the myth of the dynasty's origins on an adventurer who had risen from the gutter, the founder of their lineage, thanks to his military accomplishments. This was Tertullus, son of Torquatius, keeper of the woods of Charles the Bald, who derived from a humble family driven out of Brittany in the time of the Roman Empire. Tertullus 'the Forester' opened his way into the nobility of the Loire valley by his defeats of the Vikings in the army of the king of France, who gave him a wife and lands as a reward. His son Ingelger, a better warrior than his father, was made a knight. The *Deeds of the Lords of Amboise* make a point of the rocket-like rise of Tertullus, whose humble origins predetermined his steady loyalty with respect to Charles the Bald, who favoured more 'new men . . . become great and distinguished,' than, 'the men of old stock with too many ancestors.'[108] Tertullus, the dynastic originator of the Plantagenet dynasty, was characterized as a young and penniless man who made his own name amongst the aristocracy by his great feats of arms and who, in marrying a rich heiress, found the necessary means to set himself up. No one ever invented for the Angevins an ancestor drawn from the imperial Carolingian line, as if their knightliness counted for more than royal blood. It is worth noting that King Arthur – whom the Plantagenets endeavoured to claim as one of their ancestors – became a 'most virtuous knight' endowed with every physical and moral virtue in the work of their official historiographer, Wace.[109] Knightly greatness made an integral part of the discourse of Henry II and his men on the origins of their lineage.

Like their mythical ancestors, several members of the Angevin dynasty posed more as individualistic knights famous for their deeds of arms and personal record in battle than as kings of ancient descent, masters of generalship and public affairs in their people's service. The very embodiment of the 'knightly king' was Richard the Lionheart. Poets and chroniclers alike paid deferential homage to the outstanding qualities of this great crusader warrior. The Cistercian abbot, Ralph of Coggeshall, his biographer, described Richard as *rex bellicosus* ('king of war') in admiration for his achievements at Jaffa in 1192. If we believe him, Richard routed three thousand Saracens with only six or seven knights.[110] His idealization of Richard is not at variance with the real king: a cool and methodical military leader, always in advance of others in siege techniques and careful about logistics.[111] But it mattered little because his own propaganda painted him as the best soldier of his age: tough, courageous and high-minded.

At the age of sixteen in the spring of 1173, a year after his installation as duke of Aquitaine, Richard was invested as a knight in Paris by Louis VII. There is no doubt that the king went on to encourage him to join in the revolt of his brothers and a large section of the aristocracy against Henry II. It was through arms that Richard looked to break free of his father, like so many of the *juvenes* of his day. He surrendered in September 1174, defeated by a royal army. He moved on to labour for the next ten years to pacify the Poitevin and Limousin nobility. He particularly distinguished himself in sieges, such as the one in 1179 at Taillebourg, a stone-built fortress on top of a crag overlooking the river Charente, supposedly impregnable, that he stormed at the head of his men. From 1183 onwards he began fighting with his brothers over the future succession to Henry II, who died in 1189 harried by the armies of Richard and his ally Philip Augustus. Crowned king of England, he promptly left on a crusade whose direction he quickly commandeered. He took possession of Cyprus and the principal places on the coast of Palestine. The Anglo-Norman chronicles all talk of his direct participation in the press of battle and of his storming of towns and skirmishes, accompanied only by a token escort. His household believed he took unneccessary risks in combat. When he had returned to France in 1194, Richard fought against Philip Augustus on whom he inflicted defeats at Fréteval (1194) and Issoudun (1195). Apart from this, better to defend himself against the French king, he used his expertise to build Château-Gaillard, one of the most impressive fortifications yet built. In 1194, having had long experience of how tournaments trained men for war, he permitted them once again, with a new framework of regulation, in England, where they had been forbidden by his father who was troubled by the idea of the revolts that such aristocratic gatherings might foster. It was in March 1199, during the course of a siege of a castle of the vicomte of Limoges at Châlus that he was wounded by a crossbow bolt in the shoulder: he died some days later, aged barely forty-one. His short life was dominated by warfare.

While he was alive, his flatterers described him as a hero, worthy of the *chansons de geste*. This image is found widely across his realms. For example, in 1186 an act of the Gascon monastery of La Réole talked of him as most accomplished knight (*miles probissimus*).[112] This title was all the more unusual for a prince as it appeared in the final clause with the date of the document, a place where phrases are generally formulaic. Does the charter carry a resonance of the literary themes spread about by songs in the vernacular or by the Latin chronicles composed in honour of Richard?

Around 1195, the Norman poet Ambroise was commissioned to tell the tale of the great deeds done in the Holy Land. When he described Richard's exploits in Jaffa, Acre or Arsur, he did not hesitate to compare him to Roland or any other hero of the epics. Ambroise described the king's great deeds with some deliberation: 'You would have seen the king, sword in hand, pursuing the Turks so ruthlessly that those whom he reached had no armour that could be counted on to protect them, so they ran from him like sheep who had seen a wolf.'[113] Ambroise pressed his praise of the daring and intrepidity of the king to the point of exaggeration, but there is the following confirmation from the lips of Saladin himself: 'The king is very valiant and hardy, but he charges around like a fool!

However high a prince I may be, I would like better to have liberality and judgement with restraint than hardihood without it.'[114] The *Itinerary of the Pilgrims and the Deeds of King Richard*, a work of the 1210s, deriving from the same French source followed by Ambroise, trawls the classics to give the king: 'the power of Hector, the magnanimity of Achilles and an energy no less than that of Alexander or Roland.'[115] Thanks to Ambroise, Richard was equipped with the reputation of a warrior beyond compare and a crusader as courageous as he was determined.

This – and the heraldic tradition of the Angevin dynasty – is why Richard was called the 'lion', the unchallenged king of animals, irrepressibly daring; and also called 'the Lionheart' a surname with which Ambroise was the first to adorn him in his report of the taking of Acre (1191).[116] Ever at the head of his troops, heedless of risks, this most courageous of kings increased his honour by his arms, building up a capital of esteem unequalled by any of his contemporaries.[117] The reputation of those who followed him into the heart of the battle was no less great. Every knight of his realm had much to gain by joining his army, and not just in prestige but in rewards, because Richard's generosity was notorious amongst the chroniclers and poets committed to his side. Broadcast by professional writers in Latin and singers in French, their enthusiasm guaranteed Richard the loyalty of his nobility and influenced their political as much as military allegiance in his cause.

Even today the military reputation of Richard the Lionheart over-shadows that of his elder brother, the Young Henry, who nonetheless enjoyed a similar degree of fame in the twelfth century. Less well known than his younger brother, his biography is worth reconstructing.[118] Henry was crowned in 1170 by the archbishop of York, an act which forced the crisis of Thomas Becket's assassination. Just before his coronation his father had knighted Henry. In 1173, William the Marshal, who had been his tutor in arms and had toured many tournaments with him, girded Henry anew with a sword and embraced him.[119] Richard the Lionheart was knighted that same year, as if these rites might add a certain advantage to the two brothers in the rebellion recently unleashed against their father. Henry was to live on a decade afterwards, engaged in family quarrels and the tournament circuit. In 1183, in the Limousin, he rebelled for the last time against his father. He succumbed to an illness that June. His premature and unexpected death at the age of twenty-seven, earned him much sympathetic attention.

Several writers praise his military abilities. They picture him as a warrior without equal, imbued with knightly values. Speaking of his inexhaustible love of tournaments, the chronicler Ralph de Diceto goes so far as to chastise him for 'putting to one side his royal dignity to play the knight'.[120] His participation in jousts earned him a great reputation as a fighter, which some thought incompatible with the exercise of kingship. In a more positive mood, Walter Map likewise praised his contribution to knighthood: 'Henry was a creative warrior who awakened knighthood as if from sleep and took it to its peak.'[121] A similar elegy was written by Gervase of Tilbury, who mantained that his premature death heralded the ruin of knighthood.[122] If we believe John the Trouvère, William Marshal, Henry's tutor in his adolescence whose reputed liaison with his wife shattered their friendship, said that Henry's death marked the end of all knightliness. According to the same author, Philip of Alsace, count of Flanders (1168–1191) who was, like the Marshal, Henry's mentor in the tournament world, said likewise that never after his death would there be anyone to offer dinners and arms to young knights in need.[123] For John this generosity to penniless warriors became naturally enough one of the chief qualities of the young king, the enthusiast for tournaments who had taken knighthood to its very height.

More surprising is the posthumous cult which gathered round the Young King's person. Thomas of Earley (died c.1191) archdeacon of Wells, a man closely connected with William Marshal, was the author of a small hagiographical tract to commemorate Henry's death. The gates of heaven were opened to him because he managed to overcome his anger against his father, as proved by the sapphire ring, the gift of Henry II, which he held tightly on his deathbed in token of filial love; and so his mother Queen Eleanor dreamed of him crowned by a double halo. There followed a list of numerous miracles accomplished by physical contact with his mortal remains: cures of sick people with ulcers, facial sores, leprosy, dropsy, fevers and blindness. His body found its final home in Rouen Cathedral, to the great regret of the people of Le Mans who had hung on to it for a month before being forced to give it up against their will.[124] Object of dispute between churches, Henry's body became a relic, into whose presence came the sick and crippled.

William of Newburgh came to hear of this cult, and poured scorn on those who repeated tales of his miracles as if the Young Henry had been pardoned all his sins. William criticized them for believing that Henry had an excuse for offending his father or that his final repentance had been accepted by God. The spectacular manifestation of popular devotion towards Henry was offensive to William, who was without doubt the most considered and balanced of the chroniclers of his day. He had no sympathy for the rebel son of Henry II, 'a turbulent young man, born to ruin much yet so beloved by his vassals, for it is written that "the number of fools is infinite" (Ecclus. 1: 15)'.[125] Perhaps he had in mind the desecrations of the monastery of St Martial of Limoges and the sanctuary of Rocamadour, which the Young King had permitted just before he died, with the purpose of acquiring the treasure needed for the success of his second revolt. The pillaging is described in great detail by Roger, rector of the collegiate church of Howden, a writer who is usually less circumstantial than Newburgh, but not in this case.[126] The two clerics were unhappy that when he took up arms against his father, Henry put an obstacle in the way of his father's programme of establishing a peaceful society. The Young Henry was becoming a bad example for the nobility, inspiring resistance to lawful authority. There was an entirely different perception of his motives among his military household and among many of the young knights, who were the devoted promoters of his posthumous cult in Anjou and Normandy.

Far from earning him the reputation of a traitor, it is evident that Henry's rebellions against his father seemed lawful in the eyes of contemporary knights. In the atmosphere of the time, such rebellions were only the outburst of a *juvenis*, the son of a family of bachelors short on resources who, while awaiting his inheritance, wandered and pillaged the countryside in a group in an unending quest for glory, adventure and plunder.[127] In his *planh* in Henry's memory, Bertran de Born made him out to be 'the father of the young', that is, the generous protector of a class of knights of differing ages but all awaiting marriage.[128] True, Henry had married Margaret of France, but, as Roger of Howden said, the marriage had not freed him from dependency on his father, who had not allowed him his own lands to rule: 'he took it badly that his father did not give him any of his lands, where he could have lived with his queen.'[129] Roger was habitually uncritical of Henry II, but he seems to take the part of the son here. Was Roger perhaps maintaining that generosity – the same generosity which gave away deaneries such as those he held – was an essential quality of the king and a key element in good government? Whatever the case, he did not approve of the miserliness with which Henry II approached the patrimonial endowment of his eldest son.

It was in just this spirit that Jordan Fantosme, a historian close to Henry II, described the war of 1173 in which the Young Henry, *li gentilz debonaire*, allied with William the Lion, king of Scotland (all the more of a *juvenis* as he was as yet unmarried), and with other younger members of noble families to recover the rights that their fathers were slow to hand over to them. Jordan says that at the moment of deciding to attack England, the king of Scotland's council split into two camps: the young knights (*la gent jeufne et salvage*) of William the Lion's military household, keen for plunder and conquest, wanted war while the landholding lords chose prudently not to invade. The latter in the end went along with the hawks rather than be accused of cowardice.[130] When he fought his royal father, the Young Henry was the princely archetype of the young knight. It was the same with his brothers. It was because they had a high ideal of warrior youth that conflict between the generations became the rule, and Tertullus the Forester, mythical founder of their dynasty, was the perfect avatar of their ideal.

The intimidating character of these youthful, armed gangs served to an extent the purposes of the Plantagenets, who made a show of this sort of fury to daunt their enemies. Gerald of Barry and Peter of Blois emphasized the aggression at the heart of this dynasty of 'the sons of anger,' born in dark times from a demonic mother. They stressed also this hereditary quality which drove them irresistibly into internecine fighting. This quasi-congenital aggression surfaced just as much in the family love of the hunt. The family name 'Planta-genista' which Geoffrey of Anjou assumed, referred, according to Wace, to his love of woods and forests where he could let loose his passion for hunting.[131] Passion like this recalled the 'fury of the Normans' which Orderic Vitalis often regretted, comparing the Norman tendency to eat up its own to that of the Beast of the Apocalypse.[132] But was perhaps the Latin word *furor* used in Orderic, as with other authors, recalling the old Norse word *ódor* (*wut* in German)? It was a state of mind Scandinavian berserkers reached under the influence of intoxication so as to deploy their full strength in combat.[133] But it is pointless to speculate how far these clerical authors condemned such unfettered and violent rage.

If Angevin aggression was at the root of their numberless family disputes, when it found an outlet against an external enemy it could very often become a decisive trump card through the fear it fostered. Suitably staged, it formed part of their propaganda for war. When he told the story of the last rites of Richard the Lionheart on his deathbed, Ralph of Coggeshall said that the king had been forbidden by his confessor to take communion for seven years 'due to the mortal hatred of the king of France he harboured in his heart.'[134] Ralph made much of the respect that Richard felt towards the sacramental mystery as a way of explaining his estrangement from penance and the eucharist. However the king's attitude might savour less of piety and more of 'hubris', the Promethean defiance exhibited by some heroes of pagan Antiquity towards their gods. It might seem in fact like the disdain of a conscienceless warrior towards God and his law, so as to let loose his rage, his thirst for vengeance, and slaughter his enemies.

The supposed 'fury' of the Plantagenets is quite a contrast with the outright pacifism of clerical discourse. There are two examples which are sufficient to prove that at the end of the twelfth century English priests had adopted the restrictions brought in by the Augustinian theory of the just war through Gratian's *Decretal* (1140). From now on they would barely stomach it even against pagans and heretics.[135] Firstly, William of Newburgh congratulated the peacemakers who had achieved a truce between Henry II and Louis VII: 'for the envy and arrogance of the two kings would no longer inflict massacres on innocent folk.' He wrote later on: 'These two kings never agreed for long, and they accustomed their people to the punishment for their own insane pride.'[136] Secondly, John of Salisbury raised the question of royal anger when dealing with the curbing of crime: 'The prince punishes wrongdoers in the most measured way, not just when he is angered, but at the direction of reasonable laws.'[137] The mild benevolence of the king, dear to the hearts of ecclesiastical intellectuals, was the very opposite of that rage which the Plantagenets exhibited in battle, in the words recorded by chroniclers and in the formulas of the charters of their chancery.[138]

The contrast between Plantagenets and Capetians could not be more striking. Gerald of Barry put it neatly. In his old age, deceived by the Angevins, he transferred all his hopes on to the royal house of France with the intention of encouraging, in one of his poems, Louis VIII when he landed in force in England.[139] He concluded that the superior virtue of the Capetians was the better since the demonic dynasty of the Angevins only dragged the English relentlessly into war. He compared the bears, lions and leopards, wild beasts chosen by the Angevins for their heraldic symbols with the fleur-de-lis of the Capetians: on one side was arrogance and on the other humility.[140] But was Gerald simply trying to balance his personal score with the Plantagenets, who had always refused to allow his election to the bishopric of St David's? That would be to jump to conclusions.

Other clerks remarked on the same dichotomy between the two royal dynasties. John of Salisbury, the constant supporter of Becket against Henry II, in one of his letters states that Louis VII lived at peace amongst his people, without so much as a bodyguard.[141] According to the less biased Walter Map, the king of France replied to the count of Champagne, who had taken him to task for only having two guards while he slept, that no one had any designs on his life.[142] This contrast is also to be found in the works of the French contemporaries of Louis VII. Peter Riga (died 1209), exegete and canon of Reims, wrote a Latin verse dialogue in 1157 where a representative of the king of France disputed with one of the king of England. The Frenchman gloried in the peace that the Capetians had caused to reign in their lands, scorning the English taste for war.[143] These comparable pieces of evidence always cite the same themes: the serenity, moderation and piety of a Louis VII (as a mature elder) is opposed to the aggression of the Plantagenet *juvenes*.[144] The peacable discourse of the priests did not necessarily match the preoccupations of the lay aristocracy.

The Angevins – most particularly the Young Henry and Richard the Lionheart – undeniably embodied the warrior values most cherished by the nobility of their day. They were descended from Tertullus the Forester and Arthur, their mythical ancestors, whose feats of arms where gloried in by both Latin historiography and Anglo-Norman song. Tournaments, victorious battlefields in the west, crusade in the east and sieges, in the skilful hands of poets and writers, attracted noble sympathies towards the Plantagenets. Although very effective, their propaganda could often be a double-edged weapon, which might often have unfortunate consequences for the royal government. In embracing the ideal of war, the 'youth' of Henry II's family spread aristocratic revolt everywhere they opposed their father's will. These rebellions did not arise entirely from a nobility that resolved on them to resist the inexorable increase of royal power; they arose from the convergence of personal ambition and motiveless anger. Often they were unleashed by a son or grandson of Henry II, the holders of territorial principalities where they had raised squadrons of knights in their service. As a result they did not quite fit the scheme of things where revolt arose out of the irreconcilability of the public power of the king and the private power of the aristocracy.

Following the example of the 'youth' of his court, the king loved to personify the scholar-knight, an image particularly sought after at his court where warlike laity and learned clergy lived in symbiosis. Fond of his noble household, the Angevin prince wanted to appear as first among its equals. Whether or not he was as learned or warlike as they were, could he ever go so far as to be their equal? Of course he could not be. Anointing and coronation had given the king a sacred aspect and it is appropriate at this point to analyse the complex connections which linked this sacred character to the profane.

The king crowned, the duke enthroned

It was a woman, the empress Mathilda, daughter of Henry I of England and mother of Henry II, who brought kingship to the house of Anjou. It is hardly necessary to stress the greatness which this new royal title represented for the Plantagenets – so superior in the contemporary mind to the dignity of duke or count, which made them second rank. The chronicler, Richard the Poitevin, said no less: after he had listed the many continental principalities of Henry II, he wrote that 'by reason of the honour and reverence of the royal style, he is called "king of the English".'[145] Without doubt Richard considered that Great Britain was insular, marginal and peripheral. He had to believe this, as it explains his need to justify the choice of Henry II, who preferred the symbolic heritage of his mother to that of his father.

The case of Henry II was not unique in the West in the middle of the twelfth century. In 1162 in the dynasty of Barcelona, Alfonso II, son of Count Ramon Berengar IV and Petronilla, queen of Aragon, dropped the forename of his father for that of his maternal great uncle and took the royal title which his mother brought him. As it happened, the child Alfonso II was at this date in Henry II's wardship. This must be why William of Newburgh and Robert de Torigny dwell on Alfonso's assumption of the title and symbols of the throne of Aragon in their two chronicles; it must have reminded them of their own king's case.[146]

The limits of the sacred

One of the advantages of kingship, and not by any means the least, was the prestigious royal status which derived from consecration: a ceremony which included election, oath, anointing, the reception of the regalia (sword, spurs, sceptre and other insignia) and the coronation.[147] The ritual offered the king the legitimacy of a sacralization performed on him by the epis-copate and a collective acclamation of his authority by subjects. A grand tableau, staged by professionals, was the climax of its performance. It displayed the majesty of the king, placed high above other laymen. In a world where literacy was still not established, the language of symbols, like speech and song, served to express the king's power, and witnessed to his pre-eminence above common mortals.

At the time when Henry II took the throne of England, the ceremony of consecration already had a long history.[148] It followed a particular Anglo-Norman ritual which was a strong contrast to earlier Anglo-Saxon (largely

derived from Carolingian ritual), Norman, and Romano-Germanic cere-
monials, the three liturgical traditions from which the Ango-Norman derived.
The *ordo*, the Anglo-Norman liturgical book which laid down the coronation of the first Angevins, has not come down to us. But we have a good
idea of what it was like thanks to three detailed sources: the text of the
coronation promise of Henry II (1154),[149] the extremely detailed account
of the coronation of Richard the Lionheart at Westminster (1189) by
Roger of Howden[150] and finally the description by Gervase of Canterbury
of the ceremony of the crown-wearing by Richard at Winchester (1194) on
his return from captivity.[151] These documents, and certain other scattered
references in chronicles of the time, allow us to follow the sequence of
the consecration of the kings of England.

Apart from a few variations, the ceremony was always performed in
the following way. A solemn procession formed of bishops, abbots and
clergy met the king at the door of his chamber to lead him to the altar
of Westminster, the abbey where the relics of Edward the Confessor
(1042–1066) rested. The procession followed a route where the ground
had been covered with carpet. This is the order which Roger of Howden
gives for the coronation of Richard: at the front, clergy carrying asperges,
cross and censers; these were followed by priors, abbots and bishops surrounding four barons holding four golden candlesticks. There followed
Geoffrey de Lucy with the king's cap; John Marshal with his two golden
spurs; William Marshal with the sceptre and, next to him, William of
Salisbury with the golden rod topped by a dove. David of Huntingdon, the
king of Scotland's brother, Count John, the king's brother and Robert de
Breteuil each carrying a sword, preceded six earls and barons who had on
their shoulders a great chequered board on which were placed the regalia
and the royal robes. William de Mandeville carried the crown. At the end,
between bishops Reginald of Bath and Hugh of Durham, in the shade of
a palanquin of silk held by the four barons of the Cinque Ports, Richard
finished the procession. The crowd of earls, barons, knights and clergy
followed the procession up to the church. In its marshalling, the procession reflected the hierarchy of the two highest orders of English society
even if it kept to no strict order of precedence.

According to Ralph de Diceto – who in his capacity as dean of St Pauls
represented the bishop of London at the coronation during the vacancy of
the see – the solemn acclamation came first. The congregation expressed
as one its will to have Richard as king. Ralph considered that this approval
was 'a solemn and formal election by clergy and people,'[152] necessary
before the rest of the ceremony. This ancient acclamation, which is found

among the old Celtic and Anglo-Saxon tribes, played upon the interplay of the principles of heredity and election. At a time when the rules of hereditary succession were not yet fixed, there was a real need for the acclamation. When Henry II proceeded to the consecration of his son the Young Henry while he himself was still alive, he was trying to go beyond the elective principle, or at least he was trying to make it no more than a relic of past practice. In the Angevin dynasty this anticipation of hereditary succession persuaded no one. In fact it just gave his eldest son yet another reason to rebel.[153] It was not a practice as well assimilated as it was in the Capetian dynasty.

Kneeling, with his hands resting on the gospels and relics, which were set on the altar, the king then took a triple oath: the protection of the Church, justice towards the people and the suppression of bad customs. He promised to respect the privileges or 'private laws' (*privatae leges*) of his subjects. Some medieval historians think that Henry II took upon himself a fourth obligation reflecting his determination to strengthen royal authority (especially in regard to the claims of the Church): the inalienability of royal rights and Crown estates.[154] Following the oaths, the charter recording the text of his profession was placed upon the altar. Parchment copies of it were later despatched throughout the country.[155] Later, just after the anointing and the belting with the sword and placing of the spurs, the king undertook once again to observe what he had sworn.

The central place of the oath in the English coronation ceremonial was once seen as a peculiarly English practice. Some noted the similarity between the coronation oath and the text of Magna Carta (1215) as if the two belonged to the same legal world.[156] It is not really a sustainable view. The oath is to be found in every continental monarchy, including the French.[157] It was, for example, a component in the Aragonese idea of kingship, based on 'consensualism', the mutual contract of respect between king and the orders of his people, whose privileges were ratified at the coronation.[158] It was part of the traditional idea of kingship as being the king linked by a contractual duty to his subjects and the higher law of God.[159]

After the oath, the king was divested of his robes except for shirt and breeches. The archbishop of Canterbury anointed him on the head, breast and arms, the respective repositories of his glory, knowledge and strength.[160] At that time, the anointing was probably the high point of the ceremony, or at least the polemic surrounding its significance spawned a rich literature among the clergy. Works of fiction, intended more for a lay public, gave anointing little attention.[161] Ecclesiastical intellectuals discussed its sacramental character: was the anointing of a king the equivalent of an episcopal ordination? Did the man who received it acquire a cure of souls, a role of intermediary between God and the people whom Christ had died to save? Did it make the king comparable to Christ, whose name meant 'the Anointed One'? Did the indelible nature of anointing make sinful the deposition of a king, or indeed making rebellion against him or even disobeying him?

In the twelfth century theories were often expressed which stressed the powerful sacramentality that anointing conferred on the king. The Anonymous of York – who it may be possible to identify with William Bonne Ame (1079–1110) archbishop of Rouen – asserted that consecration gave the king the right to intervene in ecclesiastical law and even to absolve the sins of his people.[162] Similar ideas were still to be found among the courtiers of Henry II, apparently unaffected by the wide success that the Gregorian programme and the conclusion of the Investiture Contest had achieved amongst continental intellectuals. Bishop Gilbert Foliot of London, the royalist opponent of Becket, made a point of this at the end of 1166 in his letter *Multiplicem* which he addressed to Thomas in an effort to change his mind. He suggested that the king, having become a second Christ by a fivefold anointing, was so placed above other men that he was able to make judgements on every case, even if it were ecclesiastical.[163]

A circular letter that Peter of Blois sent around 1185 to his friends at court went far beyond these simple legal claims to confer on his royal master thaumaturgical qualities: 'I confess on the king's part that a cleric only may accomplish a holy thing; for the king is holy; he is Christ the Lord; not for nothing has he received the sacrament of anointing whose significance – should anyone be ignorant of it or doubt it – should be well attested by the cleansing of that disease which affects the groin and be the cure of scrofula.'[164] When Peter established a link between the ritual of consecration and pre-Christian beliefs about the curative powers of the king,[165] he firmly placed the king in a supernatural world. Besides that he established the link between royal anointing in the style of the Old Testament, carried out by a bishop, and popular, indeed pagan, religion. His mention of scrofula refers to the 'royal sickness', an abscess disfiguring the face caused by inflammation of the ganglions in the neck, which the kings of France and England were supposed to cure.

In England and France the touching for scrofula would only become a systematic practice at the end of the thirteenth century as a ceremony on the occasion of a coronation.[166] But Henry II himself did not neglect to touch for it from time to time, so as to justify the thaumaturgic powers with which some of his people credited him. The proof of this is a source which has only recently come to notice. It is in a list of miracles of Frideswide (died 735) written by Philip, Augustinian prior of her ancient monastery in Oxford. Philip says that he wrote it in 1180, to mark the solemn translation of the relics of the saint, which Henry II had sponsored. He tells of a rather surprising miracle, which concerns 'scrofula under the throat, commonly called "glands", that was said to have been cured by the touch of the royal hand.'[167] A knight's daughter, afflicted with this disease, had sought out Henry II who had cured her. But the same evening she became all at once totally paralysed. She was laid on the tomb of Frideswide, who restored her to health. Philip had nothing to say about the reasons for her paralysis, in which it is not hard to detect a divine punishment for having made resort to the thaumaturgical powers of a king.[168] Such an outcome is sure evidence of the hostility of reforming clerics of the end of the twelfth century to a belief in the sacrality of the monarch, incompatible with a Gregorian outlook. The example is nonetheless a significant one of the recourse of laypeople to the miraculous power of one who had received anointing. Whatever the case, Philip's story might be used to deny any speck of sacrality to the Angevin kings in the common consciousness of the twelfth century.[169]

The miracle story of St Frideswide is worth putting alongside another text. In his funerary eulogy for the Young Henry, a consecrated king for a dozen years before he died, Thomas of Earley described the cures of fistulas, of a leper and of a man suffering from sores by contact with his remains.[170] Although not strictly scrofulous, the men were all afflicted by illnesses with external symptoms and disfiguring sores, just like those of scrofula. So, to conclude, the first Angevin kings had on occasion cured the 'royal sickness': their supernatural aura was in this way strengthened.

Opposing the supporters of Henry II who defended the superior powers of royal anointing were ranked a group of clerks who wished to play down the political consequences of the ritual. This latter group went much further when they came into conflict with the king. For Thomas Becket, it was ecclesiastics who had initiated the anointing of the king and had delivered to him the sword by which he was to defend the Church. If he showed himself unworthy, they would naturally deprive him of his undeserved power.[171] Stephen Langton, another archbishop of Canterbury (1207–1228), completely denied that the anointing of a king had any sacramental dimension.[172] He was of the generation of Innocent III who, in a decretal of 1204, made a clear distinction between episcopal anointing and royal anointing. The first, on head and hands, was interior and invisible acting on the heart; the second, on arms and shoulders, was exterior and material and affected only the body. This theology followed logically from Lateran III (1179), which, in fixing the sevenfold nature of the sacraments, demoted royal anointing to the level of 'sacramental' – which was not a sacrament, properly speaking, but a simple rite of the Church which, although it brought some spiritual advantages, did not produce grace in its recipient in any systematic way.[173]

The debate between supporters and opponents of the sacrality of royal anointing spilled over into the choice of oils. For supporters, the king ought to be anointed with holy chrism, oil mingled with balsam. For opponents, it should be the oil of catechumens, an ordinary oil. These two oils, consecrated by a bishop in the same chrismal mass on Maundy Thursday, did not enjoy the same status. Their function was different: the first was administered just after baptism for those entering into the community of the Church, for those being confirmed and also, during an ordination, on the hands of the priest and the head of the bishop. The second oil, of less value, was applied on the breast before baptism and on liturgical objects.

In the twelfth century, the king of France was anointed with holy chrism, a privilege that he maintained despite an attempt of Innocent III to withdraw it from him. This chrism was mixed with the oil in the Holy Ampulla, a phial that it was said had miraculously appeared with a dove at the baptism of Clovis.[174] In England, the situation was less straightforward. The Anglo-Saxon kings would have received anointing by chrism on the head, and the Anonymous of York asserts at the beginning of the twelfth century that the king could intervene in ecclesiastical affairs since he had been consecrated with the same oil as a bishop. Nevertheless, at this time, the modification of the Anglo-Saxon coronation order under the influence of the Romano-Germanic pontifical, introduced the oil of catechumens into the consecration, although it was administered on the head in the manner of bishops.[175] Henry II and Richard the Lionheart had probably received anointing of this sort.[176] It was perhaps otherwise with the Young Henry, according to a text which hints at the use of holy chrism in his consecration in 1170.[177] If that were the case, the bishops opposed to Thomas Becket would have done it, probably in collaboration with Henry II, in a way deliberately provocative to Alexander III and the archbishop of Canterbury, but nonetheless true to their caesaro-papist colours.

Roger of Howden informs us further that after the anointing, the archbishop of Canterbury placed the cap, carried by Geoffrey de Lucy, on the head of Richard the Lionheart. This cap was the same as the one by which the anointed heads of the baptized were covered, having been clothed in a simple white robe. An alb and a dalmatic, two clerical vestments, were then given to the king. The archbishop delivered to the king a sword in an act whose theocratic significance is obvious. It was not the king himself who took up this symbol of his sovereign exercise of justice, but the prelate who gave it to him under the guise of an investiture. Two earls then fixed spurs on his feet, the signs of his knighthood. The intervention of these two laymen in a ceremony conducted up to that point by prelates symbolized the world of horseback aristocratic warriors, the world to which the king also belonged. At last, enveloped in a mantle, the king moved up to the altar where the archbishop asked him to repeat his oath once more. These brief intermediate rites, between the anointing and the coronation, comprise two categories: clothing and delivery of insignia. With the exception of the fixing of the spurs, which belonged to the lay world of knighthood, the lion's share of them belonged to the clergy, even though the king received the symbols of his power passively.

It was not quite the same with the coronation. According to Roger of Howden it was Richard the Lionheart who himself took the crown and handed it to the archbishop, who placed it on his head. This act of the king, taking the initiative, was not without significance. It put the role of the prelate into proportion. This part of the ceremony was all-important, for it related to an object of deep significance. In the twelfth century, the crown did not any more represent a simple item of royal insignia, descendant of the laurels and diadems of Antiquity. In political language, it had assumed by now an 'invisible' sense: it represented the entire kingdom.[178] When the king took the crown, it was his subjects and all his territories that he was taking. Another point is that the Plantagenet crown came from the Holy Roman Empire. A list of regalia drawn up in 1207 tells us that King John's crown came from Germany. There is a strong likelihood that it was one of the two brought by the Empress Mathilda when she came back to England in 1125, the year she was widowed of Henry V.[179] The use by the kings of England of these emblems drawn from the imperial treasury is not without importance. On the one hand it coincides with the aggrandizing influence of the Romano-Germanic coronation order on consecration in England. On the other, it fits into an expanded political conception of the insular and continental territories of the house of Anjou which bordered upon an imperial ideology.

The coronation proceeded with the delivery of two other symbols: the sceptre and the rod. These two emblems of government were charged with symbolism of some antiquity. Leaving aside their possible reference to the episcopal pastoral staff – as was conceivably still the case in the ninth and tenth centuries[180] – they had obviously been reinvented in the twelfth century as a classic allegory of command which is to be found in many civilizations, under the guise of batons and staffs. At that time English earls, marshals and seneschals used the rod as their particular symbol of authority.[181] Another point to make is that the Angevin coronations – unlike the Anglo-Saxon – show no trace here of the giving of a ring, which in an episcopal consecration represents the union of the prelate with the Church. Most definitely, the king, crowned by a bishop, was not one himself.

In a text written in hexameters celebrating the imminent accession of Henry II, Henry, archdeacon of Huntingdon (1080/90–c.1160) stressed the powerful symbolism of the sceptre and rod: 'Not yet king . . . you are the most worthy of guiding the reins of the kingdom! You may not yet carry the sceptre, but with or without you – being detained overseas – England rejoices in peace . . . Your rods (*radii*) as you approach radiant (*radians*) are sure confidence, cheerful clemency, prudent power, merciful judgement, heavy vengeance, gentle correction, chaste love, balanced honour and moderation in appetite. With these rods, when you are endowed with the fair sceptre, you will be more of an ornament to the crown than the crown is ornament to you.'[182] In listing all the attributes and manifestations of royal power, Henry of Huntingdon raised the sceptre and rod into the chief insignia of command.

The ceremony of consecration ended with the king's enthronement. A mass followed. At the offertory, Richard the Lionheart left his throne so as to place a mark of fine gold on the altar. Roger spoke as the dean of the collegiate church of Howden in making a point that this gift ought to be offered at each coronation: the point of this offering (not unlike the dues paid on entry to a lordship) is that it marks one more time the submission of the king to the Church. The banquet which followed afterwards featured the precedences and services whose performance followed the hierarchy of recognized groups in the kingdom, just as in the opening procession.

The queen too was crowned. Eleanor of Aquitaine was crowned at the same time as her husband, 19 December 1154. It may be, however, that she was not anointed on that occasion, for she had already experienced it with her first husband, the king of France.[183] The Young Henry received anointing and the crown, on his own, 14 June 1170. The absence of his wife, Margaret of France, was because of the unique nature of the consecration, carried out for the first time in English history on the person of a royal heir while his father was still alive. Another pressing reason was the dispute reignited by the consecration, which both Thomas Becket, archbishop of Canterbury, and the pope condemned. It is probable that Margaret's exclusion was the wish of Henry II, so as to influence her father, the king of France, into putting pressure on Becket to preside at the coronation.[184] Whatever the case, it was only on 27 August 1172, at Winchester cathedral, that Margaret was at last consecrated and crowned. Her husband was with her, since the invalidity of his earlier anointing had been recognized after Thomas's murder and the reconciliation of his father, Henry II, with the Church.[185] On 27 May 1199, King John did not associate Isabel of Gloucester with his coronation. He had already anticipated perhaps the result of his first marriage, which ended in an annulment some months later. Finally, Berengaria of Navarre and Isabel of Angouleme, married to already-crowned husbands, were crowned respectively at Limassol (Cyprus) on Berengaria's marriage day, and at Westminster, when Isabel arrived in England.[186]

Two conclusions can be drawn from those examples of the coronation of queens. Firstly in normal circumstances, the queen was consecrated at the same time as her husband. Secondly, her regalia included like the king's the sceptre and rod. But, unlike her husband, she experienced the placing of ring on finger and was given no sword.[187] In conclusion, consecration and coronation performed jointly with her husband, conferred on the queen a corresponding status of sovereignty. Eleanor of Aquitaine and Isabel of Angouleme undeniably drew prestige and authority from their anointing, in particular after they were widowed. However, royal dignity was not the same as royal power, especially as rank (the place in the hierarchy of power) and role (the effective use of power and its social acceptance) would not have been confused in the Middle Ages. The proof of this is the sword, symbol of military command and judicial power, which would otherwise have been given to the queen during the consecration. The king's wife was associated with the throne, which made her 'consort', in the full sense of the word, acknowledging their sharing the same fate, honour and dignity. But her actual power was never formalized: it entirely depended on her influence over her husband, on the power she still retained in her native realm, or on the circumstances of her widowhood.

During the time of the Norman dynasty, the king wore his crown solemnly at least three times a year, invoking the consecration that was the basis of his authority. These 'showings' always happened in church during a votive mass. They might have included a renewed coronation, delivery of regalia and chanting of the *laudes regiae*, the hymn in praise of the king which recalled his election and acclamation. Anointing was not renewed because of its indelible nature. King Henry I, however, decided to abandon these ceremonies, probably because of their cost and the distance of his residence at Woodstock from any large church worthy of that sort of liturgy.[188] After his imprisonment and then liberation during the civil war, Stephen de Blois organized in 1142 a sumptuous ceremony of re-coronation to wipe out the disgrace he had suffered. The same thing happened in 1194 with Richard the Lionheart at Winchester Cathedral on his return from his German captivity.[189] In much the same way, King John multiplied this sort of ceremony in the first three years of his reign so as to establish and publicize his power, contested by Arthur of Brittany.

In comparison with the first Norman kings, however, the Angevins were willing to let go of these crown-wearings, as they had a practical use only where their legitimacy was under threat. On Easter Day 1158, in the course of the offertory of a mass held at Worcester, Henry II and Eleanor placed their crowns on the altar, swearing that they would wear them no more. The meaning of their renunciation has led to much spilling of ink amongst historians, who have offered several explanations. They include the psychological (an act of humility, need for economy, an aversion for display or for the tediousness of the ceremonies); symbolic (the bishops predominated when they handed over the crown and stole the scene from the king); and political (avoiding the enormous assembly of the aristocracy at the court).[190] Let us set aside the unverifiable psychological theories, which refer back, so far as royal modesty is concerned, to the description of imperial elections by Suetonius (70–128),[191] and also the political motives, for when the nobility joined in the ceremony and acclaimed the king it recognized the submission it owed him rather than advancing its own power. The most probable explanation concerns the uselessness of these crown-wearings and re-coronations, as in the spring of 1158 there was no one to dispute the power of Henry II. At that time the rulers of the Scots and Welsh had made peace after the king's successes over the last dissident English lords.[192] The crown-wearings – whose theocratic implications were all too obvious – had then no practical purpose in imposing a lawful authority which was already widely accepted. The kings would turn back to them only in a major crisis.

The weakness of the vassal

If the Plantagenets were no longer bound to repeat the rites inaugurating their royal status in England, they gave more prominence to the ceremonies which made them masters of their continental duchies, where they had to assert themselves against the king of France. Such was the case when Richard and John caused themselves to be enthroned as dukes of Normandy at Rouen Cathedral, before crossing the Channel to be crowned. The archbishop of Rouen presided over this ceremony. He gave the future king the sword, the primordial symbol of ducal power, although we know that Richard had taken it off the altar himself. It was the archbishop, however, who placed on their heads the golden circlet fashioned of roses, and who delivered the ducal banner fixed to a lance. The new duke then swore to the clergy and people to protect the Church, preserve the peace and uphold justice, immediately before the homage which his subjects paid him during the ceremony.[193]

The importance which clung to the title of duke of Normandy in the hierarchy of French principalities was considerable. It is probable that at the end of the twelfth century ancient Neustria was considered as the leading region of the kingdom. To know this we should remember that, in the opening procession in the coronation of the boy Philip Augustus in November 1179, the Young Henry, duke and king, was at the head of the procession carrying the crown: 'as of his right, reckoned from the duchy of Normandy', followed by Count Philip of Flanders with the sword.[194] It is true that Henry was also seneschal of France in so far as he was Count of Anjou and that he was himself a king, factors adding to his precedence.

The ritual of ducal enthronement in Aquitaine is particularly well known. There exists a description of this ceremony for Richard the Lionheart in June 1172, thanks to the Limousin chronicler, Geoffrey de Vigeois, as well as a very detailed *ordo* of a rite enacted at Limoges that Elias Aimeric, the precentor of the chapter, may have written in 1218.[195] This latter text contains prayers taken from the Romano-Germanic consecration, perhaps because of the close links between William V of Aquitaine (996–1030) and the Emperor Henry II (1002–1024). It seems that it was under this particular duke that the ceremony was instituted, around the year 1000.[196]

The Aquitainian rite was, however, considerably enriched under the Plantagenets. They reflected the extent of its political significance in the context of a deep-seated Aquitainian irredentism. On the first occasion the ceremony was carried out at Poitiers in the basilica of St-Hilaire, of which the duke was titular abbot. He was enthroned on the abbatial seat, then he received the lance and banner from the hands of the archbishop of Bordeaux and the bishop of Poitiers. The hymn O *princeps egregie*, composed at St-Martial of Limoges, was then sung. On a second occasion, at Limoges at the door of the cathedral of St Stephen, the bishop of the city offered him holy water as a greeting and clothed him in a tunic of silk. Then he placed on the duke's finger the ring of St Valeria. The ring was central to medieval hagiographical stories about this third-century regional protomartyr. Valeria, only daughter and heir of Duke Leocadius of Aquitaine, was converted to Christianity by Martial at a time when she had been promised in marriage. She had been decapitated for refusing her prestigious match.[197] After the ring, the bishop placed on the duke's head a circlet of gold, and then he gave him a banner. At this point they entered the cathedral and approached the choir, where the duke was invested with sword and spurs. A mass followed his oath to protect the church of Limoges. At the end he placed on the altar the *ducalia* he had been given during the ceremony. A similar rite of enthronement must assuredly have been conducted at Bordeaux.

Ancient though they were, these ducal ceremonies had never had the pomp and circumstance that the Plantagenets wanted to endow them with. They were principally about the investiture with certain insignia: a gold circlet, a sword, spurs, lance and banner. The sword and the spurs, which were given to the new knight on his dubbing, were to be found in the royal consecration. The specificity of three other of the *ducalia* are worth remarking on. The circlet seems to be a pale image of the royal crown; the form of the lance approximates to the staff of command, and the banner is the symbol of troops led by a commander to victory. The jewelled engagement ring taken from Valeria recalls the most prestigious local cult. To borrow an argument of Edina Bozóky: 'the symbolic marriage of the dukes of Aquitaine with Valeria, by her ring-relic, bestowed a sacral legitimacy on their investiture.'[198] By this token, the ring of Limoges had no resemblance to the quasi-episcopal ring that kings may once have received on consecration so as to symbolize their union with their people.

For the Plantagenets, the increased magnificence of their ducal investiture rituals was partly related to their wish to play down the implications of the homage they owed the king of France for their continental domains. Proof of this is the contemporary tendency to abandon the ceremony of crown-wearing in England, where their rule was scarcely opposed. In the kingdom of France, by contrast, the display at their enthronement made believe that their power came directly from God through the intercession of the local saints. Their submission to the king of France as a consequence was all the more reduced in importance. The political strategies behind these ceremonies are laid bare in the *Deeds of Philip Augustus* by Rigord (*c.*1158–*c.*1209), monk of St-Denis, the mausoleum of the kings of France where their regalia were kept. Rigord records that the spoils of Waifar, duke of Aquitaine, defeated and killed by King Pepin the Short in 768, were preserved at St-Denis and with it, as a sort of trophy, several items of ducal insignia supposed to be given the dukes on their enthronement. This source does not just cast doubt on the attempt of the clergy of Limoges to make their city the capital of Aquitaine; it was also a formal challenge to Plantagenet propaganda and a decisive riposte to their separatist pretensions.[199]

In this war of rites, the Angevin kings were bound to affront others apart from the Capetians. They were equally in conflict with the Church in England, in particular under the archbishops Thomas Becket and Stephen Langton. The role that the archbishop had acquired – mastery of a large part of the consecration – was not to the advantage of the king, a passive recipient not only of the oil but also the crown from the prelate's hands. When he swore to protect the Church the king considerably reduced his room for political manoeuvre. At the height of his dispute with Henry II, Archbishop Thomas Becket did not fail to point out to the king the consequences: 'Remember the profession to preserve the liberties of the Church of God which you made, whose text you placed on the altar when you had been consecrated and anointed by my predecessor at Westminster.'[200] More prosaically, Gerald of Barry, a critic of royal conduct, regretted that 'the prince has lost his understanding of the royal sacrament of anointing, of the crown, sceptre and other insignia of kingship.'[201] For Gerald as for so many others, the coronation provided an opportunity to preach to the king. It presumed there were more duties than rights for the king, which tied his hands.

Anointing was, in conclusion, more of a theocratic than a caesaro-papist act. All the more, the supporters of royal sacrality attempted to resurrect the good old days of the Anonymous of York in comparing royal to episcopal consecration, or in attempting to introduce the holy chrism into the ceremony and in arguing that it gave the king thaumaturgic powers. But this rearguard action seemed already doomed to defeat.

The king nonetheless managed to associate the coronation with some signals of subordination designed for his subjects. During the ceremony, acclamations and the *laudes regiae* represented these marks of acknowledgement. More significant yet, John received the homage of his barons and the fealty of the bishops of his realm the day after his coronation in May 1199.[202] Their vassalage involved considerable constraints on the nobility. Apart from traditional military service it also opened the possibility of the surrender of baronial castles at the king's request. So in 1176 Henry II sent envoys to a number of private castles in England and Normandy, of which they symbolically took possession, effecting in the king's name solemn rites of entry, replacing the lord's banner with that of the king and taking the keys. Thanks to this advanced form of royal feudalism, the castle network came under strict royal control.[203]

It was with John that collective oath-swearing at coronations became an institution in England. These promises applied to every subject of the king, including the non-nobles. During Henry II's reign the assize of Norhampton (1176) stipulated that everyone, from earls to peasants, must swear allegiance to the king either in his presence or in that of his local justices. This legislation probably recalls the ancient Carolingian custom of the general oath, adopted by the Vikings after they took over Neustria. When the Angevin dynasty reinvented this traditional ceremony, which it adapted to suit a rapidly evolving State, the king became the undisputable and direct lord of all the inhabitants of Normandy and England. The collectivism of the oath taken to the king by gatherings of his subjects loosened the contractual implications of feudal relations, since it was a common imposition on every man, rather than respecting the privilege of each to choose his lord. For the vassal, the duties towards the king thus became more important than his rights, and feudal links would no longer be acceptable excuses in a dispute with the king.[204] This new liege homage made the king the principal lord of every vassal in the kingdom, whom he could now charge with perjury and felony if they revolted. The coming together of coronation ritual and the different sorts of homage and collective oath at this time were integral to this process of evolution.

Outside England, the first Angevin kings drew to themselves the kings and lesser rulers of other British realms by certain rites of allegiance that they drew usually from feudal vassalage. Following campaigns in the north of Wales at the beginning of his reign, Henry II gained the homage of Owain (1137–1169), prince of Gwynedd, and Rhys ap Gruffudd, prince of Deheubarth. Malcolm IV, king of Scotland (1153–1165), was present with these princes at Woodstock in July 1163, where he was obliged to submit with them to this humiliating ceremony and leave his younger brother David as hostage. By the treaty of Falaise (1174) Malcolm's successor, William the Lion (1165–1214), prisoner of Henry II, became according to its terms his 'liege man' for all his lands, and had to give up to Henry Scotland's chief castles. All his subjects witnessed the reclamation of his homage by the king of England.[205] Assuredly, the king of Scotland did not interpret the ceremony the same harsh way as his new master did, but as no more than a simple act of homage establishing a peace between comparable powers. This ambiguity was not quite as evident in Ireland, where traditional ceremonies were observed. Following the conquest of the eastern part of the island, the king and the local magnates recognized the supremacy of Henry II in their own native way: the building of huts of wood with banquetting chambers, the taking of gifts with no reciprocity, the paying of tribute, the delivery of hostages, the oath of loyalty taken next to rivers on the borders of kingdoms, the king's progress following ancient itineraries, and the calling of assemblies by Henry II on the occasion of traditional feasts. As Marie-Thérèse Flanagan says, these treaties, truces and alliances did not weigh heavily on the parties to them.[206] It was much the same with the Welsh and Scottish leaders, who looked for the least excuse to assert their independence over the king of England, and so break the homage that they had been obliged to swear after military defeats. It was to avoid this that the Angevin kings demanded from them hostages and castles.

In feudal law, royal anointing offered an extra advantage to the recipient. It put him theoretically above all other civil power. No lay authority was superior to him. He held of no one. He was emperor within his own kingdom. A result of this was that no homage could be performed by a consecrated king. Henry II, who took homage from his sons so long as they were dukes and counts, would not take it from the Young Henry after 1170.[207] Anointing and feudal subordination were mutually exclusive where his eldest son was concerned. The argument was probably employed by the legal minds in King John's household in 1202 when Philip Augustus condemned him for contumacy on confiscating his continental lands when he did not appear before his tribunal. At that time, the English argued that their king could be judged only on the march, on the frontier of Normandy, because of ancient custom.[208] In 1216, John found himself once more in a bad situation, when French troops invaded England, thinking themselves able to free it from his tyranny. But Innocent III defended him in a letter where he attacked the Capetians for taking the realm from him: 'for he is an anointed king and so is above all others.'[209] This theory, which gives a high regard to the consequences of a prestigous ritual, might well seem decisive.

In practice, however, the theory of anointing did not work. The three first Angevin kings had to submit to the somewhat humiliating ceremonial of entry into vassalage. They paid homage a dozen times to the king of France for their continental domains, usually to confirm their rights during a succession struggle or to gain the edge over a relative in their frequent family disputes. In doing this they increased their displays of subordination over those of the Norman dynasty, which had been more economical in attesting to their status as vassals.[210] Geoffrey Plantagenet as count of Anjou, at Paris in 1151 asked his son Henry II, already then duke of

Normandy, to become the liege man of the king, an act previous Norman rulers had never accepted as necessary. The Normans had always known how to avoid doing homage. When they had had no other choice, however, they had always rendered homage on the march, that is, on the frontier of the river Epte in the Vexin – the usual location of their wars with the French kings but also the place of their meetings, negotiations and truces. Homage on the march was 'personal', involving an interchange between two people; it was not 'real' homage, done for a fief, a material support for a contract. Personal homage was closer to the oath of fealty, pledged as an act of peace and implying a degree of equality between the parties. Having become kings of England, the Plantagenets used it in their turn, because they well knew all its political implications.

Homage was often done between Gisors and Trie on the French river Epte. More precisely it was performed under an elm tree (*orme*) which had given its name to the actual place, Lormeteau-Ferré. An elm tree offered a complex symbolism. It served to demarcate a frontier, as is found in *chansons de geste*. It could also feature as a place for village social gatherings, sheltering popular festivals or the lord's court.[211] Again, it was an image of Pride, because of the height and beauty which hid its barrenness. On this heading, a homily attributed to St Augustine, mentioned in medieval preaching, contrasted it with the more modest vine, which for all its small size gave in abundance.[212] In a slightly more positive light, Gregory the Great made the barren elm tree the support for the vine, which was attached to it so that it could grow and produce, in the same way as laypeople assisted monks to attain a rich spiritual harvest by their generosity.[213] The view of the sterility of the elm would undoubtedly have been disputed by Hildegard of Bingen (1098–1179) who suggested in reference to it several uses for medicinal purposes.[214] In the Middle Ages, the learned and popular significances of the elm were as rich as they were varied.

It was for this reason that Philip Augustus's decision on 18 August 1188 to cut the tree down was heavy with meaning. The failure of the negotiations which had been held over three days with Henry II under the elm of Gisors would be – if we follow Ralph de Diceto – the reason for his decision, which the Angevin king promptly avenged with the pillage of the royal demesne as far as Mantes. For William le Breton (*c*.1165–*p*.1226), the continuator of Rigord, the motive was a dispute over precedence. Henry II had sheltered himself under the shade of the elm, leaving Philip Augustus out in the heat of the sun. Its felling was all the more significant as the king of England had long before had it circled with a belt of iron on which was inscribed that on the day he would lose the elm, he would also lose his land. According to John the Trouvère, the idea of cutting it down came from the French knights without Philip Augustus's knowledge, who was himself very much against it. The amount that these three writers have to say about this episode says a lot about how they viewed its significance. The felling of the elm of Gisors symbolized a point of no return between the French king and Henry II. Henry would die the following year in the course of a campaign against Philip, allied with his own son.

Behind the violence of the Gisors incident can be sensed all the ideological implications of the homage of the duke of Normandy to the king of France. In the 1140s, the legal scholars of the north of France analysed this point of feudal law. Suger, abbot of St-Denis and mentor of Louis VII, was very much into the construction of a new political theory, according to which all the territorial principalities were fiefs of the kingdom. Homage done for them, taken on the border, was not just personal but well and truly real. Maybe Suger was borrowing the image of feudal hierarchy from the pyramid of Pseudo-Dionysian light, which he applied also to the rebuilding of his abbey, to become the first Gothic building work in the West.[215] In 1166, Stephen, abbot of Cluny, pushed the reasoning further in a letter in which he considered France to be a 'single body' where Burgundy, like all the other territories, belonged to the king without any intermediary lords.[216] These theories put together by intellectuals surfaced in the acts of princes. In 1173, forced to pay homage to Henry II, Raymond V of Toulouse inserted a reservation of fidelity to the king of France, his chief lord.[217] The kingdom of France would appear from now on as a single region in the hands of the Capetians, and the Crown as a complete and indivisible concept.

The Plantagenet response to the Capetians was pretty feeble, on the level of political theory and feudal doctrine. In 1139, Robert de Torigny copied a passage developing the idea of the allodial nature of Normandy from the *Brevis Relatio* (1114 × 1120), a work drawn up by a monk of Battle: an 'allod', held as simple property, was the opposite of a 'fief' held from a lord. This concluded that therefore the duke could be asked for no feudal service for it. At very most the duke was obliged to render to the king of France his good faith and an act of homage containing only negative obligations about not threatening the king's life or patrimony. For his part, the king swore faith to the duke, promising the same conditions in his turn. Robert was echoing the spirit of independence which was dominant at the time when Henry I defeated Louis VI in the battle of Brémule (1119). Henry had already refused Louis the homage of his son William Atheling.[218] Some years later, having become a close counsellor of Henry II, Robert made serious modifications to his thought on the subject. He accepted that ancient Neustria belonged to the kingdom of France. So he was the only Plantagenet author to mention 'the homage of Duke Henry for the duchy of Normandy' in 1151.[219] There is a strong possibility that his thinking, like that of other intellectuals in the household of the first Angevin king of England, exhibited from then on a hierarchical view of feudal society, one which subordinated ancient Neustria to West Francia.

More proof of this view of Normandy is in the *Roman de Rou*, when Wace, historian and protégé of Henry II, wrote that before he left for good for the Holy Land, Duke Robert the Magnificent (1027–1035) entrusted his son, William the Bastard, to the Capetian king: 'He placed him with the king of France and delivered him to the king by his hand; he caused him to become his man and take possession of Normandy.'[220] This literal translation of the Anglo-Norman verse shows how 'real' was the homage, in the legal sense of the term, taken for a fief, in this case Normandy. Expressing the idea of the feudal subordination of ancient Neustria to the king of France was not therefore necessarily viewed as an unpardonable slur on the duke's authority. It could be suggested that Wace's work was not tied to Henry II's goodwill, generous patron though he was, and that his independence of spirit would earn the author one day a fall from grace at the royal court.

These new legal concepts did not seem to bother Henry II much. At least a letter, dictated in 1164, about an item of business external to Normandy allows an assessment of the degree of subordination that Henry II himself said he stood in towards Louis VII. Henry wrote to Louis to ask him to release Counts William VII and William VIII of Auvergne, his vassals, whom the king of France had captured. Henry II's turn of phrase was hardly ambiguous: 'I have given up to you all my land on this side of the Channel for you to keep as being my lord.' . . . 'by the faith which you owe me, your man and your friend, as my lord.' In a second letter sent on the same subject thanking Louis for releasing the counts, Henry writes likewise: 'I will be delighted to be of service to you, my dearest lord, wherever and however you please, it matters not in what way.'[221] This is not an isolated example. A letter of the same year sent to ask him not to assist the exiled Thomas Becket in France is addressed 'to his lord and friend, the illustrious King Louis.'[222] Leaving to one side the rhetoric of letter-writing and diplomatic politeness, it is permissible to say that Henry II accepted all the consequences of the homage due to Louis VII, heavy though they might be.

The only work which argues the feudal superiority of the Plantagenets over the Capetians comes from Stephen of Rouen (*fl.*1143–1170) monk of Bec and panegyrist of Henry II. His long Latin poem of 4,390 verses, the *Draco Normannicus* (1167–1168), pictures Frederick Barbarossa sending Henry the Lion, duke of Saxony and Bavaria and Henry's brother-in-law, as ambassador to request him not to pay homage to Louis VII. Louis was less than 'his equal in power, honour and dignity', a descendant of usurpers of the Carolingian throne, whose true and sole heir was really the German emperor. Frederick goes so far as to offer France to Henry II and his successors. He plans to help Henry dispossess the Capetians. It is significant that in his vast historical panorama of the dukes of Normandy, Stephen of Rouen fails to mention the homage done by Rollo, of whom he is an admirer because of his damaging conquests of the Franks, as he fails also to mention the wardship of William the Bastard in the hands of the French king.[223] Nevertheless Stephen's work, more a pamphlet, remains the exception which proves the rule. Neither the Plantagenets nor the writers close to their court hid the homage they did to the king of France, neither did they ignore the political consequences which stemmed from it.

Other marks of subordination punctuated the history of relations between the first Angevins and the Capetians. At a time when hypergamy (marrying a woman above your station) was still unusual in princely dynasties, the Plantagenets contracted marriages or engagements with Margaret and Alice of France: as 'the giver of brides' Louis VII was demonstrating that he was their lord. When he refused the hand of his sister Joan to Philip Augustus, Richard the Lionheart made a serious political mistake. He passed up the chance of turning the situation to his advantage and drew on himself the perpetual enmity of his recent ally. Furthermore, the frequent travels to and stays at Paris by Henry II and his sons, where they enjoyed the hospitality of the king, was evidence of the role of courtier which they adopted towards the Capetians. Finally, certain gifts that the Plantagenets offered to the king amounted to pledges of their fealty. Rigord, the official historian of the Capetians, cites, for example, the eagerness with which Henry II despatched wild stags, deer and goats captured in Normandy and Aquitaine to stock the hunting grounds that Philip Augustus reinstated in the Parisian forest of Vincennes. It has been noted that England never provided game for Philip, while the continental domains of the Plantagenets were obliged to deliver these animals, the hunting of which symbolized the domination of the king of France over the provinces of his kingdom. There was a powerful warlike symbolism behind hunting. The violent subjection of wild animals, whose skins were displayed like trophies of victory, were just a metaphor for plunder taken from the defeated on the battlefield.[224] Just as with homage and hypergamic marriage, the stays at court and gifts put the Angevins within the Capetian orbit.

Did the men of those days appreciate the implications of these open marks of respect towards the king? Had they chosen to ignore the consequences of the ritual language of submission? Did they fully realize the meaning of the unfavourable interpretation of that same act that their own courtiers had done to them? And did they have to wait until the proclamation of the seizure of King John's fiefs to understand the importance of feudal relations in the structure of the Capetian state?

The reply to these questions can be kept short. It calls for two different responses. Firstly, relations between Plantagenets and Capetians were often expressed through rites of friendship that tended to lessen, and indeed disguise, the subordination involved in homage. Eating at the same table, sleeping in the same bed, demonstrating affection, grieving pathetically over a lost friend . . . In the aristocratic ambience of the twelfth century, these public and conventional marks of alliance could refashion the old arrangement between the kings of France and England to make it look like equality.[225] Secondly, the Angevins had conducted the relationship of allegiance, which marked their subordination to Louis VII and Philip Augustus, unsystematically and with no overall political objectives. What most frequently obliged them to resort to those demeaning rituals had been the need for a truce, a territorial concession, or an alliance to fight father or brother. More pragmatic than ideological, the Angevins thought perhaps that royal anointing, the new rites of ducal enthronement and the formal expressions of friendship with the king were enough to efface every external sign of vassalage. Their assessment turned out to be baseless in the end.

More of this indifference can be found in the readiness of the Plantagenets to accept dependency on other powers. There were two occasions on which they became men of the German emperor. First in 1157, at least according to a letter of Henry II of dubious authenticity, reported only by Rahewin of Friesing, continuator of the chronicle of his master Otto (1115/18–1158), the emperor's uncle, Henry may have abandoned all his kingdom and subjects to the overlordship of Frederick Barbarossa. In return he supposedly kept the hand of St James, a relic formerly in the imperial treasury and brought by his mother Mathilda to England. The precious hand had lent prestige to the Cluniac abbey of Reading, founded by Henry I, who was buried there with William, eldest son of Henry II and Eleanor.[226]

More certain is the resignation by Richard the Lionheart in 1193 of his kingdom and the island of Cyprus to the Emperor Henry VI (1190–1197). But these were different circumstances. The king, his captive, was ready to concede anything. He delivered his lands to the emperor, who gave them back to him, offering Richard a double cross of gold as a sign of investiture. Henry added to this fief the kingdom of Arles and Burgundy, an imperial domain. But it seems that he released the king of England from all these obligations on his deathbed, because of a bad conscience.[227] If his father had ambitions to secure a political primacy over the West, the ambition of Henry VI was even greater. He wished to be emperor and feudal lord, not just of Germany and Italy, but of all the kingdoms of Europe and the Holy Land.[228]

In some respects the submission of King John to Pope Innocent III (1198–1216) resembles that of Richard the Lionheart to the emperor. But the context, heavy with intimations of the theocracy of the popes of the middle of the thirteenth century, was quite different. England found itself from 1208 under interdict due to the confrontation between the king and Cardinal Stephen Langton, archbishop of Canterbury, an intimate of the pope since their days studying in Paris. Although it compromised his authority, the interdict did John's financial policies no harm; he confiscated ecclesiastical lands and enjoyed their revenues. In 1213 the threat of a French invasion forced John to open negotiaitions with Innocent III. He gave up the kingdom of England and lordship of Ireland to the pope, who returned them to him as a fief for an annual rent of 1,000 marks.[229] At this period, the temporal authority of Innocent III, tireless preacher of the crusade and mediator of many disputes between Western monarchs, was at its peak. The submission of John reflects the universal claims of the pontificate of Innocent, who took Melchizedech, priest and king, as his model. The episode of John's submission was not unique: it recalled the papal coronation and homage of the kings of Aragon and Portugal. Its significance should be kept in proportion.

It did not much burden the spirits of King John who, like Henry II and Richard the Lionheart, took the ceremony of homage on himself becoming, on his knees in an act of self-giving, the vassal of another lord. The Plantagenets identified themselves more with the line of counts of Anjou than of dukes of Normandy, by the frequency with which they acted out their dependency on the king of France, even doing it at Paris. They submitted alike to pope and emperor, to whom they ceded England in fief. The circumstances in which these rites of subjection were introduced were unique, and besides, the homage to the French king was mostly on the frontier. But every such ceremony carried an element of humiliation, experienced as such within a noble and princely society where honour was the ultimate asset. In conclusion, the Plantagenets had not been able to make much on the continent of the ideological impact consequent on their consecration. Their degree of power seems to have derived more from being a duke than being a king.

This leads inevitably to one last question: what was the degree of display they exhibited during their reigns? Was the image of themselves that they projected on high feasts royal or princely? Did their appearance favour pomp or simplicity? On this, a difference in style could be pointed out between the reign of Henry II, the son of a count, and those of his sons, raised in a royal family. Richard the Lionheart liked to endow his public appearances with a little theatre. His coronation, described in detail by the pen of Roger of Howden, was the result of very sophisticated stage management. Like his brother John, Richard revived the grandeur of the past with the ceremonial crown-wearings which his father had done away with in his reign. Richard enjoyed daily displays of his majesty. Bishop Hugh of Lincoln found him attending the mass seated on a throne at the door of the chapel of Château Gaillard, the bishops of Durham and Ely stationed at his feet.[230] Richard had a powerful sensibility of his kingship and he was fond of making it known.

The image of his father Henry II given in the sources is somewhat different. Signs of his interest in royal ceremonial are rare. According to Walter Map, he would have learned from his mother, the Empress Mathilda, to delay any business that his subjects clamoured for him to deal with promptly. A hawk that is fed little, she said, is more easy to tame. She also advised him to stay often in his chamber and to make few decisions in public. Henry II seems to have learned the first lesson, if Peter of Blois is to be believed; he reproached the king for dragging out decisions that he could have made on the spot.[231] On the other hand, in contrast to his mother's preferences, Henry liked big crowds. According to Walter Map, his relations with his people were very warm: 'Whenever he went out the crowds tugged at him and hustled him where he did not want to go. But what was astonishing was that he heard each of them with patience and in spite of the press of people which pushed him about, he did not rebuke anyone and showed no sign of irritation.'[232] This evidence was confirmed by Peter of Blois who put in Henry II's mouth the following complaint in his conversation with the abbot of Bonneval: 'At the mass I am petitioned not just by laypeople but also by clerics and monks, who do not cease from harrassing me with their demands despite the reverence due to the holy sacrament.'[233] The king went beyond etiquette on his subjects' behalf. He was undeniably open to them. His household never acted as a barrier between Henry and the common folk.

Naturally Henry's courtiers could gain access to him more easily. The places where the king enjoyed a certain privacy were in fact few within his palace. His bedchamber was no refuge from those who wanted to see him. Some of them succeeded indeed in waking him up, despite his chamberlain's efforts to keep them out. If we are to believe Jordan Fantosme, the messenger carrying news of the victory at Alnwick did just that, in the middle of the night.[234] Henry II knew nothing of the formality and inaccessibility which would be invariable for kings at the end of the Middle Ages. Henry's son, John, adopted a very different image, that of a timorous king avoiding contact with his people. The *History of William Marshal* portrays him as distrustful and suspicious, always afraid of an assault on his person and the approach of strangers, travelling by night and cutting short his stays in towns and villages so as not to have to meet the people.[235] John preferred to keep to himself and make his decisions in secret. Were these problems in his personality or actual expressions of a new and more effective way of governing and gaining respect?

A final trait appears to be characteristic of Henry II's public appearances. His dress was never showy. Gerald of Barry said that he introduced to England the Angevin fashion for short cloaks, which contrasted with the long robes and trains of the reign of Henry I, which the monk Orderic Vitalis thought characteristic of decadent and effeminate courtiers.[236] William fitz Stephen records how Henry II, plainly dressed and laughing at Thomas Becket's furs, would have taken them to give to a beggar in London, as a way of criticizing his love of luxury.

Before he was ordained priest, Becket affected a degree of ostentation considerably more spectacular than the king's. Proof of this is the sumptuousness of the embassy described by William, which Thomas led to Paris in the summer of 1158 in his capacity as envoy of Henry II to negotiate the marriage between the Young Henry and Margaret of France. His entry into Paris outdid a king's. Two hundred and fifty footmen sang as they pulled his coach; others held his greyhounds on leashes. Six carts carried his baggage and two others were loaded with beer. Each cart, guarded by chained dogs, was pulled by five horses ridden by a monkey on its collar-piece. Twenty-eight palfreys followed carrying gold, silver, bales of silk, books and liturgical ornaments. By itself, the chancellor's immediate entourage consisted of two hundred squires keeping shields, and likewise knights mounted on warhorses, riding in pairs, and also falconers. Thomas rode last with a few of his intimates. As had been calculated, faced by such a show, the Parisians cried out: 'How magnificent must be the king of England, if his chancellor travels in such style!'[237] Displaying his wealth was an effective way of exciting the respect and inspiring the fear of an enemy. Paradoxically, it was the minister not the king who was personifying luxury and largesse here.

Royal dignity was not incompatible with open displays of good fellowship and sustained trust. Adam of Eynsham records that Henry II, angry with Hugh of Lincoln, who had excommunicated a royal forester, summoned him to Woodstock. On his arrival, the bishop threw him completely off balance: 'How much you resemble your cousins of Falaise!', an open allusion to the bastardy of his ancestor. Contrary to expectation, Henry gave a roar of laughter.[238] This good humour was the very opposite of the edgy susceptibility in matters of honour that might have been expected in a king whose dignity and authority was being defied. But the laughter can be explained. It was a response, in part, to a comment which, apparently impertinent, in fact only served to point out the dynastic legitimacy of the accession of Henry II to the throne of Normandy.[239] But more important still, it appeared to be a way of dispersing a powerful tension, at least for a while.

The same reaction could have well been provoked also by the words of a jester, a person charged to say aloud what everyone was thinking to the man who had supreme power. This sort of entertainer is frequent in the sources. In 1180 the Norman Exchequer paid forty shillings to one of them, Roger, to meet Henry II with two horses and seven dogs. Henry also confirmed a serjeanty in Suffolk to a certain Roland on condition that he performed his antics and his scatalogical jokes before him at Christmas.[240] In 1200, John granted to the fool William Picolf the manor of L'Oisellerie and the lands of Champeaux and Mesnil-Ozenne in the county of Mortain.[241] These jesters, expected to stay at court, enjoyed a precise social and political role. They amused the king and in passing sometimes poked fun at him, with the intention that he come down off his pedestal and be closer to his subjects. A certain liberty of tone prevailed at court, where professional comedians at times defused quarrels in the royal household. Jesting seems to have been a safety valve for the frictions and rivalries at the heart of power. In a way, their freedom to speak was not unlike the outspoken criticism of the reformists at court, who were hardly putting their lives on the line when making their moral point to the king. The king took it in good part and displayed a genuine sociability towards his subjects so as to gain their trust.

This image of the king, communicating something of an air of unself-consciousness and definite friendliness towards his subjects, had its political consequences. The image matched up with a period when the concept of kingship related more to 'consensualism' than to 'absolutism'. Respect for law and his subjects' protection made up part of the contract that the king entered into with his people in his coronation oath. The anointing, which might be understood as a source of supernatural power, tied the hands of the king who received it from the bishops. Magna Carta, imposed on the king in 1215 by the nobility and the clergy, features in this context, considerably limiting the recognized executive power of the king. To gain their wider ends, the Plantagenets subjected themselves to higher authorities by fealty and homage. For one or other reason, the king of France, the German emperor and the pope became their lord. The majesty of the first Angevins was neither inaccessible nor all-powerful. It bore little resemblance to the absolute monarchy of the modern period. The Plantagenets embodied a transitional idea of monarchy.

The stuff of legend

The Plantagenets maintained a special link with the past, which they wanted to make their own for the purposes of propaganda. The numerous historians who had been recruited to their cause committed their exploits to writing. They also dealt with the Plantagenet lineage, recalling the high deeds of their ancestors. Some of them did very well out of royal patronage. Wace and Benoit de Sainte-Maure were commissioned by Henry II to write down in French the history of their Norman forebears.[242] Peter of Blois's letters tell us that he had drafted a history of the deeds of Henry II, which either he did not finish or is now lost.[243] It was perhaps either Wace or Benoit's work that King John ordered to be brought from Westminster to Windsor on 29 April 1205, which proves that the kings did look at and use them.[244] Other chroniclers kept up occasional links with the court, without being in royal service. Such was Roger, rector of Howden (Yorkshire), justice of the forests in the north and sometime ambassador to the pope for Richard the Lionheart, whom he accompanied to the Holy Land.[245] The most reputedly independent-minded of historians turn out in the end to have some sympathy for the Plantagenet dynasty, through connections with its courtiers. So William of Newburgh was friends with Philip de Poitou, the intimate of Richard the Lionheart.[246] The list of chroniclers in more or less direct contact with the Angevin dynasty could be further extended.

The example of these writers shows, if it were really necessary, that historical writing was all too often a job for hire in the king's interest.[247] Manipulation of memory was another integral part of the propaganda that the Plantagenet monarchy fostered so as to pass on a positive image of its dynasty.[248] It concerned the political conduct of the kings then in power, naturally enough. But it also had a lot to do with what happened in times long before the period 1154–1224. We will analyse here the method which led the chroniclers of the Angevin empire to defer to them, according to a chronology which begins with the latest of them and ends with the earliest, a method borrowed in many of its respects from the genealogy of Wace, known as a 'reverse chronicle'.

The Plantagenets carefully nurtured the memory of their more recent maternal ancestors, whether Anglo-Saxon or Norman. Edward the Confessor, who had died in an odour of sanctity in 1066, was the first to benefit from this dynastic link. Henry II urged Pope Alexander III to begin Edward's canonization process, which came to fruition in February 1161. On 13 October 1163, two years later, there was a translation of Edward's relics at Westminster, the place of the coronation. The cult of Edward in the abbey's sanctuary added further distinction to the coronation ceremony and stressed the sacred character of Edward's successors on the throne, endowed, as he was, with thaumaturgical powers.[249] It is no coincidence that the translation ceremony happened while a council was also being held at Westminster in which Thomas Becket for the first time openly opposed the king over ecclesiastical justice. In the context of his bitter dispute with the clergy, the sainthood of an English king, ratified at Rome, had its uses for Henry II.

In the context of genealogy, the king's interests were just as well served by the hagiographical tracts composed for the occasion of Edward's translation. They asserted that Henry II was truly the legitimate successor of the last Anglo-Saxon king of England. Already around the year 1138, Osbert de Clare, prior of Westminster, in his *Life of Edward*, had ignored the role of Godwin, father of Harold, and his family in royal government, so as to bring to the fore the rights of the dukes of Normandy to succeed the Confessor.[250] The Cistercian abbot, Ailred of Rievaulx (*c.*1110–1167) writing a new *Life of Edward*, just before his translation in 1163, laid stress on the ancestors of Henry II, to whom he dedicated the work. Ailred said that Henry was the cornerstone joining two walls, that is, the English and Norman races. Henry fulfilled in his person the prophetic vision Edward the Confessor experienced on his deathbed: the fruit of a tree which had been riven in two, and so recovering its unity and flower again, was none other than Henry himself, the son of the Empress Mathilda, who successfully brought together in her lineage claims to the lands on either side of the Channel.[251] Ailred's interpretation of the prophecy countered the pessimism of Osbert, for whom the image of the shattered tree symbolized a unification which was not achievable.[252] Ailred wrote his *Genealogy of the Kings of England* in the same period in much the same sort of spirit. It opens with a poetic eulogy on Henry II, whose family origins Ailred has determined to trace. Among his ancestors and kinsfolk feature St Margaret of Scotland, the pious King Alfred the Great and Edward the Confessor, whose example the new king ought to follow assiduously so as to enjoy eternal blessedness.[253] The coincidences between the two little tracts is very striking. It can probably be explained as the result of a commission from the king or his household to Ailred, who was one of the best Latinists of his day and age.

Some months after this, a nun of Barking – who can perhaps be identified with Clemencia, author of the life of St Katherine – adapted and translated into Anglo-Norman Ailred's *Life of St Edward*.[254] She inserted in her text some elements of the genealogy of 'the glorious king Henry', liberator of England and benefactor of the Church, borrowed from Ailred's other tract. In it, Henry belongs on one side to the holy line of Normandy, represented by Count Robert, Richard the Good and William the noble bastard, and also by Emma, mother of St Edward. On the other side he was the heir of the Anglo-Saxons through the marriage of Henry I, his maternal grandfather, to Mathilda of Scotland, whose maternal great-grandfather, King Edmund (1016) was half-brother of Edward the Confessor. Such vague links did not prevent the nun from asserting that this marriage restored the ancient dynasty of the Confessor, not by fear or by force, but by love. At once both English and French, Henry II was 'born of a holy lineage' (v. 108) that he continued through his children: 'So God save our king, their father, and our queen, their mother. May he keep them in true sanctity, peace, joy and prosperity, and give them power to defeat those who planned to make war on them.' (vv. 4996–5006). This prayer would have been written rather differently some years later, when Henry's sons had rebelled on several occasions against him. But on the poet's side, it shows an open intention to construct propaganda in favour of the Angevin dynasty.

This wish to exalt the power of the Plantagenet dynasty is scarcely odd in the abbey of Barking, whose abbatial election was under royal control. At the beginning of the twelfth century, Mathilda of Scotland herself, the wife of Henry I, and the other Mathilda, wife of King Stephen, had appointed the abbesses there. At the time when the anonymous nun was writing in honour of Henry II, the head of the convent was Adela, sister of Eustace fitz John, faithful supporter of the Empress Mathilda during the civil war. Mary, sister of Thomas Becket, would succeed Adela in 1173. She would be nominated by Henry II as recompense for the persecution he had launched against Becket's family before the archbishop's murder. A third Mathilda, illegitimate daughter of Henry II and a certain Joan (whose name is all we know about her), would be abbess of Barking in the last quarter of the twelfth century.[255] Such royal control of a nunnery's affairs was scarcely exceptional in the political and religious context of the time. It partly explains the obsequious treatment given Henry II's genealogy under the abbacy of Adela fitz John.

On 11 March 1162, a year and a half before the translation of Edward the Confessor's relics at Westminster, Henry II was present at a ceremony at the abbey of Holy Trinity of Fécamp, which was situated in a port of the Pays de Caux and which was one of the mausoleums of the dukes of Normandy, right next to their palace.[256] A prestigious relic was venerated there, the Holy Blood of Christ, acquired in one of two ways according to varying historiographical traditions. According to certain sources, it derived from a miracle which happened during a mass that a priest called Isaac was celebrating on 5 June 989 in a village near Fécamp, as the duke was attending the dedication of the abbey church. The oldest version of this story is drawn from the work of a monk of Fécamp writing at the end of the eleventh century, at the time when the eucharistic debate around Berengar of Tours was reaching its peak. In another version of around 1120, the precious Blood of Fécamp derived from the wounds of Christ and had been acquired by Nicodemus as Christ was placed in his tomb.[257] In 1162, the remains of Richard I (942–996) and his son Richard II (996–1026) were exhumed and placed together behind the high altar of the abbey.[258] The reputation for sanctity of these two ancestors of Henry II, particularly the first of them, was already established. Dudo of St Quentin (died a.1043) said that the father enjoyed eternal bliss because in life he had personified the gospel beatitudes, while William of Malmesbury (c.1080–c.1142) portrayed Richard II as a would-be monk and generous restorer of ruined monasteries.[259] On 19 July 1171, a dozen years after the translation of his remains, the links between Richard I, the indirect agent of the miracle of the consecration by the priest Isaac, and the Holy Blood were once more strengthened. On that date, Abbot Henry de Sully, cousin and friend of Henry II, future abbot of Gloucester and bishop of Worcester, discovered on beginning repairs to his fire-damaged abbey a reliquary phial set in a column where the saintly duke may well

have hidden it to avoid its desecration.[260] This discovery undeniably added
to the reputation of Richard I, Henry II's Norman ancestor, venerator and
protector of the Holy Blood. Just as with Edward the Confessor, Henry II
fostered – indeed commissioned – a vernacular history of Duke Richard's
life and, along with him his son Richard II, aiming at a similar elevation
to sainthood.

This vernacular history in question came from the head of Wace, sometime knight, turned clerk,[261] born of a noble family of Jersey. His *Roman
de Brut* (1155), a French verse adaptation of the *Historia Regum Britanniae*
(1138) of Geoffrey of Monmouth, had become an outright sensation. It
may be that Wace, great grandson of Thurstan, chamberlain of Robert
the Magnificent, through his mother, had hopes of imitating his ancestor
and finding a post in the ducal court by attracting the attention of Eleanor
of Aquitaine, the likely dedicatee of his first book.[262] However that may
be, Henry II summoned Wace to court in 1160 and he obtained a canon's
prebend at Bayeux so that, free from material concerns, he might tell the
story of Henry's ducal predecessors.[263] Wace devoted his time to reading
Norman chronicles, listening to epic poems, researching local oral traditions
and even studying the charters of the archives of his own cathedral and
of St Stephen of Caen.[264] Using this material he began the *Roman de Rou*
('Rou' being Rollo, the first Norman duke), where he tells us that he had
been present at the translation of the ducal remains at Fécamp in March
1162. He records, amongst other things, three of the miraculous doings
of Richard I, who in his lifetime drove off three demonic manifestations.
Unfortunately this was not enough, apparently, for his patron the king.

As Jean-Guy Gouttebroze points out,[265] in comparison with the early
Norman chroniclers or Ailred of Rievaulx, Wace never made much of
the sacral status of the dukes, as Henry had expected that he would. Wace
avoided the sort of dynastic promotion which suggested hereditary supernatural powers within the houses of England and Normandy. Does his
silence betray a Gregorian attitude to kingship, stripped of its sacramental
powers so as to promote those of the clergy? Was it influenced by the same
ecclesiological stance, inimical to royal sacrality and supportive to clerical
freedom, which is revealed by the letters between Henry de Beaumont,
bishop of Wace's church of Bayeux, and John of Salisbury, leader of the
company of clerics exiled by the king? If this was the case, Wace's position
of offical historian to Henry II was untenable during the years 1164–1170,
dominated by the Becket affair. Although it was hardly outspoken, Wace's
distancing himself from the king brought his activity as court historian
into question. Wace was not politically correct.

Wace was less than enthusiastic about certain early members of the dynasty. This had its origin perhaps in the distance that he knew an objective historian must maintain with regard to personalities and events. Wace disliked the sort of panegyric that the king wanted in return for his generosity. He was no blind admirer of William the Conqueror, whose right to the succession to England over Harold did not seem to him all that obvious. In this view he was perhaps following the *History of the English* (1135–1138) of Gaimar, who criticized the cruellest features of the Norman conquest of England. Wace also implied that Robert Curthose had a better right to England than his younger brother Henry I, who was of course the grandfather of Henry II.[266] Wace's pen slashed off the fairest flowers of the Plantagenet family tree. Apart from this, Wace was a member of the aristocracy of Lower Normandy and his flattering treatment of the history of several Norman families was not particularly appropriate after 1173, when they had rallied to the rebellion of Eleanor of Aquitaine and her sons.[267] All these attitudes betrayed Wace's strong independence, and his freedom of spirit scarcely befitted a canon provided for out of the good offices of the king. The disagreement between Henry II and Wace was more ideological than artistic.[268]

This disagreement was why Henry II dispensed with Wace. At his instruction, he abruptly stopped writing the *Rou*, while discretely expressing his regret at the attitude of his late patron.[269] He was soon replaced by Benoît de Sainte-Maure, a writer born in the Touraine whose recent *Roman de Troie* (1165), a French epic of the Homeric wars, had attracted some enthusiasm amongst the nobility. Perhaps Benoît had some plan of eventually getting a benefice from the king of England for writing the *Roman*. At the end of a long misogynistic rant he went on to add a eulogy to 'the rich wife of the rich king' (line 13,469) 'who is brimming with all knowledge' (line 13,466), as a sort of apology towards the sex he had been running down. Doubtless this was intended as a dedication to Eleanor of Aquitaine, whom he would have really liked to have as a patron.[270] If such was his hope it would be fulfilled one day at the expense of Wace.

The new official historian of the dukes of Normandy accomplished his commission with sustained energy, which in no way displeased his patron. His work contained the story of Norman history up to 1135, in more than 44,000 verses. Compared to him Wace, who stopped at the year 1106 after some 16,000 verses, might seem to have been a bit of a dilettante.[271] But as Elisabeth van Houts has explained, Benoît confined himself to translating Robert de Torigny's version of the *Deeds of the Dukes of Normandy*, livening it up with some long rhetorical digressions, which explains the frenetic nature of its composition. Wace, for his part, worked like a real historian, piecing together a lot of thin source material to construct an original text in which it is still possible to detect his own individual touch.[272] His supposed slowness should be put down to his scrupulosity.

Unlike Wace, Benoît was a devoted royalist. He was the mouthpiece of his master and padded out his work with flattering references to Henry II and his ancestors, the dukes of Normandy.[273] He stressed the affection that the dukes showed their barons, who repaid it with staunch loyalty and obedience.[274] More significant is his sketch of Duke Richard I. Firstly he makes much of the initiative of 'the good king, the son of the good Empress Mathilda, Henry II, flower of the world's princes' (vv. 32058–32061) in exhuming the duke's remains in 1162, whereas Wace does not so much as mention that Henry was present at the ceremony. In Benoît's work, Henry's maternal ancestry restored his Norman ascendancy. Secondly, Benoît criticizes Wace for passing over in silence the faith and love Richard I had for God: 'It makes me unhappy that his deep learning has been ignored, as Master Wace did and as I never would have done' (vv. 25836–25839). According to Benoît, Duke Richard drew on his theological knowledge and his native intelligence to instruct and convert his Viking followers. He was like Edward the Confessor in his piety, his charity and the attention he devoted to the welfare of his people.[275] Benoît recovered for kingship the religious authority that Wace had wanted to forget. Nothing is more obvious in this vernacular work which he had commissioned, overseen and directed, than the fingerprints of Henry II.

Although the Plantagenets found deep Anglo-Saxon and Norman roots, thanks to the complaisance of certain Latin chroniclers and French poets, they did not ignore their Angevin ancestors. Encouraging the writing of historiography to recall the great deeds of their paternal lineage was not without its dangers. The reputation of the house of Anjou had been low in Normandy in the 1130s when the chronicler, Orderic Vitalis (1075–1142) monk of St-Evroul, had described its members and soldiers during their raids on the Norman frontier as barbarians capable of unheard-of violence.[276] The work which Wace and Benoît had been commissioned to do had as its purpose the ending of this old rivalry, by restructuring the Norman view of history to the benefit of the new king of England.

This work was not, however, incompatible with the patronage of the Angevin historiography which Henry pursued. He mobilized the monks of Marmoutier, close to Tours, to work on the history of his father's lineage, as they had done in earlier times.[277] At the beginning of the reign of his father, Geoffrey Plantagenet, Eudes, abbot of Marmoutier, had begun the first version of the *Chronicle of the Counts of Anjou*. In the 1160s this text was copied, modified and brought up to date by Thomas, prior of Loches, Robin, Breton d'Amboise, and John of Marmoutier. John added a dedication to Henry II as a preamble to two manuscripts of the chronicle which he had revised.[278] A number of interventions of the king of England, or people close to him, in the *chansons de geste*, bringing the ancient Angevin rulers to the fore in the vernacular should not be ruled out. The *chansons* circulated the Latin historical tradition of Marmoutier rather further than just the local region. In some ways they can be compared with the works commissioned from Wace and Benoît.

It is interesting to find in an epic of the end of the twelfth century the ancient claim of the count of Anjou to the stewardship of the king of France, which also appears in the chronicles of Marmoutier. In 1158, Hugh de Claye, a knight of the countryside around Angers and faithful member of Henry II's household, dedicated an entire tract to the subject. In his version Robert the Strong, ancestor of the Capetians mentioned in 866, gave the command of the French army in heredity to Count Geoffrey Grisgonelle of Anjou (958–987).[279] Now, the oldest known version of the *Song of Roland*, written down *c*.1160–1170 in a manuscript now in the Bodleian Library in Oxford, was probably altered at the court of Henry II. In the *Song*, Count Geoffrey of Anjou – in whose proximity the scribe of the Bodleian *Song* twice introduced a kinsman called Henry, not found in other versions – was seneschal and banner-bearer of Charlemagne. In support of these attributions, Geoffrey overrules the royal court's decision to release Ganelon, whose treason was proved during a judicial duel where his champion was defeated by Thierry, Geoffrey's own brother.[280] The taste for the *Song* can be found in Mathilda, daughter of Henry II and wife of Henry the Lion, duke of Saxony and Bavaria, who commissioned a German translation of it from Conrad the Priest.[281] The Plantagenets' rule of Aquitaine made the *Song of Roland* even more of their family's business. The relics of those who fell at Roncesvaux were venerated at Bordeaux, Blaye and Belin, in northern Gascony. Local churches also preserved Durendaal and the oliphant. The *Pilgrim's Guide to Santiago de Compostella*, probably written by Aimery Picaud, a clerk of Parthenay (Poitou), dwelt at some length on these relics.[282] So by the sleight-of-hand of using their ancestors, the Plantagenets succeeded in hijacking a fair amount of the legend of Roland, which might have been supposed to be the exclusive property of the kings of France.

The literary success of the Angevin companions of Roland did not stop there. Many other *chansons de geste* of the end of the twelfth and thirteenth century make a point of echoing the exploits of Geoffrey Grisgonelle and his brothers: *Aspremont, Gaydon, Renaud de Montauban, Fierabras,* the *Chanson de Saisnes* and *Girart de Rousillon.*[283]

The relevance of the *Chanson d'Aspremont* for our purposes is clear. Its most recent editor goes so far as to assert, maybe too decisively, that it was 'a political song to the glory of a great royal dynasty, the Plantagenets.' He sees its patrons in Baderon of Monmouth (died 1190/1) and his wife, Rohese de Clare, great Anglo-Norman nobles.[284] The *Chanson d'Aspremont,* telling of the war between Charlemagne and Roland against the moslems in Calabria, has Geoffrey amongst the immediate retinue of the emperor. Another of his warriors, Girart de Fraite, lord of Gascony and Auvergne and enemy of the archbishop of Canterbury, bears the nickname 'Lionheart'. The comparison with Richard the Lionheart – whose familiarity with *Aspremont* is well-attested by the many quotations made from it by the poet, Ambroise[285] – is all the more easy to make as the song includes allusions to the Calabrian dower lands of Joan, Richard's sister, and to the heroism of a duke of Bavaria, who recalls Richard's brother-in-law, Henry the Lion.

A certain Richard of Normandy plays a fundamental role in *Gaydon.* The title of this epic *chanson* picks up on the nickname of Richard's brother, Thierry duke of Angers, seneschal of Charlemagne and husband of the queen of Gascony. A 'jay' (*gai* in Old French) perched on two occasions on the helmet that Thierry wore during the judicial duel with Pinabel, champion of Ganelon. His family's vengeance against the Angevins is the key part of the book.[286] In passing it is worth noting the ironic portrayal of Charlemagne, making absurd military decisions under the influence of drink. Examples of positive references to the legendary ancestors of the Plantagenets in Carolingian epics might be extended far beyond *Aspremont* and *Gaydon.*

The passages noted here show that Charlemagne, the lord of their Angevin ancestors, was not by any means distant from them. Did they have an ambition to adopt Charlemagne as a prestigious avatar for their own kingship? It is worth mentioning that in 1165 Henry II upheld the case for Charlemagne's canonization to Frederick Barbarossa and the antipope Paschal III.[287] But this manoeuvre came about in special political circumstances. These were those during the alliance between Henry and the German emperor against Louis VII: Henry's request to the imperial antipope seems as though it were a way to put Alexander III under pressure in the context of the Becket affair. A few comparisons between the English kings and Charlemagne can be found in the writings of Peter of Blois, Ralph de

Diceto, Jordan Fantosme and the troubadours Giraut de Borneil and Bertran de Born, men connected to the Plantagenets.[288] But two of them, Bertran de Born and Jordan Fantosme, were more ready to compare Louis VII or Philip Augustus when they brought up the legendary emperor, as if he were French more than anything else. Furthermore, in his *Instruction of Princes*, Gerald of Barry, who made no secret of his respect for the Capetians, asserted that the kings of France were of the line of Charlemagne, a king to whom the Britons and Scots had anciently submitted.[289]

In conclusion, the *chansons de geste* which grew up in the twelfth century around the legendary emperor furthered his appropriation by the Capetians. The reappropriation of Charlemagne by the descendants of Hugh Capet – who might have been considered a usurper on the throne that belonged of right to the Carolingians – was firmly established during the reign of Philip Augustus. The beginnings of this new genealogical sensibility was heralded by the *reditus ad stirpem Karoli*; the marriages by the Capetians into the Carolingian line. It was asserted by the marriage of Philip Augustus with Isabel of Hainault, who, unlike her husband, was directly descended from the mythical emperor.[290] Charlemagne, now seen as an ancestor of the king of France and even its tutelary and emblematic figure, belonged from then on more to St-Denis than to Aachen. He had become more Capetian than Hohenstaufen. Although depicted as a drunk, he remained the lord of the Angevins in the epics, who owed him their obedience and service.

This was why the Plantagenets' use of Charlemagne as a political cat's-paw was so very dangerous. It was therefore worth their while to devote themselves to a different prestigious dynastic forebear, one with more capacity to be useful to them. Under Henry II, and even more after the beginning of the reign of Richard the Lionheart, this role fell on Arthur, king of the Britons. The transplantation of Arthur into the ideological sphere of the Plantagenets became a major political strategy to which the historian Amaury Chauou has recently dedicated an entire book.[291] Of course, we know very little about the historical Arthur, who lived in the sixth century, and the story of his life is obscured by many medieval additions and alterations. The *Annales Cambriae* (950), which can be filled out by some earlier but less reliable sources, tell us that Arthur was the commander of a British army at Mount Badon (516) in the south of England against the Saxons. He fell some years later with a certain Mordred at the battle of Camlann (537).[292] He was an important military chief of the Celtic resistance to the Germanic invaders, whom the chroniclers elevated to the rank of hero of the British independence struggle.

Legend very quickly caught hold of Arthur. A number of stories were current on the subject in the Celtic-speaking area, drawn in their turn from ancient folkloric sources going back beyond the sixth century. *Culhwch ac Olwen*, a Welsh story in prose dating probably to the eleventh century, dressed up Arthur in the guise of a demigod whose underground court, where he reigned as a generous provider of banquets, was the home of outstanding warriors able to fight giants and monsters and to produce cauldrons full of treasure.[293] Professional bards circulated these tales. These poets often knew Latin and the Romance languages, which enabled them to travel far and wide on the continent. So Bléhéri, who can be identified with the Welsh magnate Bleddri ap Kadifor (*fl.*1116–1135), visited the court of Poitiers. Bleddri's stay, mentioned by the Flemish writer Walcher de Denain at the beginning of the thirteenth century, explains how Macabru (*fl.*1130–*c.*1149) and Cercamon (*fl.*1137–*c.*1149), two troubadours of the entourage of William IX of Aquitaine, mention Arthur and Tristran in their songs.[294] Well before the time of Henry II, several wandering singers were spreading the Arthurian myth throughout the West.

The circulation of the legend might have stayed limited without the work of Geoffrey of Monmouth (*c.*1100–1155). Geoffrey, master and canon of Oxford and later elected to the see of St Asaph (Llanelwy, in Wales) was, in 1130, the author of the prophecies of Merlin, which he incorporated eight years later in his *History of the Kings of Britain*, destined to have a remarkable literary future. The *History*, a work in Latin, mixed outright fiction drawn from its author's fertile imagination with facts trawled from Celtic oral traditions and ancient histories.[295] Geoffrey followed the great deeds of ninety-nine kings of Britain over two thousand years, from the arrival of the Trojans (supposed founder of their dynasty) up to the expulsion of the Britons by the Anglo-Saxons. A third of the book is taken up with the deeds of Arthur, son of King Uther. He defeated the Saxons and crushed the Picts and Scots before conquering not just Ireland but France, Scandinavia and Iceland. He married Guinevere, a woman of the ancient Roman nobility with whom he went on to endow the life of his court with considerable style. But Arthur was betrayed by his nephew Mordred who seduced Guinevere, made an alliance with the Saxons and defeated him. He retired stricken to the Isle of Avalon. In his *Life of Merlin*, written around 1150, Geoffrey added some more precision to his work. It was the fairy, Morgana, who carried off Arthur in her boat to tend his wounds.[296] As he left it, Geoffrey's body of writing and tales enjoyed an unheard-of success. There remain two hundred and fifteen medieval manuscripts of the *History of the Kings of Britain*, of which fifty or so belong to the twelfth century, a total unmatched for any other historical work of the same period.[297]

Translations of the *History* into Anglo-Norman raised the total further. Six of them seem to have been in circulation during Geoffrey's own lifetime.[298] The most influential was the *Histoire des Bretons*, now lost, written a little before 1140 by the clerk Geoffrey Gaimar, who had got hold of Geoffrey's *History* not long after its first appearance. Gaimar was an active member of a literary circle within the higher nobility of England, centred on Robert of Gloucester, Geoffrey's patron and dedicatee of the *History*. Gaimar says that he had borrowed his manuscript of the *History* from Constance, wife of Ralph fitz Gilbert, who had got it herself from Walter Espec, a Yorkshire baron. Walter was the patron and founder of the Cistercian abbey of Rievaulx, where lived the scholar, Ailred. We have already met some of these nobles, who belonged (with their wives) to the class of 'literate knights' (*milites litterati*), patrons of Anglo-Norman literature in the daily language of the ruling élite employed as a sign of social distinction and cultural domination.[299] They came into contact with the young Henry Plantagenet, come to England to regain the heritage of his mother the Empress Mathilda by arms with the support of Robert of Gloucester, his guardian.

Wace, late comer to holy orders after an early life as a soldier, might very well have been one of this circle. Just like the rest, he was enthusiastic about Geoffrey of Monmouth's book, which he undertook around 1155 to put into French octosyllabic verse in the *Roman de Brut*. Wace produced a very free adaptation of the *History*, rather than a translation. He expanded on Geoffrey's descriptions, adding numerous passages of his own invention, picturesque details to capture the public imagination. He transformed the image of Arthur – just lately presented to the public by Geoffrey as a high-handed autocrat and ruthless warrior, who had his enemies massacred. With Wace Arthur became a feudal monarch, full of consideration towards his vassals, whom he respected, protected and to whom he listened: a king who sat with them at a round table, something mentioned for the first time in his *Brut*.[300] When Arthur went to war he was no longer a ruthless murderer, sparing neither man nor horse and perfectly capable of sending the corpse of its defeated emperor back to Rome as a sign of complete contempt. In a mirror image to Geoffrey's portrayal, Wace pictured an Arthur who did not go to war except in the last resort, and with the single aim of restoring peace. His Arthur was chivalrous in combat, he was now devoid of aggression towards his enemies – even whose horses were not deliberately injured. He had the emperor's remains buried with the respect owed to an enemy fallen on the field of honour. His Arthur was condescending and generous towards all who came before him 'to learn of his courtesy,' (v. 1235) the prime virtue in the magnificent courtly world imagined by Wace in the *Brut*. Arthur's court became a magnet for every young warrior with ambitions to be a knight.[301] Wace made Arthur into the 'most virtuous, famous and glorious of knights' (vv. 477-8), endowed with every physical and moral virtue, whom kings and lords could only admire and imitate. Completely transformed in his manner, Wace's character became the paragon of the chevalier-king.

Arthur was also subjected to an equally significant makeover as to his nationality. Geoffrey of Monmouth wrote in praise of the Britons and even more so of his Welsh fellow-countrymen, whom he portrayed as an unconquerable race of British Celts who had survived every invasion. This was how he tried to make the Welsh respectable, when contemporary English intellectuals were fashioning a reputation for them as cruel barbarians, barely past the pastoral stage of civilization.[302] It is in the light of this double vision concerning the British past that the rejection of Geoffrey's work by William of Newburgh may best be understood. He poured scorn on the 'ridiculous fictions', good only to flatter Welsh vanity. The same was true of Gerald of Barry, who said that the demons who fled from a Gospel of John fell with enthusiasm on a copy of the *History of the Kings of Britain*.[303] It is true that Geoffrey on occasion showed open hostility towards the Normans, the latest of the invaders of Britain. A prophecy of Merlin, inspired by old Welsh poems attributed to his Celtic homonym, Myrddin, or just invented by Geoffrey in the period Stephen was fighting Mathilda and the knights she had brought with her from Normandy, did not spare the Normans: 'Out Neustrians! Cease from bearing arms and oppressing the free man by aggressive warriors! There is nothing left for you to devour, for you have consumed everything that fertile Nature has produced in its goodness. O Christ, come to the aid of your people! Subdue the lions, end the war and give peace and prosperity to the kingdom.'[304] The same anti-Norman spirit can be found in the prophecies collected by John of Cornwall in 1153-1154.[305] Merlin was definitely no friend of the Normans.

Like a good Anglo-Norman, and like a writer eager to attract the favour of Queen Eleanor, Wace decided to give Merlin a facelift. Rather than present him as Arthur's holy and quasi-royal alter ego and the agent of his policies, Wace portrayed him as a magician in royal service. He declared that he would not translate Merlin's prophecies, and it is possible to uncover what was behind his literary prejudice. The lack of Merlin's prophecies in Wace went some way to cancel out the politics in Geoffrey of Monmouth's book, particularly the idea of the imminent salvation of the Britons from Norman oppression. The *Description of England*, written by an anonymous Norman in the 1140s, illustrates something of the current spirit of the British Celtic peoples: 'The Welsh have taken their vengeance. They have massacred many of us French. They have taken many of our castles. They are threatening us fiercely. They openly say that they will take everything. It is thanks to Arthur that they will take back all their land . . . that they will call New Britain.'[306] The *Description* openly talks of the help that the return of Arthur will bring to a Wales in rebellion. So far as Wace is concerned, suppressing Merlin's prophecies and the Celtic nationalism of the mythical king was all the more understandable as in 1155, just before the *Brut* was published, the Welsh princes Owain of Gwynedd and Rhys ap Gruffudd had successfully attacked Norman garrisons in Wales and as the new king Henry II had prepared a counter-attack.[307] Wace was in fact constructing an Arthur who was no longer a king of the Britons but a king of all the English – Celts as much as the Anglo-Saxons and Normans – races which were at that time beginning to find a common identity.[308]

At the time, Arthur and the knights of the Round Table stimulated a considerable fashion amongst French writers who, by distancing them from their British origins, slowly fashioned them into cosmopolitan heroes belonging to the corpus of Western literature. These writers had some links with Henry II, the former ward of Robert of Gloucester, the patron of Geoffrey of Monmouth. The famous and brilliant Chrétien de Troyes (*fl.*1160–1190) worked at the court of Mary of Champagne, daughter of Eleanor of Aquitaine's first marriage. Chrétien knew England well and he had lived there perhaps.[309] Marie de France, the author (*c.*1160) of the Celtic lays *Lanval* and *Chèvrefeuille* had very probably also been invited to Henry II's court. It is possible that she was a member of the powerful Beaumont-Meulan family, which held lands on either side of the Channel.[310] At much the same time two other poets introduced King Arthur into their tales of the love of Tristran and Iseult as an incidental character. One was Thomas, who tells us that the source of his tale was Bléhéri and who wrote passionately in praise of London where he had probably met the royal family. The other poet, Béroul, also knew England well and Cornwall in particular, although he used a continental Norman dialect.[311] These works, too often surviving only in fragments, surely only make up a small part of the Anglo-Norman stories once in circulation concerning Arthur.

In the Plantagenet Empire these Arthurian tales were not just written down in the northern French dialects. Around 1175, Robert de Torigny, godfather of one of Henry II's daughters, was the probable author of two Latin Arthurian works: *The Birth of Gawain*, the knight who defended the northern frontier of the kingdom of his uncle Arthur heroically; and a *History of Meriadoc*, another champion of King Arthur, with whose help he avenged the murder of his father.[312] It is known that Robert had access around 1139 to a copy of the *History of the Kings of Britain* at the library of Bec, which was at the time under his care. Between 1191 and 1205, Layamon, priest of Ernley (Worcestershire), adapted the *Roman de Brut* into Middle English, although there is no way of determining any link between his work and the court. Finally, around 1195, the German *Lancelot* of Ulrich von Zatzikhoven was composed from an Anglo-Norman version of the romance, doubtless brought into the Empire by Hugh de Moreville, companion in captivity of Richard the Lionheart.[313] The conclusion can only be that the kings of England were in contact, more or less regularly, directly or indirectly, with the writers who composed the Arthurian corpus.

The Arthurian tales circulated widely, especially in the enormous area that the Plantagenets ruled in Britain and on the continent. It was quite natural that on the level of poetry, the Poitevin, Limousin and Gascon troubadours invoked Arthurian characters. Bertran de Born lamented the death of Geoffrey of Brittany saying that neither Arthur nor Gawain resurrected could replace him. Rigaud de Barbezieux (*fl.*1140–1163) said that he was so enamoured of his lady that he dared ask nothing of her, and compared his dumbness to that of Perceval before the Grail. The lament of Gaucelm Faidit for Richard the Lionheart made him out to be the equal of Arthur. Bertran de Born the Younger (*fl.*1192–1223) celebrated the adventures of Gawain and suggested that he would be a good example for King John if he was to imitate his valour in battle rather devote himself to hunting and wordly diversions and 'allow himself to be disinherited in his own lifetime.'[314] The troubadours of Aquitaine, a region far from the centres from which the Arthurian legend spread, demonstrate a clear familiarity with its matter, which they incorporated in their Occitan *chansons*. To go over the distinction established in their day between the three chief literary themes, the troubadours had mastered the 'matter of Britain', concerning Arthur and his knights, 'the matter of France' concerning Charlemagne, Roland and his companions, and the 'matter of Rome,' which set the romance in ancient times.

The troubadours were not the only ones who developed a passion for the knights of the Round Table, whose stories would come to be the sphere of novelists writing for a lay public. In his *Book of Sacramental Confession*, Peter of Blois could only regret the tears and emotion which afflicted those who heard of the misfortunes of Arthur, Gawain and Tristran, when the same people were not in the least moved by sermons on the love of God.[315] Ailred of Rievaulx said much the same.[316] The Cistercian, Caesarius of Heisterbach (*c*.1180–1240), compiler of a book of sermon *exempla*, chose to go along with it and told the story of an abbot of his monastery who preferred to tell stories of Arthur in his sermons to the lay brothers, to stop them falling asleep and snoring.[317] The use of an Arthurian iconography within religious buildings betrays the same interaction between the sacred and the profane. Two Italian examples are enough to prove it. An archivolt of the cathedral of Modena, carved around 1130, shows Arthur and his warriors in a troop. Thirty or so years later Arthur riding a he-goat was inlaid in a pavement mosaic in a church at Otranto.[318] Widely diffused, the stories of the Round Table were undeniably popular amongst the aristocracies all across the West, but also amongst the clergy and beyond them, in every social and cultural context.

It did not take long for the Plantagenets to attempt to appropriate the Arthurian cycle for themselves. To do this they had an ambition to endow the tomb of Arthur with all the lustre which they could assemble.[319] First they had to find it, because the popularity of this obscure petty king of the sixth century was so recent that time had obliterated all physical trace of him. But despite everything, the tomb's discovery took place in the Benedictine abbey of Glastonbury, located on a hill surrounded by drained marshes – that had the look of an ancient island – in Somerset, a county separated from Wales by the Bristol Channel. Glastonbury was closely linked with the king, who had the nomination of the abbot and had provided to Glastonbury several faithful supporters of his policies. The discovery of Arthur's remains was tellingly described by Gerald of Barry in a section of his *Instruction of the Prince*, written before 1192 and also in his *Speculum Ecclesie*, written around 1217. His account was repeated by two Cistercian sources, Ralph of Coggeshall (*c*.1224) and the chronicle of Margam Abbey in Glamorgan (*c*.1234), whose main significance is that they provide the date of 1191 for the discovery. Gerald's texts give more detail. They might be taken as models of deeply partisan historiography.

The accounts make much of Henry II's initiative, 'who suggested that the body would be found buried six feet or so deep in a hollowed oak trunk, according to the traditions he had heard from a British singer of historical tales.'[320] It was the king who promoted the excavations in the cemetery of Glastonbury, as conveyer of the prediction of the Welsh bard to the monks, rather like an intermediary between Celtic and monastic culture. The legend of a marvellous discovery of the corpse of a warrior at the monastery of Clonmacnoise, attested in the eleventh century, possesses a similar narrative structure. The legend was probably freely adapted by storytellers on either side of the St George's Channel. Gerald's story fuses together British folklore, hagiographical texts on the finding of saints' relics and Latin chronicles telling of the discovery of tombs of emperors, kings and other founders of lineages.

The monks of Glastonbury, under the direction of Henry II, found the remains of a giant bearing ten wounds on his body, and of a woman with blonde hair. So that there should be no doubt about their identity, an inscription was with them: 'Here lies the famous king Arthur, buried with Guinevere his second wife, in the Isle of Avalon.' The bodies were transferred to the abbey church and laid in a marble tomb. Gerald of Barry remarks how this discovery contradicted the legend of the king borne away by spirits into a land of dreams. This myth, hostile to religious orthodoxy, was just as dangerous on the political level, for it left the hope of a messianic return of Arthur to the Britons. This was why, in Gerald's writings, Morgana was only a noble kinswoman of the king, piously concerning herself with Arthur's burial, a woman that the undisciplined imagination of the superstitious bards alone had transformed into a mysterious goddess. The pragmatism of this Gerald, maintaining the outlook of a scholastic clerk, contrasts with the credulity that he usually regarded marvellous tales in his descriptions of Wales and Ireland. Gerald knew how to adapt to the literary genres that he borrowed, to his public, and to the travelling politicians that he was chasing after at the time he wrote.

Keeping in the same scholarly voice, Gerald launched into a long digression on the linguistic evolution of local toponymy to demonstrate that Glastonbury in Anglo-Saxon and Avalon in Brittonic meant precisely the same place, for they both meant 'Isle of Glass'. Gerald added a further detail to his argument. The Virgin painted on Arthur's shield was a reference to the Marian dedication of the abbey, the object of his patronage. In this way Gerald makes use of the tale of the discovery of the relics of the popular King Arthur in two ways: as an elaborate and intellectual disquisition on the identity of Glastonbury and on the absurdity of the British legends concerning the fairyland Isle of Avalon. His emphasis on the active role of Henry II in the discovery establishes yet again, if needed, the efforts of the house of Anjou to promote the public veneration of Arthur's relics.

The king's programme corresponded neatly with that of the monks of Glastonbury, who had long wanted to possess sufficiently famous relics to attract pilgrims and patrons. Already, at the beginning of the twelfth century, the monks had commissioned William, librarian of Malmesbury abbey near Bristol (a member of Robert of Gloucester's literary circle and one of the sources of inspiration for Geoffrey of Monmouth), and other hagiographers to assert the antiquity of their abbey and the prestige of their saints, with the intention of increasing their fame. These authors had never contemplated locating Glastonbury as Arthur's burial place. But nonetheless they did prepare the way involuntarily for its discovery. In his *Deeds of the Kings of England* (1125), William of Malmesbury wrote that, during the reign of the Conqueror, the tomb of Gawain, the son of Arthur's sister, was discovered in Wales, and he added that the tomb of the king of Britain himself had never been found, which gave rise to many legends about his return.[321] At the same period, another of the writers employed by the abbey, the Welshman Caradoc of Llancarfan, composed a life of Saint Gildas, an ascetic long ago resident in a hermitage on the Bristol Channel, then later at Glastonbury where he died and was buried. Caradoc was the first to draw a connection between Glastonbury and Arthur, in telling the story that the king had marched there with a powerful force to recover Guinevere from Melwas, king of Somerset, who had carried her off. The abbot of Glastonbury and Gildas negotiated a reconciliation between the rival kings who, as an acknowledgement, made generous gifts to them.

After 1184, the date when Glastonbury was devastated by a fire, these gifts were, more than ever, sadly lacking. In September 1189, Henry de Sully was summoned from Fécamp to assume the abbacy of Glastonbury, thanks to the personal intervention of Richard the Lionheart – if Adam of Domerham, a monk of the abbey who finished its chronicle at the end of the twelfth century, is to be believed. Henry was well aware that Richard, engaged in a crusade that was swallowing all the Crown's financial resources, would not help him rebuild his abbey. In 1191 he made the discovery of Arthur's tomb which resembled in many respects the finding of the Holy Blood which Henry had promoted at Fécamp nearly thirty years before. At Fécamp and Glastonbury, there were coincidences between the measures taken following an abbey fire and a religious discovery which were striking, to say the least. The discovery of Arthur's remains, following the hints of Welsh bards to the recently deceased Henry II, happened at a turning point. It served two purposes. Firstly, as far as the abbey was concerned it now possessed the remains of the most famous of the British kings; and secondly, so far as the members of the house of Anjou were concerned, they were now the authentic discoverers of the tomb of their mythical forebear. They could no longer be dissatisfied with the antiquity of their lineage. That same year of 1191 at Messina, Richard the Lionheart named his three-year-old nephew, Arthur of Brittany, as his heir to the throne of England. The choice of Arthur was not perhaps that odd following the discovery at Glastonbury, for it brought a name heavy with significance into the heart of the Angevin dynasty.[322] So archaeological discovery and genealogical nostalgia went hand in hand. There was another political benefit: the Plantagenets had now a weighty argument to use against the aristocracies of Wales and Brittany who evoked the 'hope of Britain' – the idea of the messianic return of Arthur – to raise rebellion.

The Plantagenets, discoverers of Arthur's burial, also had an ambition to recover some of his possessions. They carried the swords of legendary heroes, in line with the old belief that the power of its original possessor transferred by means of a weapon. From a Christian perspective, the power of the sword was all the more great as it had been placed on an altar, blessed and delivered on the day of his coronation. In rebellion against his father, the Young Henry took violent possession of Durendaal Roland's sword, kept in the treasury of Rocamadour. His brothers preferred an Arthurian sword gained more lawfully. Richard the Lionheart possessed Excalibur, Arthur's very own sword, which had perhaps come down to him from his grandfather Geoffrey Plantagenet, who may have received it in his turn from Henry I of England on his knighting in 1127.[323] However that might be, the only evidence of Richard's owning Excalibur comes from the Chronicle of Roger of Howden, who wrote that in 1191 Richard offered it to Tancred, king of Sicily, in exchange for twenty ships for the crusade. Arthur enjoyed great popularity in the south of Italy, where Gervase of Tilbury, Caesarius of Heisterbach and the anonymous author of an Occitan Arthurian romance called *Jaufre* (c.1160–1190) all say that Mount Etna, the dwelling place of Morgana la Fay was his last resting place.[324] The name of Excalibur or *Caliburnus* first appears in the work of Geoffrey of Monmouth. Its Celtic etymology perhaps derived from *Chalybs* (steel) or *Caled-fuwulch* (heavy cutter). Wace said that it had been forged on the Isle of Avalon and Layamon added that its swordsmith was the elf, Wygar.[325] The legend of the stone from which the young Arthur supposedly pulled it, was inspired by an edifying anecdote about St Wulfstan (1062–1095) told by Osbert de Clare around 1138. Wulfstan defied his opponents by placing his cross on the tombstone of Edward the Confessor and telling them to pick it up, which they were incapable of doing. The transfer of this story into the Arthurian corpus had occurred by the 1210s in the work of Robert de Boron.[326] It is yet more evidence of the vitality of the Arthurian myth, a constant object of adaptation and accretion.

Just like Richard, his brother, John also had a sword which drew its fame from the Arthurian cycle. He had since 1189 enjoyed the appanage of the county of Cornwall, the legendary kingdom of Mark, husband of Iseult, in the south-west of England. An inventory of 1207 talked of the 'sword of Tristan' amongst his regalia. Around 1250 it is called Curtana. Tristan had used it against the Irish giant, Morholt, breaking it in his skull where one of its pieces remained embedded. This is why later sources on the coronation of modern kings of England tell us that it featured a notch.[327] The episode of the fight with a giant was all the more central to the romance of Tristan in that it was Iseult who dressed his wounds and it is with this that certain versions of their romance began. Another indication of the adoption of this particular hero by the Plantagenets might be the mention, around 1225, of Tristan's shield being of golden lions on red in a Norse saga, the same arms carried by the Angevin kings of England. This coincidence is still a matter of debate, however:[328] around 1270 the pavement of Chertsey abbey, showing the victory over Morholt, features a lion rampant on Tristan's shield. The conclusion is that John and his successors had understood how to turn a great hero of the Arthurian cycle to the benefit of their dynasty.

The image of Arthur, as it was transmitted by the romances whose writing the Plantagenets fostered, matched neatly with their military policy of hegemony abroad and consolidation at home. Arthur, their mythical predecessor, was a warrior, a military chief (*dux bellorum*), to quote William of Malmesbury and Geoffrey of Monmouth, a king armed on horseback surrounded by a solid and disciplined household.[329] The purpose of his ceaseless warring was not just to defend his lands but also to conquer new ones. Geoffrey of Monmouth told at great length the story of Arthur's campaigns in Great Britain, and then of his conquest of Gaul from the Romans, and following him so did Wace, although in a more chivalric spirit. The imperialism of Arthur was of significance first of all in the British Isles. Gerald of Barry had nothing but praise for him in his *Conquest of Ireland*, written to glorify the campaigns of Strongbow and Henry II.[330] At the time of the war against William the Lion of Scotland, Robert de Torigny repeated how in days gone by Arthur had ridden gallantly to the relief of the Chateau des Pucelles, besieged by a pagan king in the north of Great Britain.[331] During the reign of King John, Layamon invented a tribute of sixty boats full of fish which the king of the Orkneys was supposed to send annually to Arthur, a passage not found in his source text by Wace.[332] Examples of political exploitation of the Arthurian past could be multiplied.[333] Intellectuals in favour of the territorial expansion of the Plantagenets found in it the material to justify their conquests, in addition to undermining the Celtic realms in their efforts to exploit the Arthurian heritage.

A major part of Geoffrey of Monmouth's *History* was dedicated to the exploits of Arthur in Gaul, especially his siege of Paris and elimination of the tribune Frollo, the governor there of the emperor Leo, whom he would go on to depose in Rome. Arthur awarded Anjou and Normandy to commanders in his army. His ability to dispose of the great fiefs of France, which up till then literature had reserved to Charlemagne, is full of significance. The reasoning behind it is repeated in the 1160s by the Loire valley chroniclers, John of Marmoutier and Breton d'Amboise, who proposed a territorial condominium of principalities under Arthur which broadly coincided with the area ruled by Henry II.[334] At first sight, the employment of the Arthurian myth by the Angevin kings is obvious. It consolidated their hold on their newly-acquired continental lands while taking a sideswipe in passing at their feudal subordination to the Capetians.[335]

The Arthurian narrative was loaded with harsh criticisms of the French, who were very often crushed in it by the Britons. Evidence of this is in the *Roman des Franceis*, a harsh Anglo-Norman satire in verse written by Andrew de Coutances, possibly a monk of Mont St-Michel, author of the *Gospel of Nicodemus*, dedicated to his cousin the lady of Tribehou, near St-Lô.[336] The *Roman des Franceis* is addressed to the different peoples ruled by the Plantagenets: 'English, Bretons, Angevins, Manceaux, Gascons and Poitevins.' It was responding in a burlesque way to a similar sort of *chanson* composed by a supporter of the Capetians so as to do down the English, ruled, as he said, by one Arflet of Northumbria (probably meant to be Bede's Aldfrith) 'king of the beer-drinkers' and by Arthur, eaten by the cat Chapalu. Andrew hit back by describing the conquest of France by Arthur, as it had likewise been conquered before by Maximus, Constantine, Brennius and Belinus, his predecessors on the throne of England. Arthur had barely any trouble in taking Paris at the first assault and in defeating Frollo in single combat on the Île de la Cité. Frollo was as ridiculous as he was lazy, keeping his shoes on in bed just like the rest of the French, according to Andrew. Before leaving for the combat, Frollo had dictated a sort of testament encouraging impiety, lying, cruelty, greed, gaming, blasphemy, loose talk, vanity and hatred. His first command, which the French adhered to like the others with obedience, was 'Live like dogs!' Following Frollo's death and his cremation – a first taste of the fires of hell – Andrew described the subjection of the French to the status of peasants: they became *culverts*, a lower status of serf, giving homage to Arthur and paying him a poll tax of four pence. At the end, Andrew gave lengthy consideration to French greed, particularly outstanding at the banquets where each thieved from and fought the others after food.[337] Beyond these stereotypical insults, a reversed list of the virtues of knight-liness and courtliness, the importance of the *Roman des Franceis* is in its bringing together (admittedly in a parody) of Francophobia with one par-ticular episode drawn from Geoffrey of Monmouth.[338]

Attacks on the subjects of the king of France bring to mind the long diatribe of the chronicle which continued the *Roman de Rou* of Wace when it talked of the failed siege of Rouen by Louis VII in 1174. 'The treachery of France ought not to be covered up. The French have always wanted to disinherit the Normans, and always they have persecuted them . . . They are false and treacherous and in no way can be trusted. They are so greedy for possessions that they can never be satisfied. They are miserly with their own goods and stingy in their entertainment. Look at the histories and books! The French have never kept faith with the Normans . . . The Normans have always known how to deal with them, not by treachery but by dealing them great blows.'[339] Hatred against France festered amongst the Norman writers on the continent, where their lands were often sub-ject to Capetian raids. The Norman chroniclers in Britain were not far behind in their xenophobia. On occasion, Richard of Devizes and William of Newburgh slip in some sneers on the French, sometimes the sneers were credulous and sometimes arrogant.[340] These sort of barbs, which they unleashed with even more viciousness against the Welsh and Irish, were the dark side of the English national identity which was forming throughout the twelfth century.[341] While they were discovering their Englishness as different from being Celtic, Anglo-Saxon or Norman, they needed a scapegoat to better further their emerging national feeling.

Hostility to the French was also the background to the *Draco Normannicus*. Let us remember that Stephen de Rouen, the author of that Plantagenet panegyric around 1168, urges the king of England to over-throw the Capetian usurpers with the help of Frederick Barbarossa. On several occasions Stephen suggested to Henry II ('the indomitable lion') that he throw off the yoke of the pathetic Capetians with their poverty-stricken domain, a mere shadow of the Carolingians, themselves no more than usurpers of the Merovingian dynasty. Stephen, a monk of Bec and nephew of Bernard, abbot of Mont St-Michel (1134–1149), had on his desk the Norman chronicles and the writings of Geoffrey of Monmouth as the principal sources of his historical information.

Just like the other court intellectuals, Stephen was freely inspired by the deeds of Arthur. He imagined an exchange of letters between the mythical king of Britain and Henry II. The first letter was from Roland, count of Brittany, begging Arthur to come to his help to defend his lands from Henry II's invasion. In his reply, Arthur wrote to Roland that he had nothing to fear from the king of England, for he would be shaken for a while when he learned of his mother's death. He then wrote once more directly to Henry II, introducing himself as king of the Britons, the English and French, conqueror of Rome and the traitor Mordred, and immortal resident of the Isle of Avalon. He threatened Henry that he would return from across the sea with his fleet and his invincible army to defend the Britons. Just before the decisive battle, Henry II replied to him with respect that Brittany, given to Rollo by Charles the Simple, was his by right but that he would not at this time invade it out of respect for the memory of his mother, and would be happy to hold it in fief from Arthur.[342] This fictional correspondence, inserted in what is obviously a political pamphlet, is certainly original, and its vagueness of genre, mixing fiction, historical references and political propaganda, makes it difficult to get to grips with.

Despite this, medieval historians have tried to construct interpretations of Stephen's Arthurian correspondence.[343] Firstly, on the level of rhetoric, it is worth mentioning the taste for the epistolary genre which character-ized Latin writers of the twelfth century. The intellectual renaissance of the time encouraged the reading of the letters of Cicero and Seneca, and also the letters of Alexander to Darius – which is explicitly mentioned in an annotated passage of Stephen de Rouen, who could have read them in the Latin translation by Leo the Archpriest which his abbey of Bec had. Stephen, author of an *Ars Poetica*, a man passionate about Latin versifica-tion, was indulging in a stylistic exercise. Secondly, the clues to a political reading of the letters are fairly clear. Count Roland of Brittany refers perhaps to the hero of Roncesvaux, the governor of the county under Charlemagne, but in the year of the Empress Mathilda's death he more likely refers to Roland de Dinan, one of the most powerful Breton barons, keeper of nine counties in England, lord of Richmond and since 1167 one of the Breton rebels against Henry II. Arthur took this Roland's petition to heart, but he was tactful in his dealings with Henry, who would in the end be invested with Brittany by his supposed good offices. Lastly, Stephen made a point of a condescending and amused attitude of Henry towards Arthur, whom he goes so far as to accuse of comparing himself to Alexander, when he was more like Darius in his savagery. Stephen takes on a burlesque tone. The problem raised by his choice of irony here, as pointed out by literary scholars and historians alike, is in the mention right at the heart of this fictional correspondence of the death of the Empress Mathilda, whom Stephen sincerely admired and who was moreover the mother of the dedicatee of his work. But the point is that the way laughter was employed by a twelfth-century intellectual was utterly different from our days, and likewise the way he regarded dead people to whom he was attached. Following on from other Anglo-Norman intellectuals,[344] Stephen simply mocked 'the hope of Britain', in an age when Roland de Dinan and his fellow conspirators were still trying to use the mythical figure of Arthur against Henry II.

The messianic hopes of the Breton aristocracy and the attempt of a Norman intellectual close to the English king to put them down, tells us all about the ambiguity of the Arthurian legend, which lent itself to political causes which were radically contradictory. In the same way, it is worth noting how the prophecies of Merlin, the core of Geoffrey of Monmouth's work, were adaptable. They could be used with ease by the supporters of the Plantagenets. Stephen de Rouen explained how they predicted the imperial coronation of Mathilda at Rome ('the eagle builds its nest on Mount Aran'); the victory of Henry II over King Stephen ('seized by the teeth of the boar') and the remarriage of Eleanor of Aquitaine ('the eagle is reunited in the broken union').[345] They also explained away some of the responsibility of the Plantagenets for their defeats, such as the repeated rebellions of the sons of Henry II against their father (as looked at here earlier) or the loss of Normandy in 1204, which Ralph of Coggeshall explains by the prophecy 'the sword is separated from the sceptre'.[346] But the prophecies were of more use to rebels than the establishment. During the 1140s they supported the critics of the Norman presence in Britain, sustaining the warfare that the Welsh engaged in against them. As we have seen, the subversive tendency of the prophecies was the reason why Wace had no intention of translating them in his *Brut*. In the 1160s, John Marshal (deprived of Marlborough Castle by Henry II), John of Salisbury and Herbert of Bosham (whom he had exiled) interpreted Merlin in a light hostile to the Angevins.[347] The spread of the matter of Britain, encouraged by the Plantagenets, was not without risks to them. Their ideological domestication of Arthur was never entirely achieved.

The change in the image of Arthur in the vernacular literature of the end of the twelfth century and beginning of the thirteenth proved that it was more than they could control. Arthur's role as conquering hero took second place. Following on from Chrétien de Troyes, his kingship became more curial and courtly than warlike. Arthur barely left his palace, from which he despatched his knights of the Round Table on quests. A remote figure, he sometimes appeared as a cipher; but sometimes, at the opposite extreme, he appeared overbearing.[348] Despite fading into the background, his royal majesty maintained a certain prestige; the emphasis had now passed to the young knights, whose military exploits are praised by the romances while they deplore the impoverishment of knighthood at the expense of merchants and peasants. Overlaying this Arthurian fiction on contemporary society, the noblemen of the Plantagenet Empire could identify with those knights of Arthur and deprecate the distance which had, as with them too, opened up with their king, a man increasingly inaccessible to them.

The discovery of Arthur at Glastonbury had never quite disposed of the idea of his immortality and his return. In *Perlesevaus* (1200–1210, or 1230–1240), Lancelot goes to the tomb readied for Arthur at Avalon, but finds only Guinevere buried in it. In the epilogue of this work, the hermit Joseph, its supposed author writing at the dictation of an angel, distances himself from the testimony of the monks of Avalon, who claim that they are keeping Arthur's body. The *Mort Artu* (1215–1235) pictures Girflet, knight of the Round Table, who sees the wounded king borne away by Morgana in the magical ship of ladies – which is incompatible with the idea of his burial in the black chapel, which the Avalon monks asserted as a fact. The examples of Arthur's undesirable remoteness from his knights and the dogged belief in his immortality both betray the limits of the influence of the Plantagenets on the character of Arthur.[349] Coming to maturity at the turn of the thirteenth century, the Plantagenets' creation (or at least their adopted child) broke free of them. But even worse, he could turn against them when their expansion had ground to a halt and their empire had begun to fall apart. Once the nobility began to assess the repeated defeats of John against the faultless avatar of kingship that was Arthur, the legend was going to be disadvantageous to him. Indeed, it fed dissent. The powerful propaganda weapon represented by Arthur was taken up by the rebellious English nobility, or the Welsh and Irish aristocracies fighting for their independence.

If the Plantagenets knew how to use the matters of France and Britain with a certain style – writing their predecessors into them – they were just as able to put their spin on the matter of Rome. Some intellectuals went so far as to trace back their family's roots to the heroes of the Trojan war, regarded at the time as the founders of the great towns and nations of the West.[350] They had assimilated a view of history as defined by the *Translatio imperii et studii*: the gradual migration of empire and knowledge from the east to the west. The logical end of the Trojan trek into the west was the nation of the Britons, established in the westernmost countries on the Atlantic seaboard, an idea already expressed in the ninth century in the *History of the Britons*, of 'Nennius' and, in the next century, by the Celtic *Armes Prydein Vawr* (the Great Prophecy of Britain). Geoffrey of Monmouth's *History of the Kings of Britain* developed the Trojan legend. According to him, the oracle of Diana told Brutus, the great grandson of Aeneas, to leave for an island in the far west. Brutus gave his name to Great Britain (*Brutus* producing *Britannia*) where he ended up settling down and founding London. He was the originator of the royal dynasty of Britain and, as such, the ancestor of Arthur. In Geoffrey's book the genealogy of the kings of England gains in antiquity and prestige in this way.

It is not therefore a surprise that Wace's *Brut*, the Anglo-Norman translation of Geoffrey of Monmouth, should be bound with three French romances in the manuscript of the copyist Guiot, covering the history of Troy, from the Argonauts right up to the flight of Aeneas from his burning city, as they are all part of the same narrative cycle: *Thebes*, *Troie* and *Eneas*.[351] Written in the decade between 1155 and 1165, they are packed with allusions to Henry II's court. The anonymous author of the first of them says he prefers the laughter and kisses of the daughters of Adrastus at London and Poitiers – an allusion which could be taken to indicate some familiarity with the two Plantagenet capital cities.[352] Benoit de Sainte-Maure's *Roman de Troie* contains a eulogy probably intended for Eleanor, and the language of the third of them contains Norman dialect. All three romances openly promote an intellectual elitism which contrasts with the epic cycles of Charlemagne and Arthur, which are more popular in tone. It might be noted on this that the prologue of the *Roman de Thebes* limits its audience and critics just to knights and clerks. The matter of Rome, confined to a closed and select audience, was very much 'courtly', in the sociological sense of the term. It was matched perfectly with the clerical intellectuals and *milites litterati* of the households of Henry II and Eleanor.

At least two other works address the history of Troy, written in Latin but addressed to the same intellectual circles, as if the clerical and learned language might give an extra distinction to the genealogical memory of the house of Anjou and the English monarchy. Peter de Saintes, Henry II's childhood tutor, who had introduced him to these stories, was the author of a poem, now lost, on the Trojan war. The clerk, Joseph of Exeter, nephew of Baldwin, archbishop of Canterbury (died 1190), wrote an elegant *Iliad of Darius of Phrygia* (1180–1189) in hexameters, where he slips in after the death of Hector an evocation of the memory of the Young King Henry, recently deceased. Joseph went on the Third Crusade with his uncle, which he described in his Latin work *Antiocheis*, so as to promote the exploits of Richard the Lionheart.[353] In the same period, the *Architrenius* of John de Hauville (1184), master of the cathedral school of Rouen, compiled a mythological genealogy in one of its chapter rubricated as 'Generation of Arthur and the origins of the man to whom this work is dedicated', which derived the Phrygian dynasty of Cornwall from Anchises, father of Aeneas. Arthur appears in it as the fourth 'Phoebus' (another name for the sun-god Apollo) before Henry II, who is the fifth of them.[354] These three writers, close as they were to the Plantagenets, made much of the Trojan theme, which was hardly displeasing to their masters.

Many more comparisons between the heroes of the Trojan war and the Angevins could be pointed to in contemporary literature. The parallel between Hector and the Young Henry ventured on by Joseph of Exeter is not at all exceptional: Walter Map pictured Henry II as Achilles; Alan of Lille (*c.*1125–1203) had Richard the Lionheart as Ajax; Bertran de Born depicted Mathilda, duchess of Saxony and Bavaria, as Helen.[355] But it has to be recognized that we are dealing here with little more than literary style, just like the comparisons with Alexander the Great which recur so often in the works of poets who mention the Plantagenets, and, indeed, other kings. The proof is in the parallels with Achilles and Ajax, both of them Achaeans and enemies of Troy, who hardly match up to the Trojan origins of the Britons advocated by the writers of the Angevin court. The history of Brutus and his ancestors was as difficult for the kings of England to control as the Arthurian legend. Nevertheless, even if they could not control every one of their themes and manifestations, the Trojan myth undoubtedly assisted their propaganda and their political interests. It put them on the same level as the other great European monarchies which pressed their claims to have a Trojan origin.

The Plantagenet past was divided up into three periods by the chroniclers and romancers of their realms. The first period concentrated on the history of the holy kings and dukes of the dynasty, such as Edward the Confessor and Richard I of Normandy, whose remains were venerated in churches with strong dynastic associations. In their hagiographical writings, the Plantagenet clerks legitimated the succession of the house of Anjou to the throne of England with little difficulty, by means of learned genealogies which knit together the Anglo-Saxon and Norman dynasties. The second period recalled real events of the sixth to ninth centuries all mixed up with elements drawn from ancient folklore and indeed completely invented by some writers. In this the Angevin companions of Roland and, above all, Arthur, the parallel to the Charlemagne who had already been adopted by the Capetians, were the principal characters. The third period takes us into a very unlikely Trojan world, where the mythological Greek heroes, made out to be the founders of the British dynasty, are the principal figures. This threefold reading of history, heavily biased according to our modern forms of analysis, was not unlike the contemporary model of history promoted by the kings of France at St-Denis. Its aim was undoubtedly to exalt the royal dynasty of England, whose founding fathers were the holy king Edward, the conquering and courtly Arthur, or the traveller Brutus. This reading of history abruptly downgraded the idea of the modest and knightly origins of the house of Anjou, descendants of Tertullus the Forester, as developed by monastic chroniclers of the Touraine. But the more prestigious origins that the English intellectuals formulated for the Plantagenets was more royal than princely. It allowed them to occupy a place alongside the other great Western monarchies.

Historiography was only one element of many at the heart of a vast system of communication whose objective was to legitimate Plantagenet power, justify their policies and explain away their mistakes. Whether it was conscious or unconscious, calculated or spontaneous, explicit or implicit, precise or diffuse, their propaganda drew on a variety of modes of expression. Sometimes it was by iconography and sometimes by protocol, with the staging of an intelligently designed ceremonial, but most of the time it reached its audience through words. Literature in all its forms and in several languages became the chief media of its message. *Chanson* expressed in Occitan, history-writing in octosyllabic Anglo-Norman verse, marvellous Welsh tales or obscure Latin oracles all adorned the achievements of the Angevin dynasty, in denigrating its enemies, exalting its ancestors and in heralding its imminent victories.

The impact of the Angevin message was all the more great when it was broadcast by word of mouth. In the twelfth century, every written work was recited aloud; it was experienced through performance.[356] The melodies which often accompanied it and its rhythms made memorization and recitation all the more easy. Read in Latin in the coteries of clerical intellectuals; recited in the vernacular in public places by the poets, minstrels and other bards; spread by word of mouth by their public, Plantagenet literature experienced rapid diffusion. At the Plantagenet court, the power of conviction and the range of their messages is well known. Its compositions were consciously designed to pass on political ideas or to modify dissenting views on the military ventures of the kings of England. At the distance of some centuries it can be perceived that this propaganda, after taking over the most unexpected of channels of communication, did succeed in its mission. The Plantagenet dynasty and its exploits still enjoy today a high profile with modern people and with a wide public.

The widespread nature of the propaganda pouring outwards from the Plantagenet court into a huge conglomerate of territorial principalities allows us to address once again the thorny problem of relations between the centre of the empire and its periphery. The king and his household, continually on the road, criss-crossed a vast area. Only their physical presence was synonymous with their authority. Their power was delegated on the ground to their representatives, who sometimes rebelled against the king, following the example of King Henry II's children. Courtiers and local officers formed a nobility of service, increased by clerks who sometimes climbed up a social level because of their studies. This diverse administrative cadre developed its own culture. Its political discourse was very rich: abstract reflection on the exercise of power; open criticism of the defection of intellectuals who abandoned the contemplation of ideas for the sordid business of administration; eulogies affirming Plantagenet legitimacy, and so on. The literate knights and the courtier-clerks belonged mostly to a noble and ecclesiastical environment whose amenability to the king could not necessarily be taken for granted. Open revolt was frequent enough among them. The centre did not always get the periphery to accept its law. So it had to rely for day-to-day matters on local aristocracies, staking everything on their degree of loyalty, before deepening the complex links that the Plantagenets maintained with the Church, a social influence in the West impossible to ignore in the twelfth century.

For and against the king

On 19 June 1215 King John was forced to leave his castle of Windsor where he was sheltering. The leaders of a great aristocratic revolt obliged him to come before an assembly gathered in a meadow near Runnymede. There, he had no choice but to seal the Magna Carta, whose sixty-three articles considerably curtailed his royal authority.[1] His freedom of movement restored, John tried to renege on his agreement, relying on loyal troops. But this was to take too lightly the determination of his enemies, who did not disarm. They appealed to the young Louis, son of Philip Augustus, who landed in England the next spring and marched into London. Only the sudden death of King John in October 1216 allowed his son, the child Henry III, to take the throne, frustrating the plans of the future Louis VIII. The opposition to John had been more or less unanimous among the lay and ecclesiastical magnates of England.

The movement which resulted in Magna Carta had come together two years before, in 1214, with the defeat at La Roche-aux-Moines and the collapse of John's expedition to reconquer his lands along the Loire valley, which sharpened animosity towards the king. In that year, the barons of the north of England rejected the arbitrary increase in the tax called scutage, announced by Peter des Roches, the Angevin-born justiciar of England and spokesman of the French exiles, whose hawkish programme aimed at the recovery of the continental lordships occupied since 1204 by the king of France.[2] The northern rebels comprised a group of lords tightly united against John and the party called the 'Poitevins', which had gathered round Peter des Roches, and which was very determined to pull together the financial resources for military campaigns on the continent. The rebels took against this new tax increase by the king, and also against the rapacity of his officers who, following the example of the forester, Hugh de Neville, pursued it rather too greedily for their taste.[3] Beginning in Northumberland, the unrest spread south. It was particularly severe in Essex. In January 1215, the leaders of the revolt entered London. In April, they handed over to William Marshal and other representatives of the king at Brackley a first statement of their grievances and demands. When these were turned down point-blank by John, they resolved on 9 May to withdraw their homage and faith from him. A week later, the city of London rallied to their cause. Isolated, the king had no choice but to surrender.

Magna Carta, which John was obliged to ratify, still seems today in great part 'the bible of the British constitution'. A verdict like that, deriving from the legalistic and nationalistic Whiggism of the nineteenth century is undoubtedly anachronistic. It assumes an unlikely continuity – for all but a thousand years – of the institutions of State and government traditions. Magna Carta did not come out of nowhere; it had predecessors. For example, it repeated almost word for word several clauses of the coronation charter of Henry I (1100). Legal historians have noted that it is reminiscent of documents secured by his aristocracy from Peter II of Aragon and his son James I on the eve and in the aftermath of the battle of Muret (1213) , and also the Golden Bull conceded by Andrew II of Hungary in 1231.[4] Magna Carta was in the line of evolution that was unwinding in other Western kingdoms. It was not detached either in time or space.

But the enthusiastic assessment of Magna Carta by the English consitutionalists of the nineteenth century had some elements of truth. Its settlement with the barons and rebellious townsfolk brought to a stop the process of growing centralization and royal wilfulness which had to end, sooner or later, in absolute monarchy. Magna Carta considerably curtailed the king's freedom of action; his decisions had in future to be agreed by a council of twenty-five nobles (art. 61). More important still, the king himself was placed under a higher law which he ought not to break. This was made clear in the sixty-three articles of Magna Carta. Some of them are quite rightly famous: the consent of a representative assembly to taxes (art. 12); judgement of every accused man by his peers (art. 39); justice for all (art. 40); freedom of travel for merchants (art. 41); freedom to leave England without the king's licence (art. 42). Magna Carta brought some sort of stability to the complex relationship – sometimes supportive, sometimes antagonistic – that the Angevin monarchy maintained with its nobility. On its side, the lay aristocracy took a measure of institutional control over the king. The nobility, the principal force for revolt, deserves a careful study in its own right, enabling a dissection of the nature of its links with the Crown, and this will be attempted in the next chapter.

The clauses of the charter did not just affect laypeople, but also churchmen. Beginning with the first clause, it clearly proclaimed the 'liberty of the English Church' in the tenor of the old monastic and Gregorian demands which raised 'liberty' to be the inalienable right of the clergy against the lay powers.[5] The clauses elaborated this principle in a rejection of all royal influence in episcopal elections. The total commitment of Stephen Langton, archbishop of Canterbury (1207–1227), to the rebellion and his part in the drafting of Magna Carta, was an important factor in the new legislation.[6] It is evidence of the antagonism between the English clergy and the Angevin kings. Some years previously, King John had forbidden Stephen Langton to stay in England, since he would not recognize the legitimacy of his accession to the archiepiscopal see of Canterbury gained, thanks to the intervention of Innocent III. It was not a coincidence that Langton commissioned a counter-seal depicting the murder of Thomas Becket in his cathedral, the climax of ecclesiastical opposition to the king. Langton, master of the Paris schools and famous exegete, the man who divided up the Bible into chapters and verses, embodied the thinking of the secular clergy on links between priesthood and kingship. Theological movements and the Becket affair will therefore be the subject of the second chapter of this section.

The aristocracy: between rebellion and submission

Certain intellectuals had proposed an autocratic ideology for the Angevin kings. The prologue of the *Laws and Customs of the Kingdom of England*, written by a member of the royal household, repeated the famous Justinian maxim: 'The king's will has the force of law'.[1] A similar tone, as imperious as it was peremptory, was used in the numerous charters issued by the chancery for the aristocracy. The king gave them his 'orders' (*observantie*) and his 'bans' (*censure*), as expressions of his 'power and will' (*vis et voluntas*), of his compulsion (*districtio*) and of the verdicts of his court (*justicia*).[2] The formulae of these royal acts, components of the diplomas and writs calling for compliance with the king's wishes in no uncertain terms, betray a state of mind where any possibility of disobedience was out of the question. A royal ideology manufactured in the centre that was the court established the practice of government, law and administration on the periphery.

Some royal officers in the provinces echoed the ideology, broadcasting it on to the people of their districts. They worked to bolster the lordship of the Angevin kings and to assert their influence over the majority of the nobility, grateful intermediaries of central power in the localities. The methodical imposition of an Angevin programme of centralization was taken to be high-handed and was rejected by rebellious barons. The king's desire for unequivocal obedience raised the hackles of many aristocrats. It was to the benefit of other men, particularly those who would want to be involved in royal government and take for their own profit some part of its executive power and its tax revenue.

Aristocratic attitudes varied. They might show docility, loyalty and good service, but they were more likely to display resistance and counterclaims. Deeply committed to its own courts and the autonomy of its lordships, the aristocracy took badly to Angevin encroachments on its domains. The rebellion of 1215 was the aristocratic push to the royal shove. Beginning from the 1190s, the rebellion was encouraged by the powerful political revival of the Capetians, the ancient enemies of the Plantagenets and the historical overlords of the bulk of their lordships.[3] The aristocracy, by its repeated revolts and its unreliability in diplomatic manoeuvres, was the avenue by which Normandy, the lands of the Loire and Poitou passed to the Crown of France.

A privileged nobility

Contemporary French historiography has devised a particular outlook on the aristocracy of the years 1180–1220. A first theory was put together by Paul Guilhiermoz, a legal historian interested in the appearance of hereditary privilege concerning the aristocracy. For Guilhiermoz, noble status only began in the thirteenth century. Before then every nobleman was a warrior, whatever were the antiquity and reputation of his family. His profession of arms took precedence still over his blood.[4] Thirty or so years later Marc Bloch repeated Guilhiermoz's suggestion for his own purposes. He wrote that the nobility 'only truly began to form at the end of the twelfth century; the next century saw it establishing its iden-tity'.[5] It was only then that an 'ad hoc nobility' became a 'legal entity',[6] 'the knights transformed themselves into a hereditary caste'.[7] In the period before this, 'there was not, strictly speaking, a nobility, but only men living like nobles; no hereditary knights, just horsemen proudly serving in war'.[8]

Beginning in the 1960s, German researchers of the school of Freiburg-en-Brisgau modified this sort of assumption. They famously demonstrated the remarkable genealogical continuity of a small nucleus of Carolingian families – even Merovingian and Roman – who weathered the crisis of the year 1000.[9] But they did not deny that for the most part knights of modest means would be the originators of most of the thirteenth-century noble families of the West. Georges Duby was largely responsible for spreading the theories and methods of the German school in France. But so far as the period under consideration here is concerned, he did not move far from the legal theories of Paul Guilhiermoz and Marc Bloch: 'The years on either side of 1200 do appear indeed as the point in the evolution of French society where a movement came to fruition which had long been making the aristocracy into a true nobility.'[10] Literary historians seem to go along with this theory when they perceive the appearance in the thirteenth century of a new French word, estat, which might be suitably translated by the word 'order', and which carried with it certain moral

imperatives.[11] British medieval historians have adopted an identical analytical model, either by borrowing that of the continent, or of their own
devising. David Crouch stresses, for example, the more precise way that
the English nobility was understood in this period: 'In those two generations – the time of Richard the Lionheart, John and Philip Augustus – the
aristocracy became both larger, and better defined.'[12] Overall, and despite
some attempts of later medieval historians to project it forward in time,[13]
most historians take the key years 1180–1230 as the time when the aristocracy was institutionalized into a legal category of its own.

The legal sources for the west of France for this period confirms their
point of view. The *Grand Coutumier* of Normandy, compiled around 1235,
confirms for example the existence of a specific status of hereditary nobility,
identified as a category of dubbed knights and their sons who enjoyed
some fiscal privileges:[14] 'The knights and all their children born in wedlock
are exempt from all money payments.'[15] The content of written property
conveyances tells us much the same. In order to differentiate between
groups of witnesses or list the beneficiaries of their documents, scribes
of Poitevin charters adopt a uniform categorization which divides the
'knights' (*milites*) on one side, and the 'men', 'serfs', 'villeins', and 'peasants'
(*homines, servientes, vilani, rustici*) on the other.[16] In 1199, in a confirmation
of the privileges of Sainte-Croix de Poitiers, Eleanor of Aquitaine punished
on pain of seven-and-a-half shillings the *servientes naturales* ('born serfs')
who might take wood from the abbey's forest, as opposed to a penalty of
five shillings for the *milites*.[17] The queen was responding to different fiscal
expectations on the nobility, protected here by privilege.

One of the causes of this increasing precision in the definition of nobility may be looked for in the advance of royal bureacracy. The refining of
administrative methods allowed the Plantagenets the chance to compile
lists of the emerging nobility. It was so as to make money from those liable
to military service that the king and his officers drew up lists of aristocrats,
since they believed that every nobleman must be a knight or, should he
not be knighted, a lesser soldier or squire. In the winter of 1166, an
inquest produced the *Cartae Baronum*, confiding to the pages of the
Black and Red Books of the Exchequer the names of the tenants-in-chief
who held the greater honours of England from Henry II; the number of
knights to whom they had sub-enfeoffed their lands and with whom
they must report to the royal host, and the period – whether before or
after 1135 – when they acquired these fiefs and their location. So those
who had not yet paid homage to Henry II would have to comply as soon
as possible.[18] A Norman satellite of the English *Cartae Baronum* survives

in the *Infeudationes Militum* of 1172.[19] In 1185, a comparable list was
compiled for twelve English counties, with a list of the names of widows
and under-age orphans whose fiefs owed military service to the Crown.[20]
All these official documents allowed the administration to exact from
enfeoffed noblemen annual military service for forty days or, if preferred,
its conversion into cash through scutage payments. Other lists had a more
sinister purpose. In his chronicle, Roger of Howden preserved in detail the
names of all the barons who had joined in the revolt of 1173–1174, with
the date and place of their capture.[21] Its precision can only be explained
by his consultation of an official document in the royal archives, now
lost.[22] Counting, compiling and making lists allowed the Exchequer to
collect *servitium debitum* for every fief and the better monitoring of lords
tempted to rebel. In a sense, the existence of a nobleman was from now on
linked to a written text; that nobility depended in part on the presence of
his name in the royal rolls and registers. Bureaucratization had a lot of
influence on the evolution of nobility.

Is this to say that the emergence of a legally defined nobility wiped out
the social differences so significant within the traditional de facto nobility?
In the year 1000, the dichotomy between 'nobles' (*nobiles*) and 'knights'
(*milites*), between the members of the old Carolingian lineages and the
horsemen in their service, was a major fact of aristocracy.[23] Around
1200, while personal status was becoming fixed, this duality found a legal
existence. The difference between *barones* and *milites*, signalled by the
inquest of 1166 on tenants-in-chief was part and parcel of the way that
English bureaucracy defined the nobility.[24] It continued up to the modern
period in the two quite distinct groups of 'lords' and 'gentry'. In Poitou,
charters attest likewise to the existence of a lesser category of knights
in the service of castellans and great lords. In 1196, for example, Hugh IX
le Brun de Lusignan renounced the customary meal that he used to exact
from the priory of Prémay by means of a charter in which he said he was
surrounded 'by my knights then present'.[25] The ancient dichotomy was
more than ever in evidence.

This duality did not stand in the way of the hereditary descent of other
prestigious titles within the nobility. In England, the most prized of these
was the earldom. Before the Norman conquest the title of earl was borne
by a dozen or so holders supervising one or more Anglo-Saxon shires,
where they administered justice in exchange for a third of the profits. The
Normans replaced most of the earls and reduced their functions. After
1154, an earldom did not imply any longer an administrative responsibility,
which was by then administered by replaceable sheriffs appointed directly

by the king for a short term of office. At most the Plantagenets awarded earldoms as rewards for one or other of their particularly loyal kinsmen, and that more and more rarely.[26] The strictly honorific character of the earldom is clear in the importance which began to attach to its investiture ceremony, by sword and belt, which is mentioned for the first time in 1189 when Richard the Lionheart made Hugh de Puiset, bishop of Durham, the earl of Northumbria.[27] A similar evolution is evident in household offices, by now hereditary. In Normandy the offices of chamberlain, butler and constable were recognized as belonging to the families of Tancarville, Aubigny and Hommet;[28] in Anjou, William des Roches received the stewardship from Arthur of Brittany in fee for himself and his family in 1199.[29] These offices, stripped of their ancient administrative associations, only existed around 1200 as ornaments to the families who held them.

As has already been suggested, it was during the royal coronation that the prestige of these noble titles was made most real in the common gaze. The procession that escorted Richard the Lionheart to Westminster was headed by the clergy, with the earls and their three swords coming next, and then the barons who surrounded the members of the Exchequer with the regalia and robes. At the end the king walked under a silk canopy which the barons of the Cinque Ports and Dover held. The procession closed with some knights.[30] This staging reflected social categorization and displayed the hierarchy of honour within the nobility. Strict attention to precedence, fixed in this ritual way, held up a mirror in which the nobility saw itself reflected with all the internal levels in its condition.

Divisions that seem clear on the level of law, administration and protocol were perhaps just as clear in the consciousness of courtiers. Their writings are evidence of this hardening of social levels, more marked than it had been in the past.[31] For Gerald of Barry in particular the end of the world would not efface the social order, or the highest and lesser degrees of men. Gerald's point of view was a radical contrast with the traditional ideas of most churchmen, which maintained a deep eschatological egalitarianism: the sweeping away of all distinction between men at the end time, following the apocalyptical destruction of this unjust world.[32] In the twelfth century, Gerald's sharper and harder perception of social difference was not a unique phenomenon. It went alongside changes in religious sensibilities, where everyone wanted to be a member of a particular community and fill a particular role in it. This closer appreciation of the variety of religious vocations is part and parcel for church historians of the contemporary stress on the individual's search for his God, and also of the new expansion of religious orders and the relationships between them.

A new consciousness of self and group identity surfaces in this period of intellectual renaissance and humanism.[33]

Whatever the relationship might be between a more precise understanding of the social status of individuals and the increase in religious orders, a view as radical as Gerald of Barry's had been established in the historiography, which harked back to the 'good old times' when the court offices were exclusively reserved for the nobility. In his *Chronicle of the Dukes of Normandy*, Benoît de Sainte-Maure recalled with nostalgia the legendary household of Richard II, which he suggested might be a model for his contemporaries: 'He desired to give his household offices only to gentlemen. His chaplains, scribes, chamberlains and attendants were, every one of them, noble knights.'[34] Benoît was talking here more about his own day around 1175 than about the past that he was supposed to be describing. Proof of this might be the discussion that Walter Map, another member of Henry II's household, claims that he had had with Ranulf de Glanville so as to criticize the political rise of serfs, thanks to their educational attainments. It ended with a quotation from Claudian (*c*.400): 'No one is more brutal than a peasant when he is raised on high, and no monster more repulsive than the frenzy of the slave who is let loose on free men.'[35] Ralph Niger who hated the king for the murder of Thomas Becket, upbraided him for having entrusted high office in his administration 'to slaves, bastards and common soldiers'.[36] A contrary wind was blowing at the English court, which it would be easy to link with the new fixation about noble status.

This development inspired powerful reaction. Peter of Blois took issue with the slanderers who had presumed to criticize – in a manner as inaccurate as it was unjust – the modesty of his social origins: 'It is well known that my father and mother were descended from the aristocracy (*optimates*) of Brittany. I say that not to boast, but to silence those who weave mischief, coupling great arrogance to their own degenerate birth'.[37] Such polemics about the antiquity of families can be found at any period, but it is intriguing to find them appearing at a time when the link between nobility and birth was consolidating itself.

In the world of the court, Peter shared in another debate, this time less personalized and more abstract, along with Gerald of Barry.[38] The key to this can be found in a maxim of Juvenal (*c*.60–140) that both Peter and Gerald quote: 'Nobility of soul is the one true virtue.' Juvenal, who was liberally commented on by William de Conches, John of Salisbury's master, was also cited by Thomas Becket in his attack on Gilbert Foliot. To help appreciate the vanity of the glittering prizes of the world, Becket turned to good account Juvenal's famous question: 'What good are family trees?'[39] Peter of Blois located himself in a tone more theological than philosophical when he referred to the free choice of Christ to be born to a poor family. For these medieval thinkers, educated in Ciceronian rhetoric, this ethical sensitivity and theoretical commitment to the ideal of aristocracy arose out of the eloquence and perusal of Classical poets. Just as Augustus had Virgil and Horace as friends, every prince ought to maintain contact with men of letters. Meditation on the idea and characteristics of nobility grew up by this route.

Amongst noblemen, this intellectual movement was certainly coupled to a consciousness of self and descent greater than had ever been before. For this reason, it is important to note the appearance in the Anglo-Norman aristocratic world of the first biography of a layman who was not a king, a work composed with no link to any clerical hagiography. This was the 19,214 verses of the life of William Marshal, written by John the Trouvère at the end of the 1220s. The biography clearly uses a Latin account roll in which Wigan, clerk of the kitchen of the Young Henry, recorded one by one his martial accomplishments in the tournament, at William's own request.[40] The model of conduct which William embodied owed nothing to the Church, and arose out of the epic and the chivalric romance. It was the image which his children wanted preserved for posterity: that of a courageous soldier, accomplished, loyal and generous. Such a noble consciousness of being warriors above all perhaps explains changes in their tomb effigies. The civilian effigy, still noticeable around 1150, was replaced for good around 1200 by sculptures of armed men.[41] From this point on noblemen wanted to be seen as warriors.

From the beginning, heraldry was not just a military identification device. It started on battlefields as a means of identifying combatants whose faces were obscured by helms. In passing it betrays also an individualistic perception of people akin to autobiography, linked as it was to genealogical identity. The territorial princes of northern France (especially the counts of Anjou) and of England were the ones who began to carry armorial devices in the years between 1120 and 1150. The fashion for heraldry spread through society from the highest down to the simple knights by the end of the twelfth century. Engraved on a matrix which was pressed on to wax, the armorial shield served to validate charters. To the end of the twelfth century, the armorial seal seems to have maintained an air of high status. At least the chronicle of Battle Abbey puts in the mouth of Richard de Lucy (died 1179), justiciar of England, the following complaint: 'It was not lately the custom for every petty knight (*militulus*) to possess seals, which belong properly to kings and great men.'[42] Richard de Lucy's bitter diatribe reveals in fact the success of heraldry in all strata of nobility. In his account of the war against the king of Scotland, Jordan Fantosme comments on the bright colours of banners and pennants, but more particularly those of the surcoats or coats of arms, expensive cloth figured with heraldic devices worn over the hauberks of the nobles.[43] After this, knighthood could not be separate from heraldry. It was only from the 1230s that lesser landowners aspired to the privilege and used seals to authenticate their documents, especially in Normandy.[44] Heraldry was beyond question a sign of belonging to the aristocracy.

It was the same thing with tournaments in England. Sensitive to the Church's prohibitions, Henry I and Henry II, who feared the losses in horse and mutilations of knights as much as the meetings of armed and conspiratorial noblemen, forbade tournaments in England. But according to William of Newburgh, Richard the Lionheart understood the technical edge that they gave to French knights. When he got back from his period of captivity, he decided to lift the ban, while imposing strict regulation on the tournament designed to limit the risks involved. It particularly laid down a group of organizers and judges, under the supervision of William of Salisbury, and fixed the five sites where the contests should be held. More interesting for our argument, the regulations confined the tournament to the nobility. They pledged a level of fee for each contestant – from the earl who deposited twenty marks to the knight without a fee who paid two marks for it.[45] It paved the way as a result for the appearance of heralds of arms, with the job of assessing the precise nobility of the contestants.

From the 1150s to the 1230s, the nobility therefore became a more precisely defined legal category. Its members, gathered into a social estate, enjoyed from then on a status confirmed by the king and his officers. Custom, later fixed by written codes, reserved for the nobles a particular rank in the society which in return they were bound to defend. Lists of their names were at the king's disposal when he wanted to call them up for his army. In return they had places of honour at his court, despite a reactionary movement which would have liked to confine government only to those of the highest birth. The king gave them also a select role on the day of his coronation, in a ceremony which respected the hierarchy now existing within the nobility itself. Codes defining noble status became more obvious, with the image of heraldry (still then a class privilege) and elitist tournaments. The appearance of the aristocratic biography was an additional symptom of this collective consciousness, getting clearer by the day, of a higher level of society. It was by the argument of their military skills, on which they claimed a monopoly, that the nobles argued for their pre-eminence. War was their own realm.

War domesticated

Around 1200 the identity between knighthood and nobility, evident in the *Grand Coutumier* of Normandy, in charters and funerary monuments, had widely penetrated the contemporary mindset. But the idea of knighthood has to be framed within a dual meaning. On the one hand, it meant a group of professional soldiers (*milites*) whose resources and prestige was rather less than those of the old landed nobility, in whose service they made war in return for a fief. On the other hand, knighthood as 'chivalry' referred to an ideal and to a system of values, heavily Christianized, which dictated the aristocratic warrior ethic. This second definition was inextricably linked to the idea of courtliness, for the knight had access to a secular culture whose most intellectual and literary manifestations appeared in the royal court.

At the end of the twelfth century, the growth of royal power represents a decisive step towards the building of the modern State, a State often defined in Weberian terms as 'a monopoly on violence'. In such a context, the king and his counsellors sought exclusive control of the agencies of warfare with the assistance of a still-embryonic administrative structure; and with them the prerogative of deciding who were the enemies of the realm, what were the aims of military campaigns and the objectives of territorial conquest. They wanted to concentrate decisions about making war and peace at the top of the political hierarchy, to the disadvantage of the nobility which had all too often begun their own wars at the local level. So they forbade, or at least attempted to limit, all sorts of spontaneous or wilful noble violence.

What was more, the officers of the Crown insisted that knights put their skills in the king's service. In the *Policraticus*, John of Salisbury said this clearly: the *milites* should serve the common good (*res publica*) in the profession of arms (*officia belli*) in the service of the Church and Peace, under the guidance of a prince, whose orders they enforced.[46] The notion of a commonwealth and of a military sphere of which knights took charge – always in the service of a higher authority – is by no means independent of the process of state monopolization of violence. The clauses relating to the surrender of Pacy, following on the treaty of Louviers (1196) agreed between Richard the Lionheart and Philip Augustus, used the expression 'public war' (*guerra publica*) to describe the hostilities between the kings of

England and France.[47] So far as we know, its occurrence there was one of the earliest incidences in the medieval West of 'public war', the open equation between warfare and its control by the State. The king, embodying supreme authority, retained the power to declare a just war in the light of the common good of his subjects. He alone might make the use of arms lawful.

It goes without saying that this change in the understanding of the state monopoly of violence ran up hard against the methods of the aristocracy, accustomed to wage war and fight whenever it wished, following a logic which excluded interference of the king's power. Furthermore, the nobility kept the right to halt its hostilities according to the methods which were usual for managing them.[48] This rivalry with the king is most striking at the level of the castellan. In England, Henry II secured the greater fortresses, to avoid his authority being defied as the authority of King Stephen recently had been. Henry allowed the English nobility only harmless fortified manors.[49] He was doing here as he had done in the exercise of justice and the suppression of crime at the local level. The king wanted his justices in eyre to take control of the most important legal cases and to punish the crimes which involved the shedding of blood, while the lords meant to preserve their honour courts and the power of coercion they had over the peasantry.[50] So, during the years between 1154 and 1224 the objectives of the king (embarked on a process of military and judicial centralization) and those of the nobility (within which each family sought to increase its power) became contradictory. Within the Plantagenet lands, noble revolt against the king was common currency. These periodic uprisings betrayed the hostility of the aristocracy to a kingship whose ability to act and to oppress kept growing. In this period, the dialectic between public and private was at the heart of every explanation of its warfare.

For most of the nobles, taking arms against the monarch would seem to be a response to the growing power of the king. Whichever way you look at it, rebellion remained an expression of political discontent, that is, the answer of the aristocracy to intrusions on the autonomy of their lordships, intrusions resented as impositions, inexcusable attacks on family honour. In a nobleman's eyes, revolt could easily be justified. To excuse his revolt, the rebel would offer the encroachments of royal officers on lordly jurisdictions, their flagrant money demands and the authoritarian nature of government decisions and their execution. Reading between the lines, Ralph de Diceto analyses the justifications of the rebels of 1173, so that, loyalist as he was, he could try to distort them without losing their sense, to show their internal contradictions. The rebel nobles, he wrote, violently upbraided Henry II for the confiscation of the lands of aggressive lords, the commital of castles whose owners were suspected of hostility to the Crown, heavy fines against the oppressors of the poor and the exiling of traitors.[51]

This last comment deserves a bit more consideration, for the way that royalist writers understand it is in a very wide sense. For Ralph, treason covers probably those serious wrongs committed by nobles against the peasants on their estates. Another example of the big semantic field that treason occupied is to be found in a letter addressed in 1166 to Thomas Becket by an anonymous author who deals with the terrifying wrath of Henry II against his courtier, Richard du Hommet. Richard had dared to talk to him in favourable terms of the king of Scotland: 'The king has openly called him a "traitor". Possessed by his usual fury, the king threw down the cap from off his head and ripped off his belt. Then he hurled away his cloak and clothing. He seized in his hand the silken bed cover, and as though squatting on a dung heap, began chewing on the straw with which the ground was covered.'[52] In those days, the dramatization of the king's anger was a usual way to convey and instil obedience to his orders.[53] The anger of Henry II was a more social and political expression of it than a real one. But the accusation of treachery here is interesting. The king defined the offence very broadly. One word only sufficed for treachery; it was not necessary to take up arms to commit it. Refusal to serve in the army, the surrender of a castle, and also the abrupt departure from court without permission, marked out the traitor. But it is apparent that the qualifications to be treacherous, what the texts called *proditio*, were rather more restricted in the understanding of many warrior aristocrats, for whom rebellion did not always appear in a bad light.[54] These knights believed that, if the Crown had overshot its rights to their disadvantage, their rebellion was lawful. They took arms all the more readily over it when the king had suffered humiliating military reverses, losing him respect and prestige.[55] The aristocratic conscience seems to have been only faintly troubled by treason to the king.

The view of the king and his faithful intimates was entirely different. They believed that by its very nature sedition approached sacrilege. It was an assault on a being clothed in the supernatural dignity of anointing, in contempt of God's commandment revealed to the prophets: 'Touch not the Lord's anointed' (*Nolite tangere christos meos*, 1 Chronicles 16: 22; Ps. 104: 15).[56] The sacred character of kingship was at the time reinforced by the rediscovery of Roman law, which stressed the idea of majesty. The king, sole fount of law, had to be obeyed blindly. Resistance to his commands constituted the heinous crime of *lèse-majesté*.[57] For its part, feudal law, although less autocratic and contractual in its nature, considered rebellion to be an act of felony, as an arbitrary breach of the oath of faith and homage.

Suppression of this treason was relatively harsh. The punishments applied to the troublemakers were devastation of lands; confiscation of some lordships; heavy fines; and imprisonment or exile.[58] The following are some examples. Guy de Lusignan was perhaps obliged to flee to the Holy Land following the assassination of Patrick of Salisbury. There he eventually became king of Jerusalem.[59] Two hundred and forty two supporters of Arthur of Brittany, defeated at Mirebeau, were imprisoned in Corfe Castle (Dorset) where twenty two of them died of hunger.[60] In 1157, Henry of Essex, the king's standard bearer ran away from a Welsh ambush which led to his being accused of treason by Robert de Montfort, who defeated him in a judicial duel. The king forced him to become a monk at Reading and confiscated his patrimony.[61]

Unlike their predecessors, the Plantagenets generally refrained from inflicting crueller punishments, like mutilation and execution.[62] Doubtless this restraint had been inspired by the fashionable new chivalric values.[63] If that is what had happened, the murder in prison of Arthur of Brittany by King John all the more outraged public opinion in its very exceptionality. Another sign of softening attitudes was that the decisive appropriation of rebel honours became unusual, since the idea of their hereditability was incompatible with the punishment of heirs for the rebellion of their father.[64] The Norman lords of L'Aigle, masters of the region bordering Perche, had their English lordship confiscated for their participation in the revolt of 1173, but Henry II made no bones about delivering them their ancestral lordship.[65] But if the king took less stern measures of repression than in the past, the actual indiscipline of his knights lessened in no way the fixed nature of the royal ideal of what obedience should be.

Henry II's harshness in the face of the misdeeds of certain noblemen did not affect his toleration of the terrible impositions committed on campaign by his mercenaries. With the purpose of putting down noble revolts, he used ever more willingly Brabazons, Basques, Navarrese, Scots and Welsh, who cared little for the tacit conventions which regulated chivalric warfare. Hiring them seemed to Henry to be the lesser of two evils, but unavoidable in the face of the treachery of noblemen with a high opinion of their talents in sieges and on the battlefield. The Celtic tribesmen hired en masse and the professionals enlisted by Mercadier, Falkes de Breauté and Louvrecaire were generally hated because of their brutality. The condemnations of papal bulls and councils of the 'brutes' 'beasts' and 'sacriligious brigands' seem less to do with literary convention and ecclesiastical terrors than to be the consequence of genuine atrocities. The mercenaries ignored the immunity of non-combatants and particularly that of knights, who they knew to be merciless towards humble infantry. The king allowed their pillaging and aggression in the lands of rebels and towards communities which resisted his siege. He resorted to mercenaries to deliver those harsh punishments during campaigns which the king could graciously put a stop to in the aftermath of victory, so that blame for the violence should not fall directly on him. But the use of mercenaries was not entirely to his benefit. It created more problems in the long term than it resolved in the short term. With the revolt crushed, he had to neutralize the troublesome bands, usually by expelling them with force of arms from the principalities where they had fought.[66]

Use of mercenaries in the royal army did not just happen at the end of the twelfth century. In 1066, mercenaries had crossed the Channel at the invitation of William the Conqueror. Later, Henry I recruited Bretons to pacify England, while King Stephen preferred to employ Flemings during the period called the Anarchy. But under Henry II the recruitment of mercenaries became the practice, even the systematic practice. Gerald of Barry and Geoffrey, prior of Vigeois, bitterly criticized the king for this, accusing him of draining the royal treasury to the neglect of alms, of mortgaging the crown and sword of his coronation, so as to pay the Brabazons.[67] They pinpoint an important fact: cash had become the sinew of war. Better finances and a better financial administration sustained the heavy burden of military wages on the royal budget. In England, the increased role of scutage, which would one day provoke the rebellion which would culminate in Magna Carta, helped the change. The rising income from this new tax in the receipts of the Exchequer matched the rising demand for mercenaries in the royal army. The possibility of changing *servitium* into *scutagium* goes back probably to William I, but became common under Henry I.[68] Under Henry II, the tax appears in the Pipe Rolls almost biennially. But the historian, Thomas K. Keefe, has demonstrated that a direct link between the widespread exaction of scutage and aristocratic revolt did not exist any more in his reign, so it became a routine imposition on the nobility.[69] The king was all the more inclined to exact it as he knew that the English barons could not meet their castle-guard obligations in England while fighting on the continent. Around 1200, the 'monetarization' of English feudalism is the key data in understanding the transformation of the army, in which preference was given to the mercenaries.

Despite this change, it is not possible to talk yet of a professional army on modern lines.[70] The unsystematic nature of the payment of mercenaries, in line with the response to the rhythm of occasional recruitment and the subsequent haste of the king to get rid of mercenaries once the campaigns were over, proves, if there was any need, that the conduct of war was still far from resting on a corps of professional soldiers. The heart of the king's army was in contrast made up of around a hundred *milites de familia regis*, a household of warriors and advisers, who filled the role both of his life guard and his permanent household.[71] Holders of knights' fees were of course a more numerous source of fighting troops, but they only fought for a while. Their lands obliged them to do homage to the king and to answer his summons and join the royal host for no less than forty days in a year. If they were tenants-in-chief or bannerets they did not come alone, but rode with their own retinue of knights. Their retinue of knights was more or less fixed according to the size of the honour of the tenant: Roger Bigod, one of the most powerful English lords, whose family possessed the earldom of Norfolk, served the king with a hundred-and-twenty-five knights; the high chamberlain, William de Tancarville, whom Walter Map praised as 'the father of knights' because of the fame of his retinue, served with ninety-five.[72] The use of feudal service by the Crown was not effective in all the Angevin lands. The system worked in England and Normandy, where it answered to the king or his agents, but it was largely ineffective in Aquitaine, Anjou and Brittany. It was only in 1185 in Brittany that Duke Geoffrey solemnly proclaimed the principle of parage which reserved to the eldest son the doing of homage to the king and the service owed for each of the baronies and knights' fees of his honour.[73] It is another illustration of the difference of the impact that the Plantagenets had on their various lands.

The closest relationship between feudalism and the royal army is found in England and Normandy. Legislation and administrative control achieved the highest level of sophistication in the lands on either side of the Channel, the epicentre of the Plantagenet Empire till 1204. With the *Assize of Arms* (1181), Henry II legislated on military matters and laid down the precise equipment that each knight should have in relation to the income from his fee.[74] He often took what was called 'general' homage, which included every able-bodied man capable of carrying arms. He increased inquisitions on knights' fees, particularly the *Cartae Baronum*, on ecclesiastical baronies and those of heirs. These enquiries and legislative moves all witness the considerable part of the enfeoffed knight in the king's host.

Beginning around 1200, something new and interesting affected feudalism in the Plantagenet lands: the appearance of the fief rent, an annual cash payment to castellans and knights in exchange for their loyalty. This was the particular strategy of King John and Henry III, who were happy to buy the obedience of the continental nobility in the face of the aggression of Philip Augustus and Louis VIII.[75] The first mention of the fief rent in Poitou dates from 1199, and concerns a hundred marks a year that John undertook to pay to Eschivard de Preuilly for his homage and service,[76] laboriously trying to ensure his succession to his brother Richard the Lionheart. In due course this practice became so prevalent that the kings of England and France entered into a virtual auction to buy the alliance of the more powerful Poitevin lords. It is unnecessary to say how beneficial to him the king found this arrangement. It was so easy for him to cancel a fief rent to a disloyal vassal of whom it was more or less impossible to deprive landed estates.

At the same period, kings made lesser knights the recipients of cash payments and other gifts in the form of liveries,[77] as if the king wanted to obtain their loyalty and military service direct, circumventing the tenants-in-chief.[78] These knights accommodated themselves all the more readily to this exploitation by cash as it may have seemed to them, from the close of the twelfth century onwards, that inflation and economic depression was chipping away at the standard of living of the lesser nobility.[79] Walter Map mentions serfs who climbed the rungs of the social hierarchy at the expense of the old aristocratic families, in decline because of their idleness.[80] In his *Dialogue of the Exchequer*, Richard fitz Nigel noted similarly their financial difficulties and debts.[81] The hatred for the Jewish moneylenders amongst these indebted knights tends to explain the brutality of the pogrom in York in 1190.[82] One of the causes of this fall in their income might well be found in consecutive divisions of fiefs after 1130.[83] If this is the case, the bad financial situation would have helped along the cash nexus in the military service of the lesser knights through indirect payments, livery and fief rents.

Did the nobility's caution concerning these striking and problematical cash payments – which could have undermined the feudal link between lord and tenant – set back the development of the fief rent and particularly of salaries during military campaigns? In his *sirventes*, Bertan de Born does say that the cash nexus is to knightly warfare what prostitution is to romantic love. But nonetheless he praises a generous lord who likes to retain lots of knights in his household, paying them for their service by wages. Fiction reflects the same attitude to money.[84] Meriadoc, an imaginary king of Wales, has no hesitation about entering imperial service in return for a salary. Robert de Torigny, the likely author of the story, makes a point of the honour Meriadoc obtained from being put 'among the leading stipendiary soldiers in his household'. There is no hint of any slighting verdict here, quite the opposite in fact, on the paid service of this mythical

Plate 1 The four first Angevin kings of England (thirteenth-century). The artist gives each a positive look, as the churches which they had generously caused to be built demonstrates. But he has no qualms about ridiculing the unpopular John (*bottom left*) in painting his crown falling to one side. In the same way his father Henry II (*top left*) appears in profile – a position often intended to be critical. On the other hand his eldest son, Richard the Lionheart (*top right*) carries the sword, which reflects his love of war. The fourth king is Henry III, son of John. (© AKG)

Plate 2 Effigy of Eleanor of Aquitaine (painted sculpture in stone, 1204), abbey of Fontevraud (Maine-et-Loire). Eleanor is represented reading a book of hours, symbol of eternal life, but also of her love of letters. The tombs of her husband Henry II, her son Richard the Lionheart, her daughter Joan of England with her husband Raymond VII of Toulouse, not to mention her daughter-in-law Isabel d'Angoulême, were all located in the family necropolis of the Angevin dynasty. (© AKG)

Plate 3 Portrait of Henry II on the tomb effigy commissioned to cover his grave at Fontevraud. The effigy probably dates to soon after the king's death in 1189 and is an attempt to portray his face as he would have been in his thirties, the idealised age given to the dead as Christ died at the age of 33. The portrayal of the king lying supine in regalia on a bed may echo ancient Roman portrayals of the departed on couches. (© AKG)

Plate 4 At Hastings on 14 October 1066, King Harold was fatally wounded by an arrow. With him, the greater part of the Anglo-Saxon or Anglo-Scandinavian aristocracy died on the battlefield, leaving to the Norman conquerors the option of taking their lordships. Bayeux Tapestry, c.1070. (© AKG)

Plate 5 In arranging useful marriage alliances, Henry II forged links with the German princes. Painted between 1185 and 1188, this German miniature shows his son-in-law Henry the Lion, duke of Saxony and Bavaria, with his wife Mathilda, daughter of Henry II, accompanied by her grandmother, the Empress Mathilda and, most probably, her mother Eleanor of Aquitaine. In this way Duke Henry associated the Plantagenets and their protector saints (Thomas Becket carrying the palm of martyrdom appears in a medallion above Eleanor) with his dynastic consciousness. (© AKG)

Plate 6 Deriving from a manuscript from the Romano-Germanic empire, this miniature dated 1195–1197 is hostile to Richard the Lionheart, whose arrest by the duke of Austria it shows, as he is riding in disguise. Then, his riding clothes removed and his crown recovered, Richard prostrates himself at the emperor's feet to beg for his release. This humiliation makes him the emperor's vassal. (© AKG)

Plate 7 King Arthur of Britain is dying as the ship with its fairies approaches the shore to bear him away to the isle of Avalon where he will be cured by Morgana. This picture by John M. Carrick (1854–1878) shows the vitality of the Arthurian legend. It was elaborated in learned fashion by Geoffrey of Monmouth, then reformulated by Wace for the purposes of Henry II, who claimed Arthur as his ancestor. (© AKG)

Plate 8 Taken from a *Roman de Tristan* of the end of the fifteenth century, this miniature shows Arthur and his knights together around the Round Table, in the centre of which has been placed the Holy Grail. Following on from the Plantagenets, the kings of England borrowed themes and symbols from this legend to give additional prestige to their dynasty. (© Bridgeman Art Library)

Plate 9 The English regard Magna Carta (the Great Charter), extorted by the great barons from King John after their revolt of 1215, as the foundation deed of their constitutional monarchy. This facsimile was created in the nineteenth century to commemorate the clauses limiting the monarchy's arbitrary power. (© Bridgeman Art Library)

Plate 10   Between 1180 and 1220 a chapel with stained glass was added to Canterbury Cathedral (Kent) as a continuation of its east end. It is called the *corona*, a term which referred not just to the finishing touches to the church but to Becket's tonsure which the murderers hacked. (© Bridgeman Art Library)

Plate 11   The murder of Becket, after the *Life of St Thomas* composed around 1180 by his friend John of Salisbury. On the morning of 29 December 1170, Thomas was enjoying a meal with his friends in the archiepiscopal palace of Canterbury, when the four murderers insisted on speaking to him. That evening Fitz-Urse and his companions carried out the crime in the cathedral, while John of Salisbury and other clerks hid behind the altar. (© Bridgeman Art Library)

Plate 12 A little after the murder, around fifty caskets were created and decorated with Limoges inlay to house Becket's relics. They were scattered across Europe. This casket shows Becket's murder beside an altar on which is a chalice. In vaguely associating the crime with the celebration of the mass, the sacrificial dimension of Thomas's martyrdom is compared with Christ's death on the cross. (© Bridgeman Art Library)

Plate 13 Pilgrims travelling to Canterbury to Becket's tomb to beg his spiritual help or a cure for an illness. The pilgrimage to Canterbury was one of the most popular in the West in the Middle Ages, comparable to those to Rome or Compostella. Stained glass from Canterbury, thirteenth century. (© Bridgeman Art Library)

Plate 14 This mural of the end of the twelfth century, recently discovered at Chinon on the wall of the underground chapel of Sainte-Radegonde, has inspired many interpretations. Probably to be seen (*from right to left*) are Henry II, one of his daughters, Eleanor of Aquitaine, and their two sons, one of whom carries a hawk. It might be a simple hunting party; a pilgrimage to St Radegund, a Frankish queen for whom Eleanor showed a certain devotion; or the departure of the captive Eleanor for England after the failure of her revolt against Henry II in 1174. (© Art Archive/ Dagli Orti)

Plate 15 The cathedral at Poitiers had been built at the initiative of Henry II and Eleanor of Aquitaine. It was decorated with a *Crucifixion of St Peter*, which shows at its lower levels the royal couple, surrounded by their children, their knees bent in adoration. They are themselves carrying the window, symbol of their artistic patronage. (© CESM-Poitiers)

Arthurian knight, whose name oddly enough recalls that of Cadoc, one of the French king's mercenaries.[85] Epic and romance, which both reflected and created models of knightly behaviour, show that the appearance of money in warfare seems not to have unduly disturbed the noble conscience.

Other sorts of reward might have seemed more compatible with the noble stem of values. They were more in agreement with knightly traditions and the things that their literature often dwelled on: in particular, the 'youth' (*juvenis*), who succeeded in marrying a rich heiress and who brought him her father's castle where he founded his own lineage. Only luck, a great feat of arms or a long preliminary quest allowed literary heroes to take possession of such a prize. But marriage above one's station did occur under the Plantagenets. In real life, it answered to rather more basic considerations than would occur in the Arthurian legend which so entertained knights. If the king wanted to reward a knight who had been especially loyal to him through many long years of service, he would marry him to a woman of great lineage, the heiress of a tenant-in-chief, whose patrimony and following he wanted at all costs to keep out of the hands of rather less biddable lords.[86] In the winter of 1189, when he realized that his power was ebbing in the face of the rebellion of his son Richard, Henry II stirred himself to give away some fine areas of his kingdom to knights who had remained loyal to him in his illness: Heloise of Lancaster went to Gilbert fitz Reinfrid and Isabel de Clare, daughter of Strongbow and Aiofe, to William Marshal.[87] As in previous days, knights sought to establish themselves by means of a castle and lands provided by the father of his betrothed, who was often also his lord. But it was the king by this period who had the power to give away the hand of the most sought-after women in the English nobility.

Another phenomenon seems just as significant in the political and administrative evolution at the end of the twelfth century. So as better to monitor marriages, the king ordered inquests so as to uncover the names of all heirs and the extent of their patrimony. One of these surveys is known for the year 1165 but its returns are now lost. But the public records still preserve the *Rotuli de dominabus, puellis et pueris* (Rolls of ladies, girls and boys): twelve rolls of parchment compiled around 1185, each reporting on one English county. There is to be found a list full of aristocratic widows and orphaned girls, which allowed Henry II either to find them husbands or, if it was too late, to impose a fine for a marriage which might have been celebrated without his permission. The *pueri* whose names are also entered on the rolls are the orphaned boys whose guardianship and whose fiefs the king had given away at farm, a source of juicy revenue for nobles loyal to the Crown.[88] So a network of patronage, based on the share out of the possessions of widows and orphans by the Exchequer, fell into place. It brought in extra income to the aristocracy, which had every intention of maintaining the right to monitor wardship. In 1211, King John took measures to lessen the amount that guardians could draw from patrimonies. In a more general way, John's policies seemed to considerably extend royal control over the entire feudal system. In particular, John transformed the rather tenuous and vague link, based on loyalty and obedience, which brought him the homage of his vassals, into a coherent network of allegiance secured by charters and hostages.[89] John's new arrangements helped him to keep closer control over his men. But their unpopularity gave further justification to his rebellious critics who impose by means of Magna Carta a reversion to the old ways.[90]

Administrative pressure, stronger than ever under John, stimulated in turn a resistance movement on the part of the nobility, who tried to recover the power they had lost to recent reform. British medievalists usually characterize this reaction as 'bastard feudalism'. It involved the setting-up of a network of clientage: parties and pressure groups around a magnate, who rewarded his followers with gifts, cash or by obtaining favours from the Crown.[91] Around William Marshal, for example, has been noted several connections based on protection, marriage, material common interest, social climbing and local ambition, explained in the Marshal's most recent biography as the end of traditional feudal allegiance and the rise of 'bastard feudalism'.[92] Such an analysis by medieval historians shows perhaps an idealized interpretation of the personal link, which, affectionate and disinterested, might not in its early days involve an automatic grant of a fief. In this interpretation, the relationship between lord and vassal, which could seem so disinterested at the beginning, became at the end 'bastardized' or 'corrupted' because of the desire for money.[93]

This insight of today's historians about the feudal link does nothing to detract from a major question. Does legislation concerning fees and the closer definition of the nobility betray a crisis of loyalty? Do they signify a loss of mutual confidence between the king and his military aristocracy, or a calculated response to make up for the disappearance of military service tied just to the oath taken by faith and homage? Such questions refer back to the classifications worked out by legal historians, to 'the personal link' (a relationship based on reciprocal service, but also on the trust, loyalty and obedience that feudal institutions established between lord and vassal) and to 'the property link' (a relationship between the lord and the vassal based on the fief, the land or property given in exchange for military service and counsel).[94] But as the well-established epistemology of such a dichotomy between personal and property links does not always make for agreement between medieval historians, it is as well to stress that it is very useful for the purpose of analysing feudal relations and for establishing some sort of reasonable framework in the study.

The nature of the personal link between lord and vassal is very necessary in order to understand the obedience, and sometimes disobedience, of a nobleman to the king. It is a frequent theme in Plantagenet historiography. So, Jordan Fantosme said that, if the barons of Henry II had beaten William of Scotland, it was because of the trust and the loyalty that they maintained towards their master.[95] The *History of William Marshal*, written a little after the eponymous hero's death, aimed to demonstrate that his political choices, often a matter of debate in his own lifetime, had always been honest, being dictated by his fidelity to the oath sworn to his lord and to the men of his own entourage.[96] Roger of Howden recurred often enough to the subject. For instance, he exaggerated the impact of the oath sworn to the Empress Mathilda in the mobilizing of the Anglo-Norman nobility to the side of the young Henry II against Stephen of Blois.[97] Howden also noted that Richard the Lionheart, king in July 1189, far from dismissing those who had fought against him to the bitter end because of their fidelity to his father, rewarded them and retained them in his own service. In contrast he cast off the opportunists who had betrayed his dying father so as to join his army.[98] On his part, Gerald of Barry says that the greyhound of Owain, a knight of Henry II's army, had received up to seven wounds while helping its master in the heart of a battle against the Welsh. The dog was carried to the king with full honour and Gerald launched into a long eulogy about canine loyalty.[99] It was that sort of loyalty that Henry II would very much have liked to have seen in all his subjects.

One final text has a lot to say about the importance of the personal link in the political orientations of the aristocracy. Rigord, the official historiographer of Philip Augustus, says that in 1202 many of the knights of King John gave up the fight against the Capetians and preferred instead to go on crusade 'in token of the death of King Richard of happy memory'.[100] Medievalists trained in the *Annales* tradition, cheerfully taught to think in terms of structures, mentalities and social movements, might not be happy with it, but the unpopularity of King John amongst his barons counted for a lot in the loss of Normandy, just like the reputation of Richard the Lionheart explains the success of his campaigns there. It should after all be incumbent on us to penetrate the minds of those aristocratic warriors, and to fathom their hearts and their souls, so as to understand more closely the true motives for their political, personal and free choices. In its facile nature, this assertion betrays the intellectual poverty of a historian who applies the formulaic Cartesian reading of texts so as to interpret the motivation of a nobility dealing with the expansion of Plantagenet bureaucracy. Noble rebellion certainly could be analysed as a mechanism whose principal elements might be: the strengthening of the king's central government; the presence of his representatives on the fringes of empire; the surrender of castles to the Crown; the progress of royal justice against honour courts; the pressure imposed on honorial lords to perform military service or pay scutage; the brutality of mercenaries; the adopting of a 'youthful' model of conduct by the king's sons, and so on. The list could be added to, but in the present state of research it would be a difficult task to put in any order the causes of aristocratic antagonism.

It may seem over-ambitious to assess the level of compliance or defiance towards Angevin government amongst the nobility along the lines of a dialectic, or aristocratic antithesis contrasting with royal thesis, amounting to the same thing as the private being hostile to the public sphere. When Richard the Lionheart, duke of Aquitaine, made war on his father, the king of England and his feudal lord, was it in his public or private capacity? Was he harking back to traumas arising from his troubled childhood with the encouragement of his mother, Eleanor of Aquitaine?[101] Or rather, was he defending the interests of Aquitainians against the king of England who was claiming from them more than he had a right to? Where does his departure on crusade come into it? Was it for him about the expiation of past mistakes and increasing his military glory; defending Christianity in the Holy Land; increasing the prestige of the English Crown and finding new opportunities for his knights? Around 1200, the problem of the use of violence by the king or the aristocracy is so much the more complex as it is at the commencement of a period of renewal of state power. In this time of change, when the State was beginning to come painfully to gestation, the pursuit of warfare was not exclusive to one or other of these major social players. Their military activities often agreed, since the nobility made up the core of royal armies and the king was as much a warrior as his nobles.

Elusive unity

The geopolitics of the Angevin world should not be understood as comprising a single bloc. In fact, it depended mostly on the more or less narrow link that each provincial nobility associated with the king maintained towards him. The nature of this link between king and aristocracies varied widely from one region to another. In 1151, Geoffrey Plantagenet had such a deep sense of this diversity that, on his deathbed, he advised his son Henry II to respect the customs of each of the realms which fell to him by inheritance, and never to import the laws of one of them into another. In Geoffrey's eyes, it would be a serious political misjudgement to transfer the governmental structure of England and Normandy to Anjou, despite its being so efficient, as Anjou was not yet ready to tolerate such authority.[102] Almost eight centuries later it has to be admitted that Geoffrey's analysis has not lost its wisdom. Coming from a man who was himself a count, it reveals an undeniable local knowledge. The point is to assess whether Henry II and his sons had taken it on board, and whether they made it one of their key political strategies.

Modern-day historians debate the question of whether the first Angevin king of England – discovering simultaneously the energy of its administrative structures and the profits of its fiscal system – followed his father's advice or not. For Jacques Boussard and André Debord, it was possible to talk of the centralizing authoritarianism of Henry II on the continent.[103] But English medieval historians emphasize rather the delegation of power to the characteristic institutions of each province, arguing against the idea of a Plantagenet attempt to marshal their individual realms under an over-mastering 'Empire'.[104] This diversity of opinion is witness to the complexity of the question, and also to two different historiographical traditions. It is permissible for us to put this difference in simple terms by noting how the thesis of modern French medieval historians – product of a Jacobin, centralizing republic – contrasts with their British colleagues' position, used to the autonomy of the differing lands under the Crown. To attempt to respond, so far as we can, to the question of Henry II's respect for the last wishes of Geoffrey Plantagenet, it is necessary to review each of the realms of his empire. We will start with the more 'uncontrolled' regions where the aristocracy manifested most clearly its desire for independence, and move on to those where the ruling elites not only accepted central government without a qualm, but themselves played a part in increasing its operations. As we go, we will return to our main point, discovering the dialectic between collaboration and resistance in the aristocracy confronted by a rising Angevin state.

Aquitaine: permanent rebellion

French or Anglo-Norman chroniclers at the end of the twelfth century unanimously depicted Aquitaine and its nobility as being ungovernable, rebellious and hostile to the king, whether he was Capetian or Plantagenet. There are any number of their accounts of the risings of the local aristocracy against the king. Robert de Torigny held up his hands in horror at the participants in the problems of 1168, during which the Aquitainian leaders 'rebelling wildly against the king, devoted themselves to arson, crushed the poor and wasted the entire country.'[105] Richard of Devizes, the panegyrist of Richard the Lionheart, enthusiastically described the king's military successes in bringing down the Gascon aristocrats, 'wretched brigands' (*latrunculi*) and 'incorrigible tyrants' (*tiranni indomabiles*).[106] It is much the same with Gerald of Wales who describes the seizure of Taillebourg and the efficiency with which Richard restored order to Poitou, shaken by an aristocratic rising.[107] The idea of the ancestral Aquitainian attraction to war continued at the court of King John, where the label 'Poitevin' became synonymous with the hawkish party of those French émigrés who wanted to squander English resources on dubious military adventures abroad.[108] If we believe their contemporaries, the Aquitainians of 1154–1224 were aggressive. They loved the clash of arms, which they took up whenever it suited them for their own momentary benefit, with no thought of the common good.

Another aspect of their bad reputation was the idea that the Aquitainian was not at all chivalrous in the matter of promises and given word. For William le Breton, chaplain of Philip Augustus and his court historiographer, Aquitaine was inhabited by a warlike and untamed nobility that the king could scarcely check, particularly because 'Poitevin good faith is nonexistent' and that 'changing sides is what Poitevins always do.'[109] The same view prevailed at the Anglo-Norman court. When Benoit de Sainte-Maure revised the chronicle of Dudo of St-Quentin, where William Longsword (927–942) thinks twice about marrying his sister to William III (died 963), duke of Aquitaine, he puts in William's mouth the words: 'Every Poitevin generation is slack in warfare, wimpish and lacking drive; they are the most greedy, featherbrained, disloyal and untrustworthy of people'.[110] Around 1210, the poet Raoul de Houdenc developed in his turn the theme of the treacherous Poitevin: 'What treachery there is in Poitou . . . stronghold of treason.'[111] About fifteen years later John, author of the Marshal history, repeated the same cliché when he talked of the abrupt change of side by some Poitevin barons in 1202 at King John's expense: 'Once the men of Poitou had been released, they immediately set about doing what they had to. Had to? What was it they had to do at that point? Trick their own lord and attract the alliance of foreign lordships. Such is always the way with them.'[112] A little later, Matthew Paris (1200–1259) tells how, on his deathbed, Richard the Lionheart asked that his bowels be buried in the church of Châlus (Limousin) where he had been struck down, 'as a gift to the Poitevins, to highlight their treachery, for he judged that no other part of his body was worthy of them.' Further on in his chronicle he regretted 'the innate treachery of the Poitevins'.[113] The stereotype of the duplicity, disloyalty and inconstancy of the Aquitainians is widespread in historiography. It was an old cliché, but it gathered strength at Henry II's court. It was Henry who worked so hard to put the southern lordships under his control.

But rhetorical exaggeration, in a tangle of such literary assertions, can be deceptive. It was intended to stress the difficulty of the kings' peace-keeping activities and to boost their military exploits in a region so much the more difficult to hold as its people was assumed to be violent and traitorous. It embedded itself in a deep-seated regional stereotype, through the distortion of which the northern French looked on the people south of the Loire as allergic to all forms of stable, fair and just political organiza-tion. Beginning in 1209, this theme of pervasive anarchy in the south was strengthened by the assassination of the papal legate Peter de Castelnau, and gave a solid justification to the knights of the Ile de France to join in the Albigensian Crusade, presented as a 'peace-keeping affair'.[114] This military confrontation reflected, in a spectacular way, a very deeply estab-lished antagonism between the north and south of France, which matched almost exactly the boundary between speakers of the langue d'oil and langue d'oc. The division between a Romanized world and a Germanic world was perhaps deeper than that which separated the culture of the French, English and German aristocracies.[115] Around 1200, xenophobia was undeniably influencing the perception of Aquitaine among the chroniclers and vernacular writers of the north.

It does not explain everything, however. Deconstruct it critically as much as you may, the discourse of medieval authors was based on solid reality. Their ethnic prejudices were undeniable but they do not allow us entirely to ignore their testimony. They seem balanced when they emphasize the problems that Louis VII and Henry II and his successors certainly experienced when they asserted themselves in the south. Even worse, the passionate autonomy of the southern principalities surfaced in the heart of the Plantagenet family. Eleanor of Aquitaine and the young Richard the Lionheart took their freedom to defy Henry II from their ducal title, an attitude founded on the ancient rejection of all superior authority by the count of Poitiers.[116] Further down the social scale, it is only necessary to note the small part in Henry II's government taken by Poitevin, and more so, Limousin and Gascon, nobles. They appear only occasionally in the entourage of the king of England, generally when the king was travelling round their own lands.[117] In Aquitaine, there were more who resisted the king than who accepted his rule. They were committed to the preservation of their lands from any royal intervention. The foundations of seigneurial jurisdiction were far from being undermined by any advance in ducal justice, as the formulas of certain charters show. For example, in 1160, an act of Garsire, lord of Rais (Tiffauges), mentions his 'lordship, law, jurisdiction, justice and coercion, with high and low justice of life and limbs'.[118] The house of Anjou showered gifts and favours in vain on the great local families, for they were no less reluctant to cooperate and abandon their prerogatives because of their powerful attachment to their independence.

The example of the Lusignan family is a case in point. In 1190, Richard the Lionheart supported the candidature of Guy for the throne of Jerusalem and in 1194 gave the hand of Alice, heiress of the powerful Norman county of Eu to Ralph d'Exoudun.[119] If he had done that to secure the allegiance of the Lusignans to the English Crown, it was a waste of effort. In 1202, Hugh IX le Brun de Lusignan, brother of Ralph d'Exoudun, accused King John before Philip Augustus's court of having taken Isabel of Angoulême, with whom he had already contracted a marriage by the ceremony of *verba de presenti*.[120] King Philip used it as an excuse to break the treaty of Le Goulet (1200) and invade the continental lands of the king of England, which he claimed as a forfeit.[121] The affair of Isabelle's broken engagement and its aftermath betrayed the Plantagenets' untenable situation; they had wasted their time trying to dominate the Aquitainians. It was why they had arranged for Englishmen and Normans to administer their southern lands, prefering them to the local lords. It is tempting to apply the adjective 'colonial' to describe their presence in principalities never anything other than foreign and hostile.

Aquitainian reluctance to cooperate with the king as often as not took the form of open rebellion. Roger of Howden echoes the complaints of local people against Richard the Lionheart, whom they accused of maltreating their wives and daughters before handing them over to his soldiers.[122] According to Howden, these offences against their honour justified their general uprising. Howden also relates that in June 1194 Richard the Lionheart admitted, in his reply to a request for a truce from Philip Augustus, that he had no way of checking the violence of the Poitevin magnates 'and that he had no desire to defy the customs and laws of Poitou, or his other lands, where the custom was established since ancient times that magnates settled their differences by the sword.'[123] In

THE ARISTOCRACY: BETWEEN REBELLION AND SUBMISSION   191

Howden's account, an unbridgeable chasm separated the king from the Aquitainians. They could only ever be at loggerheads.

Today's medieval historians, following Roger of Howden, have cited the Aquitainian aristocracy's fondness for resorting to arms outside state control.[124] The frequency of aristocratic rebellion in Poitou supports this idea. During Henry II's reign one broke out on average every three-and-a-half years. The flashpoints of these risings were to be found in the Limousin, where ducal demesne was non-existent, but above all in the county of Angoulême, where first the Taillefer and then the Lusignan family, perpetually at war with the duke, built up for themselves a virtual independent principality, carved out of the heart of Aquitaine.[125] The violence of these risings was such that it ended at times in the assassination of the king's lieutenant. The Lusignans were behind the murder of Patrick of Salisbury in 1168 and of one of Richard the Lionheart's close friends in 1188.[126] In 1202, at war with King John, the Lusignans again played a prominent part in the loss of Normandy. There was very often open hostility among the Aquitainian nobles toward the king of England and his officers, against whom they barely hesitated to take up arms.

In Aquitaine, the assassination of Patrick of Salisbury and King Richard's friend seems to be linked to a xenophobia specific to the English. Two texts demonstrate an insecurity – or at least a sense of definite otherness – which English clergy in Poitou experienced. Isaac, Cistercian abbot of L'Etoile, in marginalia he scribbled on a manuscript of his tract on the canon of the mass (1166), talked of his fear of a local lord who had his eye on some lands from his monastery: 'Hugh, lord of Chauvigny, shouts from the rooftops that he wants to wreak vengeance on me for all the English. Oh! If I were not English and if, in the place where I am exiled, I had never seen an Englishman!'[127] Undoubtedly, Isaac often met John Bellesmains, bishop of Poitiers, whom local charters call 'John the Englishman', like Isaac a supporter of Thomas Becket, a stance that led to an attempt to poison him. John of Salisbury sympathizes with his difficulties: 'This foreigner, educated and raised outside Poitou, did not know enough about the indigenous customs and ancient rights of the Aquitainians.'[128] The integration of an Englishman in high ecclesiastical or civil office into Aquitainian society and political life seemed impossible.

This alienation appeared continually in Aquitainian refusals to obey ducal authority. The Lusignan attitude towards the marriage of King John and Isabel of Angoulême tells us a lot about their desire to organize their own dynastic marriage strategy as it suited them. It is not the only example. In 1177, Henry II claimed wardship of Denise, only daughter of Ralph de

Déols, who had recently died in Italy returning from a pilgrimage to the Holy Land. The orphaned Denise, heir of Déols and Châteauroux, aged three or four, was the most desirable bride in Berry. Her uncle Eudes, in deciding to keep her in his castle of Châtre, was openly opposing the king, who wanted to marry her to Baldwin de Redvers (died 1188), heir to the earldom of Devon. The Young Henry, sent to Berry, surrendered in front of the walls of Châteauroux, which King Henry would take in person some months later with his own troops. Henry only obtained control of this particular heir by force.[129] The story of Denise is interesting by way of comparison. At the same time in England royal agents were hurrying around the lands of all the tenants-in-chief, compiling a list of widows and orphans available for marriage in the celebrated *Rotuli* of 1185.[130] In England, the mechanisms of the Exchequer to control the marriage of heirs were infinitely superior. The same applies to the wardship of noble boys, such as when, by contrast, Henry II experienced in 1156 great problems in getting hold of the wardship of the young viscount Aimar V of Limoges from his uncle.[131] The king encountered just as many difficulties in establishing his power over Aquitaine as he did in asserting his marital control over Eleanor, ruler of Aquitaine and the leader of the great rebellion of 1173. As ever, public and private life were inextricably mixed up.

Beginning in 1189, the date he succeeded to the kingship, Richard, son of Henry and Eleanor – a feature of the landscape in Aquitaine since he had been a boy – was more and more successful. It is remarkable that around 1190 he had not faced any particular opposition to remarrying Denise de Déols (now a widow) to his vassal, Andrew de Chauvigny, member of a knightly family in the service of the bishop of Poitiers. More important still, his officers were respected for what they were, representatives of royal authority. Richard went so far as to appoint as seneschals of Poitou (almost regional viceroys) men of modest origins, born of merchant or administrative families, men such as Robert de Montmirail and Peter Bertin.[132] But he did not succeed in completing the job, which mostly eluded him, of suppressing the autonomy of the castle-lordships and limiting their judicial privileges. Richard the Lionheart and his officers nevertheless scored some successes in their struggle to claw back aristocratic jurisdiction.

In 1199, the premature death of King Richard put a drastic full stop to the modest progress of administrative centralization. At this date, his brother John, who succeeded Richard with difficulty despite the support of Eleanor, had to resort to major concessions to the benefit of the Poitevin nobles. Comital demesne lands were squandered to their profit; fief rents poured out in exchange for their loyalty drained the English treasury; the office of seneschal of Poitou was to be monopolized from now on by Savary de Mauléon, Reginald de Pons and other local castellans. A true aristocratic tetrarchy (Lusignan, Thouars, Parthenay-Larchevêque and Mauléon) arose out of the great counties and viscounties, a tetrarchy which – all-powerful in practice – conducted itself as an equal partner with the king and subjected the castellans, the lesser nobility and the towns to its own domination.[133] Viscount Geoffrey of Thouars, for example, had a claim on the duchy of Aquitaine, for he was grandson of William IX,[134] by his mother Agnes of Poitiers. After being widowed, Agnes became the wife of Ramiro of Aragon, which also made Geoffrey the half-brother of Queen Petronilla, wife of the count of Barcelona.[135] Such was the extent and prestige of Geoffrey's network of alliances. The heads of these four vice-comital dynasties conducted their own family policy of self-aggrandizement, shifting alliances between Philip Augustus and John according to the flow of political circumstances. Until the final disaster of 1242, the choices of these dynasties made up the history of Poitou.

The career of Savary de Mauléon (c.1180–1233) is a case in point. A supporter of Arthur of Brittany and captured at Mirebeau, Savary was imprisoned by King John, who was ultimately reconciled with him and appointed him his seneschal of Poitou in 1205. From John he passed to the service of Raymond VI of Toulouse, then on to the Albigensian Crusade, from there to Philip Augustus between 1212 and 1213 and, finally, back to King John between 1214 and 1216. Savary was at Damietta with the crusaders (1219). On his return, Henry III made him the last seneschal of Poitou in the English interest. In 1224 he crossed over, bag and baggage, into the camp of Louis VIII, who gave him command of La Rochelle and L'Aunis. Nevertheless, he joined in the revolt against Blanche of Castille, and had to negotiate in 1227 a truce with Louis IX. Just before his death in 1230, he joined up with an expeditionary force led by Henry III to St Malo, for the reconquest of Poitou. His career, constrained by political about-turns and changing of alliances, appears chaotic: treason there became normal behaviour. But it did respond to a certain logic. As with the majority of Poitevin nobles, Savary drew on the profits of the wars between the kings of France and England to keep up his seigneurial power on a daily basis. He learned to play a double game in a difficult situation auctioning off his military and administrative services to the highest bidder.[136] His repeated disloyalty and his deep-seated inconstancy reveals as much the local aristocracy's wish for independence as its hostility to every centralizing authority that might threaten the autonomy of its lordships.

Further south, in Gascony, a realm annexed only in 1059 to Aquitaine, the behaviour of the nobility was even more volatile. The hold on Gascony of the dukes – natives of Poitou where their patrimony was – remained feeble. Their demesne lands there were practically non-existent other than in the city of Bordeaux and its hinterland.[137] The dukes' activities in the southern regions were modest enough. Henry II had only six charters drawn up for these territories, and the fifty or so which were issued from the chancellery of Richard the Lionheart concerned towns and monasteries on the banks of the Garonne and the Adour, whose frontier sites and strategic importance Richard knew all too well.[138] The study of Plantagenet itineraries shows that they went there rarely. The absence of ducal power allowed the power of other lords.

The counts of Bigorre and Armagnac or the viscounts of Bayonne, Dax, Lomagne, Oloron, Comargue and Gabarret, and even the majority of the castellans, were the true masters of Gascony. When Richard the Lionheart tried to reverse the situation and impose his own power on the region, they rebelled along the lines of their Poitevin, Angoumois and Limousin cousins. To counter them, the Angevins led campaigns into their lands from time to time. In May 1191, the strategic purpose of Richard's marriage with Berengaria of Navarre was precisely to gain the support of his bride's father in Gascony, where Navarrese knights fought the local lords who had rebelled during Richard's crusade and captivity.[139] In 1196, the marriage of Richard's sister Joan with Raymond VI of Toulouse – to whom she brought the Agenais as a dowry – was an integral part of the same programme of regional control.[140] The next year, the king pro-claimed statutes which aimed at imposing a peace on the country of Entre-deux-Mers, with the help of the local bishops.[141] These new matrimonial strategies reveal a greater will to intervene in Gascony. They readjusted the political marketplace in the south.

Richard the Lionheart also understood that for his Gascon policy to work, he had to count on the urban communities to help against the higher nobility. In 1175, for example, when the rebel Centulle II of Bigorre and Peter II of Dax fled to Dax, the city's population killed the latter and handed over the former to Richard, who soon after-wards confirmed the commune's privileges.[142] Much the same sort of thing happened in 1205. In that year, supported by the count of Armagnac, the viscount of Béarn and other local lords, Alfonso VIII of Castille invaded Gascony, which he claimed as the dowry of his wife Eleanor, daughter of Henry II. Bayonne, La Réole and Bordeaux closed their gates to Alfonso's troops, who had to beat a retreat.[143] These two examples highlight the significance of the alliance between the Plantagenets and the towns of the south-west.

The policy had some reasonable results in Poitou. A new town in 1130, La Rochelle saw a rapid expansion, thanks to favourable commercial circumstances. Loyal to Henry II during the revolt of 1173, the town was showered with royal privileges two years later, becoming the first sworn commune in the region. It further demonstrated its loyalty in the thirteenth century. It became the bridgehead of the campaigns of John to retake his lost possessions, and it was the last place in Poitou to fall to Louis VIII.[144] The adherence of other great regional communes (Saintes, Poitiers, Niort, St-Jean-d'Angely, Cognac and Angoulême) to the king of England was also firm. It was a response to grants of liberties by Eleanor of Aquitaine under threat from Arthur of Brittany and Philip Augustus in the period 1199–1204 after the model of the *Establishments of Rouen*.[145] It is significant that in 1220 Niort asked Henry III to be governed and defended by an English seneschal rather than a semi-independent lord with an uncertain and changing allegiance.[146] The strategy of an alliance between king and commune against the aristocracy could not be better demonstrated than in that example.

At the end of the twelfth century, the collusion between the duke and the towns against the Aquitainian counts, viscounts and castellans was a new deal in the local political marketplace. The king assisted the interests of the noble urban elite and the mercantile classes in keeping peace on the highways, abolishing aristocratic tolls and opposing lords' arbitrary exactions. The king's communal privileges granted to the rising commercial oligarchy reponsibility for part of the justice, public order and accountability of their cities. The privileges won the loyalty of the citizens and in return they acknowledged a sense of gratitude to the Plantagenets. At the same time, English and continental ports were becoming the pivotal point of the expansion of trade. Merchants increased in wealth and consequently in political power. Their loyalty was fixed on the Plantagenets, with whom they appeared to share so much in common.

It is of course a topos to talk of the role of the townsfolk of Gascony – and in particular of Bordeaux, lavishly equipped with commercial privileges and civic liberties – in the allegiance of the southern lands to the king of England.[147] Following this theory, the urban elite would become, after the 1150s, a key actor in political life, in open rivalry with the old rural castellan nobility. The theory is by no means entirely misleading. But mercantile venturing, the attractions of profits and the export of wine from the Garonne to the English ports cannot explain everything. Indeed, although expanding in political and institutional influence, the townsfolk of the thirteenth century would by no means surpass the nobility.

In Aquitaine, the real social actors remained the counts, viscounts, castellans, barons and knights, whose lordships and military expertise guaranteed their social hegemony. This aristocracy was soon made to realize that its best interests were in remaining under the rule of a distant and foreign dynasty, rather than seeing its margin of autonomy reduced by an incoming French bureaucracy. It had realized that the struggle between the Planatagenets and the Capetians was worth being stoked up by their changes of heart, treachery and treasons, which would prevent one or other of the dynasties from getting the upper hand in any decisive way, and imposing itself on Aquitaine without rivalry from the other. Used with moderation, the change of allegiance became a formidable strategy in perpetuating the stalemate between Capetians and Plantagenets. It allowed an auction, with the idea of daily rachetting up more and more lands, rents and fees in exchange for a loyalty for which the Plantagenets would pay top price. This policy – whose only result was to maintain the autonomy of Aquitainian castellans – became rapidly very unpopular at the English court. The 'Poitevin' party and its hawkish tendencies was opposed in England. Any number of Englishmen refused to join in dubious military adventures on the continent. But they did not have the last word on the subject. Up till 1224 and even till 1242, King John and King Henry III were continually active in Aquitaine. It was evidence of the dynasty's attachment to its ancestral and maternal homeland.

Was it a good idea for the aristocracy to take autonomy and privilege as their political priority? There are numerous indications of an increasing burden of ducal taxation in Gascony under John and Henry III. Among the new impositions which were levied on the nobles from now on is to be found a direct tax substituting for service in the army rather like the scutage, and direct control by the Crown over wards and wardship. Tolls on the commerce of the Bordelais were increasing even if the merchants of Bordeaux were benefitting handsomely from their privileged position with regard to English ports. The main cause of increased revenues and a tighter infrastructure was 'the shrinking of English continental possessions back to Gascony'.[148] It is a historical paradox. The king of England never ruled more effectively the south-west – up till recently a region barely governable – than when his other principalities were clasped to the heart of France. Beginning in 1224, deprived of his last continental territories, the king successfully focused his centralizing activities on the limited region between the Garonne and the Pyrenees.

Greater Anjou and Brittany: uneasy submission

Anjou, the fatherland of Henry II's family, expanded in an unprecedented way after the middle of the eleventh century. In 1152, the county included Maine and Touraine. Its territorial expansion coincided with a remarkable strengthening of comital power. After 1144, the control of Normandy put Geoffrey Plantagenet at the head of a principality administered with unusual efficiency, something which gave him ideas.[149] He was all the more successful in applying the model of Norman government in Anjou, as his dynasty had for a long time controlled substantial personal estates in the county.[150] Henry II completed his father's work, securing progressively better control of his territory on the Loire. He managed to divide Anjou and its lands in Maine and the Touraine into a dozen prévôtés, each of them well enough provided with comital castles and lands to reward his officers committed with the charge of justice, police and castle garrison. The comparison with Gascony, where there were hardly any ducal prévôts except at Bordeaux and perhaps La Réole in Henry II's time, illustrates the difference between the two regions.[151] The striking works undertaken at the fortress of Chinon, which with Loches became the most powerful fortification in the Loire valley, made the control of Henry II and his sons over the region obvious to everyone.[152] But despite these administrative advances, the local lords resisted the idea that their lordships were anything other than enclaves independent of any higher jurisdiction after the example of Bouchard, a lesser nobleman, who was still in 1189 coolly calling himself 'lord of L'Isle Bouchard by the grace of God'.[153]

It was for this reason that, up against the continual increase of comital power, the nobility of the Loire valley hovered between loyal cooperation and open rebellion. Henry II relied on certain local lords who were life-long loyalists: Maurice de Craon and Brian de Martigné were often in command of his troops. In 1173, Maurice led the royal army during the great rebellion, while Brian was given command of the castle of Thouars, seized in 1158.[154] But within the Angevin aristocracy there seemed to be rather more lords hostile to Henry II whenever a favourable opportunity offered itself, above all at the beginning of his reign. It was then that they rose up in a universal and far-reaching rebellion in a tangle of alliances and feudal loyalties. They knew that from then on, up against their count, now the most powerful king in the West, they could not pursue their claims by the single and isolated rising of one noble lineage as they had done in the past. So they banded together under powerful leaders, like Geoffrey, brother of Henry II, in 1152 and 1156 or Henry's own sons in 1173, who were in a position to raise troops within the Plantagenet Empire.

Some local barons, such as Ralph de Faye, the uncle of Eleanor of Aquitaine, or Hugh de Sainte-Maure, councillor of the Young Henry, played a key role in unleashing the great revolt of 1173. They drew in with them a number of lords, resisting the increasing authority of Henry II: William and Joscelin de Sainte-Maure, Geoffrey and Ralph de la Haye, Robert de Sablé, Geoffrey de Lavardin, Matthew de la Jaille, Philip de la Chartre, Vivian de Montevrault. These lords found solid support in the Mirebellais and the south-west of the Touraine. But the king kept the loyalty of the country round Chinon, where he was firmly in control, and in the valley of the Loire. His Anglo-Norman knights and mercenaries would give him the last word. Obedient after 1174, the aristocracy of Anjou could do nothing else thereafter but submit to the demands of comital power. In 1189, Richard the Lionheart took power by ranging himself against the nobility of the Loire region, who had remained loyal to his father. One of his first acts was to imprison Stephen de Marzai, seneschal of Anjou, and confiscate his lands for embezzlement, and to hand over his office to Robert of Thornham, an Englishman.[155] This replacement reveals the ease with which the king of England now dominated Anjou, which he could govern through a cross-Channel officer.

The history of the county of Anjou in its glory days is inextricably linked with that of Brittany. Despite what is often assumed, the duchy was by no means administratively backward before the Plantagenet takeover. Quite the contrary, Duke Conan III (1112–1148) considerably increased his power when he reformed the ducal finances.[156] It was the war which pitted his son-in-law, Duke Eudes de Porhoët (1148–1156) against his son, Hoel (1148–1156) count of Nantes, in a life-and-death struggle for succession which put a brake on administrative progress. Around 1155, the people of the Nantes region appealed to Henry II, count of neighbouring Angers up the river, a city with which they maintained close commercial links. They thus defied the government both of Eudes and Hoel. Henry accepted that his brother Geoffrey, whose second revolt in Anjou he was about to crush, should become count of Nantes, thus also solving the problem of Geoffrey's appanage.

When Geoffrey died prematurely in 1158, his inheritance passed to another Geoffrey (died 1186), his nephew and son of Henry II, whose Angevin troops helped to preserve Nantes from Conan IV (1156–1171), the new duke of Brittany. In 1166, Conan reached a lasting peace with the king of England. He espoused his only daughter and heir to Geoffrey, abdicated in his favour and retired to the county of Guincamp.[157] The agreement between Henry II and Conan IV was eased by the duke of

Brittany's possession of the vast county of Richmond (Yorkshire), for he was a member of the family of Penthièvre which had participated in the conquest of England alongside William of Normandy. If Conan IV wanted to hang on to this vast cross-Channel lordship, he had to accommodate the king.[158] Besides this, by his abdication, the duke seems to have wished to preserve the integrity of his duchy, to stop the county of Nantes being carved out of it by being annexed to Anjou. He was also maintaining the independence, theoretical and institutional as it was, which this agreement brought the duchy in regard to the king of England. Conan's great grandfather, Alan IV, duke of Brittany, who had married successively the daughter of William the Conqueror and the daughter of Fulk IV of Anjou, had already done homage for the duchy to Henry I. The Breton nobility for their part, touchy about their identity, probably supported the decision of Conan IV, stopping the territorial dismemberment of the county of Nantes and maintaining the ducal office.

Later events show that the Breton attitude was well-founded, for Brittany preserved both its territorial integrity and its ducal dynasty for a number of centuries to come. In 1181, Geoffrey married Constance, now of full age, and so made sure of her inheritance. But he died five years later, on one of his frequent visits to the court at Paris, carried off suddenly by a summer virus, and not as a consequence of an accident sustained during a tournament, as Roger of Howden sensationally makes out.[159] Philip Augustus had him buried before the high altar of the newly built cathedral of Notre Dame, where he founded two chantries for the good of Geoffrey's soul. Philip felt a true friendship for Geoffrey. Rigord praises the king's sorrow over the event, and Gerald of Wales says that the king had to be restrained from throwing himself into the freshly dug grave.[160] Such extravagant displays of affection did not only reveal a mind dealing with death or the loss of a friend: they reveal more about the public and private sphere as it then was. They show an undeniable political dimension. They follow on from the strategic understanding achieved by Geoffrey with the Capetians against the interests of his father Henry II. We should understand the staging of this friendship in a symbolical way, as dramatizing the alliance between duke and king.[161] Geoffrey had perhaps understood that the alliance with Paris was necessary to assert himself in Brittany against members of his own family?

True or not, it was Geoffrey's posthumous son, Arthur, born at Easter 1187, who embodied the alliance between the Capetians, fighting King John his uncle by Philip's side. In 1199, on the death of Richard the Lionheart, Arthur laid claim to the Crown of England against John, who defeated him at Mirebeau and imprisoned him at Rouen, where he was probably assassinated. The ducal dynasty did not disappear in this account. After the defeats inflicted on John by the king of France, Brittany continued to benefit from the friendship between the dukes and the Capetians. Brittany passed to Alix (died 1221), born of the third marriage between Constance with Guy of Thouars (died 1213). Alix married Peter of Dreux, known as Mauclerc, cousin and follower of Philip Augustus, in 1213. For many decades, the Capetian ducal line that they founded – linked now not by blood but only by marriage with the Plantagenets – maintained the independence of the duchy against the kings of France and England.[162]

The history of Brittany reveals the succession disputes within the dynasty of Anjou, with Henry II against his brother Geoffrey, and his son of the same name, and then John against his nephew Arthur. Basically, the policy of the Angevin dukes of Brittany – trapped between Normandy, Aquitaine and Anjou – was to break the links with their Plantagenet neighbours by allying with the distant, and indeed absent, Capetians. It could appear disloyal, even suicidal, on the part of the Angevin younger sons, but that is to forget that, in the Angevin family, division and intra-familial warfare were imperatives very often imposed by the territorial aristocracies that each Angevin prince ruled. The struggles demonstrate that Brittany, although peripheral, was nonetheless an important piece on a much bigger chessboard, on which the Plantagenets played the Capetians.

At a local level, these struggles also reflect geographical and political divisions in Brittany, whose counts often fought each other. It followed on from a troubled state of affairs, favourable to the assertiveness of a castle-holding and seigneurial nobility. In his lifetime, Conan IV had to confront noble revolts, principally fomented by Eudes de Porhoët, his brother-in-law; by Guilhomarc, ruler of the county of Léon, who entirely evaded the duke's jurisdiction; and by Ralph de Fougères. To counter their revolts, the duke turned to Henry II, increasing further the dependence of Brittany on its powerful neighbour, simultaneously duke of Normandy and count of Anjou. Conan's abdication and the marriage of his daughter Constance with Geoffrey was part of the logic of alliances made imperative by the plots of the local aristocracy. In 1173, Geoffrey came to a temporary accommodation with Eudes de Porhoët and Ralph de Fougères, to whom he would later grant the stewardship of Brittany. This change of direction away from his father-in-law's policy was only temporary. It occurred when he had a need for all the Breton knights as he rebelled against his own father. In 1179, with the Plantagenet family reconciled for the time being, he crushed the county of Léon.[163] These continual revolts in the vast independent counties, particularly numerous in western Brittany, resembled the situation in Aquitaine.

Despite these internal divisions, the Breton nobility showed a certain attachment to the duchy's integrity under local rule, as a sign of its independence. In contrast to the lands south of the Loire, the Breton nobility was keen to safeguard the autonomy of a principality whose identity had been forged by a long history of freedom-fighting and resistance to neighbouring principalities. As a result, they wanted to see an independent dynasty established and secure, one which took the fate of Brittany in hand. It is significant that neither Henry II or Richard the Lionheart, kings of England, had ever ventured to use the title 'duke of Brittany', nor did they appoint seneschals to run the duchy, probably so as not to upset the local aristocracy which claimed the right to be governed by one of its own.[164] This sort of feeling impregnates the *chansons de geste*. So the *Romance of Aiquin*, composed in western Brittany to celebrate the supposed expulsion of the Saracens from the duchy, attributes the biggest role in their defeat to the local count Nominoë ('Naimes' in the *Romance*), whose charisma outshone the pale figure of a feeble, ancient, indecisive and ineffectual Charlemagne. Jean-Christophe Cassard, its most recent commentator, detects in the scenario the expression of Breton independence, hostile to foreign power as embodied by the Angevin king of England.[165]

This same sentiment asserts itself all the more in 1187 around the person of Arthur, son of Geoffrey. His birth was greeted with joy by the Bretons, who had desired it for a long time.[166] If we believe the English chroniclers, Roger of Howden and Ralph de Diceto, the choice of Arthur's name agreed with a collective decision of the Bretons.[167] But it was William of Newburgh who unravelled the political stratagems behind this truly onomastic conflict: 'The king [Henry II], his grandfather, who had decided that his own name should be given to the boy, was defied by the Bretons, and by solemn acclamation he was called Arthur at the holy font. So the Bretons, who are said to have waited long for an imaginary Arthur, in this way raised up a real modern Arthur with great anticipation, according to the opinion which certain prophets expressed in their famous Arthurian legends.'[168] As the *Chronicle* (1227–1241) of Alberic of Trois Fontaines, a Cistercian of Champagne, establishes, from then on the genealogy of the boy took its roots from the person of the mythical king of the Britons.[169] The circumstances of his birth, not just posthumous but occurring on Easter Day, added to this aura, which excited hopes relating to the political messianism of his people.

At that period, the expectation of a second coming of Arthur to Britain, of his return from the Isle of Avalon or the caverns of Etna, obsessed people's imagination. It is a recurrent theme in literature between 1150 and 1200, strongly influenced by Geoffrey of Monmouth. Around 1155, Wace explicitly mentions the existence of such a hope in Brittany.[170] The same applies to Peter of Blois, who wrote to request a favour as eagerly 'as the Bretons await the coming of Arthur and the Jews that of the Messiah.'[171] But if he admired the power of this faith amongst the Bretons, he had no real belief in its object. This is so when he makes fun of an over-ambitious courtier: 'if you can have faith in such vain expectations, you can just as well await the return of Arthur with his British legions.'[172] For Joseph of Exeter, 'the faith of the Bretons and their credulosity are laughable: they are waiting for Arthur, and will wait for him for ever.'[173] Just as ironical a tone is used by the troubadours and trouvères when they use the image of Breton patience awaiting their legendary king, so as to describe the male attitude displayed before female prevarications. All the same, in a poem composed around 1187, Peire Vidal advised everyone to pause in making fun of the Bretons, 'for now the Bretons have an Arthur, in whom they have put their hopes.'[174] The bulk of these texts, written by non-Breton authors, deprecate the belief in the return of the mythical king of the Celts, too widespread in their opinion. This topos allowed them to deride the Breton separatists, whose Arthurian messianism made them seem rather ridiculous.[175]

Is it necessary to interpret the evidence of these writers as a strong rebuttal of the feeling of Celtic difference which underlies their irony? The attitude of the Breton nobility concerning Duke Geoffrey's posthumous son shows, on the contrary, that 'the hope of the Bretons', laughable as it might be to foreigners, could very much energize the independence struggle. It provided the duke of Brittany nonetheless with symbolic capital of proven value, since a collective predisposition in favour of Arthur, the warrior and conqueror, was at the time widespread. The interpretation of the history of Britain, continental or insular, turned on the independence of its people from Romans and Saxons, served the interests of a ruler who would have liked to strengthen his power in the region against the king of England. The Bretons did not refrain from stirring up this political messianism on the very day after the birth of the long-awaited post-humous heir of Duke Geoffrey.

Henry II and Richard the Lionheart tried at all costs to keep control of the exploitation of the Arthurian myth, which would deprive them of a powerful ideological weapon in their contest against the Capetians.

They claimed Arthur as their ancestor and patron in opposition to the king of France, who themselves claimed Charlemagne. As we have seen, the Plantagenets attempted to appropriate the legendary matter of Britain, whether by commissioning from Stephen de Rouen in 1168 a fictional correspondence of the king of England with Arthur, who gives Brittany to Henry II on condition that he be his vassal, or by the discovery of the relics of Arthur in the English monastery of Glastonbury (1191), demonstrable evidence of the futility of the hope of the Bretons.

More prosaically, in 1187, some months after Duke Geoffrey's death, Henry II sent troops to retake the castle of Morlaix of which Hervey of Léon was trying to take possession. Also, he imposed as the second husband of Constance, Ranulf of Chester, one of her neighbours, viscount of the Avranchin on the unstable frontier of northern Brittany, the owner of numerous estates in Lincolnshire interspersed with the lands of the Breton dukes' earldom of Richmond.[176] The king arbitrarily kept Eleanor, the eldest daughter of Geoffrey and Constance, in England as a sort of hostage to hinder any attempt on dynastic independence on the part of the duchy. In his turn, Henry's son, Richard the Lionheart, once king tried to keep his hold on the duchy by means of Constance. In 1196, he imprisoned the duchess with Ranulf of Chester's help and his armies pillaged Brittany.[177] The reasons for this attack, given a brief treatment by the English chroniclers, are difficult to work out. Was the king retaliating against the proclamation of Arthur as duke by a noble council held at Rennes, as later sources claim?[178] Was he (more probably) reacting to Constance's refusal to hand over the boy's wardship?[179] Whatever the case, the consequences of this campaign were disastrous for his policy. They opened a gulf between the Breton aristocracy and the kings of England. Moreover, Andrew de Vitré, the viscounts of Léon and Wihenoc, bishop of Vannes, succeeded in concealing Arthur and conveying him to Paris, where Philip Augustus would raise him with the future Louis VIII and betroth him to his daughter Mary.

With the duke in exile and his mother in prison, Richard still had to pacify Brittany. He was all the more able to do this as he had a means of exerting great pressure on the Breton aristocracy. The majority of the rebels, like the Fougères, Vitré, Dol, Dinan or Mayenne, were Bretons whose ancestors had taken part in the conquest and colonization of England alongside William the Bastard. They still held some lands in Britain, which the king threatened to confiscate.[180] On the unexpected death of Richard the Lionheart in 1199, his officers held Brittany. Nonetheless, as soon as the king was gone, the Breton nobility rallied almost unanimously to the cause of Arthur, the king of France's candidate for the Crown of England against John, who had been named as heir by Richard on his deathbed. The nobility's loyalty with respect to a Breton boy, who summed up in his person so many legendary expectations and hopes, was constant.

When it fought King John, the Breton nobility found itself in the same camp as the barons of Anjou, Maine, Touraine and the north of Poitou, assembled by the seneschal, William des Roches.[181] The history of these provinces became entangled after 1199 with that of Brittany. Paradoxical as it might seem, the knights of the Loire valley, who had occupied Brittany in difficult circumstances for some decades before this, from now on took the part of the duke and the nobility of the same province against which they had till lately been directing their expansionist energies.

Did they perhaps recognize, put simply, the legitimacy of the succession of Arthur of Brittany as a result of the succession customs that they themselves followed in their families.[182] But in one section of the region's nobility the norm was the custom of 'viage' or 'retour', which favoured the younger brother of the deceased over his son, a custom that at the time would have assisted John.[183] But in those days the rules of succession were far from fixed, and it does not seem a key factor in securing support for a candidate. There is proof of this in the scene described by John the Trouvère. When he heard the news of the death of Richard the Lionheart in the middle of the night, William Marshal and the archbishop of Canterbury met up at once to go over the respective rights to the throne of John and Arthur. The archbishop supported the succession of Arthur because his father Geoffrey was an older brother. But William insisted on John, as he was uncertain of the boy's personality and distrustful of his household, because of their common hostility to the English as their alliance with Philip Augustus proved. He talked hypocritically of the custom by which 'the son is the nearer heir to the father than the nephew'. But John the Trouvère's audience understood that this legal tag was just an argument to justify a decision that had already been made, one based more on personalities and political pragmatism than on succession law.[184] William Marshal had no desire to put a puppet of Philip Augustus on the English throne. Just like the Marshal's, the attitude of the aristocracy of the Plantagenet lands in the Loire valley concerning the order of succession was by no means set in stone, for it was decided pragmatically according to political circumstance.

If medievalists do not accept the legal justification, it falls to them to find other reasons for the Angevin nobility's choice of Arthur of Brittany. When it followed this boy, raised in Paris and a vassal of the Capetians, perpetual enemies of the Plantagenets, was the nobility giving free rein to its discontent with the kings of England? It is plausible that there was a reaction against a less remote administration, believed to be Norman or English. But the local aristocracy could not but be aware that the same process of centralization was going on in the frontier provinces which were directly dependent on Philip Augustus, such as Upper Berry or the Orléanais. The aristocracy did not perhaps have any long-term political insight, but it was not completely fooled either about the Capetian ambitions one day to govern every royal estate in a uniform and effective way. Disenchantment with Angevin government and a feeling of disenchantment with the Plantagenets might well count against King John, but perhaps not to the extent of preferring over him a nephew whose method of government was going to be barely any different from his.

There remains one other interpretation, that an historian of the tradition that prefers structure to accident, and society to the individual, would perhaps dislike. It has been recently restated by John Gillingham, the leading specialist in the reign of Richard the Lionheart, and it would be a pity not to examine it. It is simply about the inability of John to earn the respect of the aristocracy,[185] when in the feudal world the personal link between men largely determined the loyalty of the vassal to his lord. In autumn 1199, his first moves in Anjou comprehensively ruined his already dubious reputation. Roger of Howden said that at this date Arthur of Brittany, then heading towards Le Mans looking to find a diplomatic solution in conference with his uncle, got wind of a royal plan to take him prisoner. His fears were confirmed by the seizure of Chinon the same day, despite a truce. Arthur turned back and took refuge in Angers with his vassals and his mother, who at this time divorced the English earl, Ranulf of Chester, to marry Guy de Thouars.[186] For many, this failed ambush confirmed the reputation John had as a traitor. His bad reputation dissipated the local aristocracy's confidence in him, and, as a consequence, also their feudal allegiance. Here again Roman legal theories, which neatly separated private from public spheres, have little use. In the noble mind, what was emotional and human was preferred over vague and abstract ideas of service to the Crown.

On this level, the success of Richard the Lionheart cannot be denied. It explains how he could maintain and even increase his territorial inheritance from his father, despite his long absence on crusade and in captivity. The general loyalty towards him of the aristocracy of Anjou and the county of Nantes was acquired for a variety of reasons. His generosity attracted much good opinion towards him; his diplomatic skills extended his network of dependants; his long career as a crusader compelled admiration, as it was unusual among princes of his rank. His entire lifestyle was devoted to the knightly ideal, admired by noble warriors.[187] On his death, John the Trouvère regretted the irreparable loss of a leader of men, whom he could inspire in battle. In his time, the Normans 'were ripe corn, and now they are just straw'.[188]

The contrast between Richard and John could not be more striking. John was not equal to a struggle which the Plantagenets began with a considerable handicap. It is worth repeating once again that they were the vassals in the feudal hierachy of France of their rivals, the Capetians. The homage the count of Anjou did to them was an open acknowledgement of submission, considerably more significant than the duke of Normandy's simple oath delivered on the marches of his realm. The count of Anjou had to admit that his counties were under the Crown of France, and even that were nothing but territories within a vast realm. On this point it is significant that in the four hundred or so acts drawn up between 1170 and 1209 in Gascony and Languedoc, only twenty-six did not include a mention of the reigns of Louis VII and Philip Augustus in their dating clauses.[189] The appropriation of the mental construct of a united kingdom of France by the Capetian king was just too deeply rooted in the outlook of the subjects of the house of Anjou. It was all the more powerful as the ecclesiastical geography of the Atlantic region favoured the Capetians, thanks to their control of two metropolitan sees. Louis VII and Philip Augustus could be secure in controlling Tours, an outpost in the Plantagenet Loire valley which belonged to them up to the time of the treaty of Gaillon (1195) as much as Bourges, since the Capetians were masters of Upper Berry. The archbishops of these two sees did not refrain from exercising their rights over their suffragan dioceses, often to be found in the heart of the lordships of the house of Anjou. The Plantagenets could only retaliate by extending the jurisdiction of the archbishopric of Bordeaux and in unsuccessfully sponsoring the elevation of Dol-de-Bretagne to an archdiocese.[190] These were their only options in the face of a general European trend which, in the thirteenth century in France as elsewhere in Europe, promoted the emergence of the kingdom at the expense of the territorial principality.

All these tremors in the Angevin nobility's loyalty towards the king of England points to the large autonomy they still enjoyed. Hostility amongst the Angevins was a distinct factor in politics: in 1199, the Angevins' embracing of the cause of Arthur paved the way for the absorption of Anjou into the kingdom of France. On a significant point, William des Roches, lately the seneschal of Richard the Lionheart and ally of Arthur against John, kept his stewardship of Anjou in the aftermath of Philip

Augustus's conquest. He was typical of an aristocracy which would change sides according to a king's reputation and its own dynastic interests. The nobles of Maine, Anjou and Touraine from then on were loyal to the French Crown. The Plantagenets lost Anjou, cradle of their family, for good. It was not quite the same with the north of Poitou, conquered along with the collapse of the Loire lordships by Philip Augustus. Aimery de Thouars, appointed by the king of France as his seneschal for Poitou, changed sides in 1206. His siding with John had a lot to do with the rising level of the fief rent that the king of England paid him, as well as with the king's geographical distance which guaranteed a certain independence to the Poitevin nobility.[191] For its part, the Breton nobility was not yet ready to put up with external government. In 1213, Philip Augustus successfully took the diplomatic route in obtaining by marriage the ducal title for one of his relatives, Peter of Dreux.

Powerful comital authority, as embodied by the Plantagenets, had made it easy for the Capetians in Greater Anjou. The situation in Brittany was nowhere near the same, for the Angevin dukes there had never been able to impose their authority on the counts and barons of the north. For some centuries, paradoxical as it may seem, their failure would keep Brittany free of direct dependence on the French Crown.

Normandy and the British Isles: obedience to the tough master

Normandy and England together made up the inner core of Plantagenet rule over their vast British and continental territories. They were the centre which governed its wide periphery, the axis around which the sphere that the house of Anjou was trying to dominate rotated. Their fiscal and financial efficiency – stemming more from Carolingian than Scandinavian traditions[192] – allowed the English monarchy to draw on the resources to bring its military plans to fruition.[193] But more than that, the Anglo-Norman aristocracy was a human seedbed where the king raised the loyallest of soldiers and administrators, who preferred royal service to rebellion. Some dubious areas had appeared, however, in the picture of harmonious collaboration between the Angevin dynasty and Anglo-Norman knights, at a time when England and Normandy seemed to be losing their joyous union of former days.

In comparison with Aquitaine or Brittany, or even Anjou, Plantagenet control over the Anglo-Norman lands was tighter. This can be seen in the control of the network of castles. In 1154, Henry II caused most of the 'adulterine castles' to be dismantled, those built in England during the civil war. Only the most redoubtable and strategic had been kept to the king's advantage.[194] In Normandy, nearly every fortress, even simple mottes of earth and timber, were held in the name of the duke, who could demand their immediate surrender. Many of them were even garrisoned by royal troops.[195] A tight network of some fifty five prévôtés kept control over the seigneurial lordships, containing their extent and political autonomy.

The process of the whittling away of the feudal ban to the advantage of the monarchy was very well advanced. In England, around 1190, the reforms of Henry II and his ministers had created the most advanced judicial system in the West. The part played by manorial courts in justice was shrinking, and they barely dealt with anything more than the routine petty arguments between peasants and their minor offences. At the local level the hundred[196] and shire courts, presided over respectively by a bailiff and a sheriff, were controlled by judges in eyre, who regularly toured the country following set circuits. Every free man could appeal to the king's court (*curia regis* or King's Bench) which sat whether the king was absent.[197] Justice had become public business and the establishment of this Common Law left to the lords only lesser offences and their small fines. There is evidence for the king's desire to subvert lords' power of coercion in the *Dialogue* of Richard fitz Nigel, which treats them as 'domestic enemies' whose intolerable exactions are the most visible sign of their tyranny. The *Laws and Customs of the Kingdom of England*, in the same tone, declares that lords who abuse distraint and disseisin (the arbitrary seizure of the livestock and other goods of peasants) should undergo the same punishment as thieves and other disturbers of the peace: slicing off of the lips, death or disinheritance of their issue.[198] Doubtless such dramatic threats were not imposed in practice. Their temper is more a witness to the power of the monarchy and its increase at the expense of seigneurial justice, which was losing many of its former attributes. This dispossession mirrors the limits of the Anglo-Norman aristocracy which was not a judicial or banal one, but an aristocracy at the disposal of an emerging state.[199]

The Anglo-Norman nobility of service focused itself on the royal court. It often consisted of the upper end of the aristocracy, as calculations stemming from the inquests of 1166 and 1172 reveal. They make the limited group of close counsellors of Henry II the owners of more than two-thirds of Anglo-Norman fiefs.[200] So in comparison with the following of Louis VII, in which barely any of the great castellans of the Île-de-France appeared,[201] the Plantagenet entourage presented an undeniably noble appearance. But like the Capetian court, that of the Plantagenets contained lesser characters too. Every level of the noble hierarchy could be found in it with no exception. A recent study on the Normans who followed and advised Richard the Lionheart on his travels shows just this.[202] Hereditary officers of the palace were to be found there, men such as Hommet, Tancarville and Aubigny; there were tenants-in-chief of great political influence, such as Henry de Stuteville and Robert de Harcourt; there were ordinary undertenants who actively pursue war and crusade at the king's side, such as John des Préaux and Gerard Talbot; and there were some 'vicomtes',[203] bailiffs, justiciars and touring justices, recruited from among younger sons of the great dynasties or from less distinguished dynasties, such as Bertrand de Verdun, William de la Mare and William de Saint-Jean. Whatever the antiquity and wealth of their dynasty, the Norman barons and knights willingly served the king.[204]

The Norman zeal for service was less marked than that of the more numerous English nobles, at the royal court and in all levels of local administration, sometimes even included in court and administration on the continent. During the 1150s, after the long civil war between King Stephen and the Empress Mathilda, the great magnates of England decided to halt the conflict by truces and treaties which prepared the way for the succession of Henry II and the reunification of England and Normandy.[205] In 1154, at the moment of his coronation, their loyalty to him was secure. When they pressed for the restoration of the empress's son, had they perhaps wanted to restore at all costs the unity of kingdom and duchy, so as to regain their continental lands?[206] It was always a way that the new king could deal with them. He did not appeal to Norman and Angevin nobles by settling them in Britain.[207] He invested in the loyalty of the English, and could count on their advice, their administrative knowledge and their military support so as to rule his less securely loyal continental lordships. The Englishmen Patrick of Salisbury and Robert of Thornham featured as veritable viceroys of Poitou and Anjou for Henry II and Richard the Lionheart. In those areas, where a part of the self-governing aristocracy was all too ready to rebel against the king, the English origin of those officers was not unwelcome. It was all the more a guarantee of their good faith that these men, cut off from their alliances and networks of dependants and located faraway in a hostle region, were entirely devoted to the king.

It seems all the more remarkable to see the same thing in Normandy, where the local powers, long subjected to the duke, would not at first sight seem to oppose the Plantagenets. But let us not forget that after 1136, the house of Anjou had occupied the duchy more by force than by persuasion, to the benefit of the Empress Mathilda, and that between 1152 and 1160,

Henry II had to fight hard to keep his hold on the Norman Vexin.[208] In 1173, the revolt of the Young Henry had been supported by a large fraction of the duchy, notably in Upper Normandy, where the count of Flanders had easily been able to conquer Eu and Louis VII to lay siege to Rouen. Further south, John, count of Alençon, whose vast lands kept safe Normandy towards Anjou and Maine, also betrayed the king of England.[209] He belonged to the mercurial type of Norman marcher lords, whose double game between Plantagenets and Capetians was so integral to the easy conquest of 1204.[210] It was Henry II's English knights and Welsh mercenaries who secured the duchy under the rule of the king of England.

In such a context, with some resonances of a foreign occupation by right of conquest, some Englishmen occupied high-profile posts in Normandy. In 1176, Richard of Ilchester took control of the reform of the Norman Exchequer. Between 1178 and 1200, William fitz Ralph, who hailed from Derbyshire, became chief justiciar of Normandy; he came from the same county as Geoffrey of Repton, appointed mayor of Caen in 1200. A number of Englishmen took charge of key posts in the duchy, an external control that Lucien Musset saw as one of the reasons for the passivity of the native nobility in the run-up to Philip Augustus's invasion.[211] He was following in part the arguments of Sir Maurice Powicke and David Bates, who argued for the strength of the government of the Angevins in Normandy, forgetting sometimes how dominant the English were there.[212] Their perspective derives from that of Gerald of Barry: 'The Normans, just like the English, had been subject to the violent domination of an insular tyranny . . . How therefore might the heads of the nobility, bowed under the yoke of a cruel tyranny, be raised and how resist the unsheathed weapons and fierce courage of the French? For there is nothing that inspires the heart of men to bravery more than the joy of liberty.'[213] It is necessary, naturally, to edit the rhetoric out of this passage, as well as the prejudices of Gerald of Barry against the Plantagenets and their administration as opposed to France.[214] He does not at least refrain from saying that resistance to Philip Augustus had been sapped by an unprecedented degree of Plantagenet administrative and fiscal oppression.

The favourable unity of the Norman nobility on either side of the Channel, which in the aftermath of 1066 made up the strength of the king of England, was no more.[215] Worse still, it had not stood up under the forced separation of 1144, which had left Normandy to the Empress Mathilda and England to Stephen of Blois. The problem of the cross-Channel Anglo-Norman aristocracy deserves a pause for consideration. But the nature of such a study of 'national' identity is difficult. The difficulty lies in establishing collective feelings in medieval people. These are often impossible to penetrate, as the consciousness of belonging to a people and the emotional bond that it involves leave little trace in contemporary sources. Such emotional bonds can in any case change rapidly, often during a single lifetime or in a generation. But some elements of the sources of the second half of the twelfth century allow more precision as to how the Norman aristocracy, on either side of the Channel, defined itself. They offer some apparently contradictory data.

In his *Dialogue of the Exchequer*, Richard fitz Nigel, treasurer of Henry II, wrote: 'Nowadays, when the English and Normans live alongside each other and intermarry, the nations are so mixed up that it is difficult to establish, at least for free men, who is English by birth and who is Norman.'[216] Along the same lines, Ailred of Rievaulx underlines that the prophecy of the dying Edward the Confessor, describing a riven tree which grows back together and puts out new leaves, illustrates the reconciliation and fusion of Normans and English, which was accomplished in the person of Henry II.[217] These two authors worked in Henry II's service, of course. Richard was responsible for his finances, and Ailred's work was the result of a royal commission on the occasion of the translation of the relics of his sainted predecessor. Their work hammered away at the unity that Henry II wanted to establish within the nobility of his realms, after a period of separation and civil war.

This scarcely veiled propaganda was based on the identity of the English aristocracy which, since the transfer of properties accomplished by William the Conqueror, was mostly Norman or at least continental. The myth of the *gens Normannorum*, whose members were as evident in England, as Sicily or the Holy Land, was still alive and well amongst the twelfth-century chroniclers.[218] Around 1020, Dudo of St Quentin had echoed the dream of Rollo, founder of Normandy, who saw himself cured of leprosy after bathing in a spring where birds of all sorts gathered in harmony, the image of the diverse peoples whom he governed after his baptism and whose number would not cease to increase under his successors. A century and a half later, Wace and Benoit de Sainte-Maure repeated this anecdote, which was very popular at the Plantagenet court.[219] For his part, Henry of Huntingdon – very attached to the idea that the conquering Normans were no longer oppressors but a group integral to the English[220] – could not refrain from reporting the speech of Ralph, bishop of the Orkneys, to inspire in 1138 an army which was getting ready to oppose a Scottish invasion. To further his purpose, the bishop went through a list of the exploits of the Normans in France, England, Apulia, and from

Jerusalem to Antioch.[221] These recollections are evidence of the way the Anglo-Norman aristocracy had assimilated the Norman origin myth, and form part of the same picture as the adoption of the French language or continental courtly customs, as has been analysed above. The same goes for aristocratic naming customs, which turned away from the Anglo-Saxon names (Godwin, Harding, Aelfgiva or Edith) in favour of Norman ones,[222] amongst which William, the conqueror of England, took pride of place.[223] The Anglo-Norman nobility in no way rejected its continental roots but rather it integrated them faultlessly. Its origins bolstered its dominant position among the societies of Britain.

Is this to go as far as saying that the Anglo-Norman nobility did not want to be English? The sources are lacking to confront this question head-on, but some factors are at odds with a belief in the untroubled unity of *gens Normannorum*, as celebrated by the above-mentioned authors. Under Henry II, some Norman lords held lordships in England: the Mandevilles in Essex, the Courcy in Somerset and Cumberland, Kent and Hampshire, and the Ferrières in Rutland and Gloucestershire.[224] But their number seems to grow less. The division of estates – as a result of civil war – of noble dynasties on either side of the Channel is one of the master theses of Judith Green's book. In contrast, she uncovers an ambitious reordering of lordships in the magnates' interests, whether in Normandy or England. During the years 1135–1153, the troubled coexistence of a king and a duchess speeded up the schism within aristocratic families.[225] Despite the restoration of political unity in 1154, the process of dislocation carried on under Henry II, as is spectacularly illustrated by the story of the Beaumont twins, who went their own ways on either side of the Channel following the partition of their patrimony. Waleran of Meulan (died 1166) received the Norman lordships and followed an ambiguous policy of negotiating with Louis VII so as to keep his lands in the French Vexin, while his brother Robert of Leicester (died 1168), endowed with lands in England, raised himself, in his capacity as justiciar of England, to be the most influential amongst the royal court.[226] The parallel story of the Beaumont twins reveals the particularism of each noble grouping on the Norman and the English side of the Channel.

An English identity also appears in the manner in which continental French assessed the English nobility. Their perception is all too often xenophobic. The book of John the Trouvère, written between 1226 and 1229, at a time when the break with Normandy had been a fact for a while, gives some evidence of this. So, the Norman and Angevin knights whom William Marshal outclasses in the tournaments, describe themselves as humiliated (*abastardis*) in being defeated by *uns Engleis*.[227] By an almost nationalistic reflex, the French conspired against Marshal at the court of the Young Henry. They accused him of adultery with Queen Margaret, as well as of trespassing on royal prerogatives, and so in the end obtained his exile form the court.[228] This solidarity was expected during the famous tournament of Lagny-sur-Marne, also described by John. A number of knights of the Norman Vexin featured amongst the French but not amongst the English who formed, with the Flemings, one of the three teams.[229] Late as they may be, these descriptions of attitudes and feelings, smouldering deep in the thought world of this or that group at the end of the twelfth century, have to be taken into account.

Looking more broadly, Anglophobic stories were spreading in Normandy and also in the French lands. The English continued to be called *Angli caudati* (tailed), to taunt them as savages. The origins of this insult is alleged to go back to St Augustine of Canterbury (died 604) who tried hard to evangelize them. The English were supposed to have turned on him in derision and threatened him by disguisng themselves as animals with tails till the time came when the false tail became a real one following a miraculous punishment. This anecdote, which perhaps recalls the way that warriors and pagan sorcerers dressed up in skins, turns up again and again in the historiography of the high Middle Ages. It is to be found widely in the reigns of Henry II and Richard the Lionheart. It is repeated by Wace in the *Roman de Brut*, by the troubadour Peire d'Auvergne in 1159; in an anonymous Latin poem written around 1163, and then by Richard of Devizes, who says that in 1191, the Sicilians deployed it against the English crusaders led by Richard the Lionheart.[230] During the second half of the twelfth century such a wide circulation highlights the exist-ence of a collective consciousness of being English. On the continent, this negativity is directed against a 'national' group, whose shape from now on is clearly delineated.

Apart from this, English identity is by contrast manifested in the negative view that the English had of other peoples. So, Gerald of Barry underscores the otherness of the continental Normans, whom he describes as boasters, blasphemers, braggarts and debauchees. They had learned homosexuality from the French, he said, a vice which had by his time become part of their behaviour.[231] As a member of an old Norman family, long settled in south Wales, he himself demonstrated deep insecurities of identity, notably in his contempt for the Anglo-Saxons.[232] Gerald's attitude is significant for the rise of an English or at least insular identity, adopted by the descendants of the conquerors of 1066. For Jordan Fantosme, reckless advice from foreigners to the Young Henry and William the Lion of Scotland was the cause of their rebellion against Henry II.[233] Under John and Henry III, this xenophobia against continental courtiers is a contemporary theme in the works of Roger of Wendover (died 1236) and Matthew Paris (c.1200–c.1259), who draw a distinction between foreigners and natives.[234] But, as a new thing, Matthew Paris revives the idea of Norman tyranny in the aftermath of Hastings, and rejoices in the Anglo-Saxon roots of the monarchy.[235] On a more playful note, it is worth noting that the obsession of Latin poets – particularly Peter of Blois,[236] normally so sober – with the argument so dear to goliards about the superiority of wine to beer further widened the rift between France and England.[237] So John of Salisbury composed a eulogy of English ale against French wine, while recognizing the superiority of both to the Italian and Greek wines that the king of Sicily's chancellor served him 'to the risk of my life and salvation'.[238] Beginning in the 1150s, the English aristocracy, which had become aware of itself as an ethnic, historical and cultural group clearly distinct from the continental French, from then on kept its distance from its Norman cousins.[239]

This break was a major phenomenon in the political life of the Plantagenet Empire, which explains a good deal about the ease of Philip Augustus's conquest of 1204. The Norman nobility was ever more conscious under the domination of the house of Anjou that the influence of Englishmen in royal government was greater than their own. Some statistics confirm this change: 65% of the acts of Henry II's chancery concerned England, 25% Normandy and only 10% the other lordships of the Plantagenet realm. This trend did not alter under Richard the Lionheart and John. The proportion says a lot about the priority which the Anglo-Norman heartland still enjoyed in royal administration, since 90% of its documents make reference to it. But it particularly shows the growing preponderance of England in the Plantagenet political world. Under the house of Anjou, the centre of royal decision-making moved from Normandy to England, and more particularly to the banks of the Thames and the ancient kingdom of Wessex, where the royal domains were most concentrated. This region was also that most frequented by the kings, who owned several palaces and hunting lodges there. The resident nobility in England demonstrated a constant loyalty to the monarchy during several rebellions.[240] England became the nerve centre for the Plantagenets, who increasingly lost their Norman, and even Angevin, roots.

The English nobility, the spearhead of Plantagenet imperialism, from this time onwards outweighed any other of the British peoples. Its own opinion on this was blunter. Rather more than the Normans, the Celts became classic scapegoats for the English. Irish, Welsh or Scottish high-landers might well have been Christians, although of an unreformed Church, but they were barbarians for all that. This stereotype is often to be found in the writings of late twelfth-century Anglo-Norman intellectuals. Their chronicles and essays add to their Anglocentric clichés: habitual savagery, brutality in warfare, institutionalized pillage, deceit and treachery,[241] incest and adultery, pastoral idleness.[242] Such were the vices which served the purposes of an imperialist ideology, and justified the conscienceless conquest of these barely human tribes.[243] The subjection of the Celts was alleged to be all the more necessary as they had no respect for civil order.[244] As for the 'unmanageable tyrants' of Gascony, their pacification by military and colonial expedition was a moral duty. In its own view, the English aristocracy turned its expansionism upon neighbouring regions, an easy outlet for its aggression, and it believed itself to be behaving with more chivalry than the barbarians.

Those English knights who were the descendants of those who had conquered the south of Wales with Roger of Montgomery and William fitz Baldwin, were struggling to hang on to their lands at the beginning of the reign of Henry II. They were going under to the perpetual attacks from the still-independent north of Wales. Between 1157 and 1164 they joined in the campaigns that the king led, sometimes in person, against Owain Gwynedd and Rhys ap Gruffudd. They had only limited success. The Welsh fought off their attacks and counter-attacked even into England. In 1164, Henry II realized that he had better make peace with his Welsh opponents, whose soldiers then joined the ranks of his army as mercenaries. Also, he did not trust the English lords of South Wales, who had not genuinely supported him in his campaigns. They held large lordships removed from royal government, lands their Norman ancestors had put together as they created a marcher frontier. Passionate about their autonomy, they barely appeared at court. Just like Gerald of Barry, who was one of them, they trusted the English less than the continental Normans and Angevins. They were even less keen on Henry II's activities in Wales as he made peace with the Welsh, their hereditary enemies.

The Cambro-Norman knights turned their attention to the Irish: Celts who were quite as good as opponents as the Welsh. In 1166, they had their opportunity with the exiling of Diarmait mac Murchada, king of Leinster and of Uí Chennselaig, who recruited many of them to recover his throne. The English went further, conquering particularly Waterford and Dublin. They were led by Richard fitz Gilbert (died 1176), earl of

Striguil, who would later be given the surname 'Strongbow' and who married Aiofe, daughter of Diarmait, who himself died in 1171 after naming her as his heir. Henry II mistrusted Richard, whose family had supported King Stephen during the civil war. He looked askance on Richard's military successes and the power he acquired in Ireland, where numbers of his kinsmen joined him. In the end the king confiscated Richard's Welsh and English lands, as well as those of his relatives. So he forced Richard to submit and recognize Henry's overlordship of his lands in the east of Ireland, which became in 1185 the appanage of John. Henry allowed Hugh de Lacy and John de Courcy, the friends of Strongbow (who had gone loyally to thwart Young Henry's rebellion in Normandy in 1173) to pursue their own ambitions in Meath and Ulster respectively. The native kings and lords submitted one by one to Henry II.[245] But they had little respect for their treaties with the king of England, which they broke according to political need. Anglo-Irish relations were all the more poisonous as Henry II did not curb Strongbow's men and as he could not establish an administration in Ireland. The Cambro-Norman nobility imposed their own rule on Ireland.

The story of the Irish conquest demonstrated the dynamism of the English aristocracy, which paved the way for the seizure of Ireland by the Angevin dynasty. But the king did not completely succeed there in the way he succeeded elsewhere: he only became the real master of Ireland after he confiscated the Welsh estates of Strongbow, who participated in the struggle against the rebels of 1173. We should recall that the marriages of Strongbow's daughter and of Aiofe would be strictly controlled. Richard the Lionheart granted the daughter and all her estates on either side of the Irish Sea to William Marshal as a reward for his many services. Control of marriages reflected the true nature of relations between the English aristocracy and the king. Their relations were always dictated by the aristocracy's degree of service and compliance. For proof of this, take the English nobility's geographical mobility, deployed often enough on the continent to bolster the Angevin dynasty's power.

The loyalty of a Patrick of Salisbury, Robert of Thornham or William Marshal contrasted with the rebelliousness of a John of Alençon through his son Robert, who in 1203 opened the southern frontier of Normandy to Philip Augustus. At that date, the active collaboration of the Alençon family with the king of France was not untypical of the Norman nobility, which had barely any compunction in turning against John once he had been condemned by the court of his feudal lord. The Normans well knew the frail position of the Angevin dynasty during the 1190s, the key decade when Philip Augustus was building up his military power, consolidating the infrastructure of his kingdom and increasing his financial resources.[246] They had of course fought hard for Richard the Lionheart, a man sanctified by an aura of chivalric virtue which firmly tied them to him. But they would not put themselves out in the same way for John, whose personal authority was weak because of recent military defeat attributed to his idleness and ineptitude, and also because of his marriage with Isabel of Angoulême – regarded negatively more from feeling against him than from rational belief – and his blame for the disappearance of the young Arthur of Brittany. The few Norman families with possessions still in England chose to follow the king of France. They preferred to lose their English lands rather than continue a conflict which was devastating their lands, and which they knew was already lost anyway. In choosing to stay in the duchy, they demonstrated that a gap had opened up between the continental Normans and the English, whom one could no longer presume to call 'Anglo-Normans' as their fate was tied up now with Britain. In a few generations the followers of William the Conqueror had acquired a new identity. They knew they were Norman by descent, but they would rather be English in the service of the king crowned at Westminster and living in southern England, who was the natural enemy of the Capetians. The link between subjects and king was decisive when it came to creating a 'national' identity.

Between 1154 and 1224, political change was duplicated on the social level. During these watershed years the nobility became aware of itself, while lawyers gave it a more distinct status. A concern with the legal boundary of the nobility appeared alongside new markers and codes which (like heraldry) remained at that time a class privilege. The legalism did nothing to eliminate the class awareness at the heart of what nobility was, but rather it solidified it, particularly in England, where the king was all-powerful. In England, from tenants-in-chief to subtenants, a pyramid arising out of the feudal system widened the differences between the upper and lower aristocracy. The concentration of great lordships in the hands of a few magnates was a characteristic of the period, as much in Poitou as in England. A higher titled category of counts and viscounts stood close to the king and strengthened its links to him by marriage into the royal family. The magnates accumulated power where it was increasingly being centred: at the royal court, where they were often to be found. The court aristocracy included some men of less exalted nobility (and consequently less troublesome and more useful) often educated in literacy and accounting. At every level the aristocracy was politically powerful. The king could not govern without it, as its rebellions frequently reminded him with a grim regularity. If the State is defined as the monopoly of violence, then it already existed in the Plantagenet world in an embryonic form.

At this stage of institutional formation, it was not yet the time when the aristocracy was more than a 'noblesse de robe'. Its main business was still warfare. Every knight was a nobleman, as was symbolized by the public ritual of the delivery of arms. Within the aristocracy, military activities enjoyed a prestige superior to any other. The *History of William Marshal*, the first known biography of an aristocrat, was focused on his prolific exploits in war and on the tourney field, being scrupulously respectful of the chivalric ethic. His irresistible political and social rise was the direct consequence of his talents. But the Marshal's lifelong loyal service to the king – whoever he was – reveals a broader change in society. It ties in with the ideal, so dear to the court intellectuals, of a warrior aristocrat devoted to public war, the only lawful sort, declared by a higher and unique authority as embodied by a morally irreproachable king. Such warriors were the strong arm of the body whose head was the monarch, to take the organic image of John of Salisbury. Such an ideal was incompatible with the use of mercenaries in the royal army, which was condemned by both the clergy and lay aristocracy, the latter wanting the monopoly of at least horseback fighting. The aristocracy's decided opposition to paid cavalry and infantry was no more than a reflex of their class in a time when a warrior – however aristocratic he might be – would never shrink for payments, favours, gifts and fief rents.

More and more, the nobility marked itself off by observing the chivalric norms which mitigated its violence. Deeply marked by Christianity, chivalric values imposed tight limits on the exercise of arms that was enlisted in the exclusive service of peace and justice. The ideal was set high, too high perhaps for that day and age. Was the code put in practice on the battlefield to the benefit of anyone other than a man of blue blood? Did it bring some sort of relief to the oppression of peasants by their lords? Alas, no. Gratuitous acts of violence by knights were still numerous. In 1200, the nobleman was not really chivalrous. This was the experience of the archbishop of Canterbury, the supreme authority over the English clergy, the defining group of the unarmed in society.

The Becket affair

The murder of Archbishop Thomas Becket in his cathedral of Canterbury on 29 December 1170, was the defining event of the relationship between the Angevin kings of England and the Church, the final act in a tense drama.[1] The murder stirred high emotion all across the West. Scarcely two years after his death, it led to the canonization of Becket, recognized as a martyr. It triggered a widespread devotion shared as much by the clerical intellectuals debating the theology of the two swords as by the peasantry, the social group furthest from high culture.[2] In a few months it made Canterbury cathedral one of the most popular pilgrimage centres of Christianity, almost as popular as Rome, Jerusalem or Compostella. Becket's memory continued to be the object of strong political investment at the end of the Middle Ages and beginning of the modern period, as is demonstrated by Henry VIII's order for Becket's relics to be destroyed and his cult suppressed. By the nature of things, the attitude of the historians who studied the Becket case were saturated by its struggles and polemic. Becket could never leave anyone indifferent.

A brief biographical treatment reveals the unprecedented nature of the Becket affair. Thomas was born in 1118 in London to a wealthy family of merchants who hailed from Normandy. In 1142, now well-educated, he became a clerk of Archbishop Theobald of Canterbury. It was in Theobald's household that he was spotted by Henry II, the new king of England, who made him his chancellor by the end of 1155 at least. Some seriously important business was done in his name, such as the embassy to Louis VII in 1158 and the short-lived siege of Toulouse the next year, when he led the royal army. The confidence in his unshakable loyalty is to be seen in his tutorship of the Young Henry, the king's eldest son.

This is why Henry II in 1162 procured the archiepiscopal see of Canterbury for Becket, doubtless thinking to find an uncritical support in him for his policies. Thomas, ordained priest and bishop, took his new calling to heart and totally undeceived the king. He resigned the chancellorship against the king's will and very soon began an open conflict with him. In January 1164, Thomas went back on his decision to support the assizes of Clarendom, which lessened the Church's jurisdiction to the advantage of the king's. In November he fled to France, where he met Pope Alexander III, an exile like he was, and where he also benefitted from the protection of Louis VII. He stayed a while at the Cistercian abbey of Pontigny, from which he was expelled by a decision of the general chapter of the order, whose English possessions the king threatened with confiscation. Becket's final refuge was at the Benedictine abbey of Sainte-Colombe of Sens. In Britain meanwhile Henry II persecuted Thomas's supporters, going so far as to exile his entire family.[3] In 1166, the pope made Becket legate in England, and he excommunicated the laymen and clergy who had accepted the constitutions of Clarendon. In June 1170, the consecration of the Young Henry by the archbishop of York led Thomas to anathematize the church dignitaries who had taken part in it. There were frutiless attempts at a reconciliation with the king, who met Becket at Montmirail (January 1169), Montmartre (November 1169) and at Fréteval (July 1170). On 1 December 1170, Thomas landed with the purpose of reclaiming his see at Sandwich, where he was welcomed with delight by a crowd. The decision was to cost him his life a month later. Four of Henry II's knights took literally the king's threats against the archbishop who still refused to lift the excommunications. They cut him down with sword and axe in the cathedral, where Thomas had gone for the office of vespers.

The seven last years of Becket's life were therefore dominated by his stand-off with Henry II on the subject of ecclesiastical liberties, in defence of which he said he was ready to die. The quarrel damaged political life and social relations in England, and indeed in every Plantagenet realm. Its climax was the murder in the cathedral which crystallized in one moment many disputes, several centuries old in some cases. It is hardly surprising therefore that the Becket affair, in the man's own lifetime and in the aftermath of his death, spawned a huge literature, to which the editors of the Rolls Series dedicated seven fat volumes between 1875 and 1885.[4] The clerks involved in the conflict put their pens in Becket's service, and others, less numerous, in that of Henry II. The extent of their writings makes this dossier one of the most bulky from the twelfth century. They are striking in the detail of their accounts and their descriptions. They have often been written by eyewitnesses or those at only one remove from the action.

They can be classified in three groups. First, there exist a score of hagiographical accounts memorializing the holy martyr, composed before 1200 in Latin, but also in Anglo-Norman and Icelandic. The earliest of them is the letter *Ex Inesperato*, written barely one or two weeks after the murder by John of Salisbury, an eyewitness, and Becket's fellow exile and adviser. To be commended for their accuracy are the long *Lives* written by William fitz Stephen, Becket's secretary, which is full of details about his youth; by Herbert of Bosham, one of the finest exegetes of his day, another fellow-exile; by Edward Grim, an Oxford master, whose arm was slashed by a sword cut intended for Becket; and by Guernes de Pont-Maxence, a poet who sang an Anglo-Norman life of the saint at his tomb.[5] Then there is the English history writing whose richness is well known in that period. In their chronicles on the reign of Henry II, William of Newburgh, Gervase of Canterbury, Roger of Howden and several others were naturally drawn to the struggle between the king and the most important religious authority in England. The last group is the letter collection, all the more interesting because it was organized, for the purposes of propaganda, in the form of letters both for and against Becket.[6] Hagiography, history and letters give a deep insight into the events and the manoeuvres.

Any number of historians, especially British, have used these sources. It is worth noting how much passion was raised on a subject which was approached with a polemical end. There are numerous very decided verdicts on Becket and his actions. At the end of the nineteenth century, the Revd James C. Robertson, one of the two editors of the Becket sources for the Rolls Series, wrote that had the archbishop succeeded in pushing through his programme, its 'spirit would have led to clerical tyranny and intolerance'; England would have become 'the most priest-ridden modern country, and the least respected', instead of being, as was happily the case according to him, 'the most free'.[7] Curiously, the end of romanticism and positivism, with its corollary of historicism,[8] had not eliminated such polemical sentiments. In an argumentative, and indeed truculent, book published in 1963, H.G. Richardson and G.O. Sayles wrote: 'Henry's greatest mistake was in choosing and trusting the flashy, shallow and egotistic Thomas Becket . . . We must regard Becket not as a martyr, but perhaps as the fatuous fool that Gilbert Foliot in his anger called him.'[9] In 1973, ten years later, this prejudice had not lessened. In the solid biography of Henry II by W.L. Warren, professor at the Queen's University of Belfast, we find:

'his denunciations of the king's supposed intentions became increasingly detached from reality, and his self-justification ever more hysterical. He brought a violent death upon himself . . . Becket was too rigid, too narrow, too direct in his methods.'[10] The dossier of quotations could be extended.[11] But a small sample is enough to detect the ideological strategies which surrounded the Becket affair, even in the twenty-first century.

Of course, the consequences were more important during Becket's life. Surprising though it might appear, the murder, mutilation and imprisonment of bishops was not then uncommon. In the eleventh and twelfth centuries, no less than a dozen of them were killed just in France, without so much as one giving rise to a cult.[12] The unusual thing in the Becket affair lay in the passions that it unleashed not just in England but across Europe. It attracted a massive involvement of the intellectuals of the time, whether supporters or opponents of the archbishop. We will go on to present the context of the ideas of these clerics, before going on to analyse some of the high points of the dispute and the significance that the main actors and the witnesses read into them. The Becket affair is all the more important for the argument here in that it divided the clergy of the Plantagenet Empire between those who respected the power of Henry II and those who rejected it.

Intellectual engagement

Despite first impressions, the dispute between king and archbishop was very much an involved one. It would do it no favours to reduce it to the level of a savage quarrel between friends of fifteen years' standing, finding all at once that they hated each other. It would be just as foolish to look for the beginning of the dispute in a series of diplomatic gaffes, as if the two men had not always worked in the field of peacemaking.

It is important to assert that the confrontation between the king and Becket was principally ideological, and arose out of political theory and theology. Their quarrel made an actual duel out of the ancient dialectic between the temporal and spiritual swords, between *regnum* and *sacerdotium*, between the English monarchy in its resurgence under Henry II, and a faction of the post-Gregorian ecclesiastical hierarchy, which was ill at ease with royal control over the Church, as closely integrated as it was in the Anglo-Norman world. The ecclesiastical policy of the first king of the house of Anjou would seem all the more dictatorial as it was such a contrast to the understanding of Henry I with Rome and to the autonomy and prestige the English Church had acquired during the civil war, when royal power had been more or less extinguished. In default of central power, the bishops had taken front stage in politics: Theobald, archbishop of Canterbury between 1138 and 1161, played a leading role in the kingdom, including paving the way for the accession of Henry II.[13] In putting a stop to this episcopal hegemony and interfering in clerical life, the new king was only reviving an old Norman ducal practice of control over ecclesiastical life.[14] On this level, Henry's policy found a lot of supporters amongst clerics whose motives we should try to understand. But before we look closer at the archbishop's enemies, we need to tackle the milieu from which his supporters were drawn.

Becket himself was an unusual sort of person in his own society. He did not belong to the higher nobility, as would have been expected in a chancellor or the primate of England, but to the wealthy merchant class.[15] His father, Gilbert, a businessman from Rouen, had made a niche for himself in London society, where he was one of the two sheriffs of the city. He had contacts with the household of his fellow-Norman, the archbishop of Canterbury, Theobald de Thierceville (or Bec), who took his young son into his court.[16] Thanks to his studies in the Surrey priory of Merton and then the schools of Paris, Thomas had the grounding of an arts graduate, instructed in rhetoric and the humanities. Following that, Theobald would send him to study law at Bologna and Auxerre.[17] Thomas also acquired administrative experience at the archbishop's court. Theobald recommended him to Henry II at the time of his coronation. From 1155, when he was thirty-seven, Thomas became the king's chancellor and one of his closest counsellors.[18] The dispute would only break out seven years later, when he gave up the office of chancellor after his episcopal consecration.

There was a resemblance in the life story of John of Salisbury, Becket's mentor and faithful supporter in the storm centre of the struggle with the king. He was born between 1115 and 1120 probably to a peasant family of Old Sarum, the original site of Salisbury.[19] He pursued advanced study at Paris and Chartres, where he became acquainted with the finest minds of his day (William de Conches, Peter Abelard, Gilbert de la Porée, Simon de Poissy, Robert Pullen and Robert de Melun) engaged in the movement called 'the Twelfth-century Renaissance'.[20] Thanks to their teaching, he acquired a perfect mastery of arts and theology. From 1148, he was called on to work as secretary of Archbishop Theobald, perhaps on the recommendation of Bernard of Clairvaux.[21] He formed a friendship at this time with Becket, who was working at the same court, if he had not already when he had studied in Paris. A tranquil bureaucratic career with the archbishopric of Canterbury would seem then to have opened up to him.

In 1156, however, John fell into disfavour with Henry II, who expelled him from England. The reasons for his first exile are obscure. Three suggestions can be made. First, he might have annoyed the king by his firm opposition, which can be found in his writings, to the Toulouse campaign and the heavy taxes that went along with it.[22] Secondly, he thought up a legal device for the conquest of Ireland when at the curia of the English pope, Adrian IV (1154–1159), where Henry had sent him on a diplomatic mission, a device which the king had probably not entirely appreciated. John had made much of the forged Donation of Constantine, which gave to the Holy See control over all islands, so as to assert the lordship of the pope over Ireland, and had given the king on the pope's behalf an emerald ring to symbolize a papal investiture.[23] Again, he might well have been the draughtsman of the bull *Laudabiliter*, accepting the English expedition, but protecting the independence of the Church in Ireland in the face of primatial expansionism from Canterbury.[24] Finally, the king probably associated him, as Theobald's secretary, with the archbishop's open opposition to some of the king's nominations to sees.[25]

However it may be, John of Salisbury was obliged to stay at Rome with the pope. Cut off from public affairs, he put the final touches to his two great works, the *Metalogicon*, an apologia for the literary arts, and the *Policraticus*, returning time and again to the idea of the incompatibility of clerical life with service in public office. He warmly dedicated the latter work in 1159 to Becket, from whom he desired the king's forgiveness, and who he wanted to subscribe to his ideas about clergy.

The course of events would justify John. Thomas Becket, who did reconcile him for a while with the king, joined battle beyond all John's hopes, for the liberties of the English Church against the monarchy. John followed him into exile, his second. He stayed firm in his principles. He showed respect, diplomacy and tact towards his enemies, feelings founded on the humanism he had learned in his reading of the classics and in his theological reflection. He wrote this: 'I criticised my lord the archbishop all the more often and more decidedly than anyone, because right from the start, gripped by a misplaced zeal, he provoked the king and his men with no consideration about time, place or person.'[26] But on John's part, the subtlety of such an approach should not hide the inflexible determination of his programme. One or two of the phrases used in his letters illustrate his stubbornness: 'the Constitutions of Clarendon are nothing less than a new gospel of human making.' Becket was not to back down because he was 'a christian and not a Henrician.' The latter adjective harked back to the Gregorian jargon against the Emperor Henry IV (1054–1106), the definitive enemy of the papacy. Frederick Barbarossa would be deposed after 1168 when his antipope was no more.[27] The theory of tyrannicide, unheard of at the time, that John had presumed to articulate in his first exile – for all that his argument was nuanced and clearly distanced from Henry II – shows how extreme was his thinking, indeed in many respects, revolutionary.[28] He was mild in the way he presented his ideas, but tough in his thinking.

This was how Henry II classified John of Salisbury, perhaps counting him responsible for the radical transformation of his chancellor and old friend.[29] After Becket's murder, his own public penance, and the general amnesty awarded his critics, the king made it so that John got no ecclesiastical office in England. In 1176, John obtained the see of Chartres in the kingdom of France, probably due to the intervention of his friend William aux Blanchesmains (died 1202), then archbishop of Sens, the brother-in-law of Louis VII.[30] It was a matter of the see of a cathedral school whose intellectual dynamism and modernity of thinking was a symbol of the Twelfth-century renaissance, being embodied in its new bishop.[31] In 1179, John took part in Lateran III. He died the following year.

There are two indications of the strong imprint of John's theories on the methods of Thomas Becket. First, several passages and formulas from the *Policraticus* surface in letters written by the archbishop.[32] Secondly, it may be that one of the manuscripts of the work belonging to Becket had been annotated by himself, witnessing to his careful reading of it, and attempts at memorization.[33] In the absence of another sample of his handwriting, this theory is not verifiable. But however it may be, there is no denying the leading role in the stances and decisions taken in the course of the struggle between the king and Becket by John of Salisbury, the archbishop's veritable *eminence grise*.

Another of Becket's close friends was Herbert, born at Bosham in Sussex, a man whose social origins are unknown. He was his constant adviser, as at the council of Northampton (October 1164) when he sat at his feet and whispered to him the idea of excommunicating his enemies. It was Herbert that Becket sent ahead to France to organize his exile there.[34] Like Becket he was a royal clerk before his fall from grace, often employed by Henry II. In 1157, he acted as the king's ambassador at the court of Frederick Barbarossa in a delicate mission, at the end of which he arranged that the relic of the hand of St James would rest at Reading.[35] On that occasion, his diplomatic gifts were deployed in Henry II's interests.

Herbert's wide knowledge of power politics marked him as a man who had mastered courtly conduct in both bearing and conduct. William fitz

Stephen described the first impression he made, in May 1166, on Henry II and his court entering the hall of the palace of Angers. 'Herbert of Bosham was announced and he made his entry. The king said of him: "Look! Someone of great consequence is come!" Herbert was a tall man and good looking. He was well-dressed, wearing a tunic and a mantle of fine Auxerrois cloth on hs shoulders, arranged in the German manner, falling down to his ankles, dressed with an elegance befitting his station.'[36] The expensiveness of his clothes recalls the fine fur cloak Becket wore when he was royal chancellor, when Henry rebuked him humorously. Canon law, as the moralists pointed out, advised clergy against wearing brightly coloured clothes, especially in green and red.[37] His personal distinction arose out of the same standard of conduct that Becket instilled in Henry II's sons and the children of the higher aristocracy who had come under his tuition.[38]

Herbert's presentation before the king made a powerful impression. But his self-confidence and irony made him no friend in Henry II, any more than the quickness of his dialogue as reported by William fitz Stephen: 'The king said: "What cheek! It is not fitting that this priest's brat upsets my realm and troubles its peace." Herbert replied, "Not at all. I am no priest's son, for I was not conceived to a man in orders, since my father was ordained after that, anymore than you are son of a king, since your father was none." At this, one of the court, Jordan Taisson, said: "Whoever's son he may be, I would happily give half of my land were he mine!" ' This gift of repartee, for all it distinguished Herbert, was humiliating for the king. In an honour-bound society, as the closed circle of the court principally was, such ridicule could be a fearful weapon. It was a verbal slaughtering of a rival. Herbert turned a bad situation to his advantage, to the extent that he favourably impressed the onlookers. Jordan Taisson, a Norman nobleman owning many lordships on either side of the Channel, was charmed by his wit. It goes without saying that the text being analysed is very favourable to Herbert, as it was written by Becket's former secretary with partisan intent. But it has no less value in illustrating a certain sort of behaviour that those courtier-clerks who defected to Becket cultivated.

Herbert of Bosham had learned the use of dialectic with some distinction in the schools he had long attended. He had long been familiar with rhetoric, as well as the staged debate which was at the heart of the scholastic method. He was a recognized practitioner of exegesis, quite probably the finest of his day, and he had mastered not just rabbinic and biblical Hebrew, but even perhaps Aramaic. Around 1150, in Paris, he was under the instruction of Peter Lombard (died 1159), master of the school of Notre Dame and bishop of the city. He would remain deeply devoted to his memory, endeavouring to finish and polish the writings left uncompleted at his premature death, particularly his *Glossa* and his commentaries on the Psalms and the Epistles of St Paul. He had also been the pupil of Andrew of St-Victor, another specialist in the scriptures. He had a first-rate education, and it prepared him for the bureaucratic and diplomatic assignments which he took on without apparent demur.

On Becket's death, Herbert was torn between a life of scholarship and one of affairs. In the early days, since he would not swear fealty to Henry II, he stayed in France. There he benefitted from the patronage of Henry the Liberal, count of Champagne, the brother of William aux Blanchesmains, and there remain some letters which he wrote at some time on the count's behalf. In 1174, he was paid the arrears of his English benefice, which allowed him to devote himself to his exegetic research, and teach at St-Denis. During the 1180s, he finished up by admitting the sincerity of Henry II's penitence and returned to England. On the king's death in 1189, William de Longchamps, bishop of Ely and chancellor of Richard the Lionheart, recalled him to the court. Undoubtedly the bad relations between the new king and his father worked in Herbert's favour. In 1191, he left the world of the court for good, which in his letters he said he found debilitating, so as to concentrate on the commentary on the Psalms.[39] But it could be that his retirement might have been political in nature, a consequence of the fall of Longchamps. He returned to the continent, where he stayed in the Cistercian abbey of Ourscamp (in the diocese of Arras) till he died in 1194. His return to the world of affairs, and his rapid abandonment of them, showed the ambiguity of Herbert, as well as the irresistible lure that his Hebraic studies still had for him.

Born in 1122, John Bellesmains (died 1204) belonged to the same generation as Becket and his two closest advisers. Although his social origins are unknown, it can be said that he came from Canterbury, which would suggest an origin within a patrician or mercantile family, or even amongst artisans. In his youth he met Becket and John of Salisbury in Theobald's archiepiscopal palace. The pope supported his nomination to the archidiaconate of London, which the celebrated chronicler, Ralph Diceto, eventually got. In 1155, he became treasurer of York and then in 1163, probably at the intervention of Henry II, bishop of Poitiers, a city where he stayed for twenty years before being promoted archbishop of Lyon. In the aftermath of the crisis at Clarendon, John openly took Becket's side, which earned him the close scrutiny of the king's agents and indeed, an attempt to poison him.[40] He urged moderation on Becket, in particular on the occasion of the interview at Montmirail, where he steadfastly promoted a reconciliation with the king.[41] Absorbed by his pastoral duties, John has left no works of exegesis or theology. His level of education was nonetheless considerable. John of Salisbury, and also Robert de Torigny and Walter Map, who cannot really be suspected of bias, unanimously praise his letters and his eloquence in Latin, French and English.[42] At Poitiers, John Bellesmains was possibly linked to Master John Sarrasin, the translator and commentator on the Pseudo-Dionysius, and good-natured correspondent of John of Salisbury.[43]

Like the other clerks, Ralph Niger, a native of Bury St Edmunds, had been snapped up by the court in the intellectual headhunting dear to the Plantagenets. The royal administration benefitted from the know-how of such a man of letters, as learned Becket, John of Salisbury, Herbert of Bosham or John Bellesmains. Master of arts at Paris in 1168, he was about twenty years their junior. His letters demonstrate the links, often friendly links, between him and the Becket circle during the conflict with Henry II. It was the reason the king expelled him from England. After Becket's murder, his presence amongst the confidants of the Young Henry, at war with his father in 1173, probably did not assist his pardon. In his writings, Ralph retaliated with great coldness towards 'the king under whom the blessed Thomas, martyr of the English, suffered his passion.' Ralph showed by contrast, his gratitude towards Henry's son, '[who] died at Martel, a town of the Limousin, in a pious devotion according to the witness of many holy men.'[44] Like his companions in exile, Ralph benefitted from the protection of William aux Blanchesmains, and perhaps also Maurice de Sully (1160–1196), Peter Lombard's successor as bishop of Paris. Ralph returned to England on Henry II's death. In 1199, he received some payments from the royal court, where he certainly worked. Like Herbert of Bosham he has left exegetical works, as well as two universal chronicles and a justification of the crusade written on the occasion of the fall of Jerusalem (1187).[45]

Walter de Châtillon, born around 1135 near Lille, belonged to the same circle. He was the author of a poem in memory of Thomas Becket and dedicated his *Alexandreis*, a long epic in hexameters praising the life and career of Alexander the Great, to William aux Blanchesmains, in a fluent acrostic. Walter, an incomparable Latin poet, a graduate of the Paris schools, can be counted as one of Henry II's intellectual recruits, working in his chancery as late as 1166. But as a supporter of Becket and John of Salisbury, he distanced himself gradually from the king, and eventually returned to the continent where he became a canon of the chapter of Reims. He was reunited at Reims with William aux Blanchemains, who was archbishop there after 1176.[46] Walter's writings defended Alexander III against the emperor. He pictured the pope as Noah, piloting the ark, which was the Church, through the midst of the Flood, the ark from which Caesar was shut out because he did not submit to Alexander. After the murder of 1170, he had no qualms about stigmatizing Henry II, his former employer, as a tyrant.[47]

A frequent member of Henry II's court was John of Tilbury, likely author of the *Notarial Art*, particularly eulogistic about the 'glorious martyr' who had educated John in his work as a Chancery scribe.[48] John features with one or two of the other clerics mentioned above in the list of 'the twenty-two scholars of St Thomas' that Herbert of Bosham listed at the end of his *Life of Becket*.[49] It is an interesting point that Herbert took heed of the leading role of intellectuals in Becket's party. The influence of these *eruditi* around the archbishop was one of the principal themes of his *Life*, where Becket does not decide anything of importance without having first consulted them. Becket appears there anxious to promote these clerks to the episcopate. According to Herbert, if Becket had made the mistake at first of approving the Constitutions of Clarendon, it was because he had been too long 'at Caesar's court' rather than in monastic libraries and the cathedral schools which were the best training for the office of bishop.[50] Herbert would have preferred that the highest offices in the Church, not to mention the State, pertained to a circle of scholars, heirs of the Platonic republic of letters, an idea rediscovered by the Twelfth-century renaissance.

The prosopography of contemporary medievalists shows that Herbert of Bosham's theory underlies the action. This was the master theory of the passionate work of Beryl Smalley, significantly entitled: *The Becket Conflict and the Schools: A Study of Intellectuals in Politics*. When put in parallel, the *Lives* of Becket, his intimates and his supporters, reveal a genuine milieu, a circle of intellectuals which existed in a network on either side of the Channel. They formulated a common method and policy, as is evident from the many letters that they exchanged to keep up their spirits during the darkest days of the conflict with Henry II. Born between 1120 and 1140, this group of clerks belonged to the same generation. If they were not all noblemen, study had promoted their social rise. In their youth, they had left England for the continent, chiefly attending the schools of Paris, where they had received education in rhetoric, exegesis and theology.

These scholars had often begun their careers in ecclesiastical administration, before working at Henry II's court. But they kept a nostalgia for the continental schools, to which they usually returned in the conflict between the king and the Church. The Becket affair preceded the long interdict imposed by Innocent III on England between 1208 and 1213, which is an explanation for the important migration of Englishmen towards the capital of learning: of the forty-two Parisian masters known between 1179 and 1215, only ten came from the domain of Philip Augustus, as against sixteen of English origin.[51] The Francophilia of English bureaucrats is often exaggerated, as the writings of John of Salisbury and Gerald of Barry demonstrate. It explains in large part the opening success of the military campaigns of Philip Augustus's son in England. For the king of England, the learning of the staff of his administration was very much a two-edged sword.

But it would not do to over-emphasize the clerks opposed to Henry II. Other English churchmen, educated like them in the schools, had openly supported the king during his struggle with Becket, preferring the ease of the state-supported academic to the underground life of the active and idealistic intellectual in revolt. Gilbert Foliot (c.1105–1187) was their leader. He studied arts, exegesis and law, probably in France, before becoming a monk at Cluny. In 1139 in his capacity of prior of Abbeville, he accompanied the abbot to the council of Lateran II. King Stephen recalled him at this time to England to make him abbot of Gloucester. In 1148, at the council of Reims, he was consecrated bishop of Hereford by Theobald of Canterbury, and later he became Henry II's confessor. Gilbert openly opposed the nomination of Becket to Canterbury, maintaining that it was irregular. It could be that he had himself solicited this promotion, often given to abbots as the monastic community of Christ Church answered directly to the archbishop. He was elected bishop of London in 1163, without undergoing the oath to Becket, the new archbishop, under the pretext that Foliot had already taken the oath to Theobald on the occasion of his episcopal consecration in 1148. In fact he was claiming the pallium for the see of London,[52] which explains his refusal. According to John of Salisbury, he went so far as to cite the Prophecies of Merlin with the intention of maximizing the position of his new see. As a result it was hardly surprising that he assisted at the coronation of the Young Henry at Westminster in the spring of 1170, which earned him a papal excommunication.[53]

At the coronation, the archbishop of York whom Gilbert had assisted that day was a Norman, Roger de Pont-l'Evêque (died 1181). The coronation, which Henry II demanded as a way of managing the succession by obliging the younger sons to swear homage to the eldest, hurried on the fatal resolution of the Becket conflict. Roger had passed his youth in

the household of Theobald of Thierceville with Thomas Becket, John of Salisbury and John Bellesmains. In October 1154, two months before the coronation of Henry II, he was elected metropolitan of the north of England, a province whose rights he had every intention of defending. His opposition to Becket was part and parcel of the ancient rivalry with Canterbury over the primacy of Great Britain.[54] In Becket's absence, he consequently went ahead with the royal consecration, as two of his predecessors had done before him: in 1066, after the disgrace of Stigand of Canterbury by William the Conqueror; and in 1100 because of the exile of Anselm of Bec (who it might be said in passing was one of the spiritual heroes of John of Salisbury, Becket's biographer, and Becket himself, who asked for his canonization).[55] Now Roger believed all the more that he had the right to do this as he was in possession of a bull of Alexander III allowing him in 1161 to anoint the Young Henry. In reality, the act was conditional on there being a vacancy in the see of Canterbury, which was not the case in 1170, and it had been ruled out anyway by another papal document in 1166. It seemed that before the ceremony Roger had no knowledge of the threat of excommunication of Alexander III addressed to those who went ahead with a coronation. There was a reason, in that it had been intercepted by royal agents.[56] The coronation of the Young Henry therefore had many ecclesiological and political implications. In proceeding with it, Roger and Gilbert aimed at the strengthening of the prerogatives of their own sees against Canterbury. Their devotion to their own cathedrals explains a lot about their attitude during the conflict.

There were other prelates like them occupying senior posts in the English administration who subscribed unconditionally to Henry II's programme. Such was Richard of Ilchester, archdeacon of Poitiers, baron of the Exchequer and judge in eyre; Geoffrey Ridel, archdeacon of Canterbury and keeper of the great seal; Reginald de Bohun, illegitimate son of Bishop Joscelin of Salisbury, who made him archdeacon of his cathedral, something very anachronistic in the English Church at the end of the twelfth century; and also John of Oxford. These clerics played an important part in the crisis, leading missions and embassies to the pope, legates or to the German emperor. Their unfailing loyalty to royal policy earned them the open hostility of Becket and his supporters, who used formulas of great severity in referring to them: 'archdevil' (for archdeacon), 'son of priest', 'traitor', 'notorious schismatic', and so on. Henry II would not forget their compliance. During the 1170s, after his reconciliation with the pope, he found vacant sees for them: Winchester for Richard, Ely for Geoffrey, Bath for Reginald and Norwich for John.[57] There is no doubt that these were

rewards for their loyalty to the royalist party and for their many services. The dead archbishop's worst enemies were in this way rewarded by the king, whose methods in Church affairs hardly seem to have changed, despite his public penance for what had been done at Canterbury.

This picture of the English episcopate at the time of the Becket dispute would not be complete without mentioning the uncommitted and the supporters with divided loyalties. Roger, bishop of Worcester (1164–1174), younger son of Robert of Gloucester and consequently cousin of Henry II, was often able to be equivocal in his conduct. Assiduously attending the royal court in the darkest hours of the crisis, he still had no hesitation in taking Becket's part, visiting him on the continent, and not taking part in the Young Henry's coronation, for which the king vigorously rebuked him.[58] The attitude of Robert de Melun (c.1100–1167), a celebrated Parisian theologian who succeeded Gilbert Foliot in the see of Hereford in 1163, was more conciliatory towards the king. But he never broke his ties with Becket, whose conduct he attempted to moderate. His case is all the more complex in that, before his election as bishop, Robert had firmly professed active resistance to any king who set himself against the rights of the clergy. The Victorines of Paris, long his friends, condemned him for not putting his ideas into practice during the Becket affair.[59] The story of Arnulf (1141–1184), bishop of Liseiux, is well documented, thanks to his voluminous letter collection,[60] which showed his quandary during the crisis: supporter of the independence of the spiritual power and reform, he was nonetheless a faithful servant of the king, who had made him justiciar. His private letters demonstrate his internal attachment to Becket's cause, but he did not dare to advertise this view openly so as not to lose royal favour. He would never escape this dilemma.[61] The double game impelled him to speed up the reconciliation between Henry II and the Church. In 1173, Arnulf played the intermediary between the king and the Young Henry and the rebel Norman lords. Henry II did not like his attitude and broke with him. This dispute forced Arnulf to abandon his episcopal office and retire to St-Victor in Paris. At one in deploring Becket's intemperance, the three bishops had trouble choosing sides, or at least in revealing their sympathies publicly.

Whether hostile or sympathetic to Becket, or just peacable, this group of clerics had something in common. Monks or members of the upper aristocracy are found more frequently amongst the defenders of royal policy, while Becket's people belong rather to the secular clergy and to less well-known families. But socio-religious criteria do not always work. In either case, it is necessary to assert the importance in their careers which their studies played, often while living abroad. Their education opened the

palace doors of a king, who would reward them for their administrative work with episcopal sees or more modest canons' prebends. By contrast, the engagement of Becket's partisans, also from the ranks of the courtiers, was evidence of a radical break with the king and the world of the court, which they often diabolized in their writings. The loss of their administrative posts and ecclesiastical perks followed on from this, when they were not exiled. The steadfastness of their attitude, heavy with consequences, cannot be explained without a solid theological theory which rejected royal power or, at the least, decisively separated it from spiritual power.

The defence of clerical liberties

The ideological background of the Becket affair was enormous. It was about the very nature of authority in a Christian society and its application by means of a programme of legislation.[62] The legislation encountered the pragmatism of certain canonists, who, like the bishop of London, soon discovered common ground with the king, in the attachment to the principles of theologians which they maintained by every means so as to defend the ancient freedom of the Church, even to increase its rights, when the investiture struggle ended on the continent.

The letter *Multiplicem*, written by Gilbert Foliot and addressed to Becket, summed up the position of the bishop of London and the clerical supporters of the king well.[63] So as to convince Becket to submit to Henry II, Foliot made reference first to the religious character that coronation conferred on kingship and secondly, to the separation of the spiritual and temporal powers, even if the bishop was obliged to swear allegiance to the king for the secular business of his diocese. Such an understanding of the principles might be labelled 'Gelasian', as it has been called by some historians, so as to highlight Becket's 'Gregorian' attitude.[64] The argument of Pope Gelasius I (492–496) asserted a strict separation between spiritual authority (*auctoritas sacrata*) and secular power (*regalis potestas*) and maintained that the kingship of Christ had superseded the Old Testament figure of the priest-king.[65] On the other hand, to invoke the sacrality of anointing to defend Henry II's ecclesiastical policy, as the bishop of London had done, came close to caesaro-papism. Foliot's position was not incompatible with respect for the authority of the pope, which he had always recognized in theory (he did not hesitate to call him 'vicar of Christ') and in practice (he accepted his 1170 excommunication without complaint).[66] Nuanced though it was, his political understanding proclaimed the submission of bishops to royal authority.

The position of Becket and his *eruditi* was quite otherwise. It was to be found in the meditation on the doctrine of the two swords which developed in the Parisian schools of the first half of the twelfth century, where those young Englishmen had studied. The doctrine relied on two Gospel passages describing the arrest of Christ on the Mount of Olives. Before leaving the Last Supper for the mount, the disciples had showed Jesus two swords, of which he said that their number was enough (Luke 22: 38). As he was arrested, Peter struck off the right ear of Malchus, a servant of the High Priest, with a sword blow, which Jesus promptly healed while telling Peter to put up his sword (John 18: 10–11; cf. Matt. 26: 51; Mark 14: 47; Luke 22: 50). The importance of these foundational texts was considerable in the eleventh and twelfth centuries. It can also be said that the scene of the arrest of Christ is more frequently depicted in Romanesque sculpture than the scene of his prayer in Gethsemane, served by angels, which was to replace it in later days.

These gospel passages were widely commented upon in the French schools where Becket had studied. Their exegetes made use of them to assert the duality of the powers: spiritual and temporal. Christ had delegated them both to the pope, but asked him to rein in the temporal power because to commit physical violence was unworthy of the priesthood. St Peter's successors had delegated the temporal power to the secular powers, who were obliged to the papacy for it. They kept the spiritual sword for themselves, meaning the possibility of punishing by excommunication. The prince alone could therefore restrain by violence, since the clergy would be polluted by doing so. This reading of the gospels was a restrictive one, for by it the Church only passed on the power to coerce to the civil authorities.

After the end of the eleventh century, this interpretation had a considerable impact on the circles which opposed the inroads of lay princes into religious affairs and, more precisely, were against their tight hold on appointments to cathedral chapters and monasteries. Peter Damien (died 1072), one of the principal theoreticians behind the Gregorian reform, was the first to have compared the two swords to *sacerdotium* and *regnum*. Like him, many of the thinkers of the twelfth century considered that the totality of secular power, not just its power to coerce, was exercised by permission of the priesthood. In the 1130s, Hugh of St Victor, whose monastery occupied the hill of St-Geneviève, the home of Parisian intellectualism, argued the inferiority of kingship in comparison with the pontificate, just as the body was dependent on the soul. From this he drew the directive role which prelates had over princes. The enthusiasm with which the Victorines rallied round Becket, their recent pupil, was perfectly natural.[67]

Their ideas are explicitly rehearsed by John of Salisbury who explored in his *Policraticus* the subservience of the prince to the priests. 'The king is subject to God alone, and to the priesthood which represents God on earth.' 'All rulers are subordinate to the power of the priest,' he wrote.[68] In the letter Thomas Becket directed to Gilbert Foliot, this theory is carefully developed: 'The one who has kingship over angels and men ordained two powers, princes and priests: one terrestrial and the other spiritual; one the servant and the other the master; one to whom he has conceded power and the other the one he wishes to be revered.'[69] This extract, born out of polemic, in which can be detected the influence of John of Salisbury, is commendably clear, which is not always the case in John's theoretical writings. It advocates the subordination of the king, the servant of the clergy, quite openly. Its intention is undeniably theocratic.

To emphasize this insight, the *Policraticus* uses the organic metaphor of the State, which had a considerable and revolutionary significance. If the king was the head of the body politic, he can do nothing without the clergy, which represents the soul endowed with the grace out of which arises life.[70] John says he had borrowed this image from the *Institution of Trajan* by Plutarch, a classical authority which mitigated the revolutionary nature of the theory. In fact modern critical method has shown that he had completely invented this prestigious reference to escape criticism and retaliations against himself.[71] The practical upshot of a theory like John's was direct control of kings by priests. Had not the prophet Samuel deposed King Saul because of his disobedience to Yahweh? Furthermore, in the case of a succession dispute, it fell to the clergy to select the legitimate heir of the king.[72] Elsewhere in his book, John portrayed monarchy as the lesser of two evils, which did not arise naturally out of human society. The Old Testament (1 Kings 8) exposed the reluctance of Yahweh to give a king to the people of Israel, who forcefully demanded it of Samuel. If the Lord had given in to such a constitutional makeshift, it was because of the wickedness of his people.[73] It followed that the prestige of the Davidic monarchy was badly tarnished by this stance.

John's preference was for the previous government of judges. The Hebrews, under the guidance of their priests, had chosen their rulers for their political abilities and above all for their morality. On this, John of Salisbury's thinking was closer to the *Pastoral Rule* of Gregory the Great (590–604) than the *City of God* of Augustine of Hippo (354–430). According to John's theory, ethical behaviour among rulers and ruled took priority over the social order that such authority imposed by force on the turbulent terrestrial city. The private life of the prince could not be separate from the public sphere of his political life.[74] In this regard it is very significant that John selected Trajan to be the dedicatee of the pseudo-Plutarch's book. In terms of a highly popular current legend, it was the intercession of Gregory the Great which had secured Trajan's redemption. In his prayer the pope had reminded God that while he was alive the emperor had shown compassion for poor widows and comforted the wretched.[75] John laid more stress on the moral qualities of the statesman than on the organization of the State itself.[76]

John's thinking was deeply rooted in classical humanism, as rediscovered by the Twelfth-century Renaissance. It started from the Platonic proposition that the human spirit had difficulty in comprehending changeable reality, but that it attained knowledge by exchanging opinions and by the force of experience, transmitted by the instruction of a teacher and by perusal of the classics.[77] The Stoic writings particularly deserved, as instructive models, a careful reading by the king. These texts emphasized the eloquence aquired by study of the arts of rhetoric, more formative of behaviour and good manners than instructive in the techniques of government. The education of the young princes ought to be focused on study of written expression and accurate speech, good manners in society and a way of life marked by simplicity and self-control.[78] In this way appearance and reality came together, and aesthetics became ethics.

The resort to the classics explains the fascination of John of Salisbury with Cicero (106–43BC) and Seneca (4BC–AD65) often cited in the *Metalogicon* and *Policraticus*. Cicero, whose philosophy had long ago been adapted to Christianity in the *Offices* of Ambrose of Milan (died 397), linked the 'honest' to the 'useful', or the uprightness of the ruler and his morality to his effectiveness in the service of the common good, an idea that John regarded as essential.[79] John admired Seneca to the point of writing: 'There is scarcely any pagan moralist whose work and sentences would be more serviceable in any sort of business than Seneca.'[80] The subtitle of the *Policraticus* is very revealing, at one and the same time, of the critique of the corruption of the powerful and the enthusiasm for ancient wisdom: 'Courtiers trifles and the footsteps of philosophers'. The book contains a fine and highly conventional analysis of the apathy or quietism of the classical authors, borrowed from Aulus Gellius (2nd century AD) and Augustine; its tone remains demonstrably stoic.[81] John's message is clear. Morality must rule everything, and each act and decision of a good ruler, taking its shape from a vast field of knowledge, should be distinguished by its wisdom.

The idea of law remained preponderant at the core of such a system as John's. It was by no means incompatible with the Roman law that John (a pupil of the Bolognese jurist Vaccarius at Canterbury around 1145) so admired and knew so well.[82] It did not anticipate the two-bodies theory of kingship, neatly separating the king's private and public roles, which Roman lawyers were later to develop.[83] John repeated in his book his admiration for the Roman code and for the legislation of the man he called 'our Constantine'. He likewise, with the authority of the Julian laws on bribery, declared that the corruption of government officers was to be suppressed. If he argued against the two imperial maxims – 'what pleases the prince has the force of law' and 'the prince is not bound by the law' – he did it in the name of principles as Roman as justice, reason and equity.[84] However contractual it was, John's theory of the king as a simple 'representative' or 'vicar' of the people can be found in the *Digest*. It would be repeated by its commentators Bulgarus (died 1166) or Placentinus (*c.*1135–1192). The contract between ruler and subjects obliged the ruler not only to obey legal codes and custom but also to impose them by force, if need be. Even if it was at odds with the classical idea of the emperor as all-powerful, the doctrine of the self-sufficiency of the law which the king himself ought not to breach was not alien to Roman law.[85] Such a view was by no means displeasing to the new admirers of the Justinian Code, whose laws they did their level best to apply to the letter. This jumble of ancient material was a support to the idea of law as being eternal and pre-existing, and John of Salisbury fully subscribed to it.[86]

Law marked out the good prince, but also the bad, who because of his disdain for law became a tyrant to be overthrown. The former obeyed it as much as the latter ignored it. The good prince saw justly (*recte*), a Latin adverb which the *Etymologies* of Isidore of Seville (*c.*560–636) reckoned to be the origin of *rex* (king). The bad prince embodied tyranny which existed outside the law, in immorality and – owing to Stoic influence – epicurism. 'The will of the tyrant is the slave of his lust', said the *Policraticus*.[87] Law was thoroughly identified with the principle of liberty, for the king who lived by a strict ethic escaped the slavery to his desires; he did not crush his subjects with his own caprices. The stories of Caligula and Nero demonstrated this relationship between private debauchery and public tyranny.[88] The prince should freely surrender himself to a transcendent law. He should accept clerical morality as freely as Christ accepted the passion which the Father imposed on him. For a virtuous man, following the law became the norm, the ability to do good deeds with no hesitancy or reluctance.[89] This moral concept of *libertas* was all the more close to John's heart because it underpinned the independence which he wanted for the Church within the body politic.

There was no doubt about the subversive impact of such ideas in the twelfth century. It could allow the rejection of a prince considered to be wicked on the pretext of his misconduct and the tyranny that followed on from it. The *Policraticus* did not assess quite in those terms the young Henry II, at the time regarded rather favourably than otherwise. But in the *Entheticus*, John took a harsher tone towards the king, called Antipater and Mandrogerus, who opposed ecclesiastical freedoms and enacted tyrannical laws oppressing the clergy and people. The allusion to Henry II seems clear enough.[90] His readers would have no trouble drawing the conclusion which he was suggesting. It was legitimate to rebel against a king opposed to the privileges of the Church.

Writings of close friends of John of Salisbury generally repeat these ideas. Thomas Becket himself is a good place to start: he maintained the superiority of the spiritual sword over the temporal. The one was gold, the other lead.[91] He deduced from this the complete immunity of the ecclesiastical community, as well as the need for the bishop to rebuke wicked rulers and indeed to oppose their activities, fighting them like David fought Goliath.[92] This is an extract from a letter of Becket to Henry II: 'As the lord you are, I ought to and indeed I do offer you my advice and my respect. As the king that you are, I am obliged to revere you, but also to admonish you; and as the son which you are, because of my office, to punish and restrain you.'[93] The archbishop of Canterbury in this way asserted the pre-eminence of clergy over the king.

Becket's right-hand man, Herbert of Bosham, took a more extreme position. In a letter sent to Alexander III, he alleged that Henry II and his ally, Frederick Barbarossa, 'the great schismatic', wanted to abolish every ecclesiastical liberty. Only Thomas, he said, threw himself courageously in their way. The pope then should excommunicate the king of England and absolve his subjects of their oath of allegiance, so they might rebel.[94] This rising would be the logical outcome of Henry II's absolutism: 'the king is like a human cart, of which he is both driver and goad. He drives and directs them all. He is fearful to them as a whip. He trains, directs and urges them on.'[95] The Plantagenets took their subjects with them in the way a wagon driver might, treating them like mules on a tight rein. Accusations of tyranny naturally come from this source. Nicholas du Mont-Saint-Jacques, Becket's envoy to the Empress Mathilda, whom he would have liked to recall her son to a more amenable outlook, returned dispirited from his vain mission, for 'the woman belongs to a dynasty of tyrants.'[96]

Ralph Niger is just as critical, if not more so. Amongst his works is *The Morals of Kings* (1179–1187), a title of double significance, being a commentary on the Old Testament book of that name. There he rebukes Roman law as taught at Bologna by unscrupulous jurists, a powerful force working to strengthen royal power and legitimize royal abuses of traditional customs.[97] In his exegesis on the reluctant Yahweh's concession of a monarchy to the Jews, Ralph compared it to the enslavement of the people to kingship and its ungovernable whims. Opposed to the all-powerful English monarchy, he turns then to the wickedness of Henry II, which deserves only that his people withdraw their obedience, reducing the foundation of his power to nothing.[98] It is open sedition that Ralph is proposing.

Ralph's *Chronicle*, written in exile, literally dragged the king through the mud. The depravity of the son of the bigamous Mathilda, grandson of the likewise debauched Henry I,[99] had some terrible consequences for his subjects. Henry II is portrayed as 'the corrupter of decency, following in this the licentiousness of his grandfather', abusing women and the daughters of his subjects: 'to indulge his debauchery the more freely, he shut away the queen he had already ran off with like a satyr.' Ralph made the oppression that one such life imposed on laypeople the subject of a lengthy digression: the unheard of increase in the numbers of royal officers; lack of respect for what was right; the extension of the forest and its law; excessive control over the marriages of his aristocracy; the setting aside of custom and replacement by arbitrary law decreed by assizes; the encouragement of Jewish moneylending; the damaging rises in Danegeld, scutage, and other taxes; devaluation of the currency; forced displacement of population and replacement of honest women in England by prostitutes from Le Mans; the abolition of all liberty. But it was the Church which suffered most from autocratic government. Henry wilfully imposed the grossest flatterers of his court on episcopal sees and abbeys. Venerable prelates became kennel-keepers of his hunting dogs and saw their possessions confiscated. He forced the bishops to swear to their acceptance of a perverse law and submit their clergy to royal courts. The responsibility for the murder of Becket, his courageous opponent, rested entirely on him.[100] Ralph's list of grievances against Henry II stops here. He knew how to interpret the abstract thought of the Gregorian and Victorine theologians and canon lawyers. He brought into solid and everyday practice the theorizing of John of Salisbury.

Thomas Becket and his friends could count on the unconditional support of the papacy in their crusade. Alexander III, successor of Adrian IV, the friend of John of Salisbury, was an acknowledged jurist, whose legislation fixed for good the terms of monastic exemption, the canonization of saints and the validity of marriage. One of his programme's prime objectives became the practical implementation of canon law, assisted by the study of the Decretal of Gratian in the 1140s. The Decretal asserted the authority of the Holy See over emperors and kings in temporal matters, in which the pope was justified in meddling, as being the unchallenged privilege of the Church.[101] The long confrontation with Frederick Barbarossa bolstered the papal stand on principle. It aligned the pope with Becket when Henry II apparently played the card of an alliance with the emperor, and indeed threatened at the beginning of 1165 to remove the English Church into the obedience of the antipope Paschal III (1164–1168).[102] An extract from a letter Alexander III sent via Gilbert Foliot for the attention of Henry II shows the community of thought which united the circle of the archbishop of Canterbury: 'that the king confuses no more, as he does at present, church and state affairs, and that he does not organise the former as suits him . . . but that he confines himself to temporal matters.'[103]

It is worth adding that Becket and his companions in exile (among which appears the lawyer, Lombard de Plaisance, future bishop of Benevento) highly valued the study of canon law, which underwent a steady expansion in England beginning in the 1150s.[104] On this point, it is significant that four hundred of the eleven hundred replies of the pope on questions of law preserved from the twelfth century were made by Alexander III to British correspondents.[105] The insistence of canons on judicial centralization on ecclesiastical judges transformed the papal curia into a universal court of appeal, and could only tighten the links between litigant clergy and papacy. As the canonists in Becket's party fought their battle on a judicial battlefield they insisted on the immunity of ecclesiastical courts, fiscal exemption of their goods, and freedom of movement of papal legates in Britain and English prelates travelling to Rome.

The political discourse of Henry II and his supporters is rather more difficult to analyse than that of his opponents. The best we have is Peter of Blois making the king say, in an imaginary conversation with the abbot of Bonneval, that many times Rome had confirmed the authority and prerogatives of the kings of England over ecclesiastical business.[106] Equally, Gilbert Foliot defended the royal sacrality that came from anointing. Anti-clericalism is a different matter: more to do with the generality of people than the intellectual elite, it can be detected in certain attitudes and ideas of the Plantagenets. Gerald of Barry tells of the reply of Richard the Lionheart to Fulk de Neuilly, a preacher of the crusade, who rebuked him for having for daughters the three vices of pride, luxury and greed: 'I have already given the girls away in marriage: pride to the Templars, luxury to the Benedictines and greed to the Cistercians.'[107] But Gerald was also telling this story to denounce the decadence of the regular clergy, one of the recurrent themes in his satrirical writings, which he shared with Walter Map, like him a secular clerk.[108] But these anti-monastic witticisms teach us little of royal ideas. The same goes with King John's reputation for impiety. He took pride in wearing round his neck in front of Hugh of Avalon, bishop of Lincoln, an ancestral amulet which protected his lands.[109] These stories, redolent of the clergy that told them, do no more than illustrate the desire of princes to shock the clergy with whom they were all too frequently in conflict. They do not allow us to fathom the kings' political thinking. Royal practice towards the Church was never the subject of any theoretical treatment and certainly has not left us any treatise comparable to the *Policraticus*, which tells us so well what was the doctrine of Becket's party.

What the king did is all that can be relied on. His actions aimed at direct control of the clergy, as the older Anglo-Norman monarchy had done, but revived in new political circumstances where the king's ability to act was increased after the hiatus of a civil war. Tradition and the modern world were mingled as Henry II intervened directly in episcopal elections, of which indeed the most spectacular example was the elevation of Thomas the chancellor to the primatial see of Canterbury.[110] This royal nomination explains why Stephen de Rouen did not hesitate to compare Becket to Simon Magus.[111] He forgot to mention that Becket asked the pope to accept his resignation, conscious of the irregularity of his election, and the pope had refused to do it.[112] However it may be, the Plantagenet episcopate was made up of clerical courtiers amenable for the most part to the king's influence, the king who kept in reserve the power to delay their election so as to keep the revenues of bishoprics and other vacant beneficies for his profit. Lower down the ecclesiastical hierarchy, there was a similar hold on parish churches by local lords, who maintained a right of patronage deriving from their choice of incumbents. This situation, widespread through the Anglo-Norman Church, scandalized John of Salisbury: 'In our day and age, everything is openly bought . . . The greasy flame of avarice licks at the very sacred altars . . . The right of appointment or patronage . . . , that the blessed Ambrose charged to heretical simony . . .'[113] Many priests educated at Paris might have launched into a similar condemnation.

But they would not necessarily have been followed in this by all their colleagues. Royal patronage enjoyed a certain popularity within one group of clergy, regular clergy in particular. There is proof of this in a tract that an ecclesiastic – perhaps William de Treignac, prior of Grandmont between 1170 and 1189 – addressed to Henry II to ask him to reform the morals of Aquitainian prelates.[114] He particularly criticized the bishops of Saintes and Limoges, but he equally described the rather gloomy situation of local clergy, corrupted by nepotism, simony, hypocrisy, nicolaitism and all sorts of other abuses. In the face of this level of corruption, the author begged the king to take up the role of moral reformer of the clergy: 'If the bishop's sword falters, the king's sword will do . . . In these times where malice is everywhere, will the king of England, the ruler of Aquitaine, slumber and sleep? Surely not!'[115] Across the Channel, in 1166, Henry II suppressed with appalling ferocity the anti-sacramental heresy of the Weavers, as he believed that he was the guarantor of orthodoxy in his realm.[116] It was in this traditional spirit that Gilbert Foliot's attitude, and that of other anti-Becket prelates, needs to be understood. For these men, royal control and patronage were a guarantee of stability.

Published in January 1164, the constitutions of Clarendon, the bone of contention between Henry II and Becket, was well within the mainstream of the old ways.[117] But they did include one major novelty: the establishment in writing of practices that the king till lately had applied day by day, with no possibility of renegotiating them on the day with the Church's leaders. The Empress Mathilda had herself recognized her son's tactical error in wanting to transform working custom into statutory and episcopally approved legislation, cut free from the past.[118] A number of the clauses of the constitutions were aggressively rejected by Becket and his supporters: the king should judge disputes on the subject of presentations and collations of an incumbent of a parish (c. 1); every accused clergymen should stand before a royal court which would decide whether it was an ecclesiastical case (c. 3); to leave England, bishops must ask permission and safe conduct from the king (c. 4); bishops likewise must obtain the king's agreement before excommunicating tenants-in-chief and royal officers (c. 7); appeals to the papal curia were abolished since the king was the supreme authority in his lands (c. 8); the king reserved to himself the bulk of revenues from vacant sees and abbeys, whose nominees were to be elected in his chapel and with his consent and the newly elected man should swear faith and liege homage (c. 12). In 1169, new articles were added to these constitutions, reinforcing the control of the king over ecclesiastical justice, raising new taxes from the clergy, detaching the English bishops once and for all from Rome and suppressing with increased severity any resistance to the legislation.[119]

But the debate mainly turned on the third article, concerning criminous clerks. Becket was well aware of the king's designs. Its implementation would be followed quickly enough by the disappearance of the special jurisdiction for clergy, to the benefit of a royal monopoly of justice. So Becket clung on to the Church's liberty with ferocity. He opposed the clause all the more forcefully, as an old tradition provided that the surrender of an accused clergyman to the civil authorities depended entirely on the bishop's will. Custom allowed in the worst case the unfrocking of an accused cleric, who would be subject to royal justice only if he reoffended. When Becket defended ecclesiastical justice, he objected to the cruelty of the punishments generally handed down by civil judges. Branding particularly shocked him, for it deformed the face which was, he said, the image of God himself. For his part, Henry II, drawing on Roman law and his own stock of punitive measures, thought that punishments were still too mild to keep order in his realm.[120] The abolition of appeal to Rome, provided for in article 8, furthered the seizure of all ecclesiastical jurisdiction by the Crown. The provocative nature of this measure was flagrant at a time when the wide reading of the Decretal of Gratian, including numerous judgements of the Curia, spread the idea of papal supremacy more widely than ever before.[121] Papal primacy, so dear to the hearts of Gregorian thinkers, was scarcely compatible with the rise of an autonomous Anglo-Norman Church under royal control.

Confrontation was in the end unavoidable. The post-Gregorian concept of power was pitted against the centralizing vision of a modern-style government. On one side was liberty, privilege, the pre-eminence of an unchangeable law superior to that of men, and an ethical dialectic about government. On the other side was the coherence of institutions and the suppression of every franchise or judicial liberty, legislation at the king's pleasure and control of ecclesiastical affairs by the civil power. Such a political programme has to be summed up in concepts adapted to our heavily laicized, modern mentality. But the dialectic of Church versus State does not really comprehend it; the two phenomena were too much interpenetrated and complementary in the Middle Ages. For a twelfth-century intellectual, Church and State would be as interdependent as the human and divine nature of Christ were by their hypostatic union. We are not yet dealing here with the extreme situations which were, on the one hand, theocracy such as the papal states of Italy experienced in the thirteenth century, and, on the other hand, the caesaro-papism which had existed in the Byzantine state, totally controlled by its emperor. It is important to use the vocabulary of the opponents in the Becket conflict, which talks of temporal and spiritual swords, or kingship and priesthood. It says that a political society, or commonwealth, could not be fulfilled without the eternal salvation of each individual. To remind people of this was one of the missions of the clergy, sole keepers of wisdom and, as a result, indispensible support to government. But nothing expressed the sharpness and nature of the Becket struggle better than the words and deeds of its actors themselves.

Murder in the cathedral

Abundant and detailed sources allow the precise reconstruction of the activities of the main characters of the Becket dispute in the fatal chain of events which ended with the crime of 29 December 1170. From an anthropological and cultural perspective it is a worthwhile exercise to analyse the attitudes and words of the various characters to work out their significance. Next we must find where they are in a system, where, as individuals – each with a distinct role and identified with the group they work for – they show a sensitivity to considerations of honour. Renown, reputation, approbation by friends, or opposition to enemies, and the seeking of recognition by fellows – such were the elements which best explain the attitudes of Henry II and Thomas Becket, both of them refusing the compromise which would perhaps have ended the vicious circle of violence. Three key periods illustrate the drama, in which each event reveals a significance that, at different levels, included all those who were witness to it.

Taking up the cross (October 1164)

The scene was played out in October 1164 during the council of Northampton that the king had called so as to move on from the crisis sparked by the assizes of Clarendon ten months before. But he had no concessions in mind. He urged the bishops present to ratify the constitutions, which most of them rejected. The tension was at its highest, and Becket was afraid of a physical assault on him by the king's men. It was in this fraught environment that we find an event which the chroniclers and the hagiographers rate as highly important. Becket entered the council of bishops carrying with him a processional cross, a thing which heightened the king's anger and was followed by his self-exile to France at the end of October 1164.

William of Newburgh underlined the importance of this episode, which he dealt with briefly within his *History*. He pointed out a link between Becket's carrying of the cross and Henry's anger, as if what Becket had done was a direct insult to the royal dignity: 'The day on which Thomas should have replied to the accusations laid against him, he asked that the solemn office of St Stephen should be sung at mass, to which the introit is "Princes

also did sit and speak against me and they persecute me wrongfully"
(Ps. 119: 23, 86). Then he entered the palace himself holding the silver cross
which was customarily carried in front of him. Certain bishops suggested
to him that they should do this thing and carry it before their metropolitan,
but he refused and, despite their pleas, he did not allow anyone to take
it into the public assembly. The king, who was already very angry, had
now another reason to be enraged. This was why, the following night, the
archbishop fled overseas.'[122]

In his *Life of St Thomas* (1173–1174) William fitz Stephen returned
to this episode, but he stressed the attitude of the other bishops, particularly Gilbert Foliot, bishop of London. Thomas celebrated the office of
St Stephen on an altar that was consecrated to the saint. When he left for
the palace, he told his crucifer, Alexander the Welshman, that he wanted
to go to the king barefoot and carrying his own cross, without his signs of
office, so as to beg him to respect the peace of the Church. But his clerks
talked him out of it. Once he had entered the castle, he nevertheless took
hold of the cross. Hugh de Nonant, archdeacon of Lisieux, member of his
household turned to Gilbert Foliot who was watching the scene and urged
him to stop Becket behaving in this way. The bishop of London replied
'What's the point? He is mad and always will be!' Becket took his place
in the council under the stupified gaze of the bishops. Gilbert in the end
asked him to hand over the cross to one of his clerks, as it might appear
that he was prepared to stir up the kingdom: 'You are carrying your cross
yourself. But what if the king appeared now girded with his sword? We
would then have a king turned out for action, and an archbishop also.'
Thomas retorted, 'Were it possible I would always carry this cross. I am
convinced that this is to maintain the Peace of God in my person and in
the English Church. Say what you like, but if you were in my place you
would have a different understanding of it. If the lord king were, as you
say, to take a sword now, it would hardly be a sign of peace.' William
fitz Stephen described the arrival of Roger de Pont-l'Eveque, archbishop
of York. He had his cross carried in front of him, although he was in the
province of Canterbury where the pope had directly forbidden him to do
it. But Roger was taking advantage of the appeal against this decision that
he had sent to Rome so as to act in that way.[123]

There is much of interest in this particular text. First, it associates
the carrying of the cross with the Peace of God. In the eleventh century,
spatial manifestations of the Peace were manifested in the creation of
shelters, places of refuge where the use of arms was forbidden, whose limits
were marked by crosses. Secondly, during their discussion, fitz Stephen

tells us, Becket and Foliot make a clear contrast between the archiepiscopal cross and the royal sword, a theme we will have occasion to return to. Lastly he notes the rivalry between Canterbury and York, the latter assuming to himself the privilege of carrying his cross, even in his neighbour's ecclesiastical province.

On this last point the evidence of the monk-historian, Gervase of Canterbury, needs to be presented about an event which unfolded thirty or so years later, on the arrival of Archbishop Geoffrey of York in the council of London in 1193. Making the most of the absence from this council of Hubert Walter, very recently elected archbishop of Canterbury, Geoffrey raised a cross, an act for which he was reproached by the other bishops, condemning this open offence to the primate of the church of Canterbury. Gervase noted that the London mob had earlier thrown down the cross which Roger de Pont-L'Eveque had presumed to carry in the city. Gervase says that a discussion then began amongst the clerks of Canterbury to establish whether their archbishop, elected and consecrated but as yet without the pallium from the pope, could carry the cross. In the end it would be Gervase himself who would go to Rome to request the pallium and would hand over a cross to the new archbishop in the pope's name with the words: 'He bids you receive this church as its ruler, to cherish it and guard it in the true faith. In sign of this I give you this banner of the Sovereign King's herald, for you to carry.' Hubert celebrated mass and was enthroned.[124] The significance of the carrying of the cross can be easily seen in the rivalry between the two English archbishops as well as the powerful symbolism which went with it as liturgical object, whose reception was associated with that of episcopal office, its rights and duties.

The third text concerning the carrying of the cross at Northampton comes from Roger of Howden's chronicle.[125] He sketches the facts in much the same way as William fitz Stephen, at least so far as it concerned the bishop's positions on the business. He told of the celebration of the mass of St Stephen by Becket, which, he said, earned him the sarcasm of Gilbert Foliot on his 'magical arts'. After mass, Thomas assumed the stole and a canon's black cloak. He mounted a horse, holding the cross in his right hand. There followed a row between the bishops of London and York, the king's supporters, and Becket, defended by the aged Henry of Blois (died 1171), bishop of Winchester since 1129, the brother of King Stephen.[126] Roger of York attacked Becket for 'coming armed in this way with a cross to the court, for the king had a rather sharper sword.' Becket retorted, 'If the king's sword kills the body in the flesh, my sword strikes in the spirit and sends the soul to Gehenna.'

This exchange alludes to the functions of the two swords in their repressive aspect: physical force, the violence of the temporal sword, meets its match in the excommunication of the spiritual sword. It is worth turning to the commentaries which early twelfth-century exegetes made on the gospel scenes of Gethsemane. Robert Pullen (c.1080–1146), one of Becket's teachers at Paris, commented on the cross-like form of the sword as a sign of its exclusive use in the service of the Church. Christ had asked Peter to sheath the temporal sword, which explained why the priestly hierarchy should not shed blood. The prince of the apostles made use of the spiritual sword, by contrast, to attack Malchus (whose name meant 'king'). He cut off his right ear, meaning the spiritual ear, so preventing him in a way from hearing the word of God.[127] Excommunication, which separated from the Church community and from salvation, was rather worse than the mutilation or physical death dealt out by the royal sword. To return to Becket's words, anathema sent the soul to hell, the worst of punishments, while the temporal sword could only kill the body. It could force the king – Malchus – to submit to the bishops, in whom rested the power to pardon or to retain sins.

We know to what extent these ideas, which give pre-eminence to the episcopate over the monarchy, were adopted by Becket and his 'scholars', the former pupils of Robert Pullen. To return to the council of Northampton, the processional cross symbolized only the powers of jurisdiction which the pastor received so as to direct and correct his flock. It was solemnly delivered to the newly-elected and consecrated bishop by delegation from the pope, who confirmed the plenitude of powers to him by that act. So it symbolized the spiritual sword and the power of delivering excommunication. In wielding the cross at the critical moment in the debate at the council of Northampton, Becket showed the king that he was going to defend himself from his attacks by anathema and interdict. In a fundamental way, Becket wanted to make the king understand the superiority of *sacerdotium* over *regnum*. The bishops supporting a reconciliation with Henry II criticized him very severely.

This interpretation, based on theological and canonical twelfth-century texts, obliges us to reject two avenues of research. Firstly, the comparison with the crosses given by prelates to warriors on their departure on military campaigns, especially against Islam,[128] takes no account of the antagonism between the two swords, as those at the council of Northampton had seen it, concerning a liturgical object reserved to laymen which arose out of the circumstances of war. Guernes de Pont-Sainte-Maxence asserts, on the other hand, on the defensive, and by no means aggressive, significance of

Becket's action. When he took up the cross, 'he provided himself with the weapons of God to be in safety.'[129] Secondly, the ethnological route has been explored by the Africanist, Victor Turner, who reached an unsurprising conclusion: the king represents the masculine and the priest the feminine principle. Becket's action was all the more provocative as he reversed expectations in openly carrying a symbol of virility.[130] But such an explanation neglects the richness of twelfth-century reflection on the nature of and relations between the two powers.[131] In locating himself at the level of the collective subconsious – which seems to me personally to be undetectable after eight centuries – it neglects the key point: the conscious appreciation that Becket's contemporaries had of what he did, the understanding that they had wanted to credit him with, and that they had clearly expressed. It misleads by hypercomparativism in locating on one and the same level contemporary African animism and Christian medieval liturgy, each based on very different cultural references and social situations.[132] Becket's ostentatious taking-up of his cross at Northampton remains, before anything else, the assertion against the king of his archiepiscopal jurisdiction and his spiritual power to coerce.

The kiss of peace (November 1169 to July 1170)

Unlike the previous episode, the provocation this time was not by the archbishop but by the king. Becket was undergoing it more than provoking it. The two enemies met at Montmartre on 18 November 1169, and then at Fréteval on 22 July 1170, with the aim of reaching an agreement to end their dispute, now six years old. During the discussions, the negotiations were poised on the brink of success. Common ground had been found, and each side was ready to accept the proposals of the other. But at the moment of clinching the agreement, Henry II refused to embrace Becket. Henry affected for his part not to be holding a grudge, but he did not want to go back on an oath he had taken, in a moment of fury, never to kiss Becket. A mass was supposed to be celebrated in which, before communion, at the moment of the *Pax Domini sit semper vobiscum*, the exchange of a kiss between the two men would occur as a sign of peace. Henry II asked that the mass might be offered with the intention of the dead, as the rubric of the missal did without this ritual salute. So it was the king who was playing the active role in this impractical resolution of the conflict, indeed, in its exacerbation. Becket took the refusal as an insult: his clerks tried to persuade him to let it go, but the archbishop replied that the pope had instructed him to insist on the kiss.[133]

All the texts are unanimous on the facts, with one single exception. In his *Life of Saint Thomas*, Benedict of St Albans attributes the refusal to embrace the king to the archbishop, and not vice versa.[134] But for Benedict it was not a matter of a liturgical kiss of peace, but of the *osculum* that the vassal owed his lord in the ritual of feudalism. Around 1184, Benedict had adapted into Anglo-Norman a Latin life of Becket written by Robert of Cricklade at some time between 1172 and 1177, now lost, which he does not seem to have been following in the passage under discussion. The Icelandic translation of Cricklade, owed probably to the priest Berg Gunnsteinsson makes the king responsible for the insult.[135] Benedict was a firm partisan of Henry II. He noted the opportunity for Becket to serve 'the noble lord of his day, a king rich in objects of value', the courageous opponent of tyrants in the civil war, the first of the monarchs to place all his power at the disposal of the Church.[136] That he had an idea of the servile nature of the archbishop's submission to the king explains Benedict's more or less conscious mistake. His account must be rejected as irreconcilable.

The king's refusal calls for some discussion. It occurred in an honour-bound society where respect for a man's self, his group and his status is pre-eminent. Henry II's reputation risked being lessened in the eyes of his courtiers and, beyond them, of his aristocracy, indeed his entire people, by a volte-face. Every publicly-sworn oath overrode any sort of personal animosity. It is worth recalling the war which the king fought with his son Richard the Lionheart a score or so years later, in 1189. Forced to surrender to Richard and seek a truce, the king was obliged to exchange the kiss of peace. As he did it, Henry whispered in Richard's ear: 'May God not allow me to die before I have taken a proper revenge on you!'[137] It may be that the story is told by Gerald of Barry in 1218, three decades after the event, and Gerald kept up a grudge against the Angevins, who he was always running down. But it is nonetheless instructive on one subject: it showed that nothing stopped Henry II from embracing an enemy for whom he felt only hatred. The public enactment of a gesture of peace counted for a lot more than the states of the soul. The kiss had a social dimension but no personal one. This is why, in telling Becket that he had no animosity towards him, but that he did not want to embrace him so as not to perjure himself, Henry was behaving consonant with the standards which regulated the life of princes and aristocracy.

For his part, Becket adopted all the more firmly a position whose framework and shape was more complicated. It respected an ecclesiastical mentality whose ethical, scriptural and canonical demands outstripped his own capacities. Firstly, Becket knew that morality condemned malignant oaths, as for example that which Herod swore to Salome which cost John the Baptist his head. Henry's excuse then was not much of one, so far as Becket was concerned. Secondly, the refusal to kiss was a serious act which the Church sanctioned only with those under anathema. In 1166, when some Templars approached Henry II to greet and embrace him, the king eluded their attempt, 'saying he had no wish to give the kiss to an excommunicate.'[138] Finally, Thomas said that he was the more bound to kiss the king as the pope had laid down that he should do so. Frank Barlow notes, however, the feeble nature of this argument, for, if reconciliation was only held up by this detail, Thomas should have been able to disobey Alexander III and tell him about it later.[139] Opposition to a malignant oath, the attitude towards excommunicates and a papal injunction casts some light on Becket's obstinacy.

From an anthropological point of view, the importance of the kiss of peace appears all the greater. The act was a theatrical manifestation of the love and friendship which, in the twelfth century, often had a political aspect.[140] It 're-presented' an alliance. It was, in structuralist terms, a pertinent element of a system which cannot function without it. It was integral to the rite which regulated disputes. Herbert of Bosham reports the purposes of the pope when he insisted on the importance of the gesture in the peace ceremony, particularly if given by a member of the clergy: 'for the kiss of peace ought to be sufficient by itself for a priest wishing to maintain the cause of justice.'[141] So it was unthinkable for a clergyman to give sureties as soldiers did when exchanging hostages and castles to guarantee as truce, for the single kiss sufficed as a warrant for keeping his word. The rite of peace was impossible without the kiss. For the priest is was not only intrinsic to it, but the entire thing.

This aspect of the Becket corpus is all the more interesting as it had been overlooked by specialists in the rites which in the Middle Ages moderated reconciliations. There exist two schools of thought on the role which the kiss played in the peace ritual. Some think that it was purely formal and incidental to the ceremony. It was no more than a simple act of welcome or greeting, as the key point of the rite was the oath which the former enemies took. Others assert that the kiss, given on the mouth where the breaths which represented the soul mingled, was as important as the oath, if not more so. It was 'the central and interpretative moment of the rite'; it 'constituted the essential symbolic rite in the diplomatic rituals of civil peace . . . In literature, the ceremonial of peace was organized around the central act: the kiss.'[142] If the latter analysis is accepted, one based on the reading of numerous historiographical and literary sources, Becket's obstinacy achieves its full meaning. The archbishop, educated in theology, understood the significance of the rite, which had to be followed to the letter to have its effect. Like every canonist, Becket gave considerable weight to the proper sequence of things, which should not be marred by any error, lest it be invalidated. Becket's stubbornness stemmed from a deep conviction: no peace without the kiss.

Events justified Becket after his death. In July 1174, Henry II completed a long penance on the tomb of Thomas of Canterbury. To expiate the murder and reconcile himself with God and the saint, he had to give the kiss of peace. It was Jean Bellesmains, bishop of Poitiers, the former friend of Becket, who received it in the name of the episcopate.[143] Some years later, another prelate was involved in the business of a ritual kiss, this time with Richard the Lionheart, the new king of England. The story derives from Adam of Eynsham. In August 1198, when the king was hearing a mass in his chapel at Château-Gaillard, Hugh of Lincoln pushed forward to receive the kiss of peace from him. Richard refused to give it to him, at odds with the bishop who had refused him an aid in cash for his war against the king of France.[144] But Hugh got it in the end. That affair, purely a matter of money, was invested with less significance than one involving the kingdom's constitution. Exile and murder were not likely in this case. In his discussion of it, Gerald of Barry goes so far as to say that Richard the Lionheart had embraced Hugh of Lincoln laughing.[145] But it does not detract from the importance of the ritual kiss that the bishop of Lincoln had crossed the Channel in person to meet the king and exchange it with him. His behaviour is good evidence of the importance that medieval people gave to this act of reconciliation.

The martyrdom (29 December 1170)

Becket's murder cannot be analysed in the same terms as the carrying of his cross or the kiss of peace, highly ritualized acts which belonged to a religious ritual and lay ceremony with fixed codes. Apart from its spontaneous nature, the murder in Canterbury cathedral possessed a certain logic in its sequence. It enacted patterns of behaviour which may not have been routine in the Middle Ages, but which were not infrequent.[146] The murder may not have been ritual or sacrificial, strictly speaking,[147] but it was deeply endowed with meaning for both parties.

There are any number of accounts of the event. They might seem all the more interesting as they come from eyewitnesses who recalled their memories in a vivid way. John of Salisbury watched the murder from a distance; William fitz Stephen was at the archbishop's side; Edward Grim was wounded trying to come between Becket and his murderers; Benedict of Peterborough and William of Canterbury, at the time monks of Christ Church, the community attached to the cathedral, were waiting for Becket in the church for the office of vespers. Other authors rely on first-hand accounts, such as Herbert of Bosham, part of Becket's embassy in France at the time of the murder, or the trouvère, Guernes de Pont-Sainte-Maxence, who did his research at Canterbury and with Mary, abbess of Barking, Becket's sister.[148] Each writer gave a mass of detail on the way the crime unfolded.

Textual comparison allows a very plausible reconstruction of the event. According to the accounts, Henry II may have one time said that he seemed to maintain only traitors in his household, since none of his barons had been able to unembarrass him of Becket.[149] Four knights took him at his word. They arrived unarmed at the episcopal palace, where they had a first interview with Becket of whom they demanded that he lift the excommunication against the bishops who had crowned the Young Henry. Thomas told them that he could not absolve them on the pope's behalf. Tempers got heated and soon the archbishop was accused of treason. Becket told them that they were his vassals, for they had sworn liege homage to him when he was chancellor. The knights responded that their only lord was the king and threatened him with physical violence. Thomas replied that they would find him there, a defiance that put his head on the block.

The four men came back later that evening, this time armed, and broke down a door to get into the episcopal palace. Becket, who wanted to stand up to them, was forcibly dragged along by his clerks into the cathedral, where the monks and a crowd of laypeople were waiting for vespers. Becket refused to hide or to run away, and he forbade them to bar the door behind him, for 'the Church of God shall not be transformed into a fortress.' Just as the group of clerks entered the cathedral from crossing the cloister, Becket was overtaken by the knights, armed with swords and axes. They repeated their charge of treason and once again demanded that he lift the excommunications. Thomas refused, and he was hacked to death. When the body was prepared for burial in the church, the monks discovered the horsehair shirt he wore as a penance and the traces of the strokes of discipline.

This brief account of the events is worth expanding on. Firstly, it is important to consider the way the four knights carried out their crime, and note that nothing was left to chance. Their equipment showed to everyone what their business was, their social status and their values: their knight-hood. Armed to the teeth, they were completely protected by their helm, which hid all their face apart from their eyes, and by their hauberk. It was dressed like this that they had pushed inside a religious place, 'a house of peace and reconciliation',[150] a building where everyone's right of refuge was respected and where the shedding of blood was the worst of desecra-tions. Such a trespass was equated with a serious sacrilege, which required a specific ritual before the church could be returned to religious uses. The clerks, confronted by soldiers, could hardly offer any physical resistance. The old antagonism of knights towards clergy, particularly acute in the days when the movement of the Peace of God was at full flood, appeared in sharp relief. The fashionable play on words in the clerical world, where *militia* (knighthood) was compared to *malitia* (wickedness), was fully realized. The fact that an axe – the same that was dropped there by one of the murderers and closed off by a barrier – was left by the monks of Christ Church in the north transept on the precise site of the crime, is particularly to the point in this context. This symbolic allusion, proof of the martyrdom of Becket, demonstrated in a graphic way the confronta-tion between clerk and knight.

The Becket conflict also acquired a social dimension by the origins of the knights in the nobility of blood. What amounted to class hatred permeated the murder, which Henry II worsened when, as he publicly demanded Becket's elimination, he stressed the plebeian nature of his birth. Just before dealing Becket the fatal blow, Reginald fitz Urse called the archbishop by his family surname, Becket, the only mention of it in the *Lives*.[151] In this way Reginald insulted him by throwing the profession of his merchant father in his face. By the view presented here, there was overweening noble pride towards the clergy, often intellectuals of humble origin. It was to this very category of clerks from the gutter that Becket's chief thinker, John of Salisbury, a peasant's son, belonged. It has to be that John's humble origins had something to do with the delight that the four assassins let loose for having wounded Edward Grim, for they wrongly believed that they had slashed off John's arm. Up against the archbishop and his men, the soldiers were doubly fierce as belonging to a group of professional warriors and the social category of nobles.

The knights committed a crime of unusual brutality. From the cloister they pursued Becket and the clerks into the transept. An argument occurred: the archbishop stubbornly refused to lift the excommunications. He pushed out Reginald fitz Urse, calling him 'lion'. One of the knights immediately dealt out a blow with the flat of his sword on Becket's shoulders. He fell to his knees and covered his face with his hands, while commending himself to the Virgin – whose statue loomed over the scene – and to Ss Denis and Alphege. One of the monks was wounded at this point. Reginald struck Becket on the skull: the sword sliced off his tonsure and cut into his left shoulder. He also wounded Edward Grim who tried vainly to protect his master. Seeing his blood spill, Becket said a last prayer and stretched out his arms in the form of a cross. William Tracy struck him again. The body of the victim fell to the ground. Richard le Bret split open the skull with a sword blow so heavy that it broke on striking the pavement. Hugh Mauclerc, one of the knights' serjeants, stamped on Becket's neck with his foot, then scooped out his brain with the point of his sword shouting: 'This traitor will never rise again!' In the meanwhile, Hugh de Morville had kept the crowd at a distance. After they had left the cathedral, the assassins looted the palace and episcopal stables.

The deed was done with great brutality. The knights, armed with both sword and axe, hacked at the body of their victim even after it fell to the ground. But their acts had a certain logic. It is revealing that all their blows fell on the head. The first of them sliced the crown of the tonsure, a fact which did not escape John of Salisbury who spelled out the signific-ance in the letter *Ex Inesperato*, addressed to John Bellesmains soon after the murder: 'It was the crown of the head that the anointing of holy chrism had consecrated to God.'[152] Some decades after the event, Gerald of Barry analysed the murder at length. 'He received four wounds and no more from those four dogs of the court, madder than any dog ever was, on the crown of his head, which ought to be a sign to protect the clergy. It was only on that part of his body that he suffered his passion. The courageous soldier undergoing martyrdom for Christ crossed over in this way to a better life, earning by a happy exchange an incorruptible for a corruptible crown.'[153]

The intention of such an interpretation is clear. As Gerald said, the tonsure was the sign of the setting apart of the clergy. At that date it was applied by the uprooting of the hair of part of the scalp. Judges who had to decide if a defendant belonged to an ecclesiastical court checked in the first place whether he was marked by this cut. As such, the tonsure was also a 'sign of protection', to return to Gerald's words. In the publica-tion of the constitutions of Clarendon, jurisdiction over criminous clerks featured as the central point in dispute between Henry II and Thomas Becket. From this it can be understood why the assassins, who believed they were following the king's wishes, went on to hack at the crown of Becket's skull, the visible symbol of his clerical orders, but particularly his juridical status. The clergy noted the symbolic futility of that act of violence. Benedict of Peterborough (died 1193), monk of Christ Church and witness to the murder, makes this comment on the episode of the sword which broke on striking the ground: 'This accident seems all too conformable to truth, for it did not lack a prophetic significance. If the sword of his enemies broke, what can it signify other than the defeat of the hostile power and the victory of the Church, which triumphed thanks to the blood of the martyr?'[154] In this way the spiritual power triumphed over the lay in the decisive battle. Becket's tonsure would find a symbolic manifestation in the architecture of Canterbury Cathedral. In the early 1180s, its chevet was lengthened with a chapel of the Holy Trinity, containing Becket's reliquary, and an axial tower which was called just that, the 'crown'.[155]

The ferocity of the murderers was not satisfied by the death of Becket. It is known that they prevented the monks of Christ Church holding a proper funeral and burial in the cathedral, but instructed them to throw the body secretly into a marsh or bog, and even to hang it up. They even threatened to feed it to the dogs. It is worth noting at this point the study published by Robert Jacob on the murder of lords in medieval society. In several instances, Jacob observed that the crimes were followed by a 'demeaning burial which allowed to the murderers a sort of symbolic victory.'[156] As for Becket, he noted the repeated blows by each of the assassins, and the amount of blood spilled. The collective aspect of the assassination was highlighted explicitly by Benedict of St Albans: 'each of them had a part there to play, and had spattered blood and brains about.'[157] Gerald of Barry added that three of the knights, after striking their fatal blows, told the fourth to finish it off. The last of them struck at the skull spilling Becket's brains on the ground.[158] Solidarity amongst assassins, which explains the many blows struck, follows on from their meeting to plan the murder, their promise of mutual aid in the case of resistance and their oath to finish what they had started. Becket's murder broadly demonstrates all the main features of such a Jacob's theoretical scheme. The four assassins met secretly several times to decide on their plan. Their calculation was all the more flagrant as they were in no way under the influence of alcohol, a point several hagiographers make.[159] Guernes de Pont-Sainte-Maxence notes that the four of them had sworn to carry out the crime when they were at Bures, a ducal palace near Caen, in the same room in which Harold had once promised to concede the Crown of England to William the Conqueror, before perjuring himself.[160] The Becket plot was a conspiracy squarely like those Robert Jacob has described. On the other hand the Becket murder was not a complete match to his model. It was not the consequence of a ritual sacrifice by a master unable otherwise to keep the peace and promote prosperity, a victim whose blood, spilled and restored to the land, allowed a now fertilized nature to bloom again. If there was a sacrifice in regard to Becket it was a eucharistic one, to use the same language as the hagiographers.

Before closing the file on the murderers, their justifications for the murder need to be looked at. They were of two types. Firstly, the accusation of having betrayed the king was often levelled against Becket, charged with an offence of *lèse-majesté* which was widely punished by death. Secondly, at the moment when he dealt out the *coup de grâce*, Richard le Bret shouted at Becket: 'Take this for love of my lord, William the king's brother!'[161] This last, the younger brother of Henry II, had been promised to Isabel de Warenne, the fairest heiress in England, countess of Surrey and widow of King Stephen's son. If we believe Stephen de Rouen, who completed his *Draco Normannicus* a little before Becket's murder (a man he deeply despised), the archbishop had done everything he could to prevent this consanguineous marriage being celebrated. William supposedly died of disappointment on 30 January 1164.[162] Behind the struggle between the sort of marriage aristocrats wanted and the marriage the Church preached,[163] issues about jurisdiction are obvious, since matrimonial causes, which belonged to ecclesiastical courts, were moving to the king's. The four murderers had believed they were obeying the king in executing in his name the most noxious traitor in his realm.

Their enthusiasm was all the more marked as the four of them had recently served King Stephen in the civil war and as they needed to demonstrate, by their harshness, their present loyalty to the Angevins.[164] Their eagerness to please their new master explains why they had taken to heart his infuriated utterances against Becket. It is not criminals but would-be executioners that we are really dealing with here. In any case, Henry II seemed to them to be the instigator of the murder. The king was not indeed carrying out by any means his first act of intimidation against Becket. Had he not already sent his magnates to the Council of Clarendon where, 'having thrown back their cloaks and uncovered their arms', they had threatened the bishops?[165] The king's violence was not just verbal. It went beyond the simple formulas of the chancery's charters, whose *ira regis* threatened reprisals and punishments against those who disobeyed royal orders. It could unleash frightful consequences.

After studying the murder in the cathedral from the murderers' point if view, we need to reflect on they way it affected Becket's friends. Their understanding of it was unanimous: Becket went to certain death of his own free will. At Christmas, four days before he died, he preached to his flock that they would soon lose their shepherd, for he had returned to England to give his life to preserve the liberties of the Church. He refused to flee or to hide as the murderers commanded his followers to give him up. He wanted to confront the assassins face to face. On the day of the murder, he ordered that the palace gates should not be closed against them. He reprimanded the monks who were overjoyed to see him still alive after his first interview with the knights, in the manner of the 'Get thee behind me' directed by Christ at St Peter. His last words, recollected by his hagiographers, were most explicit: 'I am ready to die for my Lord so that by my blood the Church will gain peace and liberty.' In offering his head to his murderers, he identified himself with the 'sacrificial lamb of God'. Becket did not just submit to the murder; he did not just accept it with meekness. It could be said, on the contrary, that he went looking for it, a result which he sought.

Voluntary though it may have been, Becket's act did not any the less demonstrate that he was a martyr. His supporters understood rather that his death was a heroic renunciation of life, as witness to his faith in Christ and his Church. The monks did not wash his body before burying it, since they believed that his spilled blood was sufficient to prove the purity of his soul. Several of his biographers comment that the whiteness of his brain – matching the liturgical colour of confessors and virgins – was mixed with the red of his blood, the sign of martyrdom. The chapel of Holy Trinity, which would house his mortal remains after the 1180s, echoed those two colours in the limestone and the marble of its walls. Becket's hagiographers assert that he was not indeed just a martyr, for he did not just seek his own salvation, but that of the Church.[166] The same reasoning is to be found in the fact that he called on Ss Denis of Paris and Alphege of Canterbury as he was falling under the first blow: they were both bishops and martyrs. The previous year, during the negotiations with Henry II, which had been held in the Parisian monastery of St-Denis, a priest had said to Becket: 'Today, the peace of the Church has been argued in the martyr's chapel, I believe that it is only by your martyrdom that the Church will regain its peace.'[167] The part of the cathedral chosen for Becket's burial was located in front of the altar of St John Baptist, whose head was struck off by a king's order. As a result the majority of Becket's contemporaries came to believe that his death was well and truly a martyrdom.

It followed that there was a comparison with the passion of Christ, as the connecting thread between most of the hagiographical accounts of the murder in the cathedral. The fundamentals of such a comparison were first proposed by John of Salisbury in his letter *Ex Inesperato*, which he composed very soon after the murder. Somewhat later, he gave another expanded version of it in his *Passion of Saint Thomas the Martyr*, a significant title, where he abandoned the epistolary genre for a historical narrative.[168] Most hagiographers drew their inspiration from John of Salisbury's texts. Like him, they developed, point by point, the similarity between the passions of Christ and of Becket. His triumphal return to Canterbury, after six years' exile, has resonances of Palm Sunday – the crowds throwing their cloaks on the road as he passed, all singing: 'Blessed is he who comes in the name of the Lord' (Matt. 21: 12–22; Mark 11: 8–10; Luke 19: 37–8). In preventing the doors being closed on the assassins, Becket shouted: 'So God's will be done,' as Christ did in Gethsemane (Luke 22: 42). He cried out to the four knights that he was ready to die, but sought immunity for his followers, as Jesus had asked the guards sent by the high priest to arrest him (John 18: 8–9). His executioners were obeying an order of Henry II just as immoral as that of Pilate. When the first blow was struck, Becket fell to his knees saying the last words of Christ, just as Stephen the Protomartyr had done as he was being stoned: 'Father, into your hands I commend my spirit.' (Ps. 31: 6; Luke 23: 46; Acts 7: 59). After they had looted the episcopal palace, the murderers shared out the sacred vessels, liturgical ornaments and horses, in the same way as Jesus's executioners had divided his clothes (Ps. 22: 19; John 19: 24). William fitz Stephen drew the obvious conclusion: 'As once Christ suffered in his body, he suffered anew in his champion Thomas.'[169]

The identification between the crucifixion and Becket's martyrdom recalled the mass, a sacrifice which re-presented Christ's death. 'Note the place where Thomas was sacrificed. In the church which is the capital of the realm and the mother in Christ of the rest, in front of the altar, among his priests . . . He was accustomed to offer the body and blood of Christ on the altar. Now, laid at the altar's foot, he offers his own blood shed by the hands of sinners,' John of Salisbury wrote.[170] As well as asserting in passing the primacy of the see of Canterbury, John compares Becket's sacrifice to that of Christ on the cross for the redemption of the human race, re-enacted in the eucharist. The altar, the place of sacrifice, is referred to again and again in his writings. Becket celebrated there the sacrifice of the mass, and it was there that he had been sacrificed.

Concerning this theme, it is interesting to note the evolution of the Becket iconography. Most of the forty-eight historiated reliquaries containing relics of Becket's skull and his bloodstained chasuble derived from the enamel workshops of Limoges. Becket appears there in the act of celebrating mass in front of an altar on which is resting a chalice or a ciborium, just as he is being attacked by the knights. The same interpretation occurs on frescos, which continue to show Becket murdered during the mass.[171] The idea of his martyrdom which identified the priest in the middle of the eucharistic celebration with the crucified Christ, could not be a more marked assertion of the message.

But this association between mass and martyrdom was not to the liking of all the clergy. Thomas's eventual status as saint and martyr was contested even in his own lifetime. The theologian, Robert of Melun, bishop of Hereford, began to debate during a conversation with other prelates: 'If it should so happen, which God forbid, that the archbishop was killed for the liberty of the Church, ought we to count him among the number of the martyrs? To be a martyr a man must truly die for the faith.'[172] According to Edward Grim, the very evening of the murder, a clerk argued with the idea that Thomas had suffered martyrdom.[173] If Caesarius of Heisterbach is to be believed on the subject, the question of Becket's martyrdom set Master Roger the Norman (formerly officer at the Sicilian court and law student at Bologna, dean of Rouen from 1181) against the famous moralist Peter the Chanter, at Paris. For Roger, wilful stubbornness was the cause of Becket's death, while Peter reckoned him a martyr for the liberty of the Church. Caesarius asserted that God tipped the debate towards Peter, as numerous miracles were attributed to Becket's intercession.[174] The popularity of the archbishop's cult hung chiefly on his violent death, compared to the martyrdom and passion of Christ. Apart from that, his blood became the object of a special curative ritual: mixed with water, it was used as a salve or drink to heal the sick.[175]

Becket's death gave the clergy the chance to emphasize the sacrificial role of the eucharist in the life of the faithful; the dignity of the priestly caste that made the sacrifice during the mass; the legal exemption that ought to follow on from their priesthood; and the central place of the altar, church and cathedral in Christendom. The interpretations we have looked at are perfectly evident in the struggle between *regnum* and *sacerdotium* which divided lay and ecclesiastical society at the end of the twelfth century.

In the struggle between Church and State, the Canterbury murder gave an unarguable victory, if posthumous, to Becket. When he heard the news himself, the king was distraught. A letter of Arnulf of Lisieux calls Henry's reaction a profound prostration. He wore a penitential shirt and threw ashes on himself; he made loud lamentations; he shut himself in his chamber for three days, neither eating nor seeing anyone.[176] He embarked on a penitential regime that would last for at least four years. Apart from its spiritual dimension, this conduct was the open confession of a political defeat. Without any doubt Henry II had a very clear comprehension of the implications of the Becket murder, which buried for good the last chance of implementing the constitutions of Clarendon. In acting out his despair in such an emotional way, the king was undertaking a penance which drastically set back his programme of mastering the clergy begun ten years earlier.

After the murder, the king's person was pretty much discredited among the same priests who had been most sympathetic towards him. On this point the example of the eremetical order of Grandmont – particularly supported by the Empress Mathilda – is very instructive.[177] Roger of Howden reports that in August 1170, some four months after the murder, seriously ill, Henry II had asked to be buried in the mother house of the order to the north of Limoges, at the feet of the order's founder, Stephen Muret (died 1124).[178] This is good evidence of the king's affection for the house of Grandmont, whose construction he fostered with generous gifts. But in the aftermath of the murder, a letter of William de Treignac, prior of Grandmont, told Henry that he had discharged the masons who had arrived at the king's request to work on the church building, as he did not want to be implicated along with him. It is worth recalling that it was probably William who had composed a tract denouncing the corruption of the Aquitainian clergy to Henry II, and calling on him to suppress it. William's rejection of royal patronage was as spectacular as it was unheard of. He was making concrete the ostracism of the king who had enabled the crime. On his part, Peter Bernard, William's predecessor as prior between 1153 and 1170, wrote a long letter to Henry which contrasted his generosity towards the poor men of Grandmont and the horrible murder of Becket, 'which has stained the white of his stole with the red of the sinless lamb.' 'You,' he said, 'who take care of the construction and endowment of our churches, how you have dispersed the sheep of the Catholic flock in striking down its shepherd.' Peter Bernard accounted the rebellion of Henry's own sons as a just punishment after so great a cime.[179] So, condemnation of the king was general.

Henry II had no choice but to fall on his knees, abandoning all his claims to extend his jurisdiction. In May 1172, at Avranches, the king had to swear solemnly to his acceptance of the compromise that the papal legates had presented him with. He renounced his obstruction of appeals to the Roman curia and all the new laws concerning the clergy, and he undertook to confirm the church of Canterbury and Becket's supporters in all their rights and possessions. It was a considerable success for

Alexander III, who had caused England to come under papal jurisdiction, establishing the application of canon law in Britain. Criminous clerks answered as always to ecclesiastical courts, and the Young Henry had to be crowned again.[180] Henry II and his successors kept at least a substantial influence in episcopal elections, which continued to happen – according to the witticism of Stephen Langton – not under the influence of the Holy Spirit but in the spirit of the Exchequer.[181] Finally, at Avranches, Henry II swore also to go on crusade for three years.

Henry's exile to the Holy Land was incorporated in a ritual wider than simply penitence, which the king completed in July 1174 at Canterbury. Clothed only in a loose shirt of undyed wool, the king walked barefoot from the city's suburbs as far as the cathedral. The bishops, abbots and monks of Christ Church flogged him with rods. He lay face down for a whole day before Becket's tomb eating and drinking nothing. Then he visited the different altars in the cathedral to venerate the relics of the saints kept there. He returned to Becket's crypt. He heard mass on Sunday evening. Finally, he took a drink at the martyr's well and received a flask of water mixed with Becket's blood.[182] If we follow the clerks who described this scene, God sent him a sign recognizing the sincerity of his repentance. And indeed the very day that he made his repentance, his troops captured William of Scotland at Alnwick, a decisive victory which put an end to the general rebellion in his lands.[183] Was the English Crown on the way to achieving the unexpected in claiming the Becket cult for its very own? Some other of Becket's miracles in favour of the Angevins and repeated pilgrimages of Henry II and his sons to the tomb might well favour the idea.[184] One thing is certain, between 1185 and 1188, Mathilda, daughter of Henry II, had herself pictured in a miniature in the gospels of Henry the Lion, her husband, with her parents and her grandmother and namesake, under the protection of Becket, carrying a martyr's palm and wearing episcopal insignia.[185]

However, Henry II would never really succeed in overcoming the un-popularity which the murder had caused him. William of Newburgh, usually a detached sort of writer, explained that the ignominy of the king's death was because his repentance for the murder had been incomplete.[186] The idea was that his wife's and childrens' rebellion – his 'persecution inside his family and at home', to quote Ralph of Coggeshall[187] – and the premature death of his elder sons were direct consequences of the murder at Canterbury, which he had never truly expiated. The mildness of his punishment culminated in his refusal to go on crusade, a punishment that he commuted, very advantageously, into the construction of three monasteries.[188] In 1193, Stephen Langton asserted that Richard the Lionheart was 'imprisoned due to the sins of his father', just as Genesis illustrated that the sins of Cain were avenged on his son Canaan.[189] It would be necessary to wait some decades before Becket's supposed protection began to affect Henry II's descendants.

Becket's cult was promoted above all by the clerical intellectuals who had taken his part against the king in his own lifetime. His martyrdom had apotheosized their struggle in some way.[190] Contrary to received wisdom, it was not the Plantagenets who had commissioned the fifty or so caskets of Limoges enamel to house Becket's relics, which are found widely scattered in the West. The idea more likely originated with the episcopate.[191] The church hierarchy found in Becket a model, a benefactor and protector par excellence, in the saint's defence of papal jurisidiction, ecclesiastical privilege and canon law, up against the expansionist impulses of a princely administration in full throttle.

The murder worked also to the benefit of the king of France, the inveterate enemy of Henry II and patron of the Parisian schools, the place where the clerks had developed their theories. In 1179, Becket, who had been in his lifetime a loyal friend of Louis VII, cured Philip Augustus, aged fourteen, following his father's pilgrimage to the tomb at Canterbury. William le Breton stressed that the saint had preserved the boy 'with the purpose of wiping out the dynasty of bloodthirsty parricides.'[192] Gerald of Barry, as Francophile as ever, attributed the fall of Châteauroux at the hands of Philip Augustus in June 1188 to the intercession of Becket. A chaplain of the French king had dreamed of the archbishop armed with a sword of fire, taking a blow at Henry II.[193] Evidently the spiritual sword was hostile to the Plantagenets and friendly to the Capetians, as the enemies of their enemies were their friends. The same spiritual weapon would be taken up again with great power by Stephen Langton to cross swords with King John, with whom Stephen would have the last word. This time Magna Carta – imposed in 1215 – would safeguard the liberties of the Church from royal wilfulness and meddling for centuries to come.

Conclusion

B etween 1154 and 1224, for three generations, the house of Anjou presided over an enormous Atlantic dominion. From Hadrian's Wall to the Pyrenees, from the kingdom of Ulster to the Massif Central, numerous realms submitted to the rule of one or other of its members. A territorial complex like that is worth pondering, and might be believed to have arisen out of spontaneous generation. For never before had there been such a disparate conglomeration of kingdoms, duchies, marches, counties and vicounties under the rule of a single family. Heirs of a variety of political and cultural traditions, formed from different peoples, speaking many languages, divided by the Channel, the Bay of Biscay and the Irish Sea, the conglomeration was hardly a natural one. But, badly matched as it was, the union would last against all the odds for seven decades. With some changes, it would resurface in the fourteenth and fifteenth centuries in warfare. After a brief hiatus, the Hundred Years War allowed the Plantagenet Empire to recapture some of its old features.

The medieval historian wanting to understand such a geopolitical phenomenon from a modern perspective is in for a disappointment. Whatever the intention, the evolution of kingdoms into the modern period and the triumph of the nation-state in the nineteenth century will unbalance his analysis. The Angevin overlordship of a realm as enormous as it was incoherent would make it appear to such a scholar as an historical aberration, in the distorting glass of his ideas of unified institutions and language – essential to the construction of a country – and of the natural frontier, still a fraught concept. It is only necessary to call to mind the lengthy diatribes against the Plantagenet Empire by Jules Michelet and William Stubbs to appreciate the unanimous condemnation that it gave rise to on both sides of the Channel in the age of nationalism. Partisans of 'eternal France' and admirers of the superiority of the British constitution and splendid isolation, these first professional historians deplored, around 1850, the ambition of Henry II and his advisers. Does the disapproval of Henry's enterprise – doomed in retrospect to defeat – continue to this day and age? In many ways, the misnamed Plantagenet Empire still remains unpopular. It does not relate well to the mental parameters that the later sovereign State has left us with.

But a prince of the twelfth century had a radically different political view. He believed, without a doubt – to paraphrase Walter Map – that he ruled his lands 'as the patriarch of any household'. In this way the Plantagenet Empire would look to him principally as a family business. Had Henry II not put it together through inheritance and marriage? Was he not prepared to carve it up, looking forward to his own succession which he wanted to be equitable and to the benefit of each and every one of his children? Did he not contemplate devolving his later conquests of Brittany and Ireland to his two younger sons? Did not his wife, Eleanor of Aquitaine, exercise a degree of significant control of her lands during her widowhood? Did not the premature death of several of his sons allow Richard the Lionheart and then John to maintain the integrity of the empire against all the odds? Various customs of inheritance and marriage brought it into being. Descent and family alliance were the only reasons for its existence.

This is why its integrity and even its survival depended so much on the solidarity of its ruling family. But the Angevin dynasty was quarrelsome. Its members did not enjoy the equability of the Capetians and Hohenstaufen. The passion of the Barcelona and Castille-Léon dynasty burned deep inside them. They recalled – as Richard of Devizes said – 'the disturbed house of Oedipus'. These latter-day Atreides thought only of internecine fighting. This largely inexplicable family feuding caused a lot of contemporary comment. Students of Celtic folklore at the Plantagenet court alluded – as Gerald of Barry did – to the female demon, supposedly the founder of their dynasty in legendary times. They pondered the obscure prophecies of Merlin to work out the reason for the Angevin self-destructive impulse. To these clerical intellectuals, Scripture taught that every kingdom divided against itself could not stand. If they had no clear idea of the causes, contemporaries realized that the family civil war would bring the Plantagenet-ruled dominion to collapse, whether the day of reckoning was sooner or later. It was suicidal.

Family should not be separated from vassalage, which is nothing more than a redundant metaphor for family. The eldest of the dynasty had the right to be at the apex of the feudal hierarchy. This is why he received the royal crown from his father and the homage of his younger brothers. At a lower level, he tried to secure the formal allegiance of the aristocracy, towns and peasantry. General oaths of loyalty towards the king spread wider in England and Normandy. Local magnates alone took the oaths, which shared the symbolism of the self-giving involved in the ritual of adoption. The Irish sub-kings built wooden huts in which to dine with Henry II, who gave them in return gifts which linked him to them. The great Poitevin lords made their submission on their knees, with very bad grace, in the demeaning ceremony of homage. In exchange for their obedience, they received confirmation of their power over their ancestral lands whether in a landed fief or in the form of the hard cash deriving from the fief rent. Links of submission towards the king were very weak. If they were broken so frequently it was because they depended all too often on the personal feeling between lord and vassal. Should the king lose a battle or fail to satisfy the land and legal claims of a nobleman or should he not know how basically to keep his friendship, the links flew apart. The incompetence of King John was the root cause of what happened in 1204.

But that does not account for everything. We need to go back again to the concepts of kinship and feudalism, which are more useful in analysing Philip Augustus's final success. When they accepted Margaret and Alice of France, the daughters of Louis VII, as wives and fiancées, the Young Henry and Richard the Lionheart accepted a situation of inferiority in relation to their father-in-law. When they went with their brother Geoffrey of Brittany to the court of Paris to eat at the same table and sleep in the same bed as Philip Augustus, they accepted a lordly hospitality along the lines of that which a younger brother accepted from his elder. But feudal ritual remained the most open form of a subordinating and artificial family relationship. The Plantagenets had never shrunk from performing homage to the French king. As Angevins rather than Normans, they found it normal to submit themselves to one who held supreme power in western Francia. The start of their dazzling ascent was precisely at the point of the homage for Normandy sworn in summer 1151 at Paris, when the young Henry II showed for the first time his regard for Eleanor of Aquitaine, the wife of his lord. This event relates to another one. In August 1188, the felling of the elm at Gisors by Philip Augustus was a brutal and conclusive end to the egalitarian custom of making homage on the frontier. The confiscation of John's continental lands in his lord's court over a marital irregularity affecting the interests of another vassal followed about twenty years later. Robert de Torigny, abbot of Mont St-Michel and godfather of one of Henry II's daughters, conveniently discovered an ancient document arguing that the duke held Normandy completely free of obligation. But for all that, the Angevins were the French king's men, by act of homage from time out of mind. They were never able to evade that heavy a handicap.

If the term 'Empire' is a poor description of the political enterprise of the Plantagenets, it is because their continental possessions belonged to another 'Crown', an idea whose spatial extent was defined in the spirit of the lawyers attached to Philip Augustus's court. Its duchies, marches, counties and viscounties were above all territorial principalities. It is worth pausing at this point to consider the idea. It sums up the most illuminating explanation for the geopolitics of the European twelfth century. These regional entities, arising from the breakup of the Carolingian empire, were quite numerous in western France, shaped by coherent economic, ethnic and cultural criteria. However theoretically dependent on the king – the sovereign who took the allegiance of his feudatories, who dated their own charters according to the year of his reign – these men enjoyed a wide autonomy in practice. They put together groups of neighbouring lordships. In the middle of the eleventh century the union of Gascony and Poitou, and the construction of a Greater Anjou occurred at the same time as the conquest of the kingdom of England by the duke of Normandy. These territorial groupings a century later formed the core of the Plantagenet Empire. A certain homogeneity can genuinely be found in this great agglomeration of lordships, particularly in the Atlantic arc it formed. Whatever the case, the four rulers who succeeded each other at the head of the Empire believed in its integrity.

Did the assuming of the English Crown give the ruler an additional advantage in presiding over his continental lordships? It is sure enough that kingship carried with it great prestige and also authority, which was made real in the thaumaturgic powers that were popularly attributed to the king. Consecration at Westminster made them 'the Lord's anointed', against whom all rebellion and disobedience was an act as serious as it was sacrilegous. But consecration, a rite that the Angevins shared with the king of France and the Holy Roman Emperor, carried with it some grievous problems. It forced him, on the one hand, to swear to the liberties of the clergy and people, and on the other hand it put the king symbolically at the mercy of the bishops who enjoyed the most high-profile role in the ceremony. This double aspect of coronation, both contractual and theocratic, was a step on the road to Runnymede where King John was forced to put his seal to Magna Carta, which ended his despotism. On the continent, the consequences of their coronation seems to have been rather more limited. It did not allow the Angevins to escape their formal and ritual submission to the French king, the emperor and the pope. On the other hand it did give an extra lustre to the ceremony of ducal enthronement. A ritual involving investiture with a gold circlet, sword, spurs, lance and standard, took place in Norman and Aquitainian cathedrals and basilicas. This stratagem had its significance, as is proved by the attempt of the monks of St-Denis to put the ducal insignia of Aquitaine in their treasury.

In peace time the Plantagenets carried on their ideological warfare with Louis VII and Philip Augustus on other battlegrounds. Compared to other Western monarchies, they gave evidence of a surprising precocity in the business of propaganda. They presented themselves as 'the wise king' on Biblical and rhetorical lines, but even more as 'the scientific king', learned in empirical and popular lore. Besides that, the Plantagenets' well-documented patronage and monitoring of the composition of the chronicles of Wace and Benoît de Sainte-Maure shows a will to manipulate the memory of even long-ago events, which sank deep into the obscure days of the Trojan Wars. The logical end of this 'translation of empire and knowledge' was the British Isles, which took its name from Brutus, the great grandson of Aeneas. If their maternal kin was distinguished – what with Classical heroes and the holy kings and dukes of England and Normandy – the Angevins' paternal line was rather more modest. The founder of the lineage of Anjou was strictly speaking no more than Tertullus, the forester Charles the Bald, and experienced fighter of Vikings, whose son Ingelgerius carried out exploits which made him worthy of knighthood. From such roots, knightly rather than noble, the Angevins became attractive to the lesser nobility, impressed by their great deeds of arms whose just reward was the Angevins' ascent to the top of the hierarchy of power. The Angevin family epic recalled other deeds done by Geoffrey of Anjou, seneschal and banner bearer to Charlemagne, and by his kin.

The greatest of this dynastic pantheon was always Arthur. In the high Middle Ages, Celtic bards sang the deeds of this kinglet, who in 516AD crushed the Saxon invaders of Britain at Mount Badon, before becoming a demi-god after his mysterious death. At the beginning of the twelfth century, Geoffrey of Monmouth converted the legend into a Latin romance in his *History of the Kings of Britain*, undoubtedly the most popular history book in the Middle Ages. Geoffrey's book was widely disseminated, owing to the Anglo-Norman translation of Wace and the English translation produced by Layamon, as well as the other poems and romances which took up its themes. Most of their authors were in touch with the Angevin court, in one way or other, and amused themselves in comparing members of the royal family with Arthur. The mythical Arthur's conquests – most frequently in the field against the French – were set in the Plantagenet lands. Richard the Lionheart was all for building up this new dynastic cult. He sponsored the discovery of the tomb of Arthur and Guinevere at Glastonbury, he gave the sword Excalibur to the king of Sicily and nominated as his heir his nephew, carrying the name of Arthur. In the same way, his brother John's sword was Curtana, the sword with which Tristan had thrown down the giant Morholt. Along with the Knights of the Round Table, Arthur became the most precious of the Plantagenets' forebears, at a time when a specifically English identity was influencing the various elites of Britain. In the thought world of their politics, an Anglicized Arthur was beginning to counter to the Charlemagne Frenchified by the Capetians.

All this propaganda could only help the king of England in the exercise of his power. Controlling the Plantagenet Empire was a risky business: such was its immense extent and the diversity of the principalities of which it was composed. To manage it, the Angevins had adopted a style of itinerant living, travelling their lands ceaselessly so as to impose their authority through their physical presence. In one of his letters, Peter of Blois sketches a portrait of Henry II as a centaur, with legs warped by continual riding, barely ever dismounting. When Henry wanted to make a valuable gift to Frederick Barbarossa or to William of Sicily, it was not surprising that he offered a superb silken tent, an unsurpassable lodging for such men. He hardly ever spent Christmas in the same place twice, and crossed the Channel perhaps thirty times during his reign. His son, Richard the Lionheart adopted an identical lifestyle, and indeed he left for the Holy Land during the Third Crusade, of which he was the prime motivator and principal warrior. The retreat from this vagabond life by King John, shut up within his palaces and hunting lodges on the Thames so as to avoid the crowds of commoners that he disliked as much as his father enjoyed them, says a lot about his loss of his continental possessions.

These long journeys took Henry II and Richard the Lionheart to the most far-flung outposts of their empire. But the kings did not resort to each of their principalities with any consistency. They stayed longest in England and Normandy. Kingdom and duchy provided them with the bulk of the manpower and resources with which to govern their other territories. But paradoxical as it might appear, the tight grip by which England and Normandy were themselves held down explains their docility in the face of Capetian conquest in 1204 and the Magna Carta in 1215, a double blow against what was regarded as an intolerable degree of royal control. Compared to the Anglo-Norman core, the other lordships seemed rather under-governed. In any case, the king's resources there were badly crippled by frequent rebellions of local aristocracies. In the south of Poitou they can be calculated to have happened once every forty months. Often they were very violent, as the murder of the viceroy Patrick of Salisbury proves, an act procured in 1168 by the rising house of Lusignan. Again, there was the opposition that Richard the Lionheart encountered in taking the local fortresses of Taillebourg (site of his first venture in siege warfare) and at Chalus (where a bolt fired at him by a crossbowman cost him his life). To compensate for the troublesome local lords, the Plantagenets worked hard with the urban communes whom they showered with privileges. It was hardly any different in Anjou, the cradle of the dynasty. Brittany, whose title the king of England delegated to his near kinsmen, experienced similar rebellions, especially in its northern parts. It has to be recognized that there was a political gulf separating these turbulent lordships from England and Normandy, over which the Plantagenets kept a remarkably tight control.

Recent prosopographical studies confirm this conclusion. These concern the king's permanent household which took the chief offices of the peripheral lordships. Englishmen and Normans made up the great majority of these close counsellors of the king. Although the identity of these two 'national' groups – whose lordships were cross-Channel in extent – may often be hard to establish, it can be said that the English generally tended to take precedence over the Normans. This insularity amongst the king's close advisers increased under Richard the Lionheart. It was a remarkable turnabout, since from 1066 power had been in the hands of the Normans. But in 1204 the Norman aristocracy was all the readier to go over to Philip Augustus as it knew that it had been dispossessed of a power its predecessors had enjoyed for more than a century. It might be added that Angevins, Aquitainians and Bretons barely featured in the inner circle of Henry II or Richard the Lionheart's friends. There were some of them under King John, of whom one of the chief ministers was Peter des Roches. They were called, as an insult, 'Poitevins' and the English derided their warlike plans to reconquer Normandy and the Loire valley provinces which were seriously adding to the finanical burdens on them. Continental followers such as these would have no other choice than to become English, especially in the aftermath of the defeats of 1224. From then onwards Henry III's court took on at least a geographical homogeneity.

On the sociological level, the royal household seems more mixed. The tenants-in-chief, the great magnates of England and Normandy, keeping in their hands more than half of the lordships of their countries, filled an exclusive position close to the king. Robert II, earl of Leicester, the chief justiciar of England, was undoubtedly the most powerful baron in the kingdom, and his resources were comparable to those of William de

Mandeville, count of Aumale and Essex, to mention only two of the high profile ministers of Henry II. A lesser nobility of service, traditionally loyal to the Crown, provided any number of royal counsellors, along the lines of Richard de Lucy. Some ministers had climbed from peasant origins to power, thanks to their education. Promotion due to skills was criticized by the existing nobility. But such social climbing was rare in the court of the Angevins, whose household was largely composed of the old nobility. Angevin elitism contrasted with the followings of Louis VII and Philip Augustus, where lesser knightly families and urban patricians were more in evidence. In the long view this social contrast might explain the English aristocracy's hold over the Crown, and the powers given Parliament through the nobility. This system was the very opposite of the untrammelled authority of the French monarchy.

The Anglo-Norman royal household did not just represent a group of political advisers, but also the nucleus of the army. This limited group of aristocratic warriors was often composed of tenants-in-chief, who had distributed fees to numbers of knights with whom they filled their quotas to the royal army. William de Tancarville thus served Henry II with around a hundred combatants, among whom can be found the young William Marshal. The period of forty days' annual service seems to have been observed by the Anglo-Norman nobility, while it was more difficult to secure it in the other lordships. Quite often, the nobles preferred the payment of scutage than the service. It was a heavy tax which exempted them from military service. Scutage was a real advantage for the king, who used it more and more to hire paid troops. Mercenaries sprung from frontier or mountain peoples – Brabazons, Basques or Celts – who were loathed because of their origins. But they were nonetheless a key part of the royal army, on the lines of Mercadier, the faithful lieutenant of Richard the Lionheart. They were all the more useful to the Plantagenets, as they countered the aristocratic revolts so prevalent in the Plantagenet lands, with neither conscience nor family sympathies.

The nobility showed the greatest offence towards mercenaries on this score. Since common belief had it that the nobility was a legal category set apart, whose privileges were passed on by birth and whose members were registered by the state, the aristocracy would want to keep a monopoly on the conduct of warfare. Beyond the prestige and social superiority that it drew from the knightly occupation, it did well out of royal favour in enriching itself. Being close to the king it could acquire new fees, and also pensions, gifts and other benefits. The aristocracy was indeed capable of building up its own knightly followings, sharing out its possessions and above all the favour it could attract from the kings for the benefit of its kinsfolk and friends. Embezzlement and corruption were endemic in the nascent State which the house of Anjou built up in England and Normandy, and to a lesser degree in the other principalities of its Empire.

The great numbers of clerks at the Plantagenet court would not cease to condemn this corruption. Their writings were circumspect in relation to the political system whose establishment they paradoxically had worked closely on. Their education, usually in Paris or the northern French cathedral schools, opened the doors of the royal palace to them. In this regard the house of Anjou demonstrated a remarkably modern outlook. Its court, which included twice as many officers as that of the Capetians, had a considerable advantage. These English courtier-masters, excellent Latinists, educated in Roman law, served alongside 'literate knights' who patronized and themselves wrote vernacular works. Mastery of Anglo-Norman, like the acquisition of a degree of Classical culture, was a desirable quality in the high-status behaviour of the English aristocracy. Its èlitism appears in the prologue to the *Roman de Thèbes*, which put at a distance – in the caricature of an ass playing a harp – every listener who was not a clerk or a knight.

But the alliance between *chevalerie* and *clergie* was not the whole story. Priests very often took a high tone against lay courtiers, where perversely they had themselves chosen to serve the Crown for reward. Hellequin's Hunt, to repeat one of their favourite metaphors, and the damned souls which ran with it, attracted their anger. When they denounced the opportunism, the greed for gain and the chasing after honours of courtiers, they honestly thought that they were accomplishing the pastoral duty of reformation of manners that their clerical status involved. But they demonstrated an even more disturbing problem, as the Becket affair uncovered in grand scale. Quite a few courtiers who had taken up heavy governmental responsibilities at Henry II's court featured prominently amongst the archbishop's supporters. Most of them chose to repudiate the king and go into exile. This illustrates the sharp nature of a struggle which set *regnum* against *sacerdotium*. The significance of the conflict unleashed by the constitutions of Clarendon was deep. Moving beyond the simple clerical fondness for its legal privileges, it betrayed a stiff opposition to royal control over the Church. It attested to a Gregorian view of society where the protection of ecclesiastical privileges assisted the pastoral work of clergy and, as a result, the salvation of the whole Christian people. It would end in the murder in the cathedral, one of the events most significant for the reign of Henry II and his successors.

Does the 'Empire' of the Plantagenets occupy a unique place amongst the Western monarchies of the year 1200? The intuition of Walter Map, who talked of the 'modernity' of the world in which he lived, penetrated by an intellectual renaissance and also by the rise of the apparatus of the State, has its element of truth. In the aftermath of the civil war in 1152, England and Normandy became again the best-administered political units in Europe, a sort of workshop where every governmental, fiscal and legal practice was tempered to perfection. Feudalism, under royal control, provided the royal army with many soldiers or, in default, payment of scutage to relpace them with paid mercenaries. Archaic as it might appear, Angevin patronage of its clergy prefigured the national churches of Europe – and, indeed, Anglicanism – by more than a century. Such autocratic modernity contrasts with the Plantagenets' other lordships. In Brittany, Anjou and Aquitaine, the power to constrain and judge, when it was not fragmented, lay in the hands of a few great vice-comital or seigneurial dynasties which, like the Lusignan, Thouars and Léon, were at loggerheads with the king of England. In the light of the future development of the modern State, erasing collective privileges and seigneurial franchises, this situation smacks of the archaic.

But paradoxically these lands, once under French control, would one day experience absolutism and eventually Jacobinism. The 'model' administration of Normandy taught Philip Augustus, the duchy's conqueror, the path to take towards the unitary and centralized State. But in England, the precocity of the modernizing process provoked an unexpected reaction. The numerous and powerful court aristocracy seized control of all the king's actions. It was prepared to bring to a dead stop the rise of the king's discretionary power. Its rebellion ended in the Magna Carta of 1215 which laid the foundations of English parliamentarianism. Caught in its own trap, the Plantagenet Empire died of an overdose of authority.

Notes

Introduction

1 'Topographia' p. 20, trans. BOIVIN, *L'Irlande*, p. 266. On the context of the writing of this passage, cf. BARTLETT, *Gerald of Wales*, pp. 59–60.

2 *Roman de Rou*, ed. HOLDEN, vv. 35–6, vol. 1, p. 4. R. BEZZOLA, (*La Cour d'Angleterre*, pp. 175–7) maintains that the *Chronique ascendante*, the third branch of the *Roman de Rou*, from which this passage is abstracted, is anonymous, but for another argument, PARIS, *La Littérature*, p. 45. There are similar eulogies in JOHN OF SALISBURY, *Policraticus*, vi, 18, and WILLIAM OF NEWBURGH, *Historia rerum Anglicarum*, I, p. 106.

3 'Henricus . . . *dux Normannie et Aquitanie et comes Andegavie nominatur, et a mari usque ad mare, omni guerrarum perturbatione sedata, dominatur*', 'Annales sancti Sergii Andegavensis', p. 101. Cf. Ps. 72 (71): 8, and AVRIL, *Le Gouvernement*, p. 225. Cf. also a Tours chronicle: '*volens alas suae potestatis per universas extendere regiones*', 'Chronicon turonense magnum', p. 137.

4 '*Per longa terrarum spatia triumphali victoria suum dilataverit imperium*', *Dialogus*, pp. 27–8. On the meaning of this phrase, cf. CLANCHY, *England*, p. 118 and HOLT, 'The End of the Anglo-Norman Realm', p. 229.

5 FOLTZ, *L'Idée*, p. 54.

6 'This assemblage of feudal lordships should not be talked of as a "Plantagenet Empire" or "Anglo-Angevin State"', BAUTIER, 'Conclusions, "Empire Plantagenêt"' p. 139; 'There is no doubt that we increase our own problems of arriving at the truth by tacitly accepting concepts which sound wonderful but are anachronistic. One such is the Angevin Empire', FRYDE, *Why Magna Carta?*, p. 113.

7 *Loss of Normandy*, p. 46, cited by MARTINDALE, *Status, Authority and Regional Power*, XI, p. 24.

8 GILISSEN, 'La Notion d'Empire'.

9 The expression 'Greater Anjou' signifies Anjou with Maine, annexed to Anjou in 1109 (BOUSSARD, *Le Comté d'Anjou*, p. 7), and including also the Touraine and Vendômois, held intermittently or partially by the Angevins.

10 *The Governance of Medieval England*, p. 167.

11 *Henry II*, pp. 228–30 and 559–93.

12 'The End of the Anglo-Norman Realm', pp. 239–40, cited by CLANCHY, *England*, pp. 111–12, who adds that contemporaries saw Henry's lands 'as the lucky acquisition of a quarrelsome family and not as an institution'.

13 'Conclusions, "Empire Plantagenêt" ', pp. 140, 146–7.

14 GILLINGHAM, *The Angevin Empire*, p. 32. Cf. on the same theme, HOLLISTER and KEEFE, 'The Making of the Angevin Empire', p. 25: 'The Angevin idea of empire was a broadly conceived, flexible, and multifaceted network of family connections.'

15 JOLLIFFE, *Angevin Kingship*; MORTIMER, *Angevin England*; NEVEU, *La Normandie; passim.*

16 GARAUD, *Les Châtelains du Poitou*; DEBORD, *La Société laïque; passim.*

17 '*Castella nova, quae in diebus avi sui nequaquam exsisterant, complanari praecepit*', WILLIAM OF NEWBURGH, *Historia rerum Anglicarum*, p. 102; '*munitiunculas pessimas*', GERVASE OF CANTERBURY, *Chronica*, p. 160.

18 COULSON, 'Fortress Policy', pp. 15–23.

19 'For Plantagenet castles in Poitou, there is now a *thèse de doctorat*: BAUDRY, *Les fortifications des Plantagenêt en Poitou*. Also consult for the whole empire, the conference proceedings, *Les Fortifications dans la domaines Plantagenêt*.

20 COULSON, 'Freedom to Crenellate'; BROWN, 'Royal Castle-Building'; RENN, 'Plantagenêt Castle-Building'.

21 BOUSSARD, *Le Gouvernement d'Henri II*, p. 569. The meaning of the 'feudal system' relates to the homage that the king of England swore to the king of France for his French possessions, and that he accepted from his vassals.

22 The expression is found in his thesis published in 1938, BOUSSARD, *Le Comté d'Anjou*, p. 77.

23 R. KOSSELLECK, *L'Experience de l'histoire* (Paris, 1997), p. 121.

24 '*Henricus filius Gaufredi Plantagenest comitis Andegavensis*', GEOFFREY DE VIGEOIS, *Chronique, RHF*, vol. 12, p. 438; '*Miricem plantans*', in an act in the Great Cartulary of Fontevraud, now lost, cited by BIENVENU, 'Henri II Plantagenêt et Fontevraud', p. 25, n. 1.

25 Archives Nationales, D 10.007 and D 10.008, suggestion and references generously contributed by Michel Pastoureau.

26 LE PATOUREL, *Feudal Empires*, p. 289; GILLINGHAM, *The Angevin Empire*, p. 3.

27 'Gisfrei, son frere, que l'on clamout "Planta Genest", qui mult amout bois e forest', WACE, *Le Roman de Rou*, v, 10. 269–70, vol. 2, p. 266.

28 Alone amongst his fellow-British, John Le Patourel ('Feudal Empires', p. 294) suggested using 'Plantagenet Empire', reserving 'Angevin Empire' for the lands put together by the counts of Anjou in the eleventh and early twelfth century. His idea of 'empires' wasn't very broad since one of them barely included Anjou, Maine and the Saintonge. It led him to talk about the 'feudal empires' of the counts of Toulouse and Flanders (*ibid.*, p. 282), indeed, even of a 'Capetian empire' rather than a 'kingdom of France', (*Feudal Empires*, viii, p. 308)!

29 GILLINGHAM, *Richard I*, pp. 10–14.

30 *History of England*, London, 1849 (2nd edn, 1907), p. 4, cited by GILLINGHAM, *The Angevin Empire*, p. 2.

31 *The Constitutional History of England*, Oxford, 1883, vol. 1, p. 482, cited *ibid*. A full historiographical appreciation of Stubbs – unsympathetic to say the least – can be found in RICHARDSON and SAYLES, *The Governance of Medieval England*, pp. 1–21. These two authors were not themselves exempt from national prejudice, as when they referred to the first Norman kings of England: 'they were not pioneers of civilisation. They were rather, like their Norse forefathers and contemporaries, angels of death and destruction.' *Ibid.* p. 120.

32 'The English nation is of distinctly Teutonic or Germanic origin', *Constitutional History of England*, vol. 1, p. 584.

33 GENET, 'Histoire politique', p. 622.

34 By way of comparison it might be permissible to cite at length a quite different passage to show how a nationalistic and anachronistic approach can worsen subjectivity in historical understanding: 'England was then a conquered country. It had been colonized by Frenchmen and it was exploited by its Norman and Angevin rulers for their continental ambitions. The Angevin Empire was a French Empire', LE PATOUREL, *Feudal Empires*, viii, p. 296. In defence of Le Patourel – whose roots were in the Channel Islands, and whose origins led him to an approach to medieval English history unique in his day – note the deliberately provocative tenor of the writing.

35 *Histoire de la conquête de l'Angleterre par les Normands*, Paris, 1859, vol. 1, pp. 184–6.

36   *Louis VII, Philippe Auguste, Louis VIII* (1137–1226), Paris, 1903, vol. 3
(1st part), p. 68, appearing in the collection edited by E. LAVISSE, *Histoire
de la France.*

37   *L'Essor de l'Europe*, Paris, 1841, p. 172.

38   RENOUARD, 'Essai sur la rôle de l'empire Angevin', p. 303. Cf. also,
R. BOUTRUCHE, *Seigneurie et féodalité*, Paris, 1968–1970, p. 189: 'Under
Henry II and his successors . . . the State was raised on feudal foundations
and imbued with a "public" ethos.'

39   Cf. recently, BOURNAZEL, 'La royauté féodale', SASSIER, 'L'âge féodal.
Le retour de la royauté'.

40   It is at the core of the work of J-F. LEMARIGNIER, *Hommage en marche.*

41   'The main weakness of the Plantagenets and the main strength of the
Capetians lay in the feudal suzerainty of the kings of France', Holt, 'The End
of the Anglo-Norman Realm', p. 254.

42   JOHN OF SALISBURY, Letters, no. 279, vol. 2, p. 602. Cf. POWICKE,
The Loss of Normandy, p. 26.

43   Cf. two pioneering studies of the 1980s: B. GUENEE, *Politique et Histoire
au Moyen Age*, Paris, 1981, and LE GOFF, 'L'histoire politique est-elle
toujours l'épine dorsale de l'histoire?', republished in *L'Imaginaire médiéval*,
Paris, 1985, pp. 333–49.

44   *Chronicon*, p. 10.

45   CLANCHY, *From Memory to Written Record*, pp. 7, 29–31, 41–52, 69,
156, 105–15, 258–63, for what follows. It is a matter for astonishment that
this remarkable book has never been translated into French.

46   On the English legal 'leap forward' – in particular in the field of legal
theory – and the part played by extensive monastic writings in the process,
cf. BOUREAU, *La loi du Royaume.*

47   Cf. a clear description of the Exchequer process, its accounting techniques
and registration of debts in CLANCHY, *England and its Rulers*, pp. 77–82.

48   FAGNEN, 'Le vocabulaire du pouvoir', p. 80.

49   The best survey of the appearance of the Chancery rolls is the lecture by
N. Vincent, 'Pourquoi 1199? La bureaucratie et l'enregistrement de rôles
sous le règne de Jean sans Terre et ses contemporains', delivered at the
Ecole des Chartes in April 2002.

50   PRESTWICH, 'Military Intelligence', p. 18.

51   VINCENT, 'Conclusion', *Noblesse de l'espace Plantagenêt.*

52   CORNER, 'The *Gesta regis Henrici Secundi*'. Benedict of Peterborough never
wrote the *Gesta*, which was the work of Roger of Howden. Its first editor got

confused between the chronicler and the manuscript's owner, STENTON, 'Roger of Howden and *Benedict*', and GRANSDEN, *Historical Writing in England*, pp. 222–3.

53 Although likely, the identification of *Dicetum* with Diss, a village in Norfolk, is by no means certain, GRANSDEN, *Historical Writing in England*, p. 230.

54 GRANSDEN, *Historical Writing in England*, p. 210. On the rhetorical tricks of these historians, which give their writings a certain new style of authority, cf. DAMIAN-GRINT, *The New Historians*.

55 GILLINGHAM, *The Angevin Empire*, p. 117.

56 As far as 1112, Robert copied the universal chronicle of Sigebert of Gembloux, inserting some elements of Norman history. Eighteen manuscripts of Robert's chronicle survive including his own autograph version, GRANSDEN, *Historical Writing in England*, p. 262.

57 HUBERT and LA MONTE, introduction to the English translation of AMBROISE, *L'Estoire de la Guerre Sainte*, pp. 3–22, as opposed to DAMIAN-GRINT, *The New Historians*, pp. 76–9, which pictures Ambroise as a member of Richard the Lionheart's army and as an eyewitness to the crusade.

58 LODGE, 'Literature and History'. R. Bezzola (*La cour d'Angleterre*, p. 198) said that Jordan's language reveals a Poitevin origin, but his actual analysis makes it more Anglo-Norman apart from a few Occitanisms which were owed perhaps to Jordan's Poitevin stay with Gilbert de la Porée (DAMIAN-GRINT, *The New Historians*, p. 74).

59 Cf. the introduction of CONLON to his edition and translation of *The Song of Dermot and the Earl*. There exists only in a single manuscript of this poem, copied between 1226 and 1250. Its author said he had versified in French the Latin composition of Morris Regan, the interpreter of Diarmait Mac Murchada, king of Leinster, the protagonist of the story, who appealed to Norman knights so as to overcome his problems with neighbouring kings.

60 Referring to the edition of P. MEYER [JOHN LE TROUVÈRE], *L'Histoire de Guillaume le Maréchal*, awaiting the appearance of the edition being prepared by A.J. Holden, D. Crouch and S. Gregory.

61 'What is beyond doubt is that the Angevin and Norman court milieu harboured much of most brilliant poetry of the mid-12th century . . . England was the high point of "the Renaissance of the 12th century".' DRONKE, 'Peter of Blois and Poetry', p. 185.

62 R.W. Southern (*Scholastic Humanism*, pp. 178–218) attempts to prove the existence of two men called Peter of Blois, uncle and nephew, the one a more austere writer than the other, but the evidence for such a hypothesis seems tenuous.

63 For these authors, see the list of sources in the bibliography. Egbert Türk is preparing a French translation of the numerous letters of Peter of Blois.

64 Nearly 200 manuscripts of Peter of Blois's letters survive, for instance, of which 51 were copied in fifteenth-century Germany, from which we see that Peter had made several tries at a compilation, in 1189, 1196, 1198 and 1202, REVELL, introduction to PETER OF BLOIS, *The Later Letters*, p. xv, and SOUTHERN, *Medieval Humanism*, p. 105.

65 For Thomas Becket, cf. A. DUGGAN, *Thomas Becket*, as much as for her recent edition of his letters. Arnulf had compiled his own letter collection in his last years after he had been forced to abandon his see of Lisieux, and then Richard of Ilchester, his best friend, rearranged it, SCHRIBER, introduction to her translation, pp. 1–13.

66 Edited in an appendix to *Dialogus*, pp. 129–35.

67 'Modernitatem hanc', *De Nugis Curialium* i, 30, p. 122. Cf. CLANCHY, '*Moderni* in Medieval Education', p. 671.

68 SOUTHERN, *Medieval Humanism*, pp. 29–40, and *Scholastic Humanism*; VERGER, *La Renaissance du xiie siècle*.

69 The classic by RAMSAY, *The Angevin Empire*, is full and well-referenced. A more recent and innovative approach is to be found in GILLINGHAM, *The Angevin Empire*.

70 On precedents for the Aquitainian policy of the counts of Anjou in the tenth and eleventh centuries and their dominance of the Saintonge, cf. BACHARACH, 'The Idea of Angevin Empire', pp. 295–7, and 'King Henry II and Angevin Claims to the Saintonge'.

71 On the existence of this partition at succession, disputed by W.L. WARREN, *Henry II*, pp. 46–7 and 64, and by LE PATOUREL, *Feudal Empires*, IX, p. 6, cf. KEEFE, 'Geoffrey Plantagenet's Will'. For J. Gillingham (*The Angevin Empire*, p. 21), the embassy led at that time by John of Salisbury to Rome would have as its objective the securing from Adrian IV Henry II's dispensation from the oath to respect his father's last wishes.

72 For the events of 1149–1159 in England, cf. AMT, *The Accession of Henry II*, pp. 7–29.

73 CROUCH, 'Robert of Gloucester's Mother'.

74 On relations between the Plantagenets and Toulouse, cf. MACE, *Les comtes de Toulouse*, and BENJAMIN, 'A Forty Years War', and most recently, MARTINDALE, 'An Unfinished Business'.

75 To inaugurate this alliance, he betrothed his son Richard to one of the daughters of Raymond Berengar IV, who can perhaps be identified with Dulcia, the only named daughter of the count married in 1174 to Sancho I

of Portugal (1185–1212), TORIGNY, *Chronicle*, iv, p. 200; NEWBURGH, *Historia rerum Anglicarum*, ii, p. 10. Cf. GILLINGHAM, *Richard I*, p. 29; AURELL, *Les noces du comte*, p. 378.

76 BACHRACH, 'The Idea of Angevin Empire'; 'Henry II and the Angevin Tradition'.

77 FLANAGAN, *Irish Society*, pp. 278–84.

78 BALDWIN, *Philippe Auguste*, p. 42.

79 Two rather good recent biographies allow us to follow closely events in his reign, GILLINGHAM, *Richard I*, and FLORI, *Richard Coeur de Lion*.

80 His great grandfather, Fulk V of Anjou, was king of Jerusalem 1131–1143, through his marriage to Melisent, daughter of Baldwin II of Jerusalem, but neither Geoffrey Plantagenet – too caught up in the Anglo-Norman succession war – nor Henry II – despite his vows – had followed his example.

81 On the political role acquired by Eleanor because of her widowhood, cf. MARTINDALE, 'Eleanor of Aquitaine: the Last Years', and HIVERGNEAUX, 'Aliénor d'Aquitaine'. These two authors reach the same conclusions from different sources, one of them historiographical, the other diplomatic.

82 On the myth of the supposed loss of the king of France's archive at Fréteval, BAUTIER, 'La place du règne de Philippe Auguste', p. 17. In fact the lost documents were some ephemeral administrative records and lists of Capetian and Angevin vassals who had crossed into his camp.

83 POWER, 'L'aristocratie Plantagenêt'.

84 On the marriage of Louis VIII and Blanche of Castille, whose maternal uncle was King John, following on from the treaty, cf. J.E. RUIZ DOMENEC, 'Les souvenirs croisé de Blanche de Castille'.

85 VINCENT, 'Isabella of Angoulême', pp. 174–82.

86 ALVIRA and BURESI, 'Alphonse . . . roi de Castille'.

87 CAO CARMICHAEL DE BAGLY, 'Savary de Mauléon'.

88 On this pressure group, cf. VINCENT, *Peter des Roches*.

89 J. LE GOFF, *Saint Louis* (Paris, 1996), pp. 257–64.

Government and royal will

1 *Epistulae*, no. 66, col. 197C.

2 '*Una die, si opus fuerit, quatuor aut quinque diætas excurrit et sic inimicorum machinamenta præveniens*', ibid.

3 Epistulae, no. 14, col. 44.

4 HIGGONET, 'Spiritual Ideas in the Letters of Peter of Blois'.

5 Trans. HARF-LANCNER, 'L'enfer de la cour', p. 40. Cf. BEZZOLA, *La cour d'Angleterre*, p. 43 and DRONKE, 'Peter of Blois and Poetry', p. 194.

6 SCHMITT, *Les revenants*, pp. 134, 188.

7 *De Nugis Curialium*, IV, 13, p. 370; Trans. HARF-LANCNER, 'L'enfer de la cour', p. 39, and I, 9.

8 MORTIMER, *Angevin England*, pp. 18–19.

9 LE PATOUREL, *The Norman Empire*, pp. 128–9.

10 JOLLIFFE, *Angevin Kingship*, pp. 141, 229.

11 OTTO OF FREISING, *Gesta Frederici*, III, 7, p. 406.

12 'Tentorium sericum', RICHARD OF DEVIZES, *Chronicon*, p. 17.

13 WARREN, *Henry II*, p. 302.

14 HOLT, 'The End of the Anglo-Norman Realm', pp. 229–30. In Normandy, most of his acts were transacted at Rouen, GAUTHIEZ, 'Paris, un Rouen capétien?', p. 123.

15 Letter of Henry II to York minster's chapter in August 1158, 'nec remaneat pro passagio meo quin juste cogant firmarios suos ut sint eis ad pectum de querelas quas adversus eos habuerint', cited by JOLLIFFE, *Angevin Kingship*, p. 56, n. 2.

16 *Epistulae*, no. 66, col. 198A.

17 HOLLISTER and BALDWIN, 'The Rise of Administrative Kingship', p. 868.

18 A general study of English institutions and financial administration can be found in MORTIMER, *Angevin England*, pp. 42–70.

19 RICHARDSON and SAYLES, *The Governance of Medieval England*, pp. 186–8.

20 J.A. GREEN, 'The Last Century of Danegeld', *EHR*, 96, 1981, pp. 241–58.

21 On the English chief justiciar and the evolution of England's judicial system, cf. HEISER, 'The Households of the Justiciars of Richard I'.

22 JOLLIFFE, *Angevin Kingship*, pp. 227–33.

23 RICHARD FITZ NIGEL, *Dialogus de Scaccario*, p. 2. On the theme of the king's support for the pauper against the oppression of the potentes, cf. P.R. HYAMS, *Kings, Lords and Peasants in Medieval England*, Oxford, 1980, p. 261, and HUDSON, *Land, Law and Lordship*, p. 269.

The court, its officers and their skills

1 *De Nugis Curialium*, I, 12, p. 36; V, 7, p. 500.

2 S.F.C. MILSOM, *The Legal Framework of English Feudalism*, Cambridge, 1973; F.M. STENTON, *The First Century of English Feudalism, 1066–1166*, Oxford, 1961 (2nd edn); BRAND, *The Making of the Common Law*.

3 RAMSAY, *The Angevin Empire*, pp. 76–81.

4 J. BEAUROY, 'Centralisation et histoire sociale'; BOORMAN, 'The Sheriffs of Henry II', who shows that there had already been similar inquisitions in 1159–60 and 1163–64.

5 CARPENTER, 'The Decline of the Curial Sheriff', MORRIS, *The Medieval Sheriff*.

6 AMT, 'The Reputation of the Sheriff'.

7 Cf. lately, *Les fortifications dans les domaines Plantagenêt*, not forgetting the classic H.M. COLVIN, *The History of the King's Works*, I, London, 1963.

8 MOSS, 'Normandy and England in 1180'; *idem*, 'The Defence of Normandy, 1193–1198'; PITTE, 'Château-Gaillard dans la défense de la Normandie orientale'.

9 BAUDRY, *Les fortifications des Plantagenêt en Poitou*.

10 ROCHETEAU, 'Le château de Chinon'.

11 ADAM OF EYNSHAM, *Magna Vita sancti Hugonis*, V, 5.

12 J. RICHARD, 'Châteaux, châtelains et vassaux en Bourgogne aux xie et xiie siècles', *CCM*, 3, 1960, pp. 433–47; D. BARTHELEMY, *Les Deux Ages de la seigneurie banale. Coucy aux xie–xiiie siècles*, Paris, 1984; *La maison forte au Moyen Age*, ed. M. BUR, Paris, 1986.

13 '*Nisi ex judicio curie mee*', *Chronicle of Battle Abbey*, pp. 310–11.

14 E. SEARLE, 'Battle Abbey and Exemption: the Forged Charters', *EHR*, 83, 1968, pp. 449–80.

15 Detail drawn from the insights in BOUREAU, *La loi du royaume*, pp. 112–18.

16 'Fideles et familiares regis specialiter assistentes secretis, is quorum manu consilia regis et regni negotia diriguntur', *Materials for the History of Thomas Becket*, vol. 5, p. 507.

17 'Majores quique de regno qui familiarius regiis secretis assistunt ut quod fuerit sub tantorum presentia constitutum vel terminatum inviolabili jure subsistat', *Dialogus de Scaccario*, p. 15. The three previous examples are drawn from WARREN, *Henry II*, pp. 304–5.

18 JOLLIFFE, *Angevin Kingship*, pp. 173–87.

19 In his introduction to *Recueil des actes d'Henri II*, vol. 1, pp. 351–505. The new edition of Henry II's acts about to be published under the supervision of Nicholas Vincent contains a complete volume of biographical notices of courtiers.

20 O. GUILLOT, *Le comte d'Anjou et son entourage au xiᵉ siècle*, Paris, 1972; BOURNAZEL, *Le Gouvernement capétien*; MACE, *Les comtes de Toulouse*; M. AURELL, 'Le personnel politique catalan et aroganais d'Alphonse Iᵉʳ en Provence (1166–1196)', *Annales du Midi*, 93, 1981, pp. 121–39, and *idem*, 'Els fonaments socials de la dominatió catalana a Provença sota Alfons el Cast (1166–1196)', *Acta Historica Archæologica Mediævalia*, 5–6, 1984–1985, pp. 83–110.

21 'The Court and Household of King Henry II', unpublished PhD thesis, which it has not been possible to consult. His basic conclusions are nonetheless repeated and cited in TÜRK, *Nugæ curialium*.

22 *Feudal Assessments and the Political Community*; 'Counting those who count'.

23 *Men Raised from the Dust.*

24 *Peter des Roches*; 'King Henry II and the Poitevins'; 'Warin and Henry fitz Gerald'.

25 LEGGE, 'William Marshal and Arthur of Brittany'; STRICKLAND, *War and Chivalry*, p. 257; RICHARDSON and SAYLES, *Governance of Medieval England*, p. 334; CAZEL, 'Religious Motivation', p. 109.

26 GEOFFREY GAIMAR, *L'Estoire des Engleis*, vv. 61–816, pp. 2–25, and vv. 5,461–5,465, p. 173; WACE, *Roman de Brut*, vv. 11,173–11,174, pp. 583–4. Cf. GILLINGHAM, *The English in the Twelfth Century*, pp. 233–58; R. ALLEN, 'Eorles and Beornes: Contextualising Lawman's Brut', *Arthuriana*, 8 (3), 1998, pp. 5–6 and 14; ZATTA, 'Translating the Historia', p. 154, and HOLT, *Colonial England*, p. 313.

27 *Chronicon*, pp. 2–3, following a citation of the *Thebaid* of Statius (vv. 45–96).

28 *Dialogus inter regem Henricum II et abbatem Bonnevallis*, p. 97. Cf. also *Epistulae*, no. 2, col. 3; no. 33, col. 109; no. 47, col. 457, and no. 167, col. 461, cited by BEZZOLA, *La Cour d'Angleterre*, p. 134, where Peter of Blois analyses the revolts of rebellions of Henry II's children, which he primarily attributes to their bad advisers.

29 Among the arguments brought forward by Southern: the attestation of Abbot Christian to an act of Theobald, count of Blois, in 1188; Gerald of Barry's assertion that Henry II talked more to his clerical than his lay

courtiers; the king's decision to go on crusade; and his anger at his son Richard, who swore homage to Philip Augustus, a most disloyal act in the circumstances, 'Peter of Blois and the Third Crusade', pp. 208–11.

30 It is hard to imagine Peter of Blois as a neutral reporter of the dialogue between the two men. The fictional abbot is perhaps reminiscent of the Cistercian archbishop of Tarentaise, St Peter, whose cult began on his death in 1174 and who was canonized in 1191. A monk of Bonnevaux (Vienne) in his youth, Peter intervened directly in the reconciliation between Henry II and Louis VII on Ash Wednesday 1170. His *Vita* was contributed by Geoffrey of Auxerre, *Acta Sanctorum*, 8 May (BHL 6773), at pp. 330–31 for the truce of 1170. There were other abbeys of that name in the Plantagenet lands which could have inspired the monastery of the king's improbable confidant. Bonnevaux was a Cistercian abbey founded by Hugh de Lusignan in 1119 on his estates. There were two Limousin priories of Grandmont, an eremetical order much favoured by Henry II, Bonneval-de-Montusclat and Bonneval-de-Serre. Otherwise, Bonneval-lès-Thouars was a Benedictine nunnery in the diocese of Poitiers, L-H. COTTINEAU, *Dictionnaire topo-bibliographique des abbayes et prieurés*, Mâcon, 1939, vol 1, pp. 428–31. This long list strengthens the allegorical aspect of the fictional ecclesiastic: the abbot created by Peter of Blois became all the more believable as his monastery's name was such a common one.

31 'Annales sancti Albani Andegavensis', p. 16.

32 *De Nugis curialium*, V, 6, p. 474.

33 On the – hardly friendly – relations between these two, cf. BATE, 'Walter Map and Giraldus Cambrensis'.

34 *De Principis Instructione*, III, 27, p. 303.

35 HOWDEN, *Chronica*, vol. 2, p. 366; *idem, Gesta*, vol. 2, p. 71. Cf. BROUGHTON, *The Legends of King Richard I*, pp. 88–9, and H. PLATELLE, 'La voix du sang: le cadavre qui saigne en présence du meurtrier', *Actes de 99ᵉ congrès national des sociétés savantes*, Paris, 1977, vol. 1, pp. 161–79; BOUREAU, *La Loi du Royaume*, p. 26.

36 On the origin myths of aristocratic families, cf. E. BOURNAZEL, 'Mémoire et parenté', *La France de l'an Mil*, ed. R. DELORD, Paris, 1990, pp. 114–24.

37 J. LE GOFF and E. LE ROY LADURIE, 'Mélusine maternelle et défricheuse', *Annales ESC*, 26, 1971, pp. 587–621.

38 *De Principis Instructione*, III, 27, p. 301. The refusal by Melusine to witness the mass was compared – a little rashly – with King John's refusal to take communion at his coronation, RICHARDSON and SAYLES, *The Governance of Medieval England*, p. 331.

39 'De matre phantastica descendisse', *Dialogus miraculorum*, III, 12.

40 *De Principis Instructione*, III, 27 and II, 28.

41 'Perhaps the most popular of all medieval histories', CLANCHY, *England and its Rulers*, p. 27. Preserved are 215 medieval manuscripts of the work, of which 81 were written in the twelfth and early thirteenth century, and it was translated into numerous vernacular languages, CHAUOU, *L'Idéologie Plantagenêt*, p. 234.

42 RALPH OF DISS, *Ymagines Historiarum*, vol. 2, p. 67, sees Eleanor of Aquitaine in this eagle, for her wings covered England and France, as she had broken the alliance by her divorce from Louis VII, and as her third son Richard always wanted to exalt his mother's reputation; RICHARD THE POITEVIN, 'Chronicon', p. 419; ROGER OF HOWDEN, *Gesta Henrici*, p. 42, and for a full account of the events, *idem*, *Chronica*, vol. 2, pp. 274–81. The application of Merlin's prophecies to the English royal house goes back to the years 1138–1145, when Suger applied them to Henry I, *Vie de Louis VI le Gros*, ed. H. WAQUET, Paris, 1964, pp. 98–103.

43 *De Principis Instructione*, III, 26, pp. 295–6. Cf. KENAAN-KEDAR, 'Aliénor d'Aquitaine conduite en captivité', p. 324.

44 Gerald of Barry does not explicitly make a connection between the mural and Merlin, but he goes straight on to a commentary on Micah 7: 5–6. As much as in the Merlin texts as in Gerald's description of the mural, what is involved is an eagle, its young and attacks on the neck by which it is fastened.

45 *De Nugis Curialium*, IV, 1, p. 282.

46 *De Principis Instructione*, III, 27, p. 302, trans. BEZZOLA, *La Cour d'Angleterre*, p. 85.

47 *Dialogus inter regem Henricum II et abbatem Bonnevallis*, pp. 99–100. '*Natura sum filius ire*' refers to Eph. 2: 3 ('*eramus natura filii ire*') where St Paul makes a reference to the desires of the flesh in which Christians lived before their conversion.

48 *Medieval Germany and its Neighbours*, pp. 262–3.

49 For a number of sallies on the interaction between folklore and scholastic theology, see SCHMITT, *Les Revenants*.

50 This rich source has been recently analysed in, LECUPPRE, 'L'empereur, l'imposteur et la rumeur'.

51 *De Principis Instructione*, III, 27.

52 *Ymagines Historiarum*, p. 366.

53 G.T. BEECH, 'Contemporary Views of William the Troubadour, IXth Duke of Aquitaine, 1086–1126', *Medieval Lives and the Historian*, ed. N. BULST and J-PH. GENET, Kalamazoo (MI), 1986, pp. 73–88.

54 *De Principis Instructione*, III, 27, pp. 298–9.

55 ADAM OF EYNSHAM, *Magna Vita sancti Hugonis*, pp. 184–5.

56 Add to the list of texts cited by LABANDE, 'Pour une image véridique d'Aliénor d'Aquitaine': GERALD OF BARRY, *Expugnatio Hibernica*, I, 46; PETER OF BLOIS, *Epistulae*, no. 154, col. 448D, and RALPH NIGER, *Chronica*, p. 175.

57 TORIGNY, *Chronicle*, p. 256, and PAPPANO, 'Marie de France'.

58 AURELL, *Les Noces du Comte*, pp. 110–12.

59 '*Illicita licentia*', WILLIAM OF NEWBURGH, *Historia rerum Anglicarum*, III, 26, p. 281, '*Artificioso juramento*', GERVASE OF CANTERBURY, *Chronica*, p. 149, BALDWIN, *Masters, Princes and Merchants*, p. 335.

60 In fact this marriage within the fifth degree was comparable to her first marriage with Louis VII, LABANDE, 'Pour une image véridique d'Aliénor d'Aquitaine', pp. 196, 212.

61 WALTER MAP, *De Nugis Curialium*, V, 6, p. 476. The book's title, which translates as 'Courtier's Trifles' says it all; GERALD OF BARRY, *De Principis Instructione*, III, 27, p. 300. Among Walter and Gerald's other malicious gossip can be found the bigamy of Empress Matilda following a pretended burial of her first husband, who had become a secret hermit. For these authors' distaste for Eleanor, cf. OWEN, Eleanor of Aquitaine, p. 30 and *passim* for the development of the legend of debauchery in her circle. For another opinion, G. DUBY, *Dames du xiie siècle: Héloïse, Aliénor, Yseult et quelques autres*, Paris, 1995, pp. 26–7, 34–7.

62 GERALD OF BARRY, *De Principis Instructione*, II, 3, p. 159.

63 F. LEFEVRE, *Les mariages des duc de Normandie de 911 à 1066*, master's thesis, Rouen, 1991, and M. AURELL, 'Stratégies matrimoniales de l'aristocratie (ixe–xiiie siècle)', *Actes du colloque : Sexualité et mariage au Moyen Age (Conques, 15–18 octobre 1998)*, ed. M. ROUCHE, Paris, 2000, pp. 185–202.

64 NEWBURGH, *Historia rerum Anglicarum*, III, 26, vol. 1, p. 281.

65 TURNER, 'The Children of Anglo-Norman Royalty', p. 18, and CROUCH, 'Robert of Gloucester's Mother'. Cf. likewise, C. GIVEN-WILSON and A. CURTEIS, *The Royal Bastards of Medieval England*, London, 1984, a work which gives no references, unfortunately.

66 *Expugnatio Hibernica*, I, 46, *De Principis Instructione*, II, 3, p. 159.

67 *De Principis Instructione*, III, 27, pp. 298–9.

68 *Magna Vita sancti Hugonis*, vol. 2, pp. 298–9, trans. (into French) FOREVILLE, 'L'Image de Philippe Auguste', p. 125, and see comments by BATES, 'The Rise of Normandy', p. 22.

69 *Magna Vita sancti Hugonis*, III, 10.

70 'Incesto conjugio uxorem duxit, anno MXXXII, exinde bellum gessit', 'Annales Sancti Albini Andegavensis', p. 46, cited by BACHARACH, 'King Henry II and Angevin Claims to the Saintonge', p. 119.

71 P. CORBET, *Autour de Burchard de Worms. L'Eglise allemande et les interdits de parenté (ixe–xiie siècle)*, Frankfurt-am-Main, 2001, and AURELL, *Les Noces du Comte*, p. 299. Should the serious accusation of the abuse of his ward Alice of France, the young fiancée of his son Richard the Lionheart, against Henry II be treated in the same way? The sources dealing with this affair are not really comparable, either in genre or in moralizing tone, to those which we are about to analyse concerning the marriage of Henry II and Eleanor of Aquitaine. The evidence concerning Alice of France has recently been analysed by GILLINGHAM, *Richard I*, pp. 5, 82 and 142.

72 On the basis of the psychological approach applied to Eleanor, see AURELL, 'Aliénor d'Aquitaine et ses historiens'. The following can be added to the examples cited in the article, stemming from one of the more sober historians on the question, yet still attributing a romantic disposition to Eleanor, this time her feelings come out with William Marshal: 'Although Marshal retrieved his fortunes by an unlikely stroke of luck – Queen Eleanor of England was rather taken by his youthful charm . . .', CROUCH, *The Image of Aristocracy*, p. 131. In an interview given to a wide-circulation magazine, J. LE GOFF, goes even further: 'Aliénor d'Aquitaine, qui était une vraie garce uniquement préoccupée par le pouvoir et le sexe, en a d'ailleurs profité [de la croisade] pour tromper son mari Louis VII', *L'Express*, 11 July 2002, p. 78.

73 TURNER, 'Eleanor of Aquitaine and her Children'.

74 M. CHENEY, 'Master Geoffrey de Lucy', *EHR*, 82, 1967, pp. 750–63.

75 TURNER, 'Eleanor of Aquitaine and her Children'.

76 Cf., in the proceedings of a recent conference at Norwich – published under the title of *King John. New Interpretations* – on the reasons for John's unpopularity, GILLINGHAM, 'Historians without Hindsight', and BRADBURY, 'Philip Augustus and King John', and on the comparison of their finances, BARRATT, 'The Revenues of John and Philip Augustus', responding to, TURNER, 'Good or Bad Kingship?' The comparison between Paris and Rouen's respective demographies has something to say

about the two kings' resources: it was only in 1204 that the two cities matched in population after years of the dominance of Rouen; rather more populous still in the 1180s, GAUTHIEZ, 'Paris, un Rouen capétien?' p. 131.

77 JOHN OF MARMOUTIER, 'Historia Gaufredi', p. 224.

78 BOUSSARD, *Le Gouvernement d'Henri II*, pp. 14, 583–9.

79 John Gillingham's works have made Richard the Lionheart into a character interested only in war and indifferent to government.

80 Inquests of sheriffs in England in 1170 and of *vicomtes* in Normandy in 1171; an assize about securities for debts in 1177 relative to Normandy, Anjou, Aquitaine and Brittany; in 1181, an assize of arms for England and Normandy; Geoffrey of Brittany's assize on primogeniture, triggered by Henry II's pronouncement for Normandy, HOLT, 'The End of the Anglo-Norman Realm', pp. 227–8.

81 Ed. HOLDEN, V, 77–80, vol. 1, p. 5. On the place of this passage (composed in 1174) in the *Ascending Chronicle* which Wace dates from 1160, cf. PARIS, *La Littérature normande*, p. 45.

82 'Variorum epistolae ad Alexandrum III', *PL*, vol. 200, no. 32, cols 1,389–1,390.

83 JOHN LE TROUVÈRE, *L'Histoire de Guillaume le Maréchal*, vv. 10,363–10,419. In 1173, Henry II 'pardoned his younger sons on the grounds of their youth', NEWBURGH, *Historia rerum Anglicarum*, II, 38. John le Trouvère says on more than one occasion that their advisers were to blame, *ibid.* vv. 2,327–2,382.

84 G. Duby, 'Les jeunes dans la société aristocratique dans la France du Nord-Ouest au xiie siècle', *Annales ESC*, 19, 1964, pp. 835–46, repeated in *Hommes et structures de Moyen Age*, pp. 213–26.

85 On the subject of the triggering of the revolt of 1173 by the refusal of Richard to cede Aquitaine to his brother, cf. the analysis of MARTINDALE, *Status, Authority and Regional Power*, XI, p. 22, 'There was therefore an undeniable sense of regional attachment and shared experience which crossed the generation between mother and son.'

86 BACHARACH, 'King Henry II and Angevin Claims to the Saintonge', p. 112.

87 C. ESTEPA, *El Reinado de Alfonso VI*, Madrid, 1985; J. GONZALEZ, *El Reino de Castilla en la época de Alfonso VIII*, Madrid, 1960; AURELL, *Les Noces de Comte*, pp. 182, 226–33, 625.

88 MACE, *Les Comtes de Toulouse*, pp. 74–86.

89 LEWIS, *Le Sang royal*, pp. 209–20.

90 HOLT, 'The End of the Anglo-Norman Realm', pp. 240–41; WARREN, *Henry II*, pp. 108–9, 206, 229–30; LE PATOUREL, *The Norman Empire*, pp. 184–7; GILLINGHAM, *The Angevin Empire*, pp. 119–20, 220. The differing nuances and issues between the authors are described in Flanagan, *Irish Society*, pp. 276–84.

91 GERALD OF BARRY, *Descriptio Kambriae*, I, 7; ROBERT DE TORIGNY, *The Story of Meriadoc*, pp. 3–7.

92 JOLLIFFE, *Angevin Kingship*, pp. 143–6.

93 *Chronica*, p. 291, cited by TÜRK, *Nugae Curialium*, p. 7.

94 The self-justification before the battle of Lincoln (1141) of the bastard Robert of Gloucester, as reported by Henry of Huntingdon, comes to mind: 'Myself the son of the noblest of kings and grandson of the greatest of them, cannot be surpassed in dignity', cited by CROUCH, *The Image of Aristocracy*, pp. 4–5.

95 GERALD OF BARRY, *De Vita Galfredi*, I, 3. On this person, cf. JOLLIFFE, *Angevin Kingship*, pp. 110–18; D.L. DOUIE, *Archbishop Geoffrey Plantagenet and the Chapter of York*, York, 1960.

96 TURNER, *Men Raised from the Dust*, p. 17.

97 TURNER, 'Eleanor of Aquitaine and her Children', p. 326. Cf. HUNT and GIBSON, *The Schools and the Cloister*.

98 BOUSSARD, *Le Gouvernement d'Henri II*, pp. 339–48.

99 KEEFE, 'Place–Date Distribution of Royal Charters', p. 184.

100 MUSSET, 'Quelques problèmes'.

101 BILLORE, 'La noblesse normande'.

102 VINCENT, 'King Henry II and the Poitevins'.

103 VINCENT, *Peter des Roches*.

104 *De Nugis Curialium*, I, 1–2, trans. BATE, *Contes*, pp. 79–80.

105 *Policraticus*, VII, 15, ed. WEBB, vol. 2, pp. 155–6, and LIEBSCHÜTZ, *Medieval Humanism*, p. 29.

106 TÜRK, *Nugae Curialium*, pp. 167, 191–200.

107 CROUCH, *The Beaumont Twins*.

108 KEEFE, *Feudal Assessments and the Political Community*, pp. 112–15.

109 LALLY, 'Court and Household of Henry II', pp. 367–9, 348–50, cited from TÜRK, *Nugae Curialium*, pp. 29–31, 38–9.

110 KEEFE, *Feudal Assessments and the Political Community*, pp. 93–6, 110–12, and *idem*, 'Counting those who Count'. The same point of view is taken in, VINCENT, 'Warin and Henry fitz Gerald'.

111 TURNER, *Men Raised from the Dust*, a title borrowed from, ORDERIC VITALIS, *The Ecclesiastical History*, XI, 2.

112 TURNER, *Men Raised from the Dust*, p. 13, and, *idem, The English Judiciary*, p. 292.

113 Cf. the example of Alan de Neville, chief justice of the forests under Henry II, whom his biographer says belonged to the 'knightly class but without distinction', YOUNG, *The Making of the Neville Family in England*, p. 7.

114 AMT, 'Richard de Lucy'.

115 MORTIMER, 'The Family of Ranulf de Glanville'.

116 *Tractatus de Legibus et consuetudinibus regni Angliae.*

117 *De Nugis Curialium*, I, 10, *De Principis Instructione*, III, 2.

118 CLANCHY, '*Moderni* in Medieval Education and Government in England'.

119 BARLOW, *Thomas Becket*, and CLANCHY, '*Moderni* in Medieval Education and Government in England', p. 681, on the role of education in his rise.

120 *Policraticus*, II, 28, vol. 2, p. 164, and CLANCHY, *From Memory to Written Record*, p. 194.

121 OGGINS, 'Richard of Ilchester's Inheritance'.

122 DUGGAN, 'Richard of Ilchester, Royal Servant and Bishop'.

123 Marie dedicated her fables to a certain 'Count William' which some identify with him. Y. de Pontfarcy prefers to see in him William Marshal in his edition of MARIE DE FRANCE, *L'Espurgatoire seint Patriz*, Louvain, 1995: for this author, Marie belonged to the Beaumont-Meulan family, the highest of the Anglo-Norman aristocracy.

124 BALDWIN, '*Studium et Regnum*'; CLANCHY, '*Moderni* in Medieval Education and Government in England'; TURNER, 'The *Miles Literatus*'.

125 CLANCHY, *From Memory to Written Record*, pp. 187–92.

126 CLANCHY, *England and its Rulers*, p. 147.

127 SOUTHERN, *Scholastic Humanism*, pp. 155–66.

128 TÜRK, *Nugae Curialium*, pp. 96, 126–7.

129 KUTTNER and RATHBONE, 'Anglo-Norman Canonists', pp. 289–90.

130 E.J. KEALEY, *Roger of Salisbury*, Berkeley CA, 1972, pp. 48–50; RICHARDSON and SAYLES, *The Governance of Medieval England*, pp. 158, 271.

131 RICHARD FITZ NIGEL, *Dialogus de Scaccario*, pp. 35–6.

132 For Thomas Brun (Brown) and a parallel development, with neither direct contact nor imitation, of Sicilian and English administration, cf. H. TAKAYAMA, *The Administration of the Norman Kingdom of Sicily*, Leiden, 1993, pp. 13–14, 163–9.

133 BALDWIN, '*Studium et Regnum*', p. 204.

134 BOURNAZEL, *Le Gouvernement capétien*, pp. 74, 91; BALDWIN, 'L'entourage de Philippe Auguste', p. 73.

135 HOLLISTER and BALDWIN, 'The Rise of Administrative Kingship', pp. 904–5.

136 R.H.C. DAVIS, 'What Happened in Stephen's Reign', History, 49, 1964, pp. 1–12; AMT, *The Accession of Henry II*; HUDSON, *Land, Law and Lordship*.

137 KEEFE, 'Place–Date Distribution of Royal Charters'.

138 J.H. ROUND, 'The Honour of Ongar', *Transactions of the Essex Archaeological Society*, n.s. 7, 1900, pp. 142–52; MORTIMER, 'The Family of Ranulf de Glanville'; VINCENT, 'Warin and Henry fitz Gerald'.

139 WARREN, *Henry II*, p. 367; LALLY, 'Court and Household of Henry II', pp. 138–41, cited by TÜRK, *Nugae Curialium*, pp. 43–4; TURNER, *Men Raised from the Dust*, p. 6.

140 LALLY, 'Secular Patronage at the Court of Henry II', pp. 175–6; WARREN, *Henry II*, pp. 274–5.

141 LALLY, 'Secular Patronage at the Court of Henry II', pp. 163–7' GREEN, *Aristocracy of Anglo-Norman England*, p. 266.

142 GREEN, 'Aristocratic Women in the early Twelfth Century', pp. 62–4, 73.

143 CROUCH, *William Marshal*.

144 GILLINGHAM, *Richard I*, p. 293.

145 *Rotuli de Dominabus*. Cf. E. VAN HOUTS, 'Gender and Authority of Oral Witnesses in Europe (800–1300)', *Transactions of the Royal Historical Society*, 6th ser. 9, 1999, pp. 208–9.

146 LALLY, 'Court and Household of Henry II', pp. 179–90, cited by TÜRK, *Nugae Curialium*, p. 45.

147 Edited in an appendix to RICHARD FITZ NIGEL, *Dialogus de Scaccario*, pp. 129–35. Table and comparative view in R. COSTA GOMES, *A Corte dos reis de Portugal no final de Idade Média*, Lisbon, 1995, pp. 14–15.

148 WALTER MAP, *De Nugis Curialium*, V, 5, pp. 438, 450. For a later period, cf. F. LACHAUD, 'Textiles, Furs and Liveries: A Study of the Great Wardrobe of Edward II (1272–1307)', unpubd Oxford PhD thesis, 1992.

149 *Speculum Stultorum*, vv. 2,592–2,650. The similarity of names between Nigel and William and the dedication of the works argue indeed for a family relationship, but A. Boutémy, in the edition of the *Tractatus*, pp. 85–6, remarks that William's mother was English and that he had never benefitted directly from the bishop's patronage in his career.

150 *Architrenius*, V, 4, p. 120.

151 *Chronicon*, pp. 5, 85.

152 MORTIMER, 'The Family of Ranulf de Glanville', p. 15.

153 *L'Histoire de Guillaume le Maréchal*, vv. 9,173–9,211.

154 FLORI, *Richard Coeur de Lion*, pp. 398–406.

155 *Chronica*, vol. 3, p. 66.

156 *Estoire de Guerre Sainte*, vv. 1,053–1,108, trans. BROSSARD-DANDRE and BESSON, *Richard de Coeur de Lion*, p. 104.

157 KEEFE, 'Counting those who Count', pp. 141–5, where this complex succession is followed with the help of the Pipe Rolls and the Walden Abbey chronicle.

158 MORTIMER, *Angevin Kingship*, p. 73.

159 MASON, 'The Mauduits'.

160 *Policraticus*, V, 6.

161 In his usual ill-tempered style, Gerald of Barry, attacked him for having made the Exchequer his real classroom, like so many English bishops, CLANCHY, *From Memory to Written Record*, p. 53.

162 FOREVILLE, *L'Eglise et la royauté en Angleterre*; PONTAL, 'Les évêques dans le monde Plantagenêt'.

163 LALLY, Court and Household of Henry II', pp. 252–6, 335–6, cited by TÜRK, *Nugae Curialium*, pp. 47–9.

164 SCHRIBER, *The Dilemma of Arnulf of Lisieux*. Arnulf's involvement in the 1173 revolt can be suggested from one of his letters, ed. BARLOW, no. 76, trans. SCHRIBER, no. 2.16, pp. 143–4.

165 FOREVILLE, *L'Eglise et la royauté en Angleterre*, pp. 485–7.

166 GILLINGHAM, *Richard I*, p. 259.

167 ARNULF OF LISIEUX, *The Letters*, no. 74, trans. SCHRIBER, no. 3.08, pp. 197–8.

168 BOUSSARD, *Le Gouvernement d'Henri II*, pp. 311–29.

169 Many of the texts which follow are published in his work, *Nugae Curialium*, as much as in BEZZOLA, *La Cour d'Angleterre*, but so as not to overdo the critical apparatus, the original source is referred to here.

170 *De Nugis Curialium*, I, 9–10, IV, 13.

171 *De Principis Instructione*, p. 160, *Topographia Hibernica*, no. 48.
Cf. BARTLETT, *Gerald of Wales*, p. 65.

172 *Chronica*, vol. 2, p. 167. The historian, Benoît de Sainte-Maure, who
created an Anglo-Norman history for the king, included in his story the
language of noble discontent, insofar as he regretted the good old days of
the first Norman dukes who, after having ejected the low-born from their
household, appointed as constable, seneschal, butler, marshal, despenser,
usher and chamberlain, only those who were *'estrait de buen lignage'*,
La Chronique des ducs de Normandie, v. 28,835; FLORI, *L'Essor de la
Chevalerie*, p. 314.

173 *Memoriale*, ed. W. Stubbs (Rolls Series, 58), London, 1873, vol. 2, p. 253,
cited by TURNER, 'Toward a Definition of the *Curialis*', p. 13.

174 *Tractatus contra curiales*. According to a suggestion of David Crouch,
it could be that the work was commissioned by his uncle, William de
Longchamps, so as to attack his numerous enemies at court.

175 *De Nugis Curialium*, I, 10, trans. BATE, *Contes*, p. 85.

176 HUNT and GIBSON, *The Schools and the Cloister*, p. 9; TURNER,
Men raised from the Dust, p. 12.

177 RICHE, 'Jean de Salisbury', pp. 51–2.

178 HUNT, 'The Preface of the "Speculum Ecclesiae" ', pp. 194, 198.

179 *De Principis Instructione*, p. lvii; *Expugnatio Hibernica*, preface II.
Cf. BOIVIN, 'Les paradoxes des *clerici regis*'.

180 *Epistulae*, no. 6.

181 *Carmina*, 1.5, pp. 265–74, and ed. and trans. P. DRONKE, 'Peter of Blois',
pp. 206–9, who nonetheless maintains the courtier's cleverness, for which
Peter would have felt a certain sympathy: 'He has developed a dandy's
habits, and a keen sense of irony to protect his pleasures', *ibid.*, p. 210.
Dronke argues the lively character of these Latin verse debates, which are
not just rhetorical disputes between the Virtues, but betray the tensions and
uncertainties arising from the mismatch between spirituality and secular
feeling, *ibid.*, pp. 214–15.

182 Epistulae, no. 77.

183 TURNER, *Judges, Administrators and the Common Law*, pp. 105–17, and
The English Judiciary, pp. 2–9.

184 *Epistulae*, nos. 14, 95.

185 RICHARD OF DEVIZES, *Chronicon*, pp. 10–12, 49–52, 95–6.

186 *The Letters of Arnulf of Lisieux*, no. 10, trans. SCHRIBER, no. 3.02,
pp. 189–91.

187 *Policraticus*, III, 3–4, VI, 30, VII, 24.

188 *De Nugis Curialium*, I, 12.

189 *Policraticus*, III, 3–4, p. 177. Cf. also III, 5–7, 10, 13, etc., and LIEBSCHÜTZ, *Medieval Humanism*, p. 27.

190 *Epistulae*, no. 95.

191 *Architrenius*, III, 287–95, IV, 303.

192 LALLY, 'Court and Household of Henry II', pp. 354–5, cited by TÜRK, *Nugae Curialium*, p. 41. Walter, vice-chancellor after 1173 and archbishop of Rouen from 1184, was the brother of Roger fitz Reinfrid, who is found for his part in the service of Richard de Lucy.

193 *Policraticus*, VII, 19. Cf. JAEGER, *The Origins of Courtliness*, pp. 57–61.

194 Would it be correct to go so far as to conclude that 'magic and astrology came to play an important role in the private life of the courtier'? LIEBSCHÜTZ, *Medieval Humanism*, p. 27. It seems to us rather that John of Salisbury gave a blanket condemnation of pagan superstition, which he knew well enough from the Classical texts that he read so thoroughly from his scholastic and Christian perspective.

195 'The *Entheticus* of John of Salisbury', vv. 1,473–1,474.

196 *Policraticus*, VII, prologue and 5.

197 *De Nugis Curialium*, I, 2. Cf. I, 10–12, IV, 2, 12–13, V, 7. Cf. HARF-LANCNER, 'L'enfer de la cour'.

198 Cf. in a very different context, some quite similar critiques in the Imperial China of the 2nd century BC, in D.R. KNECHTGES, 'Criticism of the Court in Han Dynasty Literature', *Selected Essays on Court Culture in Cross-Cultural Perspective*, Taipei, 1999, pp. 51–77, an article kindly provided by the author.

199 TÜRK, *Nugae Curialium*, pp. 63–6, 103–7.

200 For Arnulf, look at SCHRIBER, *The Dilemma of Arnulf of Lisieux*, and for Gerald see BARTLETT, *Gerald of Wales*, p. 57, and also BOIVIN, *L'Irlande*. Gerald of Barry was elected in 1176, but Henry II probably feared that a man of such a lineage, whose mother belonged to the fitz Gerald family, would betray a certain Welsh separatism and obtain the *pallium* for St David's, freeing it from dependency on Canterbury. In 1190 and 1194 Gerald refused the sees of Bangor and Llandaff, as he still harboured hopes for St David's, to which he was elected once more in 1198. The next year King John – whom Gerald had supported during the absence of Richard I – issued no veto on the election, but Gerald encountered the refusal of Hubert Walter, archbishop of Canterbury. In the *Speculum Ecclesie* (1219) he made a vicious onslaught on the regular orders, since a Cluniac and a Cistercian had taken the see he had so much wanted.

201 WALTER MAP, *De Nugis Curialium*, I, 10, V, 6.

202 *Ibid.*, V, 7. Indeed, this institution alone found approval in his eyes. Naturally, Richard fitz Nigel also approved of the staff of the Exchequer, *Dialogus de Scaccario*, p. 77, cited by TURNER, *Judges, Administrators and the Common Law*, p. 110.

203 BISSON, 'The Politicising of West European Societies'.

204 This formalism is taken for granted in E. Curtius, *European Literature and the Latin Middle Ages*, New York, 1963.

205 On John of Salisbury's recycling of Jerome's criticism of the senatoral class, LIEBSCHÜTZ, *Medieval Humanism*, pp. 66–7.

206 LEGGE, *Anglo-Norman Literature*, pp. 183–4.

207 JAEGER, 'Courtliness and Social Change', p. 296.

208 Unpublished sermon on Malachi, cited by SMALLEY, *The Becket Conflict and the Schools*, p. 227.

209 *Policraticus*, IV, 6. Cf. LIEBSCHÜTZ, *Medieval Humanism*, p. 57. O. GEOFFROY, 'Le Policraticus de Jean de Salisbury (livres I, II et III): une vision de la cour au xiie siècle', unpubd master's thesis, Poitiers, 2001.

210 *Invectiva in depravatorem operum Petri Blesensis*, cited by R.B.C. Huygens, *Dialogus inter regem Henricum II et abbatem Bonnevallis*, p. 93, and *Compendium in Job*.

211 *PL*, vol. 145, col. 463. Cf. BALDWIN, *Masters, Princes and Merchants*, p. 178, and for theological debate on the question, pp. 185–6. On the other hand, the Dialogue of the Exchequer defends the employment of clerics in government: ' "All power comes from God" (Rom. 13:1): there is no contradiction in clerks keeping to God's law while simultaneously serving the king as lord (1 Pet. 2: 13)', *Dialogus de Scaccario*, p. 1.

212 'A quatuor aulicis canicis', *De Principis Instructione*, III, 4,. Cf. II, 3, III, 27–31. This last expression recalls Theobald of Blois's letter to the pope: 'The dogs of the court, those close friends of the king of England, stand revealed as the true agents of his will, and they have despicably shed innocent blood', ROGER OF HOWDEN, *Chronica*, vol. 2, p. 21; *Gesta*, vol. 1, pp. 15–16.

213 *Materials for the History of Thomas Becket*, vol. 1, §5; vol. 2, §46, cited by TÜRK, *Nugae Curialium*, p. 178.

214 'Men like Walter Map and Gerald of Wales were strong supporters of the Capetian monarchy and openly said so. Although historians have been inclined to regard these two as eccentrics and unrepresentative, they may well have only been the tip of the iceberg in the inclination of the clergy

away from the Angevins, especially after the murder of Becket', *Why Magna Carta?*, p. 124.

215 'The only key role for the political theorist [John of Salisbury] is to curry deference to the king and his counsellors', LIEBSCHÜTZ, *Medieval Humanism*, p. 46.

216 'The confusion of the political and moral spheres is something found already in Seneca' and 'It had not yet occurred to them [twelfth-century clerks] that philosophical imperatives and the needs of the State were two different things. Without the desire for power, the latter would never have existed. Real life is marked by the enigmatic interplay of the two aspects, aspiration and disposition'; and 'States do not work through hard and fast rules, but by day-to-day human activity caught in a debate between what is moral and what is practical', trans. from TÜRK, *Nugae Curialium*, pp. 189, 196.

217 Among those involved in the massacre of Jews at York (1190) is found one Richard Malebisse, on the subject of whom William of Newburgh said 'vero agnomine mala bestia', and a certain Mauleverers whose punning arms featured a greyhound (*levrier*), THOMAS, *Vassals, Heiresses and Thugs*, pp. 62–3.

218 BARLOW, *Thomas Becket*, p. 248.

219 On the prevalence of aristocratic violence and its manifestations, cf. STRICKLAND, *War and Chivalry*, and the review article by FLORI, 'Guerre et chevalerie au Moyen Age', CCM, 41, 1998, pp. 352–63, which elaborates the argument by showing how knightly idealism could moderate the savagery.

220 Cf. for his summation of this, FLORI, *Chevaliers et Chevalerie*.

221 *Epistulae*, no. 94, cols 291–4; JAEGER, 'Courtliness and Social Change'; BUMKE, *Courtly Culture*.

222 Ed. R.A. LODGE, III, 135–46, pp. 80–81; VI, 244–81, pp. 934–98. Cf. SHORT, 'Patrons and Polyglots', pp. 239–40. The book is dedicated to Cecily, countess of Hereford.

223 Cf. M. AURELL, 'Chevaliers et chevalerie chez Raymond Lulle', *Cahiers de Fanjeaux*, 22, 1987, pp. 141–57.

224 FLORI, 'La chevalerie selon Jean de Salisbury', pp. 35–77.

225 *Policraticus*, VI, 8.

226 SMALLEY, *The Becket Conflict and the Schools*, p. 98.

227 STRUVE, 'The Importance of the Organism in the Political Thought of John of Salisbury'. John's organic theory is in some respects highly original, even if it was influenced by William de Conches's commentaries on Plato, DUTTON, '*Illustre civitatis et populi exemplum*', pp. 109–11.

228 *Policraticus*, VIII, 17–23, vol. 2, p. 357.

229 It is certainly the case that some passages of the *Policraticus* (such as VII, 20, vol. 2, pp. 186–8), condemning princes who attack the Church, might be interpreted in this way, as did M. Wilks, 'John of Salisbury and the Tyranny of Nonsense', pp. 282–3. N. Fryde concluded that John of Salisbury was criticizing Henry II for atrocities committed by his troops around Gloucester and Oxford, as part of his campaign to secure England, and for the dispossession of his brother Geoffrey and the conquest of Brittany, 'The Roots of Magna Carta', p. 61. But why then expatiate on Henry II's achievement in pacifying England?

230 DICKINSON, 'The Medieval Conception of Kingship', pp. 336–7.

231 T. LESIEUR, 'The "Policraticus": A Christian Model of "Sapientia" ', unpubd lecture at a Cambridge conference (Peterhouse, 24–6 Sept. 2001): 'The Plantagenets and the Church'.

232 VAN LAARHOVEN, 'Thou shalt *not* slay a tyrant'.

233 GENET, 'Le vocabulaire politique du *Policraticus*'.

234 TURCHETTI, *Tyrannie et Tyrannicide*, pp. 251–6.

235 *De Principis Instructione*, I, 16, p. 56.

236 *Policraticus*, VI, 18, trans. DICKINSON, 'The Medieval Conception of Kingship', p. 237, n. 4.

237 *Policraticus*, VIII, 21, vol. 2, pp. 394–6. Cf. LIEBSCHÜTZ, *Medieval Humanism*, pp. 52–3.

238 'Annales Sancti Sergii Andegavensis', p. 102. For Abbot Suger, tyranny was embodied in the most treacherous of the magnates of Louis VI's domain, J. VAN ENGEN, 'Sacred Sanctions for Lordship', in *Cultures of Power*, ed. BISSON, p. 224.

239 *Policraticus*, I, 4, p. 25.

240 BUC, '*Principes gentium*', pp. 320–21.

241 BUC, *L'Ambiguïté du livre*, pp. 112–22, 225–7, and more recently, P. FREEDMAN, *Images of the Medieval Peasant*, Stanford CA, 1999, pp. 48–50.

242 *Policraticus*, VI, 10, cited by CLANCHY, *From Memory to Written Record*, p. 25.

243 NYKROG, 'The Rise of Literary Fiction'.

244 *Roman de Thèbes*, ed. RAYNAUD DE LARGE, vv. 13–16, vol. 1, p. 1. Cf. NYKROG, 'The Rise of Literary Fiction', pp. 597–8. The theme of the ass and the harp, going back at least as far as Aesop, can be found in

Roman sculpture, S. GARROS, 'Les Animaux musiciens au Moyen Age', unpubd memoir de D.E.A, University of Poitiers, 1997.

245 Not forgetting the remark of CLANCHY, *From Memory to Written Record*, p. 182: 'When a knight is described as *litteratus* in a medieval source, his exceptional erudition is usually being referred to, not his capacity to read and write.'

246 J. BALDWIN, 'The Capetian Court under Philip Augustus', in *The Medieval Court in Europe*, ed. E. HAYMES, Munich, 1986, p. 81.

247 'Miles enim litteratus fuerat et, dum vixit, solebat saepius alternis versibus', *De Principis Instructione*, III, 28, p. 310, cited by CLANCHY, *From Memory to Written Record*, p. 182. On Gerald and ghosts, cf. SCHMITT, *Les Revenants*, pp. 105–6.

248 TURNER, 'The *Miles litteratus*', pp. 941–5.

249 WILLIAM OF MALMESBURY, *Gesta Regum Anglorum*, vol. 1, pp. 10–12, and *idem*, *Historia Novella*, vol. 2, pp. 252–6.

250 CROUCH, *The Beaumont Twins*, pp. 7, 97, 207–11.

251 G.S. BURGESS and K. BUSBY, *The Lais of Marie de France*, Harmondsworth, 1986, pp. 15–19; BATE, *Contes*, p. 49, introduction by T. de PONTFARCY, *L'Espurgatoire seint Patriz*, Louvain, 1995, pp. 85–96.

252 SHORT, 'Patrons and Polyglots', p. 241. On Hue de Roteland, author of *Ipomedon* and *Prothelaus*, cf. LEGGE, *Anglo-Norman Literature*, pp. 85–96.

253 SHORT, 'Gaimar's Epilogue'.

254 CLANCHY, *From Memory to Written Record*, pp. 187, 198.

255 'Cum non esset literatus, quam doleo, quamlibet literarum seriem transcribere *sciret*', *De Nugis Curialium*, IV, 1, p. 278.

256 *Ibid.*, V, 5, p. 446. Geoffrey Plantagenet was said to have freed from captivity the knight who sang him the best produced poem, BEZZOLA, *La Cour d'Angleterre*, p. 3.

257 *Speculum duorum*, cited by BARTLETT, *Gerald of Wales*, p. 15. In his second prologue to the *Expugnatio hibernica*, Gerald of Barry says that Walter Map had told him that the Latin in which he had written his great corpus of works brought him less recognition and reputation than if he had written it in the vernacular. Gerald replied that he would not mind in the least translating his works into French but that abandoning Latin would compromise his stature as an intellectual, cited by P. BOURGAIN, 'L'emploi de la langue vulgaire dans la littérature au temps de Philippe Auguste', *La France de Philippe Auguste*, pp. 769–70. Cf. also BEZZOLA, *La Cour d'Angleterre*, p. 58.

258 SHORT, 'Patrons and Polyglots', and *idem*, 'On Bilingualism'.

259 CLANCHY, *From Memory to Written Record*, pp. 214–20.

260 WILLIAM OF CANTERBURY, *Vita Sancti Thome*, vol. 1, p. 128 and vol. 2, p. 5. Cf. particularly, SHORT, '*Tam Angli quam Franci*', p. 157, which shows the complexities involved in the interpretation of the passage in the *Vita*, where the wife of Hugh de Moreville argued with her husband in English.

261 'Un faus franceis sai d'Angleterre/ ke ne l'alai ailurs quere', cited by LEGGE, *Anglo-Norman Literature*, p. 63. Cf. J. WOGAN-BROWNE and G.S. BURGESS, *Virgin Lives and Holy Deaths. Two Exemplary Biographies for Anglo-Norman Women*, London, 1996.

262 'Lingua tamen caveas ne sit materna, sed illa / quam dedit et docuit lingua paterna tibi', *Tractatus contra curiales*, vv. 165–166.

263 'Apud Merleburgam ubi fons est quem si quis, ut aiunt, gustaverit, gallice barbarizat, unde cum viciose quis illa lingua loquitur, dicimus eum loqui gallicum Merleburge', *De Nugis Curialium*, V, 6, p. 496.

264 Since its publication in *Rerum Britannicarum Scriptores*, by T. WRIGHT, under the title of *Versus ad Guillelmum Eliensem*, in *Anglo-Latin Satirical Poets*, (Rolls Series, 1859), London, 1872, vol. 1, pp. 231–9.

265 *Policraticus*, p. 1, no. 379A-B, vv. 13–16. This 'ambitious young man' might well have been an allegorical personification of his book *Policraticus*, that John directed at the court to influence courtiers towards regular religious life, BEZZOLA, *La Cour d'Angleterre*, pp. 25–26.

266 SHORT, '*Tam Angli quam Franci*', p. 156.

267 E. LEPAGE, 'Richard Coeur de Lion et la poésie lyrique'.

268 'A program of social change . . . The common issue is the move of the warrior class from violence to restraint, from irresponsibility to social engagement, a move that the clergy had advocated in varying contexts and ideologies since the tenth century', JAEGER, 'Courtliness and Social Change', pp. 301–2. Cf. by the same author, *The Origins of Courtliness* and *The Envy of Angels*.

269 *Ensenhament*, ed. SANSONE. Cf. BEZZOLA, *La Cour d'Angleterre*, p. 269.

270 JAEGER, *The Envy of Angels*, pp. 297–308.

271 PETER OF BLOIS, *Epistulae*, no. 14.

272 *De Nugis Curialium*, V, 6.

273 RAMSAY, *The Angevin Empire*, p. 191.

274 TÜRK, *Nugae Curialium*, pp. 69, 76.

275 HERBERT OF BOSHAM, *Vite Sancti Thome*, II, 1. Cf. G. GICQUEL, 'Clercs satiristes et renouveau spirituel à la cour Plantagenêt', *Noblesses de l'espace Plantagenêt*, p. 79.

276 *Policraticus*, VIII, 9.

277 *Epistulae*, no. 139.

278 BUMKE, *Courtly Culture*, pp. 61–101. The author also observes that Germany, under northern French influence, would ignore Arthurian legend, other than the *Prose Lancelot*, translated into German at the beginning of the thirteenth century, *ibid.*, pp. 95–6. Was this due to the Plantagenet, rather than the Capetian or – properly speaking – French character of the Arthurian themes?

279 *De Principis Instructione*, III, 12, p. 259. Cf. the detailed commentaries on this text by POWICKE, *The Loss of Normandy*, p. 297 and by BATES, 'The Rise and Fall of Normandy'. Alfred Richard apparently took Gerald of Barry's analysis literally. But in the aftermath of the Fashoda Incident and the breakdown of the Entente Cordiale, Richard allowed his Anglophobia to influence his analysis in quite offensive terms: 'intellectual facility was alien to English barbarity', *Histoire des comtes de Poitou*, Paris, 1904, vol. 2, p. 15.

280 HASKINS, *Studies in Medieval Culture*, pp. 36–9; 'France was the home of freedom, reason and joy; England of oppression, dullness and dreams', SOUTHERN, *Medieval Humanism*, p. 156, cf. pp. 143–5.

281 *De Principis Instructione*, 1st preface, p. 8. Cf. BARTLETT, *Gerald of Wales*, pp. 95–7.

282 *The Letters of John of Salisbury*, no. 136, vol. 2, pp. 6–7. Cf. J. LE GOFF, *Les intellectuels au Moyen Age*, Paris, 1957, p. 28.

283 CONSTABLE, *The Reformation of the Twelfth Century*.

284 'Exeat aula qui vult esse pius', LUCAN, *La Guerre Civile (Pharsale)*, Paris, 1929, VIII, vv. 493–494, cited by JOHN OF SALISBURY, *Policraticus*, V, 10, p. 330.

285 *Cartulaire de l'abbaye cistercienne de Perseigne*, ed. G. FLEURY, Mamers, 1880, no. 14 (4 April 1196, an act of dubious authenticity) and no. 15 (1198), RALPH OF COGGESHALL, *Chronicon Anglicanum*, pp. 97–8.

286 RAMSAY, *The Angevin Empire*, pp. 368–9; ANDRAULT-SCHMITT, 'Le mécénat architectural en question', pp. 258–9.

287 He also founded Cartmel, an Augustinian priory, CROUCH, *William Marshal*, pp. 188–91.

288 HOLDSWORTH, 'Peacemaking in the 12th century', p. 11.

289 TÜRK, *Nugae Curialium*, pp. 50–51. Similar criticisms have been detected in *The Owl and the Nightingale*, a work in English of around 1200, COLEMAN, 'The Owl and the Nightingale', pp. 546–9.

290 *Statuta capitulorum generalium ordinis cisterciensis*, ed. J-M CANIVEZ, Louvain, 1933, vol. 1, p. 45.

291 RACITI, 'Isaac de l'Etoile et son siècle', pp. 138–45, 204–5, who makes a coherent and documented synthesis of these events and the despatch of Issac to the Isle of Rhé. However, in the entry 'Isaac de l'Etoile' in the *Dictionnaire des lettres françaises*, Paris, 1992, p. 714, D. Poirel attributes Isaac's departure to the island more to his 'monastic desire for isolation and poverty', but in such a short article there was no opportunity for him to argue his case.

292 *De Nugis Curialium*, I, 26. Cf. HALLAM, 'Henry II, Richard I and the Order of Grandmont'; ANDRAULT-SCHMITT, 'Le mécénat architectural en question'.

293 *Policraticus*, VII, 21–3, vol. 2, pp. 192–205. LIEBSCHÜTZ, *Medieval Humanism*, pp. 56–7.

294 TURNER *Judges, Administrators and the Common Law*, pp. 105–17, and *The English Judiciary*, pp. 135–57.

295 'Itinerarium Kambriae', I, 3, p. 47.

296 CROUCH, *The Beaumont Twins*, pp. 95, 197–201.

297 DUBY, *Guillaume le Maréchal*, pp. 7–34. William had taken the decision to be buried as a Templar thirty-five or thirty-six years earlier, during his crusade to the Holy Land, CROUCH, *William Marshal*, p. 187.

298 *Policraticus*, VII, 21.

299 *De Nugis Curialium*, I, 23, trans. BATE, *Contes*, p. 102.

300 Cf. A. VAUCHEZ, *La Spiritualité du Moyen Age occidental, VIIIᵉ–XIIIᵉ siècle*, Paris, 1994 (2nd edn), pp. 118–30.

Plantagenet ideology

1 *De Nugis Curialium*, I, 28, p. 116, and V, 5, p. 451.

2 COGGESHALL, *Chronicon Anglicanum*, p. 93. Cf. CARPENTER, 'Abbot Ralph of Coggeshall's Account'. p. 1219.

3 *Le Forme della propaganda politica nel Due e nel Trecento*, Rome, 1994 (Collection de l'Ecole Française de Rome, 2001).

4 Cf. LE GOFF, 'Conclusions', in *Le Forme della propaganda politica*, pp. 519–20, repeated by CHAOU, *L'Idéologie*, p. 24.

5   On these problems, cf. R. FAVREAU, *Epigraphie médiévale*, Turnehout, 1997, pp. 31–46.

6   'Removeri lapidem quam ipse posuit in fundamento ecclesie Varenensis, de quo erat dissentio. Quare ego ipse volo esse fundator ecclesie predicte et custos et defensor', *Recueil des actes d'Henri II*, no. 124 (1159?), vol. 1, pp. 230–1. Cf. DEVAILLY, *Le Berry*, pp. 405–12.

7   L. GODRECKI, *Vitrail roman*, Fribourg, 1977, pp. 70–3, pl. 56–8.

8   Cf., particularly the works of two art historians from Tel-Aviv University, N. KENAAN-KEDAR, 'Aliénor d'Aquitaine conduite en captivité', and S. LUTAN, 'La façade septentrionale de St-Martin de Candes'.

9   GERALD OF BARRY, *De Principis Instructione*, III, 26, pp. 295–6.

10 A. HERON, 'La chasse royale de la chapelle Sainte-Radegonde à Chinon', *Archeologia*, Feb. 1965, pp. 1965; *idem*, 'La chapelle Sainte-Radegonde de Chinon', in C. LELONG, *Touraine romane*, La Pierre-qui-Vire, 1977, pp. 327–35 (3rd edn).

11 KENAAN-KEDAR, 'Aliénor d'Aquitaine conduite en captivité' and the replies to this article in *CCM*, 42, 1999, pp. 397–9, and FLORI, *Richard Coeur de Lion*, p. 496, n. 44.

12 U. NILGEN, 'Les Plantagenêt à Chinon. A propos d'une peinture murale dans la chapelle Sainte-Radegonde', *Mélanges Piotr Skubiszewski*, Poitiers, 1999, pp. 153–7.

13 Cf., AURELL, *La Vieille et l'épée*.

14 ROGER OF HOWDEN, *Chronica*, vol. 3, p. 143, and *Gesta Henrici*, p. 216.

15 'De Vita Galfredi', II, 9, p. 427. The poem, *Discat cancellarius*, attributed by P. Dronke ('Peter of Blois and Poetry', p. 221) and its most recent editor to Peter of Blois, ought to belong to this category of anti-Longchamps songs rather than anti-Becket songs, as critics have often tried to do, *Carmina*, ed. WOLLIN, no. 4.3, pp. 517–24.

16 'Campus Trossebof, quam dedit Rollandus archiepiscopus Garino Trossebof joculatori, dum viveret', cited by E. FARAL, *Les jongleurs en France au Moyen Age*, Paris, 1910, p. 288, app. III, n. 82.

17 HASKINS, 'Henry II as a patron of literature', p. 73.

18 In taking such pleasure in the death of Eustace of Blois ('Dying was the best thing he ever did'), John of Salisbury said, paraphrasing Horace, that he had only been lamented by 'crowds of dancers, charlatans, beggars, mimes, fools and that sort', *Policraticus*, VI, 18. Cf. P. ZUMTHOR, *La Lettre et la Voix. De la 'littérature médiévale'*, Paris, 1987, p. 79; J-C. SCHMITT, *La Raison des gestes dans l'Occident médiéval*, Paris, 1990, p. 266. On the

hostility towards entertainers amongst Christian thinkers before the mendicant orders, cf. C. CASAGRANDE and S. VECCHIO, 'Clercs et jongleurs dans la société médiévale (XIIᵉ et XIIIᵉ siècle)', *Annales ESC*, 34, 1979, pp. 913–28.

19 D'A.S. AVALLE, *La letteratura medievale in lingua d'oc nella sua tradizione manoscritta*, Turin, 1961, pp. 44–9, 83, 129. A list of troubadours linked to the Plantagenets is to be found in CHAYTOR, *The Troubadours*, pp. 35–70. Since the publication of this work in 1923 scientific editions of troubadour songs mentioned below have become numerous.

20 Edition in 'Richard Coeur de Lion et la poésie lyrique'. Much later though it was and heavily romanticized, the Blondel legend is full of this sort of idea, *Récit du ménestrel de Reims au XIIIᵉ siècle*, ed. N. de WAILLY, Paris, 1876, XII.

21 PEIRE VIDAL, *Poesie*, no. 6, vv. 25–32, pp. 69–70, and no. 35, p. 267, MOINE DE MONTAUDON, *Les Troubadours cantaliens*, no. 2, v. 43, p. 262.

22 'Richard Coeur de Lion et la poésie lyrique', pp. 904–5.

23 *The Political Songs of England*, pp. 1–3.

24 BERTRAN DE BORN, *L'Amour et la Guerre*, nos. 13–14, pp. 235–67; GAUCELM FAIDIT, *Les Poèmes de Gaucelm Faudit*, no. 50, pp. 415–24. More praise of Richard the Lion Heart in nos 48, 52, 54. Although Bertan de Born is often critical of Henry II and his sons he does recognize their generosity and their taste for war, which he tries to ignite further: *L'Amour et la Guerre*, pp. LXVI–LXX, and poems nos 11–19, 24–32, 36, 38, MOORE, *The Young King Henry*, pp. 48–51.

25 GACE BRULE, *Gace Brulé: trouvère champenois*, no. 67, pp. 401–4; GAUCELM FAIDIT, *Les Poèmes de Gaucelm Faudit*, no. 40, p. 385.

26 ARNAUT DE MAREUIL, *Les Poésies lyriques du troubadour Arnaut de Mareuil*, no. 2, p. 9, vv. 31–2.

27 *Poesie*, no. 38, vv. 62–64, p. 340.

28 GIRAUT DE BORNEIL, *The Cansos and Sirventes*, no. 75, vv. 65–80, pp. 473–80, FOLQUET DE MARSEILLE, *Le Troubadour Folquet de Marseille*, no. 10, vv. 33–40, pp. 50–51, and no. 18, v. 49, p. 81.

29 *Bernart de Ventadour, troubadour du XIIᵉ siècle*, no. 10, v. 45, p. 96.

30 There were perhaps less than at the court of Barcelona (M. AURELL, 'Les troubadours et le pouvoir royal: l'exemple de Alphonse Iᵉʳ (1162–1196)', *Revue des Langues romanes*, 85, 1981, pp. 53–67) and Toulouse (MACE, *Les Comtes de Toulouse*, pp. 138–44). But their number allows us to

mitigate the assertion of I. Short ('Patrons and Polyglots', p. 239): 'Nor is the evidence for the presence of troubadour poets at Henry's court enough to prove active royal patronage.'

31 'Abril issis', vv. 272–283, pp. 52–3.

32 *Jongleurs*, no. 8, vv. 7, 26–28, p. 64.

33 A, JEANROY, 'Un sirventès historique de 1242', *Mélanges Léonce Couture*, Toulouse, 1902, pp. 115–25, and for citation, p. 122, v. 21.

34 GILLINGHAM, *The English in the 12th Century*, pp. 41–58.

35 Ed and trans. G. PARIS, Paris, 1897.

36 *Itinerarium peregrinorum et gesta regis Ricardi*. For the relationship between this work and Ambroise, cf. the introduction by HUBERT and LA MONTE, to the English translation of Ambroise: *L'Estoire de Guerre Sainte*, pp. 7–18.

37 Cf. GUENEE, *Histoire et culture historique*, p. 58.

38 POWER, 'What did the Frontier of Angevin Normandy Comprise?', p. 200.

39 Ed and trans. R.C. JOHNSTON. Cf. LODGE, 'Literature and History in the *Chronicle* of Jordan Fantosme', and CLANCHY, *From Memory to Written Record*, p. 158 for the problem of his forsaking of Latin for French. Cf. BEZZOLA, *La cour d'Angleterre*, p. 198; STRICKLAND, 'Arms and the Men'.

40 TYSON, 'Patronage of French Vernacular History Writers', p. 200.

41 LODGE, 'Literature and History', pp. 263–4.

42 *Jordan Fantosme's Chronicle*, vv. 1906–7, and DAMIAN-GRINT, 'Truth, Trust and Evidence in the Anglo-Norman *Estoire*'. On the military and espionage aspects of this battle, cf. PRESTWICH, 'Military Intelligence under the Norman and Angevin Kings', pp. 19–21, and STRICKLAND, 'Securing the North', pp. 194–6.

43 This is the view of K.M. Broadhurst ('Henry II of England and Eleanor of Aquitaine', pp. 59–60), who pointed out the conventional nature of the flattery addressed to Henry II. The article rigorously tests some received ideas, in particular the literary role of Eleanor of Aquitaine, based on exiguous evidence. But the author's definition of patronage – as being exclusively based on the commission of a work, the direct intervention of the patron in its compilation and the payment of the author – seems too restrictive. Also it makes patronage and criticism of the patron incompatible, which was not so at that time.

44 Cf. AURELL, *La Vieille et l'épée*, pp. 144–7, and M. BAKHTINE, *L'Oeuvre de François Rabelais et la culture populaire au Moyen Age et sous la Renaissance*, Paris, 1970, pp. 16–19.

45 JAEGER, 'Patrons and the Beginnings of Courtly Romance', pp. 51–3.

46 COGGESHALL, *Chronicon Anglicanum*, p. 97, trans. BEZZOLA, *La Cour d'Angleterre*, p. 215.

47 *Chronicle of Jordan Fantosme*, no. 208, v. 1959, p. 144.

48 *Policraticus*, I, VI, pp. 50–1. Cf. BEZZOLA, *La Cour d'Angleterre*, pp. 28–9.

49 'Candidatrices' (*sic* for 'cantatrices'? In which case the term might be taken in a sense near to prostitution), *Epistulae*, no. 14, col. 49.

50 WILLIAM FITZ STEPHEN, *Vita sancti Thome*, p. 31.

51 HENRY OF HUNTINGDON, *Historia Anglorum*, X, 40, p. 776.

52 ROGER OF HOWDEN, *Gesta Henrici*, vol. 2, p. 76, and BEZZOLA, *La Cour d'Angleterre*, pp. 215–16.

53 'Otia imperialia', p. 447. In his *Iliade of Darès de Phrygie* (1180–1189), Joseph of Exeter closed his verses on the death of Hector with a memorial of the Young Henry, V, v. 534, ed. GOMPF, p. 177, trans ROBERTS, pp. 63–4.

54 PETER OF BLOIS, *Carmina*, I.4, 2. 3, 3.7, pp. 257–61. Cf. DRONKE, 'Peter of Blois and Poetry', p. 191.

55 'Notes', ed. KINGSFORD, no. 5, p. 321.

56 ROGER OF HOWDEN, *Chronica*, vol. 2, p. 455, vol. 4, pp. 84–5. Cf. BROUGHTON, *The Legends of King Richard I*, p. 38.

57 ROGER OF HOWDEN, Gesta Henrici, vol. 2, pp. 251–2, and FARAL, *Les Arts poétiques*, pp. 208–10, vv. 368–430. Cf. BEZZOLA, *La Cour d'Angleterre*, pp. 215–18. Geoffrey de Vinsauf also wrote a poem to complain of the Interdict imposed on England by Innocent III under John, in, FARAL, *Les Arts poétiques*, pp. 24–6.

58 'Cessent igitur invidi, cessent et incauti, amplius obstrepere Anglorum reges nullo Hiberniam jure contingere', *Expugnatio Hibernica*, II, 6. Cf. SCHRIMER and BROICH, *Studien zum literarischen Patronat in England*, p. 140.

59 *Topographia Hibernica*, p. 21, trans. BOIVIN, *L'Irlande*, pp. 165–6.

60 'De Rebus se Gestis', *Giraldi Cambrensis Omnia Opera*, ed. J.S. BREWER, (Rolls Series, 21) London, 1861, vol. 1, pp. 72–3. CF. L. THORPE, 'Gerald of Wales: a Public Reading in Oxford in 1188 or 1189', *Neophilogus*, 62, 1978, pp. 455–8, BOIVIN, *L'Irlande*, p. 287, and GUENEE, *Histoire et culture historique*, pp. 60–1 and 291.

61 CHAUOU, *L'Idéologie Plantagenêt*, p. 239.

62 Following here, R. BARTLETT, 'Political Prophecy in Gerald of Wales'.

63 'Sunt viri nonnulli quos *Awennithon* vocant [. . .] Hi super aliquo consulti ambiguo, statim frementes spiritu quasi extra se rapiuntur et tamquam arrptiti fiunt. Nec incontinenti tamen quod desideratur edisserunt sed per ambages multas, inter varios quibus effluunt sermones, nugatorios magis et vanos quam sibi cohaerentes, sed omnes tamen ornatos, in aliquo demum verbi diverticulo qui responsum solerter observat quod petit accipiet ennucleatum.' GERALD OF BARRY, *Descriptio Kambriae*, I, 16, pp. 194–5, cited, translated and commented on by BARTLETT, *ut supra*.

64 ROGER OF WENDOVER, *Flores Historiarum*, vol. 2, pp. 62–3, 76–7.

65 SCHRIBER in her introduction to ARNULF OF LISIEUX, *The Dilemma of Arnulf of Lisieux*, p. 17.

66 *Foedera, Conventiones, etc.*, vol. 1, pp. 73–8, or RHF, vol. 19, p. 277. Cf. LABANDE, 'Pour une image véridique d'Aliénor d'Aquitaine', pp. 222–3, BEZZOLA, *La Cour d'Angleterre*, p. 33.

67 DUGGAN, *Thomas Becket*, pp. 3–8, 170.

68 JOHN OF MARMOUTIER, 'Historia Gaufredi Ducis', p. 176.

69 'Tam armata quam togata, tam martia scilicet quam litterata', *De Principis Instructione*, p. 7.

70 GALBRAITH, 'The Literacy of the Medieval English Kings', pp. 213–14.

71 *Gesta Regum Anglorum*, V, no. 390, p. 710.

72 JOHN OF MARMOUTIER, 'Gesta consulum Andegavorum', p. 140.

73 *Policraticus*, IV, 6.

74 HELINAND OF FROIDMONT, *Flores*, PL, vol. 212, ch. XV, col. 736.

75 *De Principis Instructione*, pp. 5, 42. Cf. BEZZOLA, *La Cour d'Angleterre*, p. 78.

76 'Les clercs prétendent qu'ils ont une nouvelle marchandise à vendre au prince : la sagesse d'écoles. Il faut donc qy'ills clament bien haut, premièrement qu'elle est utile, deuxièment que le roi en manque', BUC, *L'Ambiguité du Livre*, pp. 184–5.

77 *Epistulae*, no. 67, col. 211. Cf. BEZZOLA, *La Cour d'Angleterre*, pp. 45–6.

78 JOHN OF MARMOUTIER, 'Historia Gaufredi Ducis', p. 218, BRADBURY, 'Geoffrey V of Anjou', p. 40.

79 *De Invectionibus*, I, 5, pp. 100–1. Gerald in his later bitterness towards the Plantagenets, contradicts himself in his other works: he goes as far as to dedicate his *De Principis Instructione* (1218) to the future Louis VIII whom he regards – unlike the Angevins – as a good Latinist (*ibid.*, pp. 6–7). He wrote indeed that 'most people, and the prince particularly, simply do not

know enough Latin' (*Expugnatio Hibernica*, 1st preface). He regretted a time when 'our princes were more literate' (*Descriptio Kambriae*, 2nd preface). He was sorry to have once dedicated his *Topography of Ireland* and *Vaticinal History* (now lost) to Henry II and Richard the Lionheart, 'who, preoccupied with other business had little time for literature' (*Itinerarium Kambriae*, 1st preface). Gerald was subject to other contradictions, as in his preference for certain members of the house of Anjou over others. As Judith Everard mentioned ('The "Justiciarship" in Brittany and Ireland', p. 89), he was more tolerant of the Young Henry and Richard, the lawful heirs of the house, than he was of their brothers Geoffrey and John, lords of conquered or usurped domains.

80 *Itinerarium peregrinorum et gesta regis Ricardi*, VI, 8, pp. 394–6. Cf. LEPAGE in 'Richard Coeur de Lion et la poésie lyrique', p. 894 and MAYER in *Das Itinerarium*, p. 140.

81 ROGER OF HOWDEN, *Chronica*, vol. 3, pp. 75–86; *Gesta Henrici*, vol. 2, pp. 151–5.

82 'Ex Anonymi chronico', *RHF*, vol. 12, pp. 120, 415 (Muratori's interpolation in Richard the Poitevin's chronicle).

83 WILLIAM FITZ STEPHEN, 'Vita Thome', no. 102, p. 104, and GERVASE OF CANTERBURY, *Chronica*, p. 125. Cf. BEZZOLA, *La Cour d'Angleterre*, p. 6.

84 *Metalogicon*, I, 5, II, 10, and III, 4.

85 This prologue's tenor is matched by a manual which a certain master sent to his old pupil (according to P. Delahaye, the expert in this work, 'Une Adaptation du *De Officiis* au xiie siècle', pp. 256–7). William of Conches's tutorship of Henry II is noted by most historians (WARREN, *Henry II*, p. 39; LIEBSCHÜTZ, *Medieval Humanism*, p. 10), the exception being RICHARDSON and SAYLES, *The Governance of Medieval England*, p. 272, which is contrary as usual. It is true that William was a master in Paris in 1146, but it hardly matches what we know of him that he should leave such a prestigious school to go to Normandy to teach an adolescent boy.

86 *Epistulae*, no. 66.

87 *Ibid.*, no. 1, and DUGGAN, *Thomas Becket: A Textual History of His Letters*, p. 7.

88 'Princeps eloquentissimus et quod his temporibus conspicuum est litteris eruditus', *De Principis Instructione*, II, 29, p. 215.

89 *De Nugis Curialium*, V, 6.

90 CLANCHY, *From Memory to Written Record*, p. 186.

91 'Salomon alter', *Topographia Hibernica*, III, 48.

92 *Dialogus de Scaccario*; *Tractatus de Legibus et Consuetudinibus*.

93 This person appears in the list of 'Saint Thomas's twenty-two scholars' that Herbert of Bosham, his hagiographer, gives at the end of the life of Becket, as 'scriba doctus', *Vita Sancti Thome*, p. 527, no. 13. The author of the *Notarial Art* was not sparing of his eulogies on the glorious martyr Thomas, who had begun his career as a notary [JOHN OF TILBURY], *Ars Notaria*, pp. 324–5. It belonged to the period when he was Becket's secretary in the chancery. Cf. BARLOW, *Thomas Becket*, p. 79; KUTTNER and RATHBONE, 'Anglo-Norman Canonists', p. 292.

94 Recent summaries on Adelard of Bath and this particular work are in NORTH, 'Some Norman Horoscopes', and POULLE, 'Le traité de l'astrolabe'. Adelard has been associated with the Exchequer by reason of his treatise on the abacus and his mathematical knowledge. It has been suggested that the master–student dialogue in one of his horoscopes might depict Adelard and the young Henry Plantagenet, in the context of the boy's studies at Bristol in 1149, COCHRANE, *Adelard of Bath*, pp. 93–6. Interesting conjectures, but difficult to prove.

95 HASKINS, 'Adelard of Bath and Henry Plantagenet', pp. 515–16.

96 ROBERT OF CRICKLADE, 'Das Exzerpt der *Naturalis Historia* des Plinius', p. 265.

97 *Le Bestiaire de Philippe de Thaün*, p. vii. Cf. SHORT, 'Patrons and Polyglots', p. 237, and LEGGE, *Anglo-Norman Literature*, pp. 22–5.

98 *The Romance of Daude de Prades*, vv. 1,929–1,934, p. 136. What value can we attach to evidence from a century later? Did this book ever exist? Was it written by the king, was he simply its dedicatee, commissioner, or owner? Henry II's taste for falconry is known from the Pipe Rolls and the prologue of the *Topography of Ireland*, HASKINS, 'Henry II as a Patron of Literature', p. 76. It is interesting to note that techniques drawn from observed practice rather than tradition is a characteristic of Emperor Frederick II's treatise on falconry, and it may be that Daude de Prades had taken this and transferred it to Henry II.

99 'De avibus tractatus', *Adelard of Bath: Conversations with his nephew*, ed. C. BURNETT (Cambridge, 1998), pp. 239–41. The confusion between Adelard himself, held to be the tutor of Henry II, and his pupil is just as evident in the spirit of Daude de Prades.

100 GERALD OF BARRY, 'Vits sancti Remigii', p. 45.

101 *The Letters of Osbert de Clare*, nos 37, 38, pp. 128–32.

102 Y. SASSIER, 'L'utilisation d'un concept romain aux temps carolingiens: la *res publica* aux ixe et xiie siècles', *Médiévales*, 1989, 15, pp. 17–30.

103 KRYNEN, *L'Empire du roi*, pp. 208–9.

104 A summary of this debate in recent literature is A. CHAOU, *L'Idéologie*, pp. 79–88. Cf. also SHORT, 'Patrons and Polyglots'; TYSON, 'Patronage of French Vernacular History Writers'; JAEGER, 'Patrons and the Beginnings of Courtly Romance'.

105 *The Letters of Osbert de Clare*, no. 38, p. 132.

106 CARMAN, *A Study of the Pseudo-Map*.

107 *La Cour d'Angleterre*, p. 3.

108 JOHN OF MARMOUTIER and THOMAS OF CONCHES, 'Chronica de gestis consulorum Andegavensium', pp. 29–31. Cf. KOZIOL, 'England, France and the Problem of Sacrality', p. 133, and BOURNAZEL, 'Mémoire et parenté', pp. 119–22.

109 *Roman de Brut*, vv. 477–478. Cf. BOUTET, *Charlemagne et Arthur*, p. 38.

110 COGGESHALL, *Chronicon Anglicanum*, pp. 45, 48–9. Cf. PRESTWICH, 'Richard Coeur de Lion'. This image is at the heart of J. Flori's significantly titled recent biography, *Richard Coeur de Lion, le roi-chevalier*.

111 'Richard was very far from being the impetuous leader of romantic legend. Rather, his usual approach was methodical and carefully prepared', GILLINGHAM, *Richard Coeur de Lion*, pp. 224–5.

112 'Anno incarnatione MC octogesimo sexto, existente . . . comite vero Pictavense probissimo milite Richardo', 'Le cartulaire du prieuré Saint-Pierre de La Réole', ed. C. GRELET-BALGERIE, Bordeaux, 1863 (Archives historiques du département de la Gironde, vol. 5), no. 108, §105, p. 150 (1186). Cf. BOUTOULLE, *Société laïque en Bordelais*, p. 568.

113 AMBROISE, *L'Histoire de Guerre Sainte*, vv. 10,459–10,466, col. 280, trans. *Richard Coeur de Lion*, ed. BROSSARD-DANDRE and BESSON, p. 195.

114 *Ibid.*, vv. 12,147–12,152, col. 326.

115 *Itinerarium peregrinorum et gesta*, p. 143.

116 AMBROISE, *L'Histoire de Guerre Sainte*, v. 2310, col. 62. Cf. BROUGHTON *The Legends of King Richard I*, pp. 115–19, FLORI, *Richard Coeur de Lion*, pp. 264–9. Count Richard, harrier of the Saracens, a hero of Jean Renart's *L'Escoufle* (1200–1202) was also called 'Coeur de Lion' (v. 298), BALDWIN, *Aristocratic Life in Medieval France*, Baltimore, 2000, p. 38.

117 STRICKLAND, *War and Chivalry*, pp. 99–103.

118 MOORE, *The Young King*, pp. 17–23.

119 JOHN THE TROUVERE, *L'Histoire de Guillaume le Maréchal*, vv. 2,071–2,096. D. Crouch doubts that this ceremony was a knighting, since a correspondent of Becket says that Henry II had knighted him in 1170. To Crouch, it was more of a blow by which a master indicated that his pupil was no longer a simple squire, but a bacheler, CROUCH, *William Marshal*, p. 46n.

120 *Ymagines Historiarum*, vol. 1, p. 428, cited by FLORI, *Richard Coeur de Lion*, p. 357.

121 *De Nugis Curialium*, IV, 1, pp. 280–3, trans. BATE, p. 222.

122 'Ita moriens universae militiae fuit exitium', *Otia Imperialia*, p. 447.

123 JOHN THE TROUVERE, *L'Histoire de Guillaume le Maréchal*, vv. 2,071–2,096, 6,987–6,988, 7,156–7,184.

124 THOMAS OF EARLEY, 'Sermo de morte et sepultura Henrici regis junioris', pp. 263–73.

125 *Historia Rerum Anglicanum*, III, 7, which also notes the ring sent by Henry II to his dying son.

126 ROGER OF HOWDEN, *Chronica*, vol. 2, pp. 277–8.

127 DUBY, *Hommes et structures du moyen age*, pp. 213–26.

128 GOUIRAN (ed.), *L'Amour et la Guerre*, pp. 237–45, and STRICKLAND, *War and Chivalry*, pp. 108–9.

129 'Ubi ipse cum regina sua morari posset', *Chronica*, vol. 2, p. 46; cf. vol. 1, p. 41, and BOUSSARD, *Le Comté d'Anjou*, p. 78.

130 *Jordan Fantosme's Chronicle*, vv. 378–406. Cf. STRICKLAND, 'Arms and the Men', pp. 213–15, and 'Securing the North', p. 196.

131 *Roman de Rou*, vv. 10,269–70, vol. 2, p. 266.

132 *Historia Ecclesiastica*, vol. 3, p. 198; vol. 4, p. 82, vol. 5, pp. 24, 300; vol. 6, pp. 450–8. Cf. LOUD, 'The Gens Normannorum', p. 106.

133 R. BOYER, ' "Dans Upsal où les Jarls boivent la bonne bière". Rites de boisson chez les Vikings', in, *La Sociabilité à table*, ed. M. AURELL, O. DUMOULIN, F. THELAMON, Rouen, 1992, p. 84.

134 *Chronicon Anglicanum*, p. 96. Without going as far as that, writers also discussed the deeper reasons for the persistent bad feeling between Henry II and Louis VII, which they found more in Eleanor's remarriage than in their rival claims to the Vexin, 'Annales sancti Sergii', p. 101; OTTO OF FREISING, *Gesta Frederici*, IV, 24; RALPH DE DICETO, *Ymagines Historiarum*, vol. 1, pp. 303–4; PETER RIGA, 'Un poème inédit'.

135 Cf. the commentary on his chapter 23, in SOUTHERN, *Medieval Humanism*, p. 56.

136 *Historia Rerum Anglicanum*, II, 12, p. 131; II, 29, p. 159.

137 *Policraticus*, IV, 2.

138 JOLIFFE, *Angevin England*, p. 100.

139 BARTLETT, *Gerald of Wales*, appendix II, pp. 222–5.

140 GERALD OF WALES, *De Principis Instructione*, III, 30, pp. 320–1; *idem*,
     Gemma ecclesiastica, London, 1862 (Rolls Series, 21), vol. 2, II, 11.
     Cf. BARTLETT, *Gerald of Wales*, pp. 91–100. Another slighting allusion to
     Henry II's leopard is in a letter of Cardinal Albert to Thomas Becket: 'non
     facile mutat . . . pardus varietates suas', *The Correspondence of Thomas
     Becket*, no. 323, p. 1340. Ralph Niger notes the dragon as banner of
     Richard the Lionheart, cited by FRYDE, *Why Magna Carta?*, p. 52.

141 *The Letters of John of Salisbury*, vol. 2, no. 277, p. 592.

142 *De Nugis Curialium*, V, 5, p. 226. Cf. LEYSER, *Medieval Germany and its
     Neighbours*, p. 249.

143 PETER RIGA, 'Un poème inédit'. Cf. KRYNEN, *L'Empire du roi*, pp. 58,
     62, BALDWIN, *Philippe Auguste*, p. 457.

144 FLORI, *L'Essor de Chevalerie*, p. 303.

145 'Ob honorem tamen et reverentiam regalis nominis rex Anglorum vocatus
     est', RICHARD THE POITEVIN, 'Chronicon', p. 417. Cf. LE PATOUREL,
     Norman Empire, p. 242, n. 4.

146 AURELL, *Les Noces du Comte*, pp. 380–8. William of Newburgh, (*Historia
     rerum Anglicarum*, II, 10), says, however, that Raymond Berengar IV
     refused the title of king: 'Since none of my ancestors was more than a count,
     I am a born count . . . and so that for me nature will not exceed my desserts,
     I set aside the name and insignia of a king . . . I had rather be the first
     among counts than no more than the seventh amongst kings.' Cf. besides
     this, ROBERT DE TORIGNY, *Chronica*, pp. 200–1.

147 Cf. recently, E. PALAZZO, *Liturgie et société au Moyen Age*, Paris, 2000,
     pp. 194–212, and J. LE GOFF, E. PALAZZO, J-C. BONNE, M-N.
     COLETTE, *Le Sacre royal à l'époque de Saint Louis*, Paris, 2001.

148 On this subject, cf. P.E. SCHRAMM, *A History of the English Coronation*.
     The solid erudition of this work is not in question though its ideological
     background should not be forgotten. It was written by a German National
     Socialist who published it at Oxford in 1937, in honour of the royal family
     with which Germany was seeking a diplomatic link.

149 *Councils and Synods*, no. 152, p. 828.

150 *Chronica*, vol. 3, pp. 9–12, and *Gesta Henrici*, vol. 2, pp. 79–83, as
     analysed by Ramsay, *The Angevin Empire*, pp. 266–9, and translated into
     French by BROSSARD-DANDRE and BESSON, *Richard de Coeur de Lion*,

pp. 66–9. Cf. RICHARDSON, 'The Coronation in Mediaeval England', pp. 131–3. SCHRAMM, *A History of the English Coronation*, pp. 69–70. Certain historians attribute the account of the 1189 coronation to Richard fitz Nigel, the baron of the Exchequer, with Howden simply as transcriber (FRYDE, *Why Magna Carta?*, p. 54). This seems unlikely as an hypothesis, when you note the strong theocratic orientation of the description, which rather suggests a clerical author.

151 *Chronica*, vol. 1, pp. 524–5. Crown-wearing was a ceremony of display, different from the first coronation on the accession of a monarch.

152 'Ymagines historiarum', vol. 2, p. 68.

153 SCHRAMM, *A History of the English Coronation*, pp. 141–62.

154 RICHARDSON, 'The Coronation in Mediaeval England', pp. 151–3; RICHARDSON and SAYLES, *The Governance of Medieval England*, p. 138; WARREN, *Henry II*, p. 218.

155 For the difference between *carta coronationis* and *carta professionis*, see FOREVILLE, 'Le sacre des rois anglo-normands et angevins', p. 111.

156 SCHRAMM, *A History of the English Coronation*, pp. 193–202, 229.

157 BARBEY, *Etre roi*, p. 35.

158 J. SOBREQUES, *El pactisme a Catalunya*, Barcelona, 1982.

159 M. DAVID, 'Le serment de sacre du ixe au xve siècle. Contribution à l'étude des limites juridiques de la souveraineté', *Revue du Moyen Age latin*, 6, 1950, pp. 5–272.

160 ROGER OF HOWDEN, *Chronica*, vol. 3, p. 10; *The Correspondence of Thomas Becket*, no. 74, p. 294.

161 Anointing fails to appear in the four verses devoted by Wace to the coronation of Arthur, much more elaborately described in Latin by Geoffrey of Monmouth, and it barely rates a mention in the coronation described in *Erec et Enide*, D. BOUTET, *Charlemagne et Arthur*, p. 65.

162 SCHRAMM, *A History of the English Coronation*, pp. 120–1, and FOREVILLE, 'Le sacre des rois anglo-normands et angevins', p. 107.

163 *The Letters and Charters of Gilbert Foliot*, no. 170, p. 236, lines 229–35.

164 *Epistulae*, no. 150, col. 440, trans. BLOCH, *Les Rois thaumaturges*, pp. 41–2. Cf. *Ibid.*, pp. 79–89, 146, 185–216.

165 J-P. POLY, 'Le Capétien thaumaturge: genèse populaire d'un miracle royal', *La France de l'an mil*, ed. R. DELORT, Paris, 1990, pp. 282–308.

166 BARLOW, 'The King's Evil'; LE GOFF, preface to BLOCH, *Les Rois thaumaturges*, pp. xv–xvi.

167 'Sub faucis scrophulis, quas vulgo glandulas vocant, vexari coepit, quae contactu regiae manus curari dicuntur', PHILIP OF OXFORD, 'Ad Acta sanctae Frideswidae', p. 575. Cf. KOZIOL, 'England, France and the Problem of Sacrality', p. 140.

168 On the frequency of such inflictions in collections of miracles, cf. E. BOZOKY, 'Les miracles de châtiment au haut Moyen Age et à l'époque féodale', *Violence and Religion*, ed. P. CAZIER and J-M. DELMAIRE, Lille, 1998, pp. 151–67.

169 That is part of the stance of G. Koziol ('England, France and the Problem of Sacrality',) whose merit is in taking account of this miracle, unknown to Bloch. Koziol's theory relies on the conflict between Plantagenets and Capetians, the latter overcoming their political handicap by their moral eminence and thaumaturgical powers.

170 THOMAS OF EARLEY, 'Sermo de morte et sepultura Henrici regis junioris', pp. 267–8.

171 KNOWLES, *The Episcopal Colleagues of Thomas Becket*, p. 154.

172 FRYDE, *Why Magna Carta?*, p. 53.

173 LEMARIGNIER, 'Autour de la royauté française', p. 14.

174 BARBEY, *Etre roi*, p. 36.

175 SCHRAMM, *A History of the English Coronation*, pp. 120–2.

176 'Infundens oleum sanctum super caput eius', ROGER OF HOWDEN, *Chronica*, vol. 3, p. 10.

177 P.E. Schramm (*ibid.*, pp. 126–7) began this theory, repeated by D. Knowles (*The Episcopal Colleagues of Thomas Becket*, p. 154), which notes the provocative nature of the coronation of 1170. He based it on the account of the Young Henry's death given by Ralph de Diceto, who mentions the body of the prince wrapped in the cloths soaked in chrism on his coronation day: 'quas habuit in sua consecratione, lineis vestibus crismate delibutis'. 'Ymagines Historiarum', vol. 2, p. 20. The problem with it is that *oleum* and *chrisma* are often synonymous ('chrisma, oleum quo fideles unguntur', AUGUSTINE OF HIPPO, *PL*, 46, II, 1161). Apart from that, it is remarkable that no trace of this chrism is mentioned in the correspondence of Thomas Becket or the bulls of excommunication against the dignitaries participating in the Young Henry's coronation. For example, Herbert of Bosham, who goes into a long diatribe against the *consecratio*, which he calls an *execratio*, fails to use the word, 'Vita sancti Thome', pp. 458–60.

178 KANTOROWICZ, *The King's Two Bodies*, p. 336; BOUTET, *Charlemagne et Arthur*, pp. 69–70.

179   MASON, 'The Hero's Invincible Weapon', p. 131; LEYSER, *Medieval Germany and its Neighbours*, pp. 215–40.

180   KRYNEN, *L'Empire du roi*, p. 24.

181   CROUCH, *The Image of Aristocracy*, pp. 211–14.

182   *Historia Anglorum*, X, 40, p. 776.

183   GERVASE OF CANTERBURY, *Chronica*, p. 160. Cf. SCHRAMM, *A History of the English Coronation*, p. 57.

184   *The Correspondence of Thomas Becket*, nos 285–6, pp. 1216–24. Cf. WARREN, *Henry II*, p. 111. SCHRAMM, *A History of the English Coronation*, p. 58.

185   Because of the context in which the 1170 ceremony was played out, it seems to us most likely that the renewal of the consecration of the Young Henry in 1172 was only a simple ritual office of crown-wearing, as according to P.E. Schramm, *A History of the English Coronation*, p. 44. For the evidence, RAMSAY, *The Angevin Empire*, p. 162.

186   GILLINGHAM, *Richard I*, p. 149; VINCENT, 'Isabella of Angoulême', p. 184.

187   RICHARDSON, 'The Coronation in Mediaeval England', p. 122; SCHRAMM, *A History of the English Coronation*, p. 84.

188   D. CROUCH, *The Normans: The History of a Dynasty*, London, 2002, p. 181.

189   RICHARDSON, 'The Coronation in Mediaeval England', pp. 113–30; RICHARDSON and SAYLES, *The Governance of Medieval England*, p. 139.

190   RAMSAY, *The Angevin Empire*, p. 15; FRYDE, *Why Magna Carta?* pp. 52–3.

191   R. FOLZ, *Le Couronnement impérial de Charlemagne*, Paris, 1974, p. 176.

192   FRYDE, *Why Magna Carta?* p. 52.

193   ROGER OF HOWDEN, *Gesta*, vol. 2, pp. 72–3, and Chronica, vol. 4, p. 87, trans. BROSSARD-DANDRE and BESSON, *Richard de Coeur de Lion*, p. 61; ROGER OF WENDOVER, *Flores Historiarum*, pp. 286–7. Cf. SCHRAMM, *A History of the English Coronation*, pp. 46–7; CROUCH, *The Image of Aristocracy*, pp. 201–8.

194   ROGER OF HOWDEN, *Chronica*, vol. 2, p. 194. Cf. FLORI, *Richard Coeur de Lion*, pp. 57–8; HOLLISTER, 'Normandy, France and the Anglo-Norman *Regnum*', p. 238; BOUSSARD, 'Philippe Auguste et les Plantagenêt', p. 267.

195　GEOFFREY DE VIGEOIS, *Chronique*, pp. 422–3 and 'Ordo ad benedicendum ducem Aquitainiae', *RHF*, 12, pp. 451–3. P.E. Schramm (*A History of the English Coronation*, pp. 48–9), the most knowledgable man in coronation orders, saw Elias's text, whose oldest known version is the edition of J. Besli in 1641, a text incorporating many later revisions.

196　TREFFORT, 'Le comte de Poitiers', pp. 422–3.

197　BARRIERE, 'L'anneau de Valérie', pp. 14–17.

198　BOZOKY, 'Le culte des saints', p. 281.

199　STOCLET, 'A la recherche du ban perdu', pp. 374–6.

200　*The Correspondence of Thomas Becket*, no. 74, p. 298. Cf. FOREVILLE, 'Le sacre des rois anglo-normands et angevins', pp. 106–7.

201　*De Principis Instructione*, p. 5.

202　RICHARDSON and SAYLES, *The Governance of Medieval England*, p. 147.

203　COULSON, 'Fortress-Policy in Capetian Tradition', pp. 15–16, 23.

204　LEMARIGNIER, 'Autour de la royauté française', p. 20.

205　RODERICK, 'The Feudal Relations between the English Crown and the Welsh Princes', pp. 204–5; FLANAGAN, *Irish Society*, pp. 220, 234.

206　*Irish Society*, pp. 173–212.

207　SCHRAMM, *A History of the English Coronation*, p. 127.

208　LEMARIGNIER, *Hommage en marche*, p. 179.

209　MATTHEW PARIS, *Chronica majora*, vol. 2, p. 657.

210　HOLLISTER'Normandy, France and the Anglo-Norman *Regnum*', pp. 235, 238.

211　LEMARIGNIER, *Hommage en marche*, pp. 85–111, and pp. 104–5 for the felling of the elm at Gisors. As a place of meeting, the elm was the equivalent of the lime tree in the Germanic lands, W. ROSENER, *Peasants in the Middle Ages*, Oxford, 1996, p. 165.

212　*Sermones*, PL, 39, col. 2,334, cited by Hrabanus Maurus, *PL*, 108, col. 1,041.

213　*Homiliae in Evangelia*, Turnhout, 1999, trans into French. A. DE VOGUE and others, Le Barroux, 2000, I, 20, 13, p. 252.

214　*Physique* or *Liber subtilitatum*, III, 44, cap. 35, PL, 197, col. 1,239.

215　KRYNEN, *L'Empire du roi*, pp. 47–50. Cf. PANOFSKY, *Architecture gothique et pensée scolastique*, Paris, 1967.

216　BOURNAZEL, 'La royauté féodale', p. 445.

217 MACE *Les comtes de Toulouse*, p. 213.

218 *The* Gesta Normannorum Ducum, vol. 2, p. 286, where E. Van Houts, the editor, asserts with some reason that Robert de Torigny may have written this paragraph, disagreeing with the assumption of F. Lot, repeated by J-F. Lemarignier, *Hommage en marche*, pp. 96–100. It could be that the monk of Battle re-copied in his turn one of a number of lost texts about William the Conqueror still current in his day. Cf. the recent edition of the *Brevis Relatio*, VAN HOUTS, *History and Family Traditions*, VII, pp. 21–2, 45.

219 ROBERT DE TORIGNY, *Chronica*, p. 62. Cf. KRYNEN, *L'Empire du roi*, p. 47.

220 *Roman de Rou*, ed. HOLDEN, vv. 2,973–76, vol. 1, pp. 271–2. Cf. GILLINGHAM, *The Angevin Empire*, p. 124. As D. Crouch notes, Wace makes a point of of Duke Richard I's minority and his submission to Louis IV.

221 *RHF*, 16, pp. 110–11, nos 341–2.

222 *Materials for a History of Thomas Becket*, vol. 5, p. 134.

223 *Draco Normannicus*, III, 4, vv. 191–340, pp. 718–3. Cf. BEZZOLA, *La Cour d'Angleterre*, pp. 127–31, 138–9; HARRIS, 'Stephen of Rouen's *Draco Normannicus*'; HOLT, 'The End of the Anglo-Norman Realm', pp. 244–5.

224 BUC, *L'Ambiguïté du Livre*, pp. 116–18.

225 VAN EICKELS, ' "Hommagium" and "Amicitia" '. It should be noted in passing that there was no ambiguity about these acts, despite what has often been said concerning the relations between Philip Augustus and Richard the Lionheart. On this, cf. GILLINGHAM, *Richard I*, 84, 264–5, arguing against J. BOSWELL, *Christianity, Social Tolerance and Homosexuality*, Chicago, 1980, pp. 231, 298.

226 LEYSER, *Medieval Germany and its Neighbours*, pp. 215–40. Curiously none of the studies consulted questions the authenticity of Henry II's letter, whose only copy comes from an imperial panegyrist.

227 ROGER OF HOWDEN, *Chronica*, vol. 3, pp. 202–3 and 225–6. Cf. SCHRAMM, *A History of the English Coronation*, p. 54.

228 R. FOLZ, *L'Idée d'Empire en Occident du ve au xive siècle*, Paris, 1953, pp. 122–5.

229 CHENEY, *Innocent III*, pp. 326–56.

230 ADAM OF EYNSHAM, *Magna vita sancti Hugonis*, V, 5, p. 101.

231 WALTER MAP, *De Nugis Curialium*, V, 6, pp. 478, 484, PETER OF BLOIS, *Dialogus inter regem Henricum II et abbatem Bonnevallis*, p. 104. Cf. LEYSER, *Medieval Germany and its Neighbours*, p. 252.

232 *De Nugis Curialium*, V, 6, p. 484.

233 *Dialogus inter regem Henricum II et abbatem Bonnevallis*, p. 105.

234 *Jordan Fantosme's Chronicle*, nos 207–10, vv. 1950–1980, pp. 144–7.

235 JOHN LE TROUVÈRE, *L'Histoire de Guillaume le Maréchal*, vol. 2, pp. 96–7, cited by GILLINGHAM, *The Angevin Empire*, p. 102.

236 *De Principis Instructione*, III, 28, p. 304; ORDERIC VITALIS, *The Ecclesiastical History*, VIII, 10, vol. 4, pp. 184–9.

237 WILLIAM FITZ STEPHEN, *Vita sancti Thomae*, pp. 24–5, 29–33.

238 ADAM OF EYNSHAM, *Magna vita sancti Hugonis*, III, 10.

239 LEYSER, 'The Angevin Kings and the Holy Man', p. 59.

240 Forthcoming edition of Henry II's charters by N. Vincent, who has generously passed on this document, no. 4739H (1177–1189) featuring in passing in an inquistion of 1331 about a concession in favour of Butley Priory.

241 M. LEVER, *Le Sceptre et la marotte. Histoire des fous de cour*, Paris, 1983, pp. 119–20.

241 GOUTTEBROZE, 'Pourquoi congédier un historiographe'.

242 *Epistulae*, no. 14, col. 45. A reference kindly communicated by D. Crouch.

243 A letter enrolled in the *Rotuli Litterarum*, cited by MASON, 'Saint Wulfstan's Staff', p. 162, which identifies this book with Geoffrey Gaimar's.

245 CORNER, 'The *Gesta regis Henrici Secundi*', pp. 135–41.

246 GILLINGHAM, 'Royal Newsletters', p. 184.

247 CINGOLANI, 'Filologia e miti storiografici'; GOUTTEBROZE, 'Henri II Plantagenêt, patron des historiographes'; SHORT, 'Patrons and Polyglots', p. 245; GUENEE, , *Histoire et culture historique*, pp. 334–5.

248 R.W. Southern noted the freedom of expression and numerous anti-royal statements in English historians of the time, as opposed to their Capetian counterparts. He explained it as the unpopularity of the English tax regime. He concluded that 'in England we have a tradition of service without affection; in France a tradition of domesticity without, at this time, much professional service', *Medieval Humanism*, p. 151.

249 The link between Edward the Confessor and the coronation is mentioned explicitly in charters granted to Westminster by Henry II and Richard the Lionheart, copied into the chronicle of Richard of Cirencester in the second half of the fourteenth century, Rolls Series, 30, vol. 2, pp. 34–5.

250 BARLOW, *Edward the Confessor*, pp. xxiv, 274, 283–4.

251 AILRED, *Vita sancti Edwardi*, cols 738, 773–4. Cf. BOZOKY, 'Le culte des saints', p. 279. BARLOW, *Edward the Confessor*, pp. 247–8. This dream is found already in the *Vita*, written *c*.1064 × 1068, and in the *Gesta* of William of Malmesbury. It is, as is well known, repeated by the nun of Barking in her French translation of Ailred.

252 F. MORENZONI, 'La Vie d'Edouard le Confesseur d'Alexandre d'Ashby', in *Culture Politique des Plantagenêt*, pp. 241–52.

253 AILRED, *Genealogia*. Cf. CINGOLANI, 'Filologia e miti storiografici', p. 824.

254 NUN OF BARKING, *Vie de Saint Edouard*. Cf. LEGGE, *Anglo-Norman Literature*, pp. 60–72.

255 *The Heads of Religious Houses. England and Wales*: I, *940–1216*, ed. D. KNOWLES, C.N.L. BROOKE and V.C.M. LONDON, Cambridge, 2001, 2nd edn, p. 208. Cf. also the thesis in progress of E. Mitchell (Cambridge) which puts forward a proposed new date, difficult to establish, of 1175–1200 for the nun's work. The discovery of Mathilda's mother's first name was established by Mitchell, MITCHELL, 'Patrons and Politics in 12th-Century Barking Abbey'.

256 A. RENOUX, *Fécamp: du palais ducal au palais de Dieu*, Paris, 1991.

257 GOUTTEBROZE, *Le Précieux Sang de Fécamp*, pp. 18–20, 29–30. At the end of the Middle Ages the two historiographical traditions were combined: the name of Isaac was given to the nephew of Nicodemus who supposedly committed the Holy Blood to the sea, carried on the trunk of a fig tree which was miraculously washed up at Fécamp (*Ficus campi* = 'Fig tree of the field'), *ibid.*, pp. 65–78. Cf. VINCENT, *The Holy Blood*, pp. 69–70.

258 *Recueil des actes d'Henri II*, nos 221–3, vol. 1, pp. 358–61; ROBERT DE TORIGNY, *Chronica*, pp. 212–13; WACE, *Roman de Rou*, III, vv. 2,241–6, vol. 1, p. 244. CF. VAN HOUTS, *History and Family Traditions*, X, p. 115.

259 DUDO OF ST-QUENTIN, *De moribus et actis primorum Normannniae ducum*, pp. 293–8; WILLIAM OF MALMESBURY, *Gesta Regum*, X, p. 115.

260 GOUTTEBROZE, *Le Précieux Sang de Fécamp*, pp. 37–8, 78–83. Precision here in establishing the link between the Holy Blood and the Arthurian Grail legend in the time of the crusader King Richard is to be avoided (CHAOU, *L'Idéologie Plantagenêt*, p. 259, following J. Marx), as it is not mentioned before Robert de Boron at the beginning of the thirteenth century.

261 BENNETT, 'Poetry as History?', p. 37. D. Crouch doubts, however, that the term *vaslet* by which Wace indentifies himself was a synonym for a military man.

262 Cf. JAEGER, 'Patrons and the Beginnings of Courtly Romance', pp. 56–7. This dedication does not appear in any version of the Anglo-Norman *Brut*. It is only known by v. 22 in Anglo-Saxon translation in one of two old manuscripts that Layamon made a quarter of a century later (*Brut/Layamon*, ed. G.L. Brook and R.F. Leslie, Oxford, 1963). This manusript (Cotton Caligula) is certainly better and closer to the original than the Cotton Otho version which does not mention Eleanor (see introduction to the translation by R. Allen, London, 1992). Benoît de Sainte-Maure would draft an identical dedication to profit from the patronage of Henry II in his *Roman de Troie*.

263 'Li reis Henris li Secunt;/ cil me fist duner, Deus lui rende,/ a Baieues une provende', *Roman de Rou*, vv. 172–174, vol. 1, p. 167. Cf. *La cour d'Angleterre*, pp. 180–3, TYSON, 'Patronage of French Vernacular History Writers', pp. 193–8; SHORT, 'Patrons and Polyglots', p. 238. E. Van Houts shows that other members of Wace's family had been canons of Bayeux in the past, which infleunced the king in his favour, *History and Family Traditions*, X, p. 105.

264 VAN HOUTS, *History and Family Traditions*, X, pp. 114–16.

265 GOUTTEBROZE, 'Pourquoi congédier un historiographe', pp. 295–6, 304–7.

266 SOUTHERN, *Medieval Humanism*, p. 155; BLACKER, *The Faces of Times*, p. 119; HOUTS, *History and Family Traditions*, XI, p. 118.

267 BENNETT, 'Poetry as History?', p. 36. Wace's supposed attachment for the rebellious queen, suggested by R. Lejeune ('Rôle littéraire d'Aliénor d'Aquitaine', p. 26), is simply not sustainable as the cause of his disgrace, cf. GOUTTEBROZE, 'Pourquoi congédier un historiographe', pp. 290–1.

268 Cf. *contra* DRONKE, 'Peter of Blois and Poetry', p. 187, which looks at the question of Benoît's supposed poetical superiority over Wace in the view of Henry II, supposedly a connoisseur of verse. On the contrary, J-G. Gouttebroze ('Pourquoi congédier un historiographe', p. 290) finds Wace's writing 'more vigorous, economical and expressive' than Benoît's. Each to his own taste.

269 *Le Roman de Rou*, vv. 11,420–4, vol. 2, p. 307. Unfortunately Wace gives no date for his disgrace, which would have better allowed us to pin down the cause.

270 BEZZOLA, *La cour d'Angleterre*, p. 289.

271 At least according to SCHRIMER and BROICH, *Studien zum literarischen Patronat in England*, pp. 86–8, where Wace's work rate is advanced as the cause of his dismissal.

272 VAN HOUTS, *History and Family Traditions*, XI, pp. 118–19.
     Cf., however, the cautionary words by P. Damian-Grint (*The New
     Historians*, pp. 194–7) on the misleading nature of his 'authorial
     self-presentation' which ought not to be interpreted as a sign of
     'honesty' or 'critical judgement'.

273 BEZZOLA, *La cour d'Angleterre*, pp. 194–7.

274 TEUNIS, 'Benoit of Ste-Maure and William the Conqueror's *amor*'.

275 GOUTTEBROZE, 'Pourquoi congédier un historiographe', pp. 308–10.

276 ORDERIC VITALIS, *The Ecclesiastical History*, XIII, 21–2.
     Cf. J. BRADBURY, 'Geoffroy V of Anjou', pp. 21, 27–8 and POWER,
     'What did the Frontier of Angevin Normandy Comprise?' p. 200.

277 S. FARMER, *Communities of St Martin: Legend and Ritual in Medieval
     Tours*, Ithaca NY, 1991, pp. 76–95.

278 *Chroniques des comtes d'Anjou*, ed. HALPHEN and POUPARDIN,
     pp. vii–viii and xxvii–lxv. Cf. CHAUOU, *L'Idéologie Plantagenêt*, p. 53;
     BACHRACH, 'The Idea of Angevin Empire', pp. 298–9.

279 HUGH DE CLAYE (CLERIIS), 'De Majoratu et senescalcia Franciae';
     Cf. MIREAUX, *La Chanson de Roland et l'histoire de France*, pp. 84–92.
     N. Vincent's forthcoming edition of Henry II's charters contain many
     mentions of Hugh de Claye, thanks to Professor Vincent for his kindness
     in helping identify Hugh.

280 MIREAUX, *La Chanson de Roland et l'histoire de France*, pp. 79–83,
     101–3. Cf. SCHRIMER and BROICH, *Studien zum literarischen Patronat
     in England*, pp. 104–8; KELLER, 'The *Song of Roland*', pp. 244, 248–9,
     256.

281 MIREAUX, *La Chanson de Roland et l'histoire de France*, pp. 98–101;
     BUMKE, *Courtly Culture*, p. 77; SOUTHERN, *Medieval Humanism*,
     p. 139; BEZZOLA, *La cour d'Angleterre*, pp. 302.

282 *Le Guide du Pélerin de Saint-Jacques de Compostelle*, ed. VEILLIARD,
     pp. 24–6, 78–80.

283 LOT, 'Geoffroy Grisegonelle dans l'épopée'.

284 *Chanson d'Aspremont*, ed. MANDACH, vol. 3, p. 1, vol. 4, pp. 12–27, 54.
     See, however, the precisely opposite view in BOUTET, *Charlemagne et
     Arthur*, pp. 474–82: 'il est exclu de voir dans Aspremont une oeuvre de
     propagande en faveur des Plantagenêt' (p. 478).

285 AMBROISE, *L'Estoire de la Guerre Sainte*, vv. 516, 4,188, 8,491–3,
     cols 15, 112, 227. Cf. VAN WARD, *Etudes sur l'origine et la formation
     de la Chanson d'Aspremont*, p. 263.

286 J. SUBRENAT, *Etude sur Gaydon, chanson de geste du XIIIe siècle*, Aix, 1974; BOUTET, *Charlemagne et Arthur*, pp. 99–100, 397–402, 530–5; MIREAUX, *La Chanson de Roland et l'histoire de France*, pp. 93–6.

287 FOLZ, *Le Souvenir et la légende de Charlemagne*, pp. 197–207.

288 *Epistulae*, no. 14, col. 45, and *Compendium in Job*, col. 810–11; 'Ymagines Historiarum', vol. 2, p. 178; *Chronicle*, no. 10, vv. 112–114, p. 11; GIRAUT DE BORNEIL, *The Cansos and Sirventes*, no. 75, v. 75, p. 476; BERTRAN DE BORN, *L'Amour et la Guerre*, no. 12, v. 70, p. 224.

289 BERTRAN DE BORN, *L'Amour et la Guerre*, no. 10, v. 42, p. 190; no. 28, v. 23, p. 576; *De Principis Instructione*, I, 17, p. 74. Cf. BEZZOLA, *La cour d'Angleterre*, pp. 80, 201–2; LEWIS, *Le Sang royal*, pp. 146, 150–1, 155.

290 SPIEGEL, 'The *Reditus Regni*'.

291 CHAUOU, *L'Idéologie Plantagenêt*.

292 JACKSON, 'The Arthur of History'. The appendices in CHAMBERS, *Arthur of Britain*, pp. 234–79, contain most of the Latin sources relevant to Arthur.

293 *The Mabinogion*, pp. 95–136.

294 WESTON, 'Waucherie de Denain and Bleheris'; ANGLADE, *Les Troubadours et les Bretons*, pp. 25, 41–2, 47; BEZZOLA, *La cour d'Angleterre*, pp. 67–8, 163–4, 291–2, and vol. 2 (pt 2) pp. 318–20; NEWSTEAD, 'The Origin and Growth of the Tristan Legend'; NYKROG, 'The Rise of Literary Fiction', p. 602.

295 WRIGHT, 'Geoffrey of Monmouth and Bede', and 'Geoffrey of Monmouth and Gildas', NYKROG, 'The Rise of Literary Fiction', p. 595.

296 There is a good context for Geoffrey in ASHE, 'Geoffroy de Montmouth', and, on the political background, GILLINGHAM, *The English in the Twelfth Century*, pp. 19–39.

297 CRICK, *The Historia Regum*.

298 DAMIAN-GRINT, 'Redating the Royal Brut Fragment'.

299 LEGGE, *Anglo-Norman Literature*, pp. 28–32; SHORT, 'Gaimar's Epilogue'; DAMIAN-GRINT, *The New Historians*, pp. 49–50.

300 The problem of the egalitarian or hierarchical nature of the Round Table has spawned a sizeable literature among medievalists. Wace indeed stresses the equality it imposed, but in practice Arthur had precedence there. He laid down that he take the seat first among the knights; his power is all the more evident there as it is around the Table that his commands put a final end to his knights' rivalries. Its circular shape might well conjure up cosmic power,

the universality of royal power, SCHMOLKE-HASSELMAN, 'The Round Table: Ideal, Fiction Reality'; GUERREAU-JALABERT, 'Alimentation symbolique et symbolique de la table ronde'.

301 FLETCHER, *The Arthurian Material in the Chronicles*, pp. 127–42; BEZZOLA, *La Cour d'Angleterre*, pp. 154–7; BOUTET, *Charlemagne et Arthur*, pp. 157–63, 185, 199–203.

302 GILLINGHAM, *The English in the Twelfth Century*, p. 20; NYKROG, 'The Rise of Literary Fiction', pp. 595–6.

303 NEWBURGH, *Historia rerum Anglicanum*, ii, pp. 11–12, 17–18; GERALD OF BARRY, *Itinerarium Kambriae*, I, 5, p. 57. Cf. BEZZOLA, *La Cour d'Angleterre*, pp. 120–2; GRANSDEN, *Historical Writing in England*, pp. 264–5; GILLINGHAM, *The English in the Twelfth Century*, pp. 22–3; ROBERTSON, 'Geoffrey of Monmouth and the Translation of Insular Historiography', p. 53.

304 *Life of Merlin*, vv. 1,511–1,515. Cf. *Ibid.*, p. 9; P. ZUMTOR, *Merlin le Prophète*, Geneva, 1973, p. 38.

305 JOHN OF CORNWALL, *Prophetia Merlini*, ed. CURLEY.

306 Cited by GILLINGHAM, *The English in the Twelfth Century*, p. 33; L. JOHNSON and A. BELL, 'The Anglo-Norman *Description of England*', *Anglo-Norman Anniversary Essays*, ed. I SHORT, London, 1993, pp. 11–47.

307 BLACKER, '*Ne vuil sun livre translater*', and, *idem*, 'Where Wace feared to Tread'. Arthurian memory was still alive and well amongst the Welsh princes at the end of the thirteenth century. In 1284, 'Arthur's jewel' was part of Llywelyn ap Gruffudd's treasure captured by Edward I, R.R. DAVIES, *Wales, 1063–1415*, Oxford, 1991, p. 355.

308 GILLINGHAM, *The English in the Twelfth Century*, p. 253.

309 BULLOCK-DAVIES, 'Chrétien de Troyes and England', pp. 59–60. Cf. BEZZOLA, *La Cour d'Angleterre*, pp. 310–11.

310 HOEPFFNER, 'The Breton Lais', pp. 116–21; BEZZOLA, *La Cour d'Angleterre*, p. 305; introduction to Y. de Pontfarcy's edition of MARIE DE FRANCE, *L'Espurgatoire seint Patriz*; CHAUOU, *L'Idéologie Plantagenêt*, p. 248.

311 NOBLE, 'Romance in England and Normandy'; NEWSTEAD, 'The Origin and Growth of the Tristan Legend'.

312 These two works were edited and translated in 1984 and 1988 by M.L. Day, who made a judicious study of the problem of authorship. The author was designated only by the letter 'R'. Robert de Torigny's responsibility is, however, contested by J-Y. Tilliette in his recent review

of ECHARD, *Arthurian Narrative*, following J.D. Bruce and R.S. Loomis, who believed the works to belong to the thirteenth century, for which see, *CCM*, 45, 2002, p. 176.

313   JONES, 'Richard the Lionheart in German Literature', pp. 76–7; CHAUOU, *L'Idéologie Plantagenêt*, p. 248.

314   BERTRAN DE BORN, *L'Amour et la Guerre*, no. 22, vv. 33–40. Cf. ANGLADE, *Les Troubadours et les Bretons*, pp. 60–77.

315   *Liber de confessione sacramentali*, PL, 207, col. 1088D. Cf. LOOMIS, *Studies in Medieval Literature*, p. 4; DRONKE, 'Peter of Blois and Poetry', pp. 198–9.

316   *Le Miroir de la charité. Sermons de l'amitié spirituelle*, trans. C. DUMONT, Paris, 1961, II, 17, p. 50.

317   *Dialogus miraculorum*, IV, 36.

318   LOOMIS, *Arthurian Legend*, pp. 4–10, 31–6; SCHMITT, *Les Revenants*, pp. 140–41.

319   For the following paragraph, refer to GRANSDEN, 'The Growth of Glastonbury'. A French translation is to be found in FARAL, *La Légende arthurienne*, pp. 437–41. Cf. likewise CHAUOU, *L'Idéologie Plantagenêt*, pp. 203–20; BARBER, 'The *Vera Historia de Morte Arthuri*'.

320   *De Principis Instructione*, I, 20, pp. 126–8.

321   MALMESBURY, *Gesta Regum*, III, 287, p. 520.

322   WOOD, 'Guenevere at Glastonbury', p. 28.

323   MASON, 'Rocamadour in Quercy above all other churches'; *eadem*, 'The Hero's Invincible Weapon', pp. 127–9.

324   BRESC, 'Excalibur en Sicile'; CASSARD, 'Arthur est vivant!', pp. 144–5; SCHMITT, *Les Revenants*, pp. 140–3.

325   FLETCHER, *The Arthurian Material in the Chronicles*, p. 162; BROUGHTON, *The Legends of King Richard I*, pp. 97–9; CASSARD, 'Arthur est vivant!', p. 143.

326   Wulfston had been nominated to his see by Edward the Confessor. His persecutors were some of the Conqueror's men who reproached him for being unable to understand French. King John made use of the anecdote before the papal legates to support his right to choose bishops in the way his sainted predecessor had, MASON, 'St Wulfstan's Staff'.

327   LOOMIS, 'Tristram and the House of Anjou', pp. 29–30; MASON, 'The Hero's Invincible Weapon', pp. 131–2.

328   The point is whether the Tristram Saga is translating a lost passage by Thomas (which is Loomis's theory in *Arthurian Legend*, pp. 44–8,

attributing the arms to Henry II, and of BRAULT, *Early Blazon*, p. 21, who attributes them rather to Richard the Lionheart) or if it was invented to flatter Haakon V (1217–1263) king of Norway, who carried similar arms (PASTOUREAU, *L'Hermine et le sinople*, pp. 280–3).

329 BOUTET, *Charlemagne et Arthur*, pp. 102–3.

330 *Expugnatio Hibernica*, pp. 18–149. Cf. FLANAGAN, *Irish Society*, p. 49.

331 R[OBERT DE TORIGNY] *The Rise of Gawain*, pp. 112–15. A *castrum puellarum*, the same name as in the romance, is mentioned in a treaty with the king of Scotland in 1175, ROGER OF HOWDEN, *Chronica*, vol. 2, p. 81.

332 FLECHTER, *The Arthurian Material in the Chronicles*, p. 154.

333 For instance these verses of around 1250, still carrying on this tradition: 'A Bruto dicti Britones timuere Ricardum [the Lionheart]/ cui velut Arhturo colla subacta dabunt,/ scilicet Arthuro qui straverat agmina Romae', JOHN DE GARLANDE, *De triumphis ecclesie*, p. 52.

334 *Liber de compositione castri Ambaziae*, p. 10.

335 CHAUOU, *L'Idéologie Plantagenêt*, pp. 44–5, 54–5.

336 The popularity of Nicodemus in Normandy comes – as has been seen – from the cult of the Holy Blood.

337 ANDREW DE COUTANCES, *Roman des Franceis*, ed. HOLDEN, cf. PARIS *La Littérature*, pp. 47–51.

338 J.C. Holt ('The End of the Anglo-Norman Realm', p. 253) plays down the political impact of the *roman*, making much of its burlesque tone and the absurdities of the English king 'Arflet'. But it could be said in reply that irony is another sort of weapon and that the 'king of the beerdrinkers', always portrayed with sympathy, is cited at the beginning of the poem in reply to the French song which Andrew means to retaliate.

339 *Roman des Franceis*, ed. HOLDEN, vv. 45–58, translated in PARIS *La Littérature*, pp. 45–6.

340 RICHARD OF DEVIZES, *Chronicon*, p. 64; WILLIAM OF NEWBURGH, *Historia rerum Anglicarum*, II, 28, p. 174. Cf. PARTNER, *Serious Entertainments*, pp. 98–9; MORTIMER, *Angevin England*, p. 239.

341 GILLINGHAM, *The English in the Twelfth Century*, pp. 3–18, 41–58, 69–162.

342 *Draco Normannicus*, II, 17–23, vv. 941–1,283, pp. 695–708. Cf. BEZZOLA, *La Cour d'Angleterre*, pp. 132–6; FLETCHTER, *The Arthurian Material in the Chronicles*, p. 145; HARRIS, 'Stephen of Rouen's *Draco Normannicus*'.

343   These were formalized in 1933 by J.S.P. Tatlock ('King Arthur in *Normannicus Draco*'), and are followed here as in the work of all our recent predecessors, especially, DAY, 'The Letter from King Arthur to Henry II', and HARRIS, 'Stephen of Rouen's *Draco Normannicus*'.

344   GREENE, 'Qui croit au retour d'Arthur'.

345   TATLOCK, 'King Arthur in *Normannicus Draco*', pp. 44–5; BEZZOLA, *La Cour d'Angleterre*, pp. 129–30. Ralph de Diceto uses the same prophecy of 'the eagle from the broken union' – undoubtedly the most popular of Merlin's prophecies in the twelfth century – when Richard the Lionheart became king to the great joy of Eleanor of Aquitaine, MARTINDALE, 'Eleanor of Aquitaine: the Last Years', pp. 142–3. Certain prophecies about the conquest of Ireland appear on the continent, where a chronicle of Tours explicitly cited Merlin, *Chronicon turonense*, p. 137.

346   RALPH OF COGGESHALL, Chronicon, p. 146; PARTNER, *Serious Entertainments*, pp. 64–6.

347   *The Letters of John of Salisbury*, nos 173, 292, vol. 2, pp. 134–7, 668–9; *Materials for a History of Thomas Becket*, vol. 5, p. 292; CROUCH, William Marshal, p. 22. Cf. BLACKER, *The Faces of Times*, p. 39; BARTLETT, 'Political Prophecy in Gerald of Wales'.

348   BOUTET, *Charlemagne et Arthur*, pp. 510–11.

349   This draws on an unpublished article of C. Girbea, 'Limites du contrôle des Plantagenêt', to whom sincere thanks.

350   BEAUNE, *Naissance de la nation France*, pp. 19–54.

351   CHAUOU, *L'Idéologie Plantagenêt*, pp. 46–9, 90–3, 171–81.

352   BEZZOLA, *La Cour d'Angleterre*, p. 271, after vv. 971–2 of the manuscript edited by L. Constans (Paris, 1890), since these verses did not match the version published by G. Raynaud de Lage.

353   A.K. Bate, the introduction to his edition of JOSEPH OF EXETER, *Iliade*, pp. 4–13, and p. 21 for Peter de Saintes. Only 22 verses in two fragments survive of the *Antiocheis*: one of these fragments a eulogy of Arthur, ed. BEZZOLA, *La Cour d'Angleterre*, p. 146, n. 2. For the Young Henry, V, v. 534, ed. GOMPF, p. 177, trans. ROBERTS, pp. 63–4.

354   *Architrenius*, V, 17, v. 443, p. 140. This 'fifth Phoebus' is not specifically identified, and for E. Wetherbee, the poem's editor, identifying him as Archbishop Walter of Rouen and making him the dedicatee of the work, *ibid.*, p. 262, n. 27. However, Henry II is the object of a previous eulogy, V, 4, v. 87, p. 120. He appears as the latest in the lineage of Anchises, then of Arthur, which ends the 'fifth Phoebus', who cannot be Walter, but only the king.

355 *De Nugis Curialium*, V, 1, p. 404; Anticlaudianus, cited by CLANCHY, *England and its Rulers*, p. 136; BERTRAN DE BORN, *L'Amour et la Guerre*, no. 2, v. 7, p. 44, and no. 3, v. 9, p. 56, cf. pp. lxxvii–lxxviii.

356 P. ZUMTOR, *La Lettre et la Voix. De la 'littérature' médiévale*, Paris, 1987.

For and against the king

1 For what follows, cf. HOLT, *Magna Carta*, and also RICHARDSON and SAYLES, *The Governance of Medieval England*, pp. 368–9.

2 VINCENT, *Peter des Roches*, pp. 114–34.

3 HOLT, *The Northerners*, pp. 61–78.

4 HOLT, *Magna Carta*, pp. 24–6.

5 FRYDE, *Why Magna Carta?* pp. 82–3, 96.

6 POWICKE, *Stephen Langton*.

The aristocracy: between rebellion and submission

1 *Tractatus de Legibus et consuetudinibus regni Angliae*, p. 2, following the adage of the *Institutes*, I, II, 6: 'Quod principi placuit legis habet vigorem'. Cf. TIERNEY, *Church law and Constitutional Thought in the Middle Ages*, IV, pp. 296–8, 315–16; JOLLIFFE, *Angevin Kingship*, p. 18; RICHARDSON and SAYLES, *The Governance of Medieval England*, p. 143.

2 JOLLIFFE, *Angevin Kingship*, pp. 5–6, 24–9.

3 BALDWIN, 'La décennie décisive'.

4 'If we study eleventh- and twelfth-century texts, it appears that nobility there is completely integrated with the idea of knighthood, that is to say that it was but necessary to be a knight to enjoy all the privileges of the class we call the nobility', *Essai sur l'origine de la noblesse en France au Moyen Age*, Paris, 1902, p. 370. At he beginning of his book, P. Guilhiermoz defined nobility as 'a social class, whose privileges were recognised by law, deriving entirely from the fact of birth', *ibid*. p. 1.

5 'Sur la passé de la noblesse française: quelques jalons de recherche', *Annales d'histoire économique et sociale*, 8, 1936, p. 366.

6 *La Société féodale*, Paris, 1968 (5th edn), pp. 445–60.

7 'Un problème d'histoire comparée: la ministérialité en France et en Allemagne', *Revue d'histoire du droit*, 1928, p. 89.

8   *Ibid.*, p. 80.

9   Cf. principally, K.F. WERNER, *Naissance de la noblesse. L'essor des élites politiques en Europe*, Paris, 1998.

10 DUBY, *Hommes et structures du moyen age*, p. 343. Cf. *idem*, *La Société au xie et xiie siècles dans la région mâconnaise*, Paris, 1979, pp. 470–4.

11 D. BOUTET and A. STRUBEL, Littérature politique et société dans la France du Moyen Age, Paris, 1979, pp. 110–14; J. BATANY, *Les origines et la formation du thème des états du monde*, unpubd thesis, University of Paris IV, 1979, pp. 533–45; V. SERVERAT, *La Pourpre et la Glèbe. Rhétorique des états de la société dans l'Espagne médiévale*, Grenoble, 1997.

12 *The Image of Aristocracy*, p. 177.

13 J. MORSEL, 'L'invention de la noblesse en Haute Allemagne à la fin du Moyen Age. Contribution à l'étude de la sociogenèse de la Noblesse médiévale', *Mélanges Philippe Contamine*, ed. J. PAVIOT and J. VERGER, Paris, 2000, pp. 533–45; P. CONTAMINE, *La noblesse au royaume de France de Philippe le Bel à Louis XII*, Paris, 1997, p. 329, n. 1.

14 On the subject of this identification, cf. D. CROUCH, *The Image of Aristocracy*, p. 141: 'It was the decisions of Henry II and his advisers that did more than anything else to establish the English knight as an aristocrat'.

15 'Sunt exempti . . . omnes milites et omnes de milite de uxore propria procreati', *L'Ancienne Coutume de Normandie*, ed. W.L. de CRUCHY, Jersey, 1881, chap. 15, p. 44. A fifteenth-century glossator made the logical comment on this passage as follows: 'Dans la division des états, l'état de noblesse est appelé état de chevalerie', GUILHIERMOZ, *Essai sur l'origine de la noblesse*, p. 145, after Bibliothèque nationale de France ms fr 2765, fol. 45.

16 HAJDU, *A History of the Nobility of Poitou*, p. 29; C. JENNEAU, 'La construction de châteaux et la 'mutation féodale', unpubd D.E.A. thesis, Poitiers, 2000. The context reveals that these *servientes* are not 'serjeants' in the military sense, but rather the equivalent of the *servi* in other regions.

17 'Documents inédits pour servir à l'histoire de l'abbaye de Sainte-Croix de Poitiers', ed. P. de MONSABERT, *Revue Mabillon*, 9, 1913–14, no. 11.

18 *Liber Niger Scaccarii*, vol. 1, pp. 49–340; *The Red Book of the Exchequer*, pp. 186–445; ROUND, *Feudal England*, p. 225; STENTON, *First Century of English Feudalism*, pp. 136–9. The most recent and authoritative study of the Inquest of 1166 can be found in KEEFE, *Feudal Assessments and the Political Community*.

19 *Les registres de Philippe Auguste*, ed. J. BALDWIN, Paris, 1992, vol. 7, pp. 267–308.

20 *Rotuli de Dominabus.*

21 *Gesta Henrici*, vol. 1, pp. 56–7.

22 STRICKLAND, 'Against the Lord's Anointed', p. 58.

23 AURELL, *La noblesse en Occident*, pp. 69–82; FLORI, *Chevaliers et chevalerie*, pp. 64–88.

24 CROUCH, *The Image of Aristocracy*, p. 141.

25 'Coram militibus meis qui tunc presentes aderant', *Recueil de documents relatifs à l'abbaye de Montierneuf de Poitiers (1076–1319)*, ed. F. VILLARD, Poitiers, 1973, no. 108, p. 176. Cf. HAJDU, *A History of the Nobility of Poitou*, p. 30, which brings together similar references.

26 Between 1150 and 1250 seven earldoms disappeared, and three new ones were created, MORTIMER, *Angevin England*, p. 79.

27 CROUCH, *The Image of Aristocracy*, p. 73. Although, as J. Gillingham notes, this ceremony was only described around 1200 by Roger of Howden, a historian with some interest in ritual. Maybe it was earlier in origin.

28 BILLORE, 'La noblesse normande', pp. 157–8.

29 *Recueil des actes de Philippe Auguste, roi de France*, ed. H-F. LABORDE, C. PETIT-DUTAILLIS and J. MONICAT, Paris, 1943, vol. 2, p. 156, no. 68. Cf. VINCENT, *Peter des Roches*, pp. 22–5, and J. EVERARD, *Brittany and the Angevins*, pp. 157–71.

30 ROGER OF HOWDEN, *Chronica*, vol. 3, pp. 9–12; and *Gesta Henrici*, vol. 2, pp. 79–83.

31 These problems are approached from another direction in J. GILLINGHAM, *The English in the Twelfth Century*, pp. 259–76.

32 *De Principis Instructione*, I, 1, pp. 8–9, a passage commented on in BUC, 'Principes gentium', p. 317, and *L'Ambiguité du Livre*, pp. 147–61.

33 BYNUM, 'Did the Twelfth Century discover the Individual?'

34 *Chronique des ducs de Normandie*, ed. FAHLIN, vv. 28,832–40.

35 *De Nugis Curialium*, I, 10, pp. 12–15. One could object that Claudian himself, around the year 400, is himself echoing a similar obsession with legal status, and that the repetition of his arguments by Walter Map is responding to the survival of an ancient rhetorical model, indeed the repetition of universal reactionary themes in all literature. But, unlike the literary scholar, it is the historian's job to look at the text as a text in its 'intertextuality' but to put it in its 'context' so as to analyse it as a reflection – however distorted and pale – of the social reality of its own day.

36 RALPH NIGER, *Chronica*, p. 67. Cf. TÜRK, *Nugae Curialium*, p. 179.

37 *Epistulae*, no. 49, col. 147.

38 *Epistulae*, no. 3, col. 8; *De Principis Instructione*, I, 15, p. 51.

39 *The Correspondence of Thomas Becket*, no. 96, p. 432 and note 15. The quotations from Juvenal are drawn from *Satires*, VIII, 20.

40 CROUCH, 'The Hidden History of the Twelfth Century'; *idem*, *William Marshal*.

41 T.S.R. BOASE, *Death in the Middle Ages: Mortality, Judgement and Remembrance*, London, 1972, pp. 73–81; CROUCH, 'The Culture of Death in the Anglo-Norman World'.

42 *The Chronicle of Battle Abbey*, p. 214.

43 CROUCH, *William Marshal*, pp. 202–3.

44 M. PASTOUREAU, *Manuel d'héraldique*, Paris, 1997, pp. 47–55.

45 *Foedera, conventiones etc*, I, i, 65. Cf. GILLINGHAM, *Richard I*, pp. 278–9; J. BARKER, *The Tournament in England (1100–1400)*, Woodbridge, 1986, pp. 11, 53–6.

46 FLORI, 'La chevalerie selon Jean de Salisbury'.

47 *Layettes du trésor des chartes*, ed. A. TEULET, Paris, 1863, vol. 1, no. 433 (2 IV 1195–13 I 1196). Cf. POWER, 'L'aristocratie Plantagenêt', p. 127.

48 Cf. *Le Reglement des conflits au Moyen Age*, ed. S.H.M.E.S., Paris, 2001.

49 BROWN, 'Royal Castle-Building'.

50 BEAUROY, 'Centralisation et histoire sociale'; BOORMAN, 'The Sheriffs of Henry II'.

51 *Ymagines Historiarum*, vol. 1, p. 371.

52 *The Correspondence of Thomas Becket*, no. 112, p. 542.

53 ALTHOFF, 'Ira regis'. Cf. also the letter of March 1165 in which Bishop Arnulf of Lisieux dwelt on the king's 'innate ferocity', *Letters of Arnulf of Lisieux*, ed. BARLOW, pp. 69–88.

54 GREEN, *The Aristocracy of Norman England*, p. 264.

55 'Military incompetence, crushing defeat, meant to contemporaries failure to act the part of a king. A defeated king lost the respect and eventually the loyalty of his barons', RICHARDSON and SAYLES, *The Governance of Medieval England*, p. 366.

56 STRICKLAND, 'Against the Lord's Anointed'.

57 On the introduction of Roman Law into England, cf. KANTOROWICZ and SMALLEY, 'An English Theologian's View of Roman Law'. John of Salisbury, instructed in the theory of opposition to tyranny, devoted a long digression to the universal duty of loyalty to the head of the body politic and to the crime of *lèse-majesté*, based on the Code and the Digest, *Policraticus*, VI, 25.

58 GREEN, *The Aristocracy of Norman England*, pp. 257–64.

59 At least if Roger of Howden is to be believed, *Chronica*, vol. 1, p. 273, but Roger undermines his own case by mentioning Patrick's unlikely return from Compostella. John le Trouvère (*L'Histoire de Guillaume le Maréchal*, n. 52, vv. 1,600–1,652) fixes the crime rather on troops of his brother, Geoffrey de Lusignan. Robert de Torigny and Gervase of Tilbury point the finger at the Poitevins in general, while Ralph de Diceto says only that Patrick was killed by the blow of a lance in Aquitaine. Cf. the excellent analysis of P. MEYER in his edition of John le Trouvère, vol. 3, pp. 25–6. n. 6, and GILLINGHAM, *Richard I*, p. 90, on Geoffrey de Lusignan's assassination of a representative of the duke of Aquitaine in 1188, which might have caused confusion in the minds of English chroniclers with the events of 1168.

60 HAJDU, *A History of the Nobility of Poitou*, p. 312; CAO CARMICHAEL DE BAGLY, 'Savary de Mauléon', p. 274.

61 TORIGNY, *Chronicle*, p. 218; WILLIAM OF NEWBURGH, *Historia rerum Anglicarum*, II, 5, vol. 1, p. 325. Cf. BARLOW, *Thomas Becket*, pp. 84–9.

62 At the beginning of the twelfth century, blinding and castration of those who plotted against the king was still widespread, C.W. HOLLISTER, 'Royal Acts of Mutilation', *Albion*, 10, 1978, pp. 330–40.

63 GILLINGHAM, *The English in the Twelfth Century*, pp. 209–32.

64 GREEN, *The Aristocracy of Norman England*, p. 264; JOLLIFFE, *Angevin Kingship*, pp. 44–5, 67–77 and 311–13.

65 THOMPSON, 'The Lords of Laigle', pp. 191–2.

66 Cf. the notable discussions on this subject in STRICKLAND, *War and Chivalry*, pp. 291–323.

67 GERALD OF BARRY, *Itinerarium Kambriae*, I, 2; GEOFFREY DE VIGEOIS, *Chronique*, p. 443. In the ascetic literature of the time, the mercenary or slave represent servile obedience in bad grace to God's will, BERNARD DE CLAIRVAUX, *On the Love of God*, PL, 182, XIII.

68 J.O. PRESTWICH, 'War and Finance in the Anglo-Norman State', *Transactions of the Royal Historical Society*, 5th ser., 4, 1954, pp. 19–43; C.W. HOLLISTER, *The Military Organisation of Norman England*, Oxford, 1965, pp. 195–204.

69 'The 1168 and 1172 levies were not a factor in the rebellion', *Feudal Assessments and the Political Community*, p. 117. T.K. Keefe distances himself here from J.E.A. Jolliffe and W.L. Warren.

70 This is the point of view of a weighty article, which could do with being better nuanced on this point, BOUSSARD, 'Les mercenaires au xiie siècle'.

71 PRESTWICH, 'The Military Household of the Norman Kings'; CHURCH, *The Household Knights of King John*, p. 14.

72 To be more precise, with $94^3/_4$ following the *Infeodationes baronum* of 1172, CROUCH, *William Marshal*, 25n.

73 EVERARD, *Brittany and the Angevins*, pp. 183–203, which demonstrates that the custom of primogeniture was already widespread amongst the Breton aristocracy, but that it was not incompatible with the laws which systematized feudal practices.

74 RAMSAY, *The Angevin Empire*, pp. 208–9.

75 CHURCH, *The Household Knights of King John*, pp. 74–99.

76 HAJDU, *A History of the Nobility of Poitou*, p. 317, which, however, remarks with some cause that the date of 1199 is likewise the date when a fief rent is first mentioned in England, and that the development might be related to the progress of charter enrolments by the English chancery.

77 JOLLIFFE, Angevin Kingship, p. 218, and for a later period, F. LACHAUD, 'Textiles, Furs and Liveries: a Study of the Great Wardrobe of Edward I (1272–1307)', unpublished DPhil thesis, Oxford, 1992.

78 THOMAS, *Vassals, Heiresses and Thugs*, p. 170.

79 This is the argument maintained by COSS, *Lordship, Knighthood and Locality*, pp. 19, 264–304, but contested by CARPENTER, 'Was there a crisis of the knightly class?' pp. 721–52.

80 *De Nugis Curialium*, I, 10, p. 12.

81 *Dialogus Scaccarii*, p. 111. Cf. CROUCH, *The Image of Aristocracy*, p. 148.

82 THOMAS, *Vassals, Heiresses and Thugs*, pp. 166–7.

83 GREEN, *The Aristocracy of Norman England*, p. 381.

84 BERTRAN DE BORN, *L'Amour et la Guerre*, no. 8, vv. 78–88, p. 135, and no. 36, vv. 25–32, p. 715.

85 ROBERT DE TORIGNY, *The Story of Meriadoc*, p. 102 and p. xiii of M.L. Day's introduction.

86 GREEN, *The Aristocracy of Norman England*, pp. 264–5.

87 CROUCH, *William Marshal*, pp. 62–3.

88 KEEFE, 'Proffers for Heirs and Heiresses in the Pipe Rolls'.

89 JOLLIFFE, *Angevin Kingship*, p. 339.

90 WAUGH, 'Marriage, Class and Royal Wardship'.

91 Cf. COSS, 'Bastard Feudalism Revised', and the discussion between this author, D. Crouch and D. Carpenter in 'Debate: Bastard Feudalism Revised', *Past and Present*, no. 131, 1991.

92 CROUCH, *William Marshal*, pp. 150–1, 166–76.

93 AURELL, 'Appréhensions historiographiques de la féodalité'.

94 F-L. GANSHOF, *Qu'est ce que la féodalité?* Brussels, 1957 (3rd edn), p. 14.

95 *Jordan Fantosme's Chronicle*, II, vv. 457–458.

96 CROUCH, 'The Hidden History of the Twelfth Century', p. 113. On the subject of William Marshal's loyalty to the king, cf. the preamble of an act which repeats the biblical image of gold in the furnace: 'Tanquam aurum in fornace, sic in necessitate probavit', *Patent Rolls, 1216–1225*, cited by HOLT, *The Northerners*, p. 254.

97 'Memores sacramenti quod fecerant imperatrici et heredibus suis', ROGER OF HOWDEN, *Chronica*, vol. 1, p. 212.

98 'Illos autem omnes, tam clericos quam laicos, qui, relicto patre suo, illi adhaeserunt, odio habuit, et a familiaritate sua alienos fecit: illos vero, qui patri suo fideliter servierunt secum retinuit et multis bonis ditavit', *ibid.*, vol. 3, p. 5.

99 GERALD OF BARRY, *Itinerarium Kambriae*, I, 7, p. 69.

100 RIGORD, *Gesta Philippi*, vol. 1, p. 153, no. 139.

101 For another view, AURELL, 'Aliénor d'Aquitaine et ses historiens'.

102 JOHN DE MARMOUTIER, *Historia Gaufridi*, p. 224; WILLIAM OF NEWBURGH, *Historia rerum Anglicarum*, vol. 1, p. 105.

103 BOUSSARD, *Le Comté d'Anjou*; and *Le Gouvernement d'Henri II*; 'Territorialisation and centralisation are the characteristics that can be discerned in Henry II's government . . . The prince's justice made some spectacular progress in Henry II's time', DEBORD, *La Société laïque*, pp. 370, 378.

104 GILLINGHAM, The Angevin Empire; BATES, 'The Rise and Fall of Normandy'. An American author, R. Hajdu, also puts forward doubts about Henry II's administrative energy in Poitou, except for the end of his reign, *A History of the Nobility of Poitou*, pp. 254–7, 266, 287–8.

105 ROBERT DE TORIGNY, *Chronica*, p. 235.

106 RICHARD OF DEVIZES, *Chronicon*, pp. 11, 76.

107 *De Principis Instructione*, III, 7, p. 235.

108 VINCENT, *Peter des Roches*, p. 28.

109 WILLIAM LE BRETON, *Historia de vita et gestis Philippi*, p. 210; *idem*, *Philippidos*, VIII, v. 451.

110 *La Chronique des ducs de Normandie*, vv. 12,059–12,064, p. 350, following Dudo 'Pictavenses semper sunt timidi frigidique armis et avari', *De moribus et actis primorum Normannniae ducum*, p. 192.

111 RAOUL DE HOUDENC, Songe d'Enfer, ed. M.T. MIHM, Tübingen, 1984, pp. 59–60. Cf. M-A DE MASCUREAU, *Les Lusignan ou l'insurrection des grands féodaux du duché d'Aquitaine entre 1154 et 1242*, unpublished master's thesis, Poitiers, 2000, pp. 97–105.

112 *L'Histoire de Guillaume le Maréchal*, vv. 12,545–12,550.

113 MATTHEW PARIS, *Chronica Majora*, vol. 2, p. 451. 'O innata Pictavensibus proditio!' *ibid.*, vol. 3, p. 84.

114 M-H. VICAIRE, ' "L'affaire de paix et de foi" du Midi de la France', *Cahiers de Fanjeaux*, 4 (1968), 1969, pp. 102–26.

115 'East–West tensions ought not to make us forget even more deep-seated tensions between North and South, which culminated in the Albigensian Crusade and was aggravated by the linguistic barrier between Langue d'oïl and Langue d'oc . . . Aquitainians might well have made up part of the regnum Francorum, but no one would have dreamed of calling them Frenchmen', C. BRÜHL, *Naissance de deux peuples: Français et Allemands (ixe–xie siècle)*, Paris, 1994, pp. 135–7.

116 On the eve of the 1173 revolt, Eleanor in Aquitaine wielded 'a recognised authority and sovereignty', but 'few means of exercising government' because of Henry II's oversight. Cf. MARTINDALE *Status, Authority and Regional Power*, XI, p. 22.

117 VINCENT, 'King Henry II and the Poitevins'.

118 Grant to the abbey of Breuil-Herbaud, 'Cartulaire des sires de Rays', ed. R. BLANCHARD, in, *Archives historiques de Poitou*, 30, 1899, no. 253, p. 343 (11 X 1160). 'Merum et mixtum imperium' is the expression of the Code of Justinian to designate high and low justice; the lord who commands 'mère et mixte empire' can, as a consequence, judge violent crime and apply corporal penalties, including hanging.

119 GILLINGHAM, *Richard I*, p. 149, HAJDU, *A History of the Nobility of Poitou*, p. 22.

120 VINCENT, Isabella of Angoulême', pp. 173–4.

121 The most recent and solid analysis is VINCENT, 'Isabella of Angoulême'. Cf. otherwise. E. CARPENTIER, 'Les Lusignans'; JORDAN, 'Isabelle d'Angoulême'.

122 ROGER OF HOWDEN, *Gesta Henrici*, vol. 1, p. 292.

123 ROGER OF HOWDEN, *Chronica*, vol. 3, p. 255. As J. Gillingham has suggested, Richard was then in a strong position in relation to Philip Augustus, and had every interest in pursuing the fight, but that he used the argument of the Poitevin revolt to reject his rival's proposal is, in itself, a strong indication that he was being factual.

124 'Before 1242 public life in Poitou had a distinctive quality: violence',
     HAJDU, *A History of the Nobility of Poitou*, p. 278. For northern Gascony
     during the reigns of Henry II and Richard the Lionheart, F. Boutoulle,
     entitles his chapters, 'Recrudescence des troubles et de l'insecurité', and
     'Déprédations de l'aristocratie laïque', *Société laïque en Bordelais*, p. 442.

125 DEBORD, *La Société laïque*, pp. 382–96. For the county of Angoulême,
     Debord goes so far as to talk of 'an embryo State', *ibid.*, p. 392. Cf. in the
     latter case, DUBUC, 'Les possessions poitevines des Lusignan', and
     BARRIERE, 'Le comté de La Marche'.

126 For Patrick of Salisbury, see above. For 1188, 'Gaufridus de Liziniaco
     quemdam familiarissimum Richardi comitis Pictavensis structis insidis
     interfecit', RALPH DE DICETO, *Opera*, vol. 2, p. 54; the revolt of 1188 is
     attested by ROGER OF HOWDEN, *Chronica*, vol. 2, p. 339, and *Gesta
     Henrici*, vol. 2, p. 34. The name of 'Richard's very close friend' is not
     known.

127 *PL*, 194, col. 1895B. Cf. RACITI, 'Isaac de l'Etoile et son siècle', p. 145.

128 *The Letters of John of Salisbury*, no. 177, vol. 2, p. 179. Cf. POUZET,
     L'Anglais dit Jean Bellesmains, pp. 9–10.

129 VINCENT, 'William Marshal, King Henry II and the Honour of
     Châteauroux'; DEVAILLY, Le Berry, pp. 409–10.

130 For an example of marriage between Norman nobles on the Perche frontier
     under Henry II's careful supervision, THOMPSON, 'The Formation of the
     County of Perche', pp. 302, 313, n. 62.

131 DEBORD, *La Société laïque*, p. 381.

132 HAJDU, *A History of the Nobility of Poitou*, pp. 23–4, 258.

133 Analyses taken from, HAJDU, *A History of the Nobility of Poitou*, pp. 26,
     45–7, 50, 63, 71–8, 210–27, 257–70, 326–30, 403. Cf. DEBORD, *La
     Société laïque*, pp. 397–8.

134 COLLET, 'Le combat politique des Plantagenêt en Aquitaine'.

135 AURELL, *Les Noces du Comte*, pp. 361–71.

136 CAO CARMICHAEL DE BAGLY, 'Savary de Mauléon'.

137 BOUTOULLE, *Société laïque en Bordelais*, pp. 163–6, 1061.

138 VINCENT, *Peter des Roches*, p. 44.

139 GILLINGHAM, *Richard Coeur de Lion*, pp. 119–39.

140 H. DEBAX, 'Stratégies matrimoniales des comtes de Toulouse (850–1270)',
     Annales du Midi, 100, 1988, pp. 131–51, and 'Les comtesses de Toulouse:
     notices biographiques', *ibid.*, pp. 215–34.

141 BOUTOULLE, *Société laïque en Bordelais*, pp. 449–54.

142 MONLEZUN, *Histoire de la Gascogne*, vol. 2, pp. 220–1.

143 ALVIRA and BURESI, 'Alphonse, par la grâce de Dieu, roi de Castille';
     MARSH, *English Rule in Gascony*, pp. 5–9.

144 FAVREAU, 'Naissance et premier développement de la ville', pp. 11–21.

145 RENOUARD, 'Essai sur la rôle de l'empire Angevin', pp. 301–3.

146 GILLINGHAM, *Angevin Empire*, pp. 64–6.

147 POWICKE, The Loss of Normandy, p. 32; MARSH, *English Rule in
     Gascony*, pp. 2–4.

148 BOUTOULLE, *Société laïque en Bordelais*, pp. 477–88, 508.

149 BOUSSARD, *Le Comté d'Anjou*, p. 64.

150 O. GUILLOT, *Le comte d'Anjou et son entourage au xie siècle*, Paris, 1972.

151 A. DEBORD, 'La politique des fortifications des Plantagenêt', p. 10;
     BOUTOULLE, *Société laïque en Bordelais*, pp. 497–9.

152 ROCHETEAU, 'Le château de Chinon'.

153 'Cartulaire de Cormery', ed. J-J. BOURASSE, in, *Mémoires de la société
     archéologique de Touraine*, 12, 1860, no. 72, cited by HAJDU, *A History
     of the Nobility of Poitou*, p. 14.

154 BOUSSARD, *Le Comté d'Anjou*, pp. 30, 74; BAUDRY, *Les fortifications
     des Plantagenêt en Poitou*, p. 300.

155 RICHARD OF DEVIZES, Chronicon, pp. 5, 85; BOUSSARD, *Le Comté
     d'Anjou*, pp. 68–70, 80–2, 105–6, 113, 117, 127–8.

156 GUILLOTEL, 'Administration et finances ducales en Bretagne'.

157 HILLION, 'La Bretagne et la rivalité Capétiens–Plantagenêt', pp. 111–44;
     EVERARD, *Brittany and the Angevins*, pp. 141–5.

158 LE PATOUREL, *Feudal Empires*, X, p. 101.

159 HILLION, 'La Bretagne et la rivalité Capétiens–Plantagenêt', pp. 112,
     128–9; EVERARD, *Brittany and the Angevins*, pp. 141–5.

160 RIGORD, *Gesta Philippi*, no. 44, p. 68; *De Principis Instructione*, III, 10,
     p. 176.

161 On this political aspect of medieval love and on texts describing passionate
     friendship, cf. JAEGER, *Ennobling Love*.

162 *The Charters of Constance, Duchess of Brittany and her Family
     (1171–1221)*, ed. J. EVERARD and M. JONES, Woodbridge, 1999.

163 POCQUET DU HAUT-JUSSE, 'Les Plantagenêt et la Bretagne';
     QUAGHEBEUR, *La Cornouaille*, pp. 358–61.

164 EVERARD, 'The "Justiciarship" in Brittany and Ireland', pp. 89–90.

165 *Aiquin ou la conquête de Bretagne*, ed. JACQUES.

166 'Natus est Arturus filius Gauffridi ducis Britanniae, desideratus gentibus', annotation on 29 March 1187, in a lost register cited by A. DE LA BORDERIE, *Histoire de la Bretagne*, Paris-Rennes, 1899, vol. 3, p. 286.

167 *Gesta Henrici*, p. 469; *Ymagines Historiarum*, p. 629. Cf. HILLION, 'La Bretagne et la rivalité Capétiens–Plantagenêt', p. 129, n. 26.

168 WILLIAM OF NEWBURGH, *Historia rerum Anglicarum*, iii, 7.

169 'De qua genuit Arturum juvenem . . . de genere antiqui Arturi', *Chronica*, p. 859. Cf. CHAOU, *L'Idéologie Plantagenêt*, p. 258.

170 'Fu el cors navrez mortelmant,/ An Avalon s'an fist porter/ Por ses plaies mediciner./ Ancor I est, Breton l'atandent,/ Si com iul dient et antandent', *Le Roman de Brut*, vv. 12,327–12,331.

171 *Epistulae*, no. 34, col. 112A; no. 51, col. 154C.

172 *Carmina*, 1.5, pp. 265–74, and DRONKE, 'Peter of Blois and Poetry', pp. 206–9, str. 8.

173 JOSEPH OF EXETER, *Iliad*, III, vv. 472–473.

174 PEIRE VIDAL, *Poesie*, no. 40, vv. 12–13, p. 366. Cf. No. 31, v. 39, p. 248, and ANGLADE, *Les Troubadours et les Bretons*, pp. 39–40.

175 GREENE, 'Qui croit au retour d'Arthur'.

176 EVERARD, *Brittany and the Angevins*, p. 157, and, *The Charters of Constance, Duchess of Brittany*.

177 QUAGHEBEUR, *La Cornouaille*, pp. 363–4.

178 HILLION, 'La Bretagne et la rivalité Capétiens–Plantagenêt', p. 119 and n. 108, who cites Dom Lobineau, after an old manuscript from Nantes cathedral.

179 GILLINGHAM, *Richard I*, p. 298.

180 M. JONES, 'Notes sur quelques familles bretonnes en Angleterre après la conquête normande', *Mémoires de la société d'histoire et d'archéologie de Bretagne*, 1981, pp. 73–91; HILLION, 'La Bretagne et la rivalité Capétiens–Plantagenêt', p. 120; EVERARD, 'Lands and loyalties in Plantagenet Brittany'.

181 On this person, cf. VINCENT, *Peter des Roches*, pp. 23–6.

182 This is the point of view in BOUSSARD, *Le Comté d'Anjou*, pp. 94–5.

183 For the right of 'viage' or 'retour', cf. M. GARAUD, 'Le viage ou le retour dans le *Vieux Coutumier de Poitou*', *Mémoires de la Société des Antiquaires de l'Ouest*, 1964, pp. 747–86, and *idem*, *Les Châtelains du Poitou*, p. 74.

184 *L'Histoire de Guillaume le Maréchal*, ed. MEYER, vv. 11,837–11,908, vol. 2, pp. 62–5. Cf. POWICKE, *The Loss of Normandy*, p. 194, n. 1; RICHARDSON and SAYLES, *The Governance of Medieval England*, pp. 139–41; LEGGE, 'William Marshal and Arthur of Brittany'.

185 'The collapse is much more plausibly to the question marks against John's personality than to any structural reasons . . . With John's accession there came to the throne a king whose reputation was even more unsavoury than Philip's', GILLINGHAM, *Richard I*, p. 340.

186 *Chronica*, vol. 4, pp. 96–7. Cf. GILLINGHAM, *Richard I*, p. 337.

187 Richard's chivalry is an integral part of the second half of the work by J. FLORI, *Richard Coeur de Lion*, subtitled, *le roi-chevalier*.

188 *L'Histoire de Guillaume le Maréchal*, v. 4,644 *et seq.*, vol. 3, p. 58, and BATES, 'The Rise and Fall of Normandy', p. 22. In 1193, when Richard was in captivity, William of Newburgh talked of the Normans as 'sheep without a shepherd' who had lost their loyalty; so they were unable to resist Philip Augustus' seizure of Gisors, POWICKE, *The Loss of Normandy*, pp. 144–5.

189 HIGOUNET, 'Problèmes du Midi au temps de Philippe Auguste', p. 319.

190 CONCKLIN, 'Les Capétiens et l'affaire de Dol-de-Bretagne'; VINCENT, *Peter des Roches*.

191 COLLET, 'Le combat politique des Plantagenêt en Aquitaine'.

192 L. MUSSET, *Autour du pouvoir ducal normand*, Caen, 1985, pp. 45–9; BATES, 'The Rise and Fall of Normandy', p. 25; NEVEUX, *La Normandie des ducs aux rois*, pp. 185, 190–1.

193 HOLT, 'The Loss of Normandy and Royal Finances'; MOSS, 'The Norman Fiscal Revolution'.

194 WILLIAM OF NEWBURGH, *Historia rerum Anglicarum*, p. 102; GERVASE OF CANTERBURY, *Chronica*, p. 160. Cf. COULSON, 'Freedom to Crenellate by License'; BROWN, 'Royal Castle Building'.

195 YVER, 'Les châteaux'; LOUISE, *La seigneurie de Bellême*; DEBORD, 'La politique des fortifications des Plantagenêt'.

196 This is the 'hundred', a subdivision of the English shire or county.

197 MORTIMER, *Angevin England*, pp. 52–73; P. BRAND, '*Multis Vigiliis Excogitatam et Inventam*'; TURNER, *The English Judiciary*.

198 *Dialogus Scaccarii*, p. 101, and *Tractatus de Legibus et consuetudinibus regni Angliae*, I, 2, and VII. Cf. HUDSON, *Land, Law and Lordship*, pp. 40–43.

199 Some regional nuances need to be brought to bear on this conclusion. If H.M. Thomas is to be followed, in Yorkshire, Henry II's judicial reforms had little effect on the local nobility, which continued to resort to extra-legal violence and to apply unrestricted justice in its seignorial courts, *Vassals, Heiresses and Thugs*, pp. 84–5. But it is true that in the northern lands towards the Scottish border, William the Conqueror had allotted vast estates to his followers, and allowed them a wide autonomy and room for manoeuvre for reasons of military security. It should be remembered that the baronial rebellion of 1214–1215 would begin with these men, HOLT, *The Northerners*.

200 KEEFE, *Feudal Assessments and the Political Community*.

201 BOURNAZEL, *Le Gouvernement capétien*, pp. 74, 91.

202 BILLORE, 'La noblesse normande'.

203 In Normandy, the *vicecomes* (*vicomte*) was not a hereditary title deriving form a Carolingian officer, but simply a local judicial and administrative official, comparable to the English 'sheriff' (also called *vicecomes* in Latin) or the Angevin *prévôt*.

204 For the reign of Henry I, cf. the royal rewards for the high and middling nobility in service, GREEN, *Aristocracy of Norman England*, who debates the 'men raised form the dust' of whom Orderic Vitalis speaks, as did R. Turner in his turn.

205 DAVIS, *King Stephen*, pp. 111–14, AMT, *The Accession of Henry II*, pp. 7–29.

206 LE PATOUREL, *Feudal Empires*, VII, p. 8; VIII, p. 293.

207 LE PATOUREL, *The Norman Empire*, p. 115.

208 POWER, 'Between the Angevin and Capetian Courts'; 'What did the Frontier of Angevin Normandy Comprise?' On the destructiveness of the Angevin military campaigns between 1136 and 1144, and on the resentment this gave rise to in Normandy, cf. ORDERIC VITALIS, *The Ecclesiastical History*, vol. 2, pp. 190, 279, and also BRADBURY, 'Geoffrey V of Anjou', pp. 21, 27–8 and NEVEUX, *La Normandie des ducs aux rois*, pp. 503–13.

209 BATES, 'The Rise and Fall of Normandy', pp. 23, 32; POWICKE, *The Loss of Normandy*, p. 158.

210 On these problems, cf. D.J. POWER, *The Norman Frontier in the Twelfth and Early Thirteenth Centuries*, Cambridge, 2004.

211 'The lay aristocracy, whatever its origins, felt less and less Norman and more and more English . . . In the end, the old equilibrium between England and Normandy was completely upset, to the benefit of the English', MUSSET, 'Quelques problèmes', pp. 293–4.

212 'Absolutism of the Angevin rule in Normandy', POWICKE, *The Loss of Normandy*, p. 438; BATES, 'The Rise and Fall of Normandy', p. 22.

213 *De Principis Instructione*, III, 12, p, 258. The link between tyranny and islands was borrowed from Greek and Latin classical texts which located the most oppressive forms of government in Ancient Sicily.

214 BARTLETT, *Gerald of Wales*, pp. 95–6.

215 J. Le Patourel (*Feudal Empires*, pp. 164–76) asserted that Anglo-Norman unity was structural: for him, the Channel was an easy means of communication, assisting exchange and communication; the loss of the White Ship (1120) appears to him to be a most unforseeable and exceptional accident. For a view taking more account of the perils of the sea and navigational difficulties, cf. BATES, 'Normandy and England after 1066', pp. 859–61.

216 *Dialogus Scaccarii*, pp. 53–4.

217 AILRED, *Vita sancti Edwardi*, col. 774. Cf. BARLOW, *Edward the Confessor*, p. 283, and SHORT, '*Tam Angli Quam Franci*', pp. 170–1.

218 DAVIS, *The Normans and their Myth*.

219 DUDO OF ST-QUENTIN, *De moribus et actis primorum Normannniae ducum*, p. 146, where J. Lair gives the references for Wace (v. 1,025) and Benoît de Sainte-Maure (v. 1,559). Cf. BEAUNE, 'Les ducs, le roi et le saint Sang', p. 718.

220 GILLINGHAM, *The English in the Twelfth Century*, pp. 69–92, 123–45.

221 *Historia Anglorum*, p. 716. Cf. DAVIS, 'The Normans and their Myth', p. 66; LOUD, 'The Gens Normannorum', pp. 105–6; GREEN, *Aristocracy of Norman England*, p. 344; CLANCHY, *England and its Rulers*, p. 57.

222 GREEN, *Aristocracy of Norman England*, p. 344; SHORT, '*Tam Angli quam Franci*', pp 160–1; CLANCHY, *England and its Rulers*, p. 57.

223 At Christmas 1172, the Young Henry invited to a banquet, as it happens in Normandy, as many as 110 knights called William, TORIGNY, *Chronica*, p. 253. Cf. CROUCH, *William Marshal*, pp. 41–2.

224 BILLORE, 'La noblesse normande', pp. 154–5.

225 *Aristocracy of Norman England*, pp. 16, 325–6.

226 CROUCH, *The Beaumont Twins*, pp. 76–9.

227 *L'Histoire de Guillaume le Maréchal*, vv. 5,214–5. Cf. BILLORE, 'La noblesse normande', p. 156.

228 CROUCH, *William Marshal*, p. 50.

229 *L'Histoire de Guillaume le Maréchal*, vv. 4481–4542.

230 BROUGHTON, *The Legends of King Richard I*, pp. 93–95; SHORT, 'Tam Angli quam Franci', p. 153; SOUTHERN, Medieval Humanism, p. 141, n. 1. It so happens that the last verse of Peter Riga's pro-French poem also contains an allusion to Englishmen's 'tails', 'Un poème inédit', ed. HAUREAU, p. 11.

231 GERALD OF BARRY, *Gemma Ecclesiastica*, p. 348; *De Vita Galfredi*, p. 423. Cf. BARLETT, *Gerald of Wales*, p. 12; MORTIMER, *Angevin England*, p. 240.

232 BARTLETT, *Gerald of Wales*, p. 50. Gerald makes no bones about directing long diatribes against the *Anglici*, which openly embrace Welsh or Anglo-Welsh sentiments: 'The English [for which read 'Anglo-Saxons'] who had long before been conquered as they were ever, as if by nature, slaves', *Descriptio Kambriae*, V, 21, p. 202; 'The English are the most despicable people under heaven . . . In their own land they the most abject slaves of the Normans. In my country the English are only cowherds, shepherds, leather workers, skinners, builders, artisans, rabbit hunters or indeed sewage farmers, *Invectiones* I, 4, p. 98, cited by BARTLETT, Gerald of Wales, p. 93. Cf. GILLINGHAM, '"Slave of the Normans"'.

233 STRICKLAND, 'Arms and the Men', pp. 196, 209–10.

234 CLANCHY, *England and its Rulers*, pp. 241–62. On the importance to royal policy of these 'foreigners' or *alieni*, continental exiles who had been given in compensation lands in England confiscated from Anglo-Norman lords who had chosen to follow Philip Augustus in 1204, cf. VINCENT, *Peter des Roches*, pp. 6–7, 28–30.

235 READER, 'Matthew Paris and the Norman Conquest'.

236 PETER OF BLOIS, *Carmina*, 1.6, p. 277; 1.7, p. 285; 1.7a, p. 289.

237 SOUTHERN, *Medieval Humanism*, pp. 142–3.

238 *The Letters of John of Salisbury*, no. 1, 33, pp. 57–8, cited by BROOKE, 'John of Salisbury and his World', p. 9.

239 Cf. GILLINGHAM, *The English in the Twelfth Century*, pp. 99, 123–44, where, following Geoffrey Gaimar, William of Malmesbury and Henry of Huntingdon, this claim to Englishness by the descendants of Norman colonists is dated 'by 1140 at the latest', p. 99.

240 KEEFE, 'Place–Date Distribution of Royal Charters'.

241 It is interesting to see here the same accusation of treachery used to smear the Poitevins, who like the Welsh shared the same taste for independence and revolt. See on this subject the little-known views of Herbert of Bosham, the companion in exile of Thomas Becket, who wrote on the Welshman, Alexander Llywelyn, another friend of the archbishop of Canterbury, 'and

what is a thing unheard of in his nation (*in natione illa*), he was not only efficient, but loyal to his master in all things and at all times', *Vita sancte Thome*, p. 528, cited by KNOWLES, *Thomas Becket*, p. 109.

242 BARTLETT, *Gerald of Wales*, pp. 16, 44; DAVIES, 'Buchedd a moes y Cymru'; STRICKLAND, *War and Chivalry*, pp. 291–340. In particular, William of Newburgh talks of these peoples with the same distaste as for the Jews, *Historia rerum Anglicarum*, II, 5, 15, 26, 28, 32; III, 36, and GRANSDEN, *Historical Writing in England*, p. 266.

243 GILLINGHAM, *The English in the Twelfth Century*, pp. 3–18, 41–58. Victorian historiography repeated the commonplace of the backward nature of the Irish, all the more readily as it both justified the twelfth-century conquest as much as nineteenth-century English rule, FLANAGAN, *Irish Society*, pp. 1–2.

244 'Quoniam inter eos [the Irish] publica potestas constituta non fuerat, quae metu poenarum impunitatem minime repromitterent, cum patres suos mutuis caedibus interfectos saepissime doluissent, ut in virtute regis pax fient in diebus suis, ei et in eum jus suum transtulerunt et potestatem', RALPH DE DICETO, *Ymagines Historiarum*, vol. 1, p. 350.

245 FLANAGAN, *Irish Society*, pp. 56–228.

246 BALDWIN, 'La décennie décisive'.

The Becket affair

1 Among the many biographies of Thomas Becket, it is appropriate to single out the best-documented and relatively recent work of F. Barlow; D. Knowles's work, less detached and more sympathetic than Barlow's, is always a stimulating read.

2 On this cult, FOREVILLE, *Thomas Becket*.

3 The sweeping nature of this measure shocked writers who were normally sympathetic to royal policy: 'Quid facis, tyranne? Quae te dementia vicit, ut sic since causa expelleres a regno tuo, qui malum non fecerunt, nec dolus inventus est in ore eorum', ROGER OF HOWDEN, *Chronica*, vol. 1, p. 241.

4 *Materials for a History of Thomas Becket*.

5 E. WALBERG, *La Tradition hagiographique de saint Thomas Becket avant la fin du xii⁰ siècle*, Paris, 1929, and BARLOW, *Thomas Becket*, pp. 5–9.

6 DUGGAN, *Thomas Becket*.

7 *Life of Becket*, London, 1859, p. 320.

8 G.O. OEXLE, *L'Historisme en débat: de Nietzshe à Kantorowicz*, Paris, 2001.

9 *The Governance of Medieval England*, pp. 267, 294.

10 *Henry II*, pp. 400–1.

11 Although published around thirty years ago, an anthology presents a good overview of this historiography: *The Becket Controversy*, ed. T.M. JONES.

12 M. SORIA, 'Les violences antiépiscopales dans la royaume de France aux xiᵉ–xiiᵉ siècles', unpublished doctoral thesis, Poitiers, 2002. Cf. also, *Bischofsmord im Mittelalter*, ed. N. FRYDE and D. REITZ, Göttingen, 2003.

13 SALTMAN, *Theobald Archbishop of Canterbury*, p. 153.

14 Z.N. BROOKE, *The English Church and the Papacy*, pp. 198–9.

15 BARLOW, *Thomas Becket*, p. 270.

16 WILLIAM FITZ STEPHEN, *Vita sancti Thome*, pp. 14–18.

17 SMALLEY, *The Becket Conflict and the Schools*, pp. 109–12.

18 WARREN, *Henry II*, pp. 56–7.

19 CLANCHY, *From Memory to Written Record*, p. 194.

20 SMALLEY, *The Becket Conflict and the Schools*, pp. 87–9; DRONKE, 'New Approaches to the School of Chartres', pp. 121–3; SOUTHERN, *Scholastic Humanism*, pp. 167–77.

21 BROOKE, 'John of Salisbury and his World', p. 5.

22 *The Letters of John of Salisbury*, no. 168, p. 104; *Policraticus*, VI, 18, trans. DICKINSON, p. 237, n. 4; *Metalogicon*, IV, 42, p. 183. Cf. LIEBSCHÜTZ, *Medieval Humanism*, pp. 13–14, 16.

23 *Metalogicon, ut supra*. Cf. CONSTABLE, 'The Alleged Disgrace of John of Salisbury', p. 75.

24 FLANAGAN, *Irish Society*, pp. 51–3; appendix II to the edition of John of Salisbury's letters by W.J. MILLOR, H.E. BUTLER and C.N.L. BROOKE, vol. 1, pp. 257–8.

25 LIEBSCHÜTZ, *Medieval Humanism*, p. 12.

26 *The Letters of John of Salisbury*, no. 150, p. 48.

27 SMALLEY, *The Becket Conflict and the Schools*, pp. 103–8; A. DUGGAN, 'John of Salisbury and Thomas Becket', pp. 429–32. Around 1159, while still chancellor, Thomas had already been accused of being a 'Henrician' by a Parisian clerk who differed from Thomas in the weight he gave to his financial ideas.

28 'Aucune autre théorie ne sera aussi péremptoire et tranchante. Le cas de Jean de Salisbury demeure unique au Moyen Age', TURCHETTI, *Tyrannie et Tyrannicide*, p. 255.

29 LIEBSCHÜTZ, *Medieval Humanism*, p. 95.

30 BROOKE, 'John of Salisbury and his World', p. 19.

31 It should not be forgotten, however, that, like Laon, the school of Chartres cut a sorry figue in comparison with Paris, SOUTHERN, *Medieval Humanism*, pp. 61–83.

32 FOREVILLE, *L'Eglise et la royauté en Angleterre*, pp. 260–3.

33 At least according to N. Fryde ('The Roots of Magna Carta', p. 62) following from MS 46, Corpus Christi College Cambridge.

34 SMALLEY, *The Becket Conflict and the Schools*, p. 63.

35 LEYSER, *Medieval Germany and its Neighbours*, pp. 215–40.

36 WILLIAM FITZ STEPHEN, *Vita sancti Thome*, pp. 99–101.

37 SMALLEY, *The Becket Conflict and the Schools*, p. 64, n. 17.

38 JAEGER, *The Envy of Angels*, pp. 297–308.

39 SMALLEY, *The Becket Conflict and the Schools*, pp. 61–2, 70–74, 82–5.

40 POUZET, *L'Anglais dit Jean Bellesmains*, pp. 22–35. The business of the poisoning is the object of a chapter in Myraim Soria's doctoral thesis, mentioned above.

41 WARREN, *Henry II*, p. 516.

42 POUZET, *L'Anglais dit Jean Bellesmains*, pp. 16–17.

43 *The Letters of John of Salisbury*, no. 194, vol. 2, pp. 268–74.

44 RALPH NIGER, *Chronica*, p. 93.

45 FLAHIFF, 'Ralph Niger'.

46 BEZZOLA, *La Cour d'Angleterre*, p. 145; DRONKE, 'Peter of Blois and Poetry', p. 190; A.C. DIONISOTTI, 'Walter of Chatillon and the Greeks', in, *Latin Poetry and the Classical Tradition*, Oxford, 1990, pp. 73–96.

47 SMALLEY, *The Becket Conflict and the Schools*, pp. 33–4.

48 [JOHN OF TILBURY], *Ars Notaria*, pp. 324–5. Cf. BARLOW, Thomas Becket, p. 79; KUTTNER and RATHBONE, 'Anglo-Norman Canonists', p. 292.

49 HERBERT OF BOSHAM, *Vita sancti Thome*, p. 527, no. 13.

50 SMALLEY, *The Becket Conflict and the Schools*, p. 78.

51 BALDWIN, 'Masters at Paris from 1179 to 1215', pp. 147–50.

52 The pallium is a lambs' wool stole or scarf granted by the pope only to archbishops who as metropolitans are at the head of an ecclesiastical province, on which depend many bishops. It symbolizes the archiepiscopal dignity.

53 KNOWLES, *The Episcopal Colleagues of Thomas Becket*, pp. 39–47; SMALLEY, *The Becket Conflict and the Schools*, pp. 168–82.

54 KNOWLES, *Thomas Becket*, pp. 72–6, 127–9; BARLOW, *Thomas Becket*, pp. 204–10.

55 BARLOW, *Thomas Becket*, pp. 85, 295. This *Vita* has been edited in *Materials for a History of Thomas Becket*, vol. 3, pp. 299–322.

56 HESLIN, 'The Coronation of the Young King in 1170'.

57 KNOWLES, *The Episcopal Colleagues of Thomas Becket*, pp. 17–20; WARREN, *Henry II*, pp. 311–13, 535; DUGGAN, *Canon Law in Medieval England*, XII, p. 2; *idem*, 'Richard of Ilchester, Royal Servant and Bishop'; KEEFE, *Feudal Assessments and the Political Community*, pp. 110–11.

58 KNOWLES, *The Episcopal Colleagues of Thomas Becket*, pp. 106–8; WARREN, *Henry II*, pp. 216, 520, 551.

59 KNOWLES, *The Episcopal Colleagues of Thomas Becket*, pp. 29–30, 59–60, 86–7, 104–6; WARREN, *Henry II*, pp. 473, 550; SMALLEY, *The Becket Conflict and the Schools*, pp. 53–6.

60 *The Letters of Arnulf of Lisieux*, ed. BARLOW; *The Letter Collection of Arnulf of Lisieux*, trans. SCHRIBER.

61 SCHRIBER, *The Dilemma of Arnulf of Lisieux*.

62 DUGGAN, *Canon Law in Medieval England*, I, p. 367.

63 *The Letters and Charters of Gilbert Foliot*, no. 170, pp. 229–43. There is no better defence of its authenticity than KNOWLES, *The Episcopal Colleagues of Thomas Becket*, p. 119. There is a comment in, SMALLEY, *The Becket Conflict and the Schools*, pp. 182–5.

64 'In practice he was more of a Gelasian than a Gregorian', KNOWLES, *The Episcopal Colleagues of Thomas Becket*, p. 42, cf. p. 146. 'Gilbert advances the moderate Gelasian attitude widely held in the church of that time', BARLOW, *Thomas Becket*, p. 154.

65 J. LECLER, *L'Eglise et la souveraineté de l'Etat*, Paris, 1946.

66 KNOWLES, *The Episcopal Colleagues of Thomas Becket*, p. 119; BARLOW, *Thomas Becket*, p. 140; SMALLEY, *The Becket Conflict and the Schools*, p. 177.

67 SMALLEY, *The Becket Conflict and the Schools*, pp. 26–30, 51–8.

68 *Policraticus*, IV, 10, 3; V, 2. Cf. NEDERMAN and CAMPBELL, 'Priests, Kings and Tyrants'.

69 *The Correspondence of Thomas Becket*, no. 96, pp. 436–8.

70 *Policraticus*, IV, 3, 7–10; V, 2.

71 LIEBSCHÜTZ, *Medieval Humanism*, pp. 24–5. B. Smalley (*The Becket Conflict and the Schools*, p. 92) believed that John had repeated this apocryphal story rather than invented it himself.

72 DICKINSON, 'The Medieval Conception of Kingship', p. 318.

73 *Policraticus*, VIII, 18, vol. 2, p. 358 and IV, 3; VIII, 17. Cf. DICKINSON, 'The Medieval Conception of Kingship', pp. 310–11; BUC, *L'Ambiguïté du livre*, pp. 246–9.

74 DICKINSON, 'The Medieval Conception of Kingship', pp. 319–20, 335.

75 C. GALDERESI, 'Le "crâne qui parle": du motif aux récits. Vertu chrétienne et vertu poétique', *CCM* , forthcoming.

76 LIEBSCHÜTZ, *Medieval Humanism*, pp. 35–6, 46; SMALLEY, *The Becket Conflict and the Schools*, p. 92.

77 LUSCOMBE, 'John of Salisbury in Recent Scholarship'.

78 *Policraticus*, IV, 6. Cf. LIEBSCHÜTZ, *Medieval Humanism*, pp. 32, 46, 49; JAEGER, 'Courtliness and Social Change'.

79 SMALLEY, *The Becket Conflict and the Schools*, pp. 91–7, 106.

80 *Metalogicon*, I, 21, cited by LIEBSCHÜTZ, *Medieval Humanism*, p. 84.

81 SMALLEY, *The Becket Conflict and the Schools*, pp. 106–7. Cf. T. LESIEUR, 'Consonantia: construction d'une raison chrétienne à l'aube de la réforme grégorienne', unpublished thesis, E.H.E.S.S., 2001, pp. 510–14.

82 RATHBONE, 'Roman Law in the Anglo-Norman Realm', p. 259; introduction to *The Letters of John of Salisbury*, pp. xxii–xxiii; LEYSER, *Medieval Germany and its Neighbours*, pp. 265–6.

83 KANTOROWICZ, *The King's Two Bodies*, pp. 94–7; 'The twelfth century is a time when an impersonal crown has been only imperfectly conceived', JOLLIFFE, *Angevin Kingship*, p. 54.

84 KRYNEN, ' "Princeps pugnat pro legibus" '.

85 DICKINSON, 'The Medieval Conception of Kingship', pp. 312–13.

86 LIEBSCHÜTZ, *Medieval Humanism*, pp. 55–6.

87 *Policraticus*, VIII, 22. Cf. DICKINSON, 'The Medieval Conception of Kingship', pp. 326–8.

88 *Policraticus*, IV, 1, 4; VIII, 16–18.

89 NEDERMAN and CAMPBELL, 'Priests, Kings and Tyrants'.

90 *Entheticus*, vv. 1378, 1389–1392, pp. 179–80. Cf. WILKS, 'John of Salisbury and the Tyranny of Nonsense', p. 285.

91 EDWARD GRIM, *Vita sancti Thome*, vol. 2, p. 398. Cf. KNOWLES, *The Episcopal Colleagues of Thomas Becket*, p. 147.

92 SMALLEY, *The Becket Conflict and the Schools*, pp. 34–5.

93 *The Correspondence of Thomas Becket*, no. 74, p. 292. Cf. JOLLIFFE, *Angevin Kingship*, p. 17. Rotrou, archbishop of Rouen, and the other Norman bishops used identical expressions in the letter they addressed to the Young Henry in 1182: 'We beg you as our lord, we urge you as king, and we instruct you as our son', PETER OF BLOIS, *Epistulae*, no. 33, col. 109.

94 *Materials for a History of Thomas Becket*, vol. 5, pp. 285–94. Cf. SMALLEY, *The Becket Conflict and the Schools*, pp. 67–8.

95 *Liber melorum*, PL, 190, col. 1,322.

96 *The Correspondence of Thomas Becket*, no. 41, p. 166. Similar charges can be found against Richard the Lionheart (POUZET, *L'Anglais dit Jean Bellesmains*, p. 44) and King John (GERALD OF BARRY, *De Principis Instructione*, p. 310).

97 KANTOROWICZ and SMALLEY, 'An English Theologian's View of Roman Law'; RATHBONE, 'Roman Law in the Anglo-Norman Realm', pp. 256–7.

98 BUC, *L'Ambiguïté du livre*, pp. 367–9, 376–8.

99 For Henry I, Ralph resorted to the *topos* of the link between the profligacy of the king and the oppression of his subjects, which he further developed at length in relation to Henry II: 'King Henry [I] as debauched as nearly all his family, brutally oppressed the English through his forest laws', RALPH NIGER, *Chronica*, p. 165.

100 *Ibid.*, pp. 167–9.

101 PACAUT, *Alexandre III*.

102 BARLOW, *Thomas Becket*, pp. 136, 147; KNOWLES, *Thomas Becket*, pp. 110–11.

103 *Materials for a History of Thomas Becket*, vol. 5, p. 157.

104 KNOWLES, *Thomas Becket*, p. 108; KUTTNER and RATHBONE, 'Anglo-Norman Canonists'.

105 DUGGAN, *Decretals*, II, p. 87; BROOKE, *The English Church and the Papacy*, pp. 212–13.

106 *Dialogus inter regem Henricum II et abbatem Bonnevallis*, p. 107, where the abbot argues that he did not intend to exploit the Holy See, but act to its profit.

107 *Itinerarium Kambriae*, I, 3, p. 44; *Speculum Ecclesie*, II, 12, p. 54. Cf. BROUGHTON, *The Legends of King Richard I*, pp. 128–9.

108 *De Nugis Curialium*, I, 16–18, 22–8, pp. 51–117. Cf. BEZZOLA, *La Cour d'Angleterre*, p. 99.

109 The saint pointed out to him kings confined to hell represented on the tympanum of the abbey church of Fontevraud, so as to influence him to abandon this practice, ADAM OF EYNSHAM, *Magna Vita sancti Hugonis*, pp. 139–41. Cf. *ibid.*, p. 412, where King John makes sport of the bishop, gambling with gold pieces from his annual alms.

110 BARLOW, *Thomas Becket*, pp. 65–7; SMALLEY, *The Becket Conflict and the Schools*, pp. 118–20. Some examples of the king's intervention in continental elections are in AVRIL, *Le Gouvernement*, pp. 240–2; BOUSSARD, *Le Comté d'Anjou*, pp. 97–102 and FOREVILLE, *L'Eglise et la royauté en Angleterre*. There is a good sketch of this in PONTAL, 'Les évêques dans le monde Plantagenêt'. By way of comparison, cf. PACAUT, *Louis VII et les élections*. Cf. the paper at a colloquium at Peterhouse, (Cambridge, September 2002) of M. Soria on the poisoning of Adhemar de Pérrat, a bishop elected against the advice of Richard the Lionheart at Limoges and murdered on return from his consecration at Rome in 1198.

111 *Draco Normannicus*, II, 8, vv. 415–488, 675–677.

112 WILLIAM OF NEWBURGH, *Historia rerum Anglicarum*, II, 16. Cf. BALDWIN, *Masters, Princes and Merchants*, pp. 171–2.

113 *Policraticus*, VII, 17.

114 [WILLIAM DE TREIGNIAC], 'Tractatus quales sunt'. The identification of the author is to be found in an anonymous note in the *Histoire littéraire de la France*, ed. P. PARIS, Paris, 1869, vol. 15, pp. 140–41, 406–8.

115 'Tractatus quales sunt', col. 1049C.

116 RAMSAY, *The Angevin Empire*, pp. 75–6.

117 The best edition is in *Councils and Synods*, no. 159, pp. 852–93.

118 *The Correspondence of Thomas Becket*, no. 41. p. 166. Z.N. BROOKE, *The English Church and the Papacy*, pp. 206–7; DUGGAN, *Canon Law in Medieval England*, I, p. 370.

119 Edited and annotated in KNOWLES and others, 'Henry II's Supplement to the Constitutions of Clarendon'.

120 DUGGAN, 'The Becket Dispute and the Criminous Clerks'; SMALLEY, *The Becket Conflict and the Schools*, pp. 123–31.

121 DUGGAN, 'Papal Judges Delegate', pp. 173–5; SMALLEY, *The Becket Conflict and the Schools*, p. 122.

122 WILLIAM OF NEWBURGH, *Historia rerum Anglicarum*, II, 16, p. 142.

123 WILLIAM FITZ STEPHEN, *Vita sancti Thomae*, pp. 56–8.

124 GERVASE OF CANTERBURY, *Chronica*, pp. 518–20, 1193 (16).

125 ROGER OF HOWDEN, *Chronica*, vol. 1, pp. 226–7.

126 On this person, cf. primarily, N.E. STACY, 'Henry of Blois and the Lordship of Glastonbury', *EHR*, 114 (1999), pp. 1–33.

127 ROBERT PULLEN, 'Sentences', *PL*, 196, cols 905–6, 919–22. Cf. SMALLEY, *The Becket Conflict and the Schools*, pp. 26, 42–3.

128 For the Iberian peninsula, cf. M. FEROTIN, *Le Liber Ordinum en usage dans l'Eglise wisigothique et mozarabe d'Espagne du v⁰ au xi⁰ siècle* in *Monumenta Ecclesiae Liturgica*, Paris, 1904, vol. 5, col. 149–153. This ritual is assuredly Visigothic in origin, but it was used in the wars against the muslims, S. DE SILVA, *Iconografía del siglo x en el reino de Pamplona-Nájera*, Pamplona, 1984, and B. CABAÑERO and F. GALTIER, '*Tuis exercitibus crux Christi semper adsistat*. El relieve prerománico de Luesia', *Artigrama*, 3, 1986, pp. 11–28, an article kindly passed on to me by E. Palazzo. One also wonders about the relic of the True Cross captured by Saladin at the battle of Hattin (1187).

129 GUERNES DE PONT-SAINTE-MAXENCE, *La Vie de Saint Thomas*, vv. 1640–1650. This passage was kindly brought to my attention by Martha Ganeva.

130 'Heavy wooden cross would confront Henry's sword and scepter, holy machismo would challenge kingly machismo', V. TURNER, 'Religious Paradigms and Social Action', p. 91. Among the factual errors in this article, we note the marriage of a daughter of Henry II to Emperor Henry VI (confused with Henry the Lion, duke of Saxony and Bavaria), and the assertion that Thomas never excommunicated the king of England.

131 On the epistemological and methodolical significance of these problems, cf. P. BUC, 'Political Ritual: Medieval and Modern Interpretations', *Die Aktualität des Mittelalters*, ed. H-W GOETZ, Bochum, 2000, pp. 255–72, and for a critique of V. Turner's suspect analysis, *ibid.*, p. 257 and n. 8.

132 On this head, M. Bloch's famous response to J. Frazer might be repeated: 'Ne transportons pas les Antipodes tout entiers à Paris ou à Londres' (Let's not drag the Antipodes into Paris or London), *Les Rois thaumaturges*, p. 54.

133 For the setting out of the facts on the basis of the texts, cf. BARLOW, *Thomas Becket*, pp. 188, 194–5, and KNOWLES, *Thomas Becket*, pp. 124–33.

134 'Ne se poeit pas acorder/ a sun seignur,/ kar pur home n'el vout baiser/ ne sun maltalent pardoner/ a icel jur', BENEDICT OF ST ALBANS, *La Vie de Saint Thomas*, vv. 1,166–1,170, p. 121. For a translation: 'He cannot come to an agreement with his lord, for he has no wish to embrace him as his man, not to forgive him his malice that day.'

135 *Thomas Saga*, § 67, vol. 1, pp. 446–9.

136 BENEDICT OF ST ALBANS, *La Vie de Saint Thomas*, no. 333, v. 1,993, p. 155, vv. 97–110. But the king was not the commissioner of Benedict's work, as he was criticized right from the introduction opening of a manuscript copy of the original, in fact it was Simon fitz Simon (died *c.*1199), and his wife Isabel, daughter of Thomas of Cuckney, born in the East Midlands, a stronghold of aristocratic vernacular patronage, SHORT, 'The Patronage of Beneit's *Vie de Saint Thomas*'.

137 GERALD OF BARRY, *De Principis Instructione*, p. 296.

138 *The Correspondence of Thomas Becket*, no. 112, p. 542.

139 BARLOW, *Thomas Becket*, p. 195.

140 JAEGER, *Ennobling Love*.

141 HERBERT OF BOSHAM, *Vita Sancti Thomae*, pp. 449–50.

142 Y. CARRE, *Le baiser sur la bouche au Moyen Age*, Paris, 1992, pp. 155, 177, 179. The first citation is from R. Trexler, and it comes from a letter sent to the author, who repeated it in his work.

143 POUZET, *L'Anglais dit Jean Bellesmains*, pp. 40–41.

144 ADAM OF EYNSHAM, *Magna Vita Sancti Hugonis*, V, 5.

145 'Sub risus modici significantia', GERALD OF BARRY, *The Life of St Hugh of Avalon*, p. 29, no. 39.

146 Cf. R. KAISER, 'Evêques expulsés, évêques assassinés aux xiᵉ et xiiᵉ siècles', in, *Le Temps des Saliens en Lotharingie (1024–1125). Actes du colloque de Malmedy (12–14 septembre 1991)*, Malmedy, 1993, and the thesis of C. Girbea.

147 V. Turner's interpretation of a ritual sacrifice, of a symbolic death whose function is – apart from a consequent but temporary turmoil – to re-establish communal harmony, is to be found in 'Religious Paradigms and Social Action'. It is a poor way of accounting for the murder of Becket. A trenchant consideration of the dangers of unguarded anthropological interpretations on ritual is in P. BUC, *The Dangers of Ritual. Between Early Medieval Texts and Social Scientific Theory*, Princeton, 2001.

148 Biographical notices and references for parallels in the *Vitae*, in BARLOW. *Thomas Becket*, pp. 5–9. Refer likewise to the book's last chapter for

an account of the assassination, as also to KNOWLES, *Thomas Becket* pp. 140–49. By referring to these two books – extremely precise and well-referenced – I have allowed myself to skimp on the critical apparatus below.

149 'A plebeo quodam clerico', EDWARD GRIM, *Vita sancti Thomae*, p. 429.

150 *Ibid.*, p. 435. Edward Grim followed his denigration of the assassins in denying them the title of *milites*, a heavily Christianized term in the clerical world: 'canes ipsi ex tunc et miseri non milites appelandi'.

151 'Ubi est Thomas *Beketh*, proditor regis et regni?', EDWARD GRIM, *Vita sancti Thomae*, p. 435. Cf. KNOWLES, *Thomas Becket*, p. 146. The name of Becket likewise appears in the letter which Peter Bernard, prior of Grandmont, wrote to Henry II after the murder, *Thesaurus novus anecdotorum*, col. 563. But it is true that it could have been inserted in the single, late copy that is available to us.

152 The letter, *Ex Inesperato*, in JOHN OF SALISBURY, *The Later Letters*, pp. 732–3.

153 *De Principis Instructione*, II, 3, p. 161. Cf. *Expugnatio Hibernica*, I, 20. In passing, the dog is a figure often used to represent a subservient courtier, who barks at his master's will.

154 Benedict of Peterborough, *Passio sancti Thomae Cantuarensis*, V, p. 13, trans. PANZARU, 'Caput mystice'.

155 C. Andrault-Schmitt very kindly brought this detail to my attention, for which I thank her sincerely.

156 JACOB, 'Le meurtre du seigneur', p. 257.

157 'Chacun d'eux l'a blessé, et a répandu son sang et sa cervelle', BENEDICT OF ST ALBANS, *La Vie de Saint Thomas*, vv. 1759–1760, p. 146, no. 294.

158 *Vita sancti Remigii*, p. 60.

159 In 1129, those who plotted against Norbert, archbishop of Magdeburg, determined *de se soûler* so that responsibility for the murder would not be fixed on them.

160 *La Vie de Saint Thomas*, vv. 5042, 5096–5100. Cf. KNOWLES, *Thomas Becket*, p. 139.

161 WILLIAM FITZ STEPHEN, *Vita sancti Thomae*, p. 142. Cf. BARLOW, *Thomas Becket*, p. 247.

162 *Draco Normannicus*, II, vv. 441–455, p. 676. Cf. BARLOW, *Thomas Becket*, p. 106.

163 There are any number of recent studies on the question: G. DUBY, *Le Chevalier, la Femme et le Prêtre. La mariage dans le France féodale*, Paris, 1981; J. GAUDEMET, *Sociétés et Mariage*, Strasbourg, 1980; *idem, Le Mariage en Occident*, Paris, 1987; AURELL, *Les Noces du Comte*; P. CORBET, *Autour de Burchard de Worms. L'Eglise allemande et les interdits de parenté (ixe–xiie siècle)*, Frankfurt, 2001. On the imprisonment of Bishop Peter of Poitiers by William IX of Aquitaine, Eleanor's grandfather, because the bishop had excommunicated him for his cohabiting with the viscountess of Châtellrault, cf. F. VILLARD, 'Guillaume IX d'Aquitaine et le concile de Reims de 1119', *CCM*, 15, 1973, p. 169, and G. BEECH, 'The Biography and the Study of 11th-century Society: Bishop Peter II of Poitiers (1087–1115)', *Francia*, 7, 1977, pp. 101–21.

164 Cf. N. VINCENT, 'The Murderers of Thomas Becket', in, *Bischofsmord im Mittelalter*, ed. N. FRYDE and D. REITZ, Göttingen, 2003, pp. 211–72.

165 'Regni principes . . . conclave quo sedebamus ingressi, rejectis palliis exsectisque brachiis', *The Letters and Charters of Gilbert Foliot*, no. 170 (1166), p. 233, lines 140–42.

166 SMALLEY, *The Becket Conflict and the Schools*, pp. 194–5.

167 HERBERT OF BOSHAM, *Vita sancti Thomae*, p. 451.

168 A. DUGGAN, 'John of Salisbury and Thomas Becket'.

169 WILLIAM FITZ STEPHEN, *Vita sancti Thomae*, p. 142.

170 Letter *In Inesperato* in JOHN OF SALISBURY, *The Later Letters*, pp. 728–9.

171 T. BORENIUS, *Saint Thomas Becket in Art*, London, 1932; M. GUARDI, 'Sant Tomàs Becket i el programa iconogràfic de les pintures murals de Santa Maria de Terrassa', *Locus amoenus*, 4, 1998–1999, pp. 37–58. I was alerted to the iconographic avenue by Myriam Soria and Eric Palazzo.

172 WILLIAM FITZ STEPHEN, *Vita sancti Thomae*, vol. 3, pp. 60–61, Cf. SMALLEY, *The Becket Conflict and the Schools*, pp. 56–8.

173 EDWARD GRIM, *Vita sancti Thomae*, p. 440.

174 *Dialogus miraculorum*, VIII, 69. Cf. BALDWIN, *Masters, Princes and Merchants*, pp. 146–7; KUTTNER and RATHBONE, 'Anglo-Norman Canonists', p. 289.

175 P.A. SIGAL, 'Naissance et premier développement d'un vinage exceptionnel: l'eau de saint Thomas', *CCM*, 44, 2001, pp. 35–44. Many of Becket's miracles have come under scrutiny from an original angle in, D. LETT, *L'Enfant du miracle. Enfance et société au Moyen Age (xiie–xiiie siècle)*, Paris, 1997.

176 *The Letters of Arnulf of Lisieux*, no. 72, trans. SCHRIBER, no. 3.06, pp. 194–6.

177 Cf. R. GRAHAM, *English Ecclesiastical Studies*, London, 1929, pp. 216–17; HALLAM, 'Henry II, Richard I and the Order of Grandmont'; and most recently, ANDRAULT-SCHMITT, 'Le mécénat architectural en question', pp. 244–8, 268.

178 ROGER OF HOWDEN, *Gesta*, vol. 1, p. 7.

179 *Thesaurus novus anecdotorum*, cols 561–569, later editions in, *PL*, 204, col. 1,168, and *RHF*, 16, p. 471.

180 Edited in, *Councils and Synods*, no. 166, pp. 942–56. Cf. M.G. CHENEY, 'The Compromise of Avranches', and FOREVILLE, *L'Eglise et la royauté en Angleterre*, pp. 329–67; DUGGAN, *Canon Law in Medieval England*, I, pp. 372–4; BARLOW, *Thomas Becket*, pp. 260–61; KNOWLES, *Thomas Becket*, pp. 152–5.

181 Bibliothèque nationale, ms latin 14,415, fol. 242v, cited by BUC, *L'Ambiguïté du livre*, p. 62. Cf. TURNER, 'Richard Lionheart and English Episcopal Elections'.

182 GERVASE OF CANTERBURY, *Chronica*, pp. 248–9; WILLIAM OF NEWBURGH, *Historia rerum Anglicarum*, III, 25, 35; ROGER OF HOWDEN, *Chronica*, vol. 2, pp. 61–2; ROBERT DE TORIGNY, *Chronica*, p. 264; GEOFFREY OF VIGEOIS, *Chronique*, *RHF*, vol. 12, p. 443; *The Chronicle of Battle Abbey*, p. 276; PETER OF BLOIS, *Epistulae*, no. 66.

183 DAMIAN-GRINT, 'Truth, Trust and Evidence in the Anglo-Norman *Estoire*', p. 63.

184 BOZOKY, 'Le culte des saints', pp. 285–6.

185 OEXLE, 'Lignage et parenté'.

186 WILLIAM OF NEWBURGH, *Historia rerum Anglicarum*, III, 26.

187 'Quae persecutio intestina atque domestica ideo ei justo Dei judicio, ut credimus, illata est quia in beatum Thomam plurimum deliquerat', RALPH OF COGGESHALL, *Chronicon*, p. 26.

188 GERALD OF BARRY, *De Principis Instructione*, II, 7.

189 Bibliothèque nationale, ms latin 14,414, fol. 118r, cited by BUC, *L'Ambiguïté du livre*, p. 62.

190 SMALLEY, *The Becket Conflict and the Schools*, pp. 191–3, 200–1, 212–13.

191 Contradicting, M-M. GAUTHIER, cited by BOZOKY, 'Le culte des saints', p. 286; CAUDRON, 'Thomas Becket et l'Oeuvre de Limoges', p. 62.

192 *Philippidos*, I, vv. 325–328, p. 20; ROGER OF HOWDEN, *Chronica*, vol. 2, pp. 192–3. Cf. BALDWIN, Philippe Auguste, p. 476; FOREVILLE, 'L'Image de Philippe Auguste', p. 126; BEAUNE, 'Les ducs, le roi et le saint Sang', p. 730. J-P. Poly and E. Bournazel ('Couronne et mouvance', pp. 213–32) note the attempt by Rigord to reserve the miraculous cure to St-Denis rather than Becket.

193 *De Principis Instructione*, pp. 251–2. Cf. BARTLETT, *Gerald of Wales*, p. 87.

Index

DATE DUE

2/26/10			

Demco, Inc. 38-293